SRA Reading Mastery

Signature Edition

Language Arts
Presentation Book A
Grade 1

Siegfried Engelmann
Jean Osborn
Karen Lou Seitz Davis

McGraw Hill **SRA**

Columbus, OH

SRAonline.com

 SRA

Send all inquiries to this address:
SRA/McGraw-Hill
4400 Easton Commons
Columbus, OH 43219

ISBN: 978-0-07-612484-8
MHID: 0-07-612484-3

5 6 7 8 9 RMN 13 12 11

The McGraw-Hill Companies

Table of Contents

Scope and Sequence *at the back of the book*

Before presenting the program, see the Placement section of the guide.

LESSON   1

Materials: For lessons 1 through 130, each child will need a workbook, a pencil, and a box of crayons that includes: red, brown, blue, green, black, orange, yellow, purple, **pink, gray.**

Objectives

- **Identify objects in a large class.** (Exercise 1)
- **Name common opposites; answer questions by generating sentences using opposites.** (Exercise 2)
- **Identify objects in the classes of plants and animals.** (Exercise 3)
- **Identify objects in the class of vehicles.** (Exercise 4)
- **Listen to and answer questions about a new story.** (Exercise 5)
- **Make a picture consistent with the details of the story.** (Exercise 6)
- **Follow coloring rules involving shapes.** (Exercise 7)
- **Follow coloring rules involving class.** (Exercise 8)

EXERCISE 1   Classification

Containers

1. This is the first language lesson. When we do language lessons, you're going to talk. You're going to name things and learn about things like opposites and rules. You'll learn facts about places and things and funny story characters. You'll learn about the calendar, difficult words, and a lot of other things. Remember to follow my directions and work hard. Let's start with a rule for containers.

2. Listen: If it's made to hold things, it's a container. Say the rule. Get ready. (Signal.) *If it's made to hold things, it's a container.*
   - Again. Say the rule. Get ready. (Signal.) *If it's made to hold things, it's a container.*
   - (Repeat step 2 until firm.)

3. Listen: If something is made to hold things, it is a container. If something is not made to hold things, it is not a container.

4. A box is made to hold things, so what do you know about a box? (Signal.) *It's a container.*
   - A cup is made to hold things, so what do you know about a cup? (Signal.) *It's a container.*
   - A basket is made to hold things, so what do you know about a basket? (Signal.) *It's a container.*
   - A suitcase is made to hold things, so what do you know about a suitcase? (Signal.) *It's a container.*

- Is a knife made to hold things? (Signal.) *No.*
- So what do you know about a knife? (Signal.) *It's not a container.*

5. I'll name some things. You tell me if they are containers. Listen: a log. Tell me: container or not container. (Signal.) *Not container.*
   - Listen: a bike. Tell me. (Signal.) *Not container.*
   - Listen: a cabinet. Tell me. (Signal.) *Container.*
   - Listen: a jar. Tell me. (Signal.) *Container.*
   - Listen: a pencil. Tell me. (Signal.) *Not container.*

6. Listen: You could say that a house, a car, or a plane are containers because they do hold things. These things are not usually called containers. A house is a building. A car and a plane are vehicles.

7. Remember, if something is made to hold things, it is a container. If something is not made to hold things, it is not a container.

EXERCISE 2   Opposites

1. Some words let you figure out things. Those are words like dry, skinny, full, young, long.
   - If something is dry, it is not wet.
   - If something is fat, it is not skinny.
   - If something is small, it is not big.
   - If something is young, it is not old.
   - If something is full, it is not empty.
   - If something is long, it is not short.

2. Your turn. If something is dry, what else do you know about it? (Signal.) *It is not wet.*

- If something is fat, what else do you know about it? (Signal.) *It is not skinny.*
- If something is small, what else do you know about it? (Signal.) *It is not big.*
- If something is young, what else do you know about it? (Signal.) *It is not old.*
- If something is full, what else do you know about it? (Signal.) *It is not empty.*
- If something is long, what else do you know about it? (Signal.) *It is not short.*

3. (Repeat step 2 until firm.)
4. Listen: I'm thinking of a chicken that is skinny. What else do you know about it? (Signal.) *It is not fat.*

- Listen: I'm thinking of a leaf that is wet. What else do you know about it? (Signal.) *It is not dry.*
- Listen: I'm thinking of a rope that is long. What else do you know about it? (Signal.) *It is not short.*
- Say the whole thing about the rope. Get ready. (Signal.) *The rope is not short.* Yes, the rope is not short.
- Listen: I'm thinking of a jug that is empty. What else do you know about it? Get ready. (Signal.) *It is not full.*
- Say the whole thing about the jug. Get ready. (Signal.) *The jug is not full.*
- Listen: I'm thinking of a duck that is young. What else do you know about it? (Signal.) *It is not old.*
- Say the whole thing about the duck. Get ready. (Signal.) *The duck is not old.*

EXERCISE 3 Classification

Plants Or Animals

1. Listen: Fruits and vegetables and trees and grass are in the class of plants. What's the big class name for fruits and vegetables and trees and grass? (Signal.) *Plants.*

- Listen: Another large class has cows and bugs and many other living things that move. That's the class of animals.

2. I'll name some things that are either plants or animals. You tell me the class they're in.

- Listen: dogs. What class? (Signal.) *Animals.*
- Listen: carrots. What class? (Signal.) *Plants.*
- Listen: grass. What class? (Signal.) *Plants.*
- Listen: rabbits. What class? (Signal.) *Animals.*
- Listen: butterflies. What class? (Signal.) *Animals.*
- Listen: beetles. What class? (Signal.) *Animals.*
- Listen: trees. What class? (Signal.) *Plants.*
- Listen: turkeys. What class? (Signal.) *Animals.*

3. Who can name some plants we haven't named? (Call on individual children.)

- Who can name some animals we haven't named? (Call on individual children.)

EXERCISE 4 Classification

Vehicles

1. I'll tell you the rule for vehicles: If it's made to take you places, it's a vehicle. Say the rule with me. Get ready. (Signal.) *If it's made to take you places, it's a vehicle.*

- All by yourself. Say the rule. Get ready. (Signal.) *If it's made to take you places, it's a vehicle.*
- (Repeat step 1 until firm.)

2. Listen: if something is made to take you places, it is a vehicle. If something is not made to take you places, it is not a vehicle.
3. A car is made to take you places, so what do you know about a car? (Signal.) *It's a vehicle.*

- A boat is made to take you places, so what do you know about a boat? (Signal.) *It's a vehicle.*
- A knife is not made to take you places, so what do you know about a knife? (Signal.) *It's not a vehicle.*

4. I'll name some things. You tell me if they are vehicles. Listen: a train. Tell me: vehicle or not vehicle. (Signal.) *Vehicle.*

- Listen: a bike. Tell me. (Signal.) *Vehicle.*
- Listen: a cabinet. Tell me. (Signal.) *Not vehicle.*
- Listen: a bus. Tell me. (Signal.) *Vehicle.*
- Listen: a house. Tell me. (Signal.) *Not vehicle.*
- Listen: a plane. Tell me. (Signal.) *Vehicle.*

5. Remember, if something is made to take you places, it is a vehicle. If something is not made to take you places, it is not a vehicle.

EXERCISE 5 Paul Paints Plums

Storytelling

1. Everybody, I'm going to read you a story. Listen to the things that happen in the story because you're going to have to fix up a picture that shows part of the story.
2. This is a story about Paul. Listen:

> Everybody has favorite colors. Some people love red. Some people love yellow. Others love blue or green. Some like brown or black. Well, Paul had his favorite colors, too. But his favorite colors were not red or blue or brown or black or even white or yellow. His two favorite colors were pink and purple. It's hard to say which color Paul liked the most. Sometimes, he would prefer pink. At other times, he preferred purple.
>
> Well, Paul also loved to paint. And whenever he painted, he'd use one of his favorite colors. One day, he was on his porch painting a picture of purple plums.

- Everybody, what was Paul's favorite color on that day? (Signal.) *Purple.*

> Paul said to himself, "Painting pictures of purple plums on the porch is perfect."

- That's hard to say. Listen again: Painting pictures of purple plums on the porch is perfect. Who can say that? (Call on a child.) *Painting pictures of purple plums on the porch is perfect.*

> But as he was painting, he dripped some purple paint on the floor of the porch. "Oh, pooh," he said. "Puddles of purple paint are on the porch, but I can fix it." So he got a great big brush and started to paint the whole floor of the porch purple.

- Listen: What did Paul start to do to fix up the puddles of purple paint? (Call on a child. Idea: *Paint the whole floor of the porch purple.*)

- Everybody, is that the way **you** would fix up the purple puddles? (Signal.) *No.*
- How would you fix up the purple puddles? (Call on a child. Praise reasonable responses.)

> But here's what Paul did: He got a great big brush and started to paint the whole porch purple. But just when he was almost finished, he backed into his painting and the painting fell against the window. It didn't break the window, but it got purple paint on the window pane.

- See if you can get a picture in your mind of that. Paul backed into the painting, his painting fell against the window pane, and now the window pane had big smears of purple paint on it.
- Listen: Why did the purple paint get on the window pane? (Call on a child. Idea: *The painting fell against the window.*)

> So now the floor of the porch is purple and there is purple paint on the window pane. "Whoa," Paul said. "Now there are patches of purple paint on the pane. But I can fix it."
>
> He tried wiping the purple paint from the pane, but that didn't work. At last Paul said, "I fixed the floor of the porch and I can fix that pane the same way."

- I'll bet I know how Paul's going to fix up that window. What do you think he'll do? (Call on several children. Idea: *Paint the whole window purple.*)

> It didn't work when Paul tried wiping the purple paint from the pane. So he said, "A purple pane may look perfectly pleasing." And he painted the whole window pane purple. But just as he was painting the last corner of the pane, some purple paint dripped on the wall.

- Uh oh. I'll bet I know what Paul will do now. What do you think he'll do? (Call on several children. Idea: *Paint the whole wall purple.*)
- Let's see what happened.

The purple paint dripped on the wall. "Wow," Paul said, "perhaps purple paint would look perfect on the wall." So you know what he did next. He painted the whole wall purple. And just as he was finishing up the last corner of the wall, his brother came out of the house. As his brother walked onto the porch, he rubbed against the wall and got a great smear of purple paint on his pants. Paul's brother tried to wipe the purple paint from the pants, but he just smeared the paint.

"I'm a mess," his brother said.

"So you are," Paul agreed. Then Paul smiled at his brother and said, "But brother, don't worry. I can fix it." And he did just that.

- What do you think he did? (Call on several children. Ideas: *Paul painted his brother purple* or *Paul painted his brother's pants purple*.)
3. Everybody, listen to the whole story one more time. Remember the things that happened, because you're going to fix up a picture that shows part of the story.

Paul loved to paint. One day, Paul was on the porch painting a picture of purple plums. He said, "Painting pictures of purple plums on the porch is perfect." But as he was painting, he dripped some purple paint on the floor of the porch. "Oh, pooh," he said. "Puddles of purple paint are on the porch, but I can fix it." So he got a great big brush and started to paint the whole floor of the porch purple.

But just when he was almost finished, he backed into his painting and the painting fell against the window. It didn't break the window, but it got purple paint on the window pane. "Whoa," Paul said. "Now there are patches of purple paint on the pane. But I can fix it."

He tried wiping the purple paint from the pane, but that didn't work. At last Paul said, "I fixed the floor of the porch and I can fix that pane the same way." So he said, "A purple pane may look perfectly pleasing."

And he painted the whole window pane purple. But just as he was painting the last corner of the pane, some purple paint dripped on the wall. "Wow," Paul said, "perhaps purple paint would look perfect on the wall."

So you know what he did next. He painted the whole wall purple. And just as he was finishing up the last corner of the wall, his brother came out of the house.

As his brother walked onto the porch, he rubbed against the wall and got a great smear of purple paint on his pants. Paul's brother tried to wipe the purple paint from the pants, but he just smeared the paint.

"I'm a mess," his brother said.

"So you are," Paul agreed. Then Paul smiled at his brother and said, "But brother, don't worry. I can fix it." And he did just that.

Workbook

EXERCISE 6 **Story Details**

1. Everybody, open your workbook to Lesson 1. Write your name on the line at the top of the page. ✔
2. Everybody, find the picture of Paul painting the window pane.
- Here's a picture of something Paul did in the story. Everybody, what's Paul doing in this picture? (Signal.) *Painting the window pane.*

- The funny lines on the window pane show how much he's already painted. But this picture shows something that happened in the middle of the story.
- Get a purple crayon and put a little purple mark on everything that is already purple. Don't put a purple mark on anything that Paul hasn't painted purple yet. Don't get fooled. The story mentioned a lot of things that were purple by the time Paul finished painting. But this picture doesn't show the **end** of the story. So you can only color those things that Paul had already painted when this picture took place.
- Name some things that are not purple yet. (Call on a child. Ideas: *The wall; the bottom of the window pane; his brother*.)
- Make your purple marks now. Raise your hand when you're finished. (Observe children and give feedback.)
3. Name the things you marked with purple. (Call on several children. Praise children who name the plums in the painting, the floor of the porch, and the top of the window pane.)
4. Raise your hand if you got everything right. Great job.
- Your turn to color part of the picture. Fix up the picture so the plums, the floor of the porch, and the top part of the window are purple. Later, you can color the other parts of the picture any colors you wish.

EXERCISE 7 Coloring Rules

1. Everybody, find the next page in your workbook. (Hold up a workbook.) Your page should look just like mine. ✔
2. Touch the first part of your page. (Point to the first half of the page.) You should be touching this part of your page. ✔

3. Find a triangle.
- Here's a coloring rule for this picture. Listen: Make every triangle red. What's the rule? (Signal.) *Make every triangle red.*
- (Repeat step 3 until firm.)
4. Make a red mark on one of the triangles to show what you do. ✔
5. Here's another coloring rule for this picture. Listen: Make every circle yellow. What's the rule? (Signal.) *Make every circle yellow.*
- (Repeat step 5 until firm.)
6. Make a yellow mark on one of the circles to show what you do. ✔
7. Some triangles have parts missing. You'll follow the dots with your pencil to make these triangles before you color them.
8. Here's the last coloring rule. Listen: Make all the squares any color you want. What's the rule? (Signal.) *Make all the squares any color you want.*
9. Pick a color and make a mark on one of the squares. ✔
- What's the rule for your squares? (Call on individual children. Idea: *Make all the squares _____.*)

EXERCISE 8 Classification

1. (Hold up workbook. Point to second half.)
2. Here's a coloring rule for this picture. Color the containers blue. What's the rule? (Signal.) *Color the containers blue.*
- (Repeat step 2 until firm.)
3. Who can name all the containers in this picture? (Call on a child. Ideas: *box, purse, dish-soap bottle, paint can*.)
- Everybody, mark one of the containers blue. ✔
4. Here's another coloring rule for this picture. Color the animals brown. What's the rule? (Signal.) *Color the animals brown.*
- (Repeat step 4 until firm.)
5. Mark one of the animals brown. ✔
6. Here's one more thing to do. Parts of the cow are missing. What parts? (Signal.) *The legs.*
- Before you color the cow, follow the dots with your pencil to make the legs.
7. Remember—the marks show you what color to make the containers and the animals.

Independent Work Summary
- Remember—the marks show you what color to make some things in your workbook. You can color the other things any color you want.

LESSON 2

Materials: For lessons 2 through 102, you will need a current calendar to present to the class. A reproducible blank calendar appears at the end of the *Teacher's Guide.*

Objectives

- **Identify objects in subclasses and classes**. (Exercise 1)
- **Follow directions and identify statements that tell "where."** (Exercise 2)
- **Name the days of the week and the seasons**. (Exercise 3)
- **Identify the class of food**. (Exercise 4)
- Answer questions by generating sentences using opposites. (Exercise 5)
- **Identify days and dates on a calendar.** (Exercise 6)
- Answer questions about a new story. (Exercise 7)
- Make a picture consistent with the details of the story. (Exercise 8)
- **Follow coloring rules involving specific objects**. (Exercise 9)
- Follow coloring rules involving class. (Exercise 10)

EXERCISE 1 Classification

Living Things

1. What's the big class name for fruits and vegetables and trees and grass? (Signal.) *Plants.*
- What's the big class name for cows and bugs and other living things that move? (Signal.) *Animals.*
- Both those classes are in a very large class. That's the class of **living things.** What's the class that has both plants and animals in it? (Signal.) *Living things.*
2. I'll name some things. You tell me if they are living things or not living things. Listen: rocks. Living things or not living things? (Signal.) *Not living things.*
- Listen: water. Living thing or not living thing? (Signal.) *Not living thing.*
- Listen: birds. Living things or not living things? (Signal.) *Living things.*
- Are birds plants or animals? (Signal.) *Animals.*
- Listen: carrots. Living things or not living things? (Signal.) *Living things.*
  Yes, carrots are living things that grow in the ground.
- Are carrots plants or animals? (Signal.) *Plants.*
- Listen: spiders. Living things or not living things? (Signal.) *Living things.*
- What kind of living things? (Signal.) *Animals.*
- Listen: sheep. Living things or not living things? (Signal.) *Living things.*
- What kind of living things? (Signal.) *Animals.*

- Listen: clouds. Living things or not living things? (Signal.) *Not living things.*
- Listen: trees. Living things or not living things? (Signal.) *Living things.*
- What kind of living things? (Signal.) *Plants.*
3. I'll name some things that are either plants or animals. You tell me the class they're in. Listen: fish. What class? (Signal.) *Animals.*
- Listen: mosquitos. What class? (Signal.) *Animals.*
- Listen: bushes. What class? (Signal.) *Plants.*
- Listen: mice. What class? (Signal.) *Animals.*
- Listen: alligators. What class? (Signal.) *Animals.*
- Listen: onions. What class? (Signal.) *Plants.*
- Listen: tulips. What class? (Signal.) *Plants.*
- Listen: oak trees. What class? (Signal.) *Plants.*
- Listen: worms. What class? (Signal.) *Animals.*
4. Who can name some plants we haven't named? (Call on individual children.)
- Who can name some animals we haven't named? (Call on individual children.)

EXERCISE 2 Where

1. Everybody, put two fingers on your elbow. Get ready. (Signal.) (Wait.) ✔
- Where are your fingers? (Signal.) *On my elbow.*
- Put two fingers on your wrist. Get ready. (Signal.) (Wait.) ✔
- Where are your fingers? (Signal.) *On my wrist.*
- Where were your fingers? (Signal.) *On my elbow.*

- Say the whole thing about where your fingers were. Get ready. (Signal.) *My fingers were on my elbow.*

2. Some statements tell **where.** Listen: My fingers were on my elbow. That statement tells where. Here are the words that tell where: On my elbow.

- Listen to the statement again: My fingers were on my elbow. Does that statement tell where? (Signal.) *Yes.*
- Say the words in the statement that tell where. Get ready. (Signal.) *On my elbow.*

3. Listen: The car was in the driveway. That statement tells where. Say the words in the statement that tell where. Get ready. (Signal.) *In the driveway.*

- Listen: The book was on the refrigerator. Does that statement tell where? (Signal.) *Yes.*
- Say the words in the statement that tell where. Get ready. (Signal.) *On the refrigerator.*
- Listen: The dog was under the tree. Does that statement tell where? (Signal.) *Yes.*
- Say the words in the statement that tell where. Get ready. (Signal.) *Under the tree.*
- Listen: The man was sad. Does that statement tell where? (Signal.) *No.*
- That statement does not tell where. There are no words in it that tell where something was.
- Listen: The dog was sleeping. Does that statement tell where? (Signal.) *No.*
- Listen: The cat was next to the garage. Does that statement tell where? (Signal.) *Yes.*
- Say the words in the statement that tell where. Get ready. (Signal.) *Next to the garage.*
- Listen: The penny was under the dresser. Does that statement tell where? (Signal.) *Yes.*
- Say the words in the statement that tell where. Get ready. (Signal.) *Under the dresser.*

4. Remember, a statement tells where if it has words that tell where.

EXERCISE 3 Calendar Facts

1. Here are facts about days and dates.
- Listen: There are seven days in a week. Say the fact. Get ready. (Signal.) *There are seven days in a week.*

- When you name the days of the week you start with Sunday. Listen: Sunday, Monday, Tuesday, Wednesday, Thursday, Friday, Saturday.
- Your turn. Start with Sunday and say the seven days of the week. Get ready. (Signal.) *Sunday, Monday, Tuesday, Wednesday, Thursday, Friday, Saturday.*

2. New fact: There are four seasons in a year.
- Everybody, say the fact. Get ready. (Signal.) *There are four seasons in a year.* (Repeat step 2 until firm.)

3. When you name the seasons, you start with the first season of the year. That's winter. Listen: winter, spring, summer, fall.
- Your turn. Name the four seasons of the year. Get ready. (Signal.) *Winter, spring, summer, fall.*

EXERCISE 4 Classification

Food

1. Humans eat food. They don't eat the same things that dogs, cats, or birds eat.
- I'll name some things. You tell me if they are food for humans or not food. Listen: bread. Food or not food? (Signal.) *Food.*
- Listen: tomatoes. Food or not food? (Signal.) *Food.*
- Listen: tables. Food or not food? (Signal.) *Not food.*
- Listen: dirt. Food or not food? (Signal.) *Not food.*
- Listen: milk. Food or not food? (Signal.) *Food.* Yes, milk is a food.

2. (Call on individual children.) Name something else that is food.

3. Here's the rule about food: If you eat it, it's food. Once more: If you eat it, it's food.
- Your turn. Say the rule about food. Get ready. (Signal.) *If you eat it, it's food.* (Repeat step 3 until firm.)

4. Listen: fruit. Food or not food? (Signal.) *Food.*
- How do you know it's food? (Signal.) *You eat it.*
- Listen: grass. Food or not food? (Signal.) *Not food.*
- How do you know? (Signal.) *You don't eat it.*

EXERCISE 5 Opposites

1. If something is fat, what else do you know about it? (Signal.) *It is not skinny.*
- If something is long, what else do you know about it? (Signal.) *It is not short.*
- If something is wet, what else do you know about it? (Signal.) *It is not dry.*
- If something is old, what else do you know about it? (Signal.) *It is not young.*
- If something is small, what else do you know about it? (Signal.) *It is not big.*
- If something is full, what else do you know about it? (Signal.) *It is not empty.*
2. (Repeat step 1 until firm.)
3. Listen: I'm thinking of a snake that is long. What else do you know about it? (Signal.) *It is not short.*
- Listen: I'm thinking of a woman who is old. What else do you know about her? (Signal.) *She is not young.*
- Listen: I'm thinking of a leaf that is dry. What else do you know about it? (Signal.) *It is not wet.*
- Listen: I'm thinking of a bottle that is full. What else do you know about it? (Signal.) *It is not empty.*
- Listen: I'm thinking of a duck that is fat. What else do you know about it? (Signal.) *It is not skinny.*

EXERCISE 6 Calendar

Note: You will need a current calendar for steps 3 through 6.

1. Everybody, how many days are in a week? (Signal.) *Seven.*
- Start with Sunday and say the days. Get ready. (Signal.) *Sunday, Monday, Tuesday, Wednesday, Thursday, Friday, Saturday.*
2. (Repeat step 1 until firm.)
3. (Present calendar. Point to the month.) Listen: This month is _____. What's this month? (Signal.)
- This is a calendar. It shows the dates. Those are the numbers of the days for this month.
- The calendar shows days of the week. The first column shows Sunday. (Point to Sunday column.) The next column shows Monday. (Point to Monday column.) The next column shows Tuesday. (Point to Tuesday column.)

4. I'll touch columns. You tell me if I'm touching numbers for Sunday, Monday, or Tuesday.
- (Touch a number for Sunday.) What day? (Signal.) *Sunday.*
- (Touch another number for Sunday.) What day? (Signal.) *Sunday.*
- (Touch a number for Monday.) What day? (Signal.) *Monday.*
- (Touch another number for Monday.) What day? (Signal.) *Monday.*
- (Touch a number for Sunday.) What day? (Signal.) *Sunday.*
- (Touch a number for Monday.) What day? (Signal.) *Monday.*
- (Touch a number for Tuesday.) What day? (Signal.) *Tuesday.*
- (Touch a number for Monday.) What day? (Signal.) *Monday.*
- (Touch a number for Tuesday.) What day? (Signal.) *Tuesday.*
- (Touch another number for Tuesday.) What day? (Signal.) *Tuesday.*
5. I'll show you the number for today. (Touch number. Say date: day, month, number; e.g: Today is Wednesday, September 15th.)
- Your turn. Say the date. (Signal.)
6. (Repeat step 5 until firm.)

EXERCISE 7 Cindy The Squid

Storytelling

1. Everybody, open your workbook to Lesson 2. Write your name on the line at the top of the page. ✔
2. Everybody, find the picture that shows some fish and a squid. ✔
- Touch the squid. It's that animal with a lot of arms. ✔
- Touch that great big fish. ✔
- Who knows what kind of fish that is? (Call on a child.) *A shark.*
- Later you're going to fix up that picture. It shows part of the story I'm going to tell you.
3. This is a story about Cindy the squid. Listen to the things that happen in this story.

Cindy was a squid who lived among the rocks with schools of little yellow fish and schools of little green fish. Cindy liked these fish, but she didn't like the sharks because when they came to the rocks, they were looking for something to eat. Those sharks loved to eat yellow fish and green fish.

- Listen: Which fish did Cindy like? (Call on a child. Idea: *The yellow fish and the green fish*.)
- Which fish didn't Cindy like? (Call on a child. Idea: *The sharks*.)
- Why didn't Cindy like the sharks? (Call on a child. Idea: *Because the sharks loved to eat the yellow fish and the green fish*.)

One day a huge shark came to the rocks. The yellow fish darted off this way and that way. The green fish darted off this way and that way. But Cindy the squid didn't move. She said to herself, "I've had enough of these sharks. It is time to teach this shark a lesson."
So she moved right in front of a big rock and started to wave her little tentacles at the shark.

- Cindy's tentacles are her arms.

Cindy started to wave her little tentacles at the shark. "Here I am, you bag of teeth. Come and get me."

- Listen: Where was Cindy when she was saying all these things to the shark? (Call on a child. Idea: *In front of a big rock*.)

- I wonder what Cindy was up to.

The shark looked at Cindy. "Come on," Cindy said. "Look at these tasty tentacles. Yum, yum. Come and get me, tooth face."
The shark was mad. He said to himself, "I'm going to eat that squirmy thing before it can move." And with all the speed and strength the shark had, he shot forward through the water, right at Cindy.
But, aha. Cindy had a trick. She sometimes used that trick to entertain the yellow fish and the green fish. She could squirt out a cloud of black ink so thick that you couldn't see anything.
And when the shark was so close to Cindy that all Cindy could see were two rows of huge teeth, Cindy squirted out the biggest cloud of ink she had ever squirted. Then she ducked to one side, just as that great shark charged full speed right into the rock.

- Listen to that part again and get a picture in your mind of what was happening.

When the shark was so close to Cindy that all Cindy could see were two rows of huge teeth, Cindy squirted out the biggest cloud of ink she had ever squirted. Then she ducked to one side, just as that great shark charged full speed right into the rock.
Bonk. The shark was knocked goofy.

- Listen: What made that bonk sound? (Call on a child. Idea: *The shark hitting the rock*.)
- Right, that shark swam right into the rock.
- Why didn't the shark see where he was going? (Call on a child. Idea: *Because Cindy squirted out a cloud of black ink*.)
- Where was Cindy? (Call on a child. Idea: *To one side of the rock*.)

That shark was so goofy he didn't know who he was or where he was. When the ink started to clear, the shark looked at Cindy and asked, "Who am I?"
Cindy said, "Why, you are a little yellow fish, of course."

- Listen: Who did Cindy say the shark was? (Call on a child. Idea: *A little yellow fish.*)
- Do you think the shark will believe her? (Call on a child. Accept reasonable responses.)

"Oh, yeah," the shark said. "A little yellow fish."

"Well," Cindy said, "you'd better join the other yellow fish."

"Okay," the shark said. And he did just that.

- Listen: What did the shark do? (Call on a child. Idea: *The shark joined the yellow fish.*)
- Oh my, a great big shark swimming around with those little yellow fish.

So if you ever go to the place where Cindy lives, you'll see something very strange. You'll see a squid that entertains yellow fish and green fish. But one of the yellow fish looks a little bit different than the others.

- Listen: Which yellow fish looks a little different? (Call on a child.) *The shark.*
- Does the shark really look just a little different or a lot different? (Call on a child. Idea: *A lot different.*)
4. Everybody, listen to the Cindy the squid story one more time. Remember the things that happened and then you're going to fix up a picture that shows part of the story.

Cindy was a squid who lived among the rocks with schools of little yellow fish and schools of little green fish. Cindy liked these fish, but she didn't like the sharks because when they came to the rocks, they were looking for something to eat. Those sharks loved to eat yellow fish and green fish.

One day a huge shark came to the rocks. The yellow fish darted off this way and that way. The green fish darted off this way and that way. But Cindy the squid didn't move. She said to herself, "I've had enough of these sharks. It is time to teach this shark a lesson."

So she moved right in front of a big rock and started to wave her little

tentacles at the shark. "Here I am, you bag of teeth. Come and get me."

The shark looked at Cindy. "Come on," Cindy said. "Look at these tasty tentacles. Yum, yum. Come and get me, tooth face."

The shark was mad. He said to himself, "I'm going to eat that squirmy thing before it can move." And with all the speed and strength the shark had, he shot forward through the water, right at Cindy.

But, aha. Cindy had a trick. She sometimes used that trick to entertain the yellow fish and the green fish. She could squirt out a cloud of black ink so thick that you couldn't see anything.

And when the shark was so close to Cindy that all Cindy could see were two rows of huge teeth, Cindy squirted out the biggest cloud of ink she had ever squirted. Then she ducked to one side, just as that great shark charged full speed right into the rock.

Bonk. The shark was knocked goofy. That shark was so goofy he didn't know who he was or where he was. When the ink started to clear, the shark looked at Cindy and asked, "Who am I?"

Cindy said, "Why, you are a little yellow fish, of course."

"Oh yeah," the shark said. "A little yellow fish."

"Well," Cindy said, "you better join the other yellow fish."

"Okay," the shark said. And he did just that.

So if you ever go to the place where Cindy lives, you'll see something very strange. You'll see a squid that entertains yellow fish and green fish. But one of the yellow fish looks a little bit different than the others.

EXERCISE 8   Story Details

1. Everybody, look at the picture of Cindy and the shark again. The picture shows part of the story.

- Does this picture take place **before** Cindy tricked the shark or **after** Cindy tricked the shark? (Call on a child.) *After Cindy tricked the shark.*
- How do you know it happened **after** Cindy tricked the shark? (Call on a child. Ideas: *Because the shark is swimming with the little yellow fish; he has a bonked head and goofy eyes.*)

2. Everybody, get a yellow crayon and put a little yellow mark on all the fish that are supposed to be yellow. Remember, the shark is swimming with the yellow fish. Raise your hand when you're finished. (Observe children and give feedback.)
- Those fish off to the side are different. Who remembers what color those little fish should be? (Call on a child.) *Green.*
- Everybody, put a little green mark on those fish so you'll know what color to make them. Raise your hand when you're finished. (Observe children and give feedback.)

3. Later, you can color the rest of the picture. I think that shark should be gray. And Cindy could be any color you want because squids can make themselves different colors.

EXERCISE 9 Coloring Rules

1. Everybody, find the next page in your workbook. (Hold up workbook.) Your page should look just like mine. ✔
2. Touch the first part of the page. (Point to the first half of the page.) You should be touching this part of your page. ✔
3. Find a dog. ✔

4. Here's a coloring rule for this picture. Listen: Make every dog black. What's the rule? (Signal.) *Make every dog black.*
- (Repeat step 4 until firm.)
5. Make a black mark on one of the dogs to show what you do. ✔
6. Here's another coloring rule for this picture. Listen: Make the leaves on every tree green. What's the rule? (Signal.) *Make the leaves on every tree green.*
- (Repeat step 6 until firm.)
7. Make a green mark on one of the tree's leaves to show what you do. ✔
8. Some dogs have parts missing. What parts? (Signal.) *The legs.* ✔
- You'll follow the dots with your pencil to make these legs before you color them.
9. Here's the last coloring rule. Listen: Make all the cats any color you want. What's the rule? (Signal.) *Make all the cats any color you want.*
10. Pick a color and mark on one of the cats. ✔
- What's the rule for your cats? (Call on individual children. Idea: *Make all the cats _____.*)

EXERCISE 10 Classification

1. (Hold up workbook. Point to second half.) Find the bear. ✔
2. Here's a coloring rule for this picture. Color the tools blue. What's the rule? (Signal.) *Color the tools blue.*
- (Repeat step 2 until firm.)
3. Who can name all the tools in this picture? (Call on a child.) *Toothbrush, scissors, saw, hammer.*
- Everybody, mark one of the tools blue. ✔
4. Here's another coloring rule for this page. Color the food yellow. What's the rule? (Signal.) *Color the food yellow.*
- (Repeat step 4 until firm.)
5. Mark one of the foods yellow. ✔
6. Here's one more thing to do. Part of the toothbrush is missing. What part is missing? (Signal.) *The handle.*
- Before you color the toothbrush, follow the dots with your pencil to make the handle.
7. Remember—the marks show you what color to make the food and the tools.

Independent Work Summary

- Remember—the marks show what color to make some things in your workbook.

LESSON 3

Objectives

- Identify objects in subclasses and classes. (Exercise 1)
- Follow directions and identify statements that tell "where." (Exercise 2)
- Name the days of the week, the seasons **and identify how many months are in a year.** (Exercise 3)
- **Identify objects in the class of tools.** (Exercise 4)
- Answer questions by generating sentences using opposites. (Exercise 5)
- Identify days and dates on a calendar, **and identify the date for today.** (Exercise 6)
- Answer questions about a new story. (Exercise 7)
- Make a picture consistent with the details of the story. (Exercise 8)
- Follow coloring rules involving specific objects. (Exercise 9)
- Follow coloring rules involving class. (Exercise 10)

EXERCISE 1   Classification

Living Things

1. What's the big class name for fruits and vegetables and trees and grass? (Signal.) *Plants.*
- What's the big class name for cows and bugs and other living things that move? (Signal.) *Animals.*
- Listen: Both those classes are in a very large class. What's the class that has both plants and animals in it? (Signal.) *Living things.*
- If it's a living thing, it's either a plant or an animal.
2. I'll name some things. You tell me if they are plants or animals. Listen: flies. Are they living things? (Signal.) *Yes.*
- What kind of living things? (Signal.) *Animals.*
- Listen: elephants. Are they living things? (Signal.) *Yes.*
- What kind of living things? (Signal.) *Animals.*
- Listen: roses. Are they living things? (Signal.) *Yes.*
- What kind of living things? (Signal.) *Plants.*
- Listen: frogs. Are they living things? (Signal.) *Yes.*
- What kind of living things? (Signal.) *Animals.*
- Listen: ladybugs. Are they living things? (Signal.) *Yes.*
- What kind of living things? (Signal.) *Animals.*
- Listen: pineapples. Are they living things? (Signal.) *Yes.*
- What kind of living things? (Signal.) *Plants.*
3. Remember, if it's a living thing, it's either a plant or an animal.

EXERCISE 2   Where

1. Everybody, hold your hand over your head. (Signal.) (Wait.) ✔
- Where is your hand? (Signal.) *Over my head.*
- Say the whole thing about where your hand is. Get ready. (Signal.) *My hand is over my head.*
- Listen: My hand is over my head. Does that statement tell where? (Signal.) *Yes.*
- Everybody, say the words in that statement that tell where. Get ready. (Signal.) *Over my head.*
2. Hold your hand in front of your nose. (Signal.) (Wait.) ✔
- Where is your hand? (Signal.) *In front of my nose.*
- Those are words that tell where. Say the whole thing about where your hand is. Get ready. (Signal.) *My hand is in front of my nose.*
- Listen: My hand is in front of my nose. Does that statement tell where? (Signal.) *Yes.*
- Everybody, say the words in that statement that tell where. Get ready. (Signal.) *In front of my nose.*
3. Listen: The car was near the city. Does that statement tell where? (Signal.) *Yes.*
- Everybody, say the words in the statement that tell where. Get ready. (Signal.) *Near the city.*
- Listen: The cat and dog were playing. Does that statement tell where? (Signal.) *No.*
- Listen: The cat and dog were playing in the yard. Does that statement tell where? (Signal.) *Yes.*
- Say the words in the statement that tell where. Get ready. (Signal.) *In the yard.*

- Listen: Her sister was sleeping under the tree. Does that statement tell where? (Signal.) *Yes.*
- Say the words in the statement that tell where. Get ready. (Signal.) *Under the tree.*
- Listen: The dog was sad. Does that statement tell where? (Signal.) *No.*
- That statement does not tell where. There are no words in it that tell where something was.
- Listen: The dog was sleeping. Does that statement tell where? (Signal.) *No.*
- Listen: The cat was next to the garage. Does that statement tell where? (Signal.) *Yes.*
- Say the words in the statement that tell where. Get ready. (Signal.) *Next to the garage.*
- Listen: The pillow was under the bed. Does that statement tell where? (Signal.) *Yes.*
- Say the words in the statement that tell where. Get ready. (Signal.) *Under the bed.*
4. Remember, a statement tells where if it has words that tell where.

EXERCISE 3   Calendar Facts

1. You learned calendar facts. Everybody, how many days are in a week? (Signal.) *Seven.*
- Say the fact. Get ready. (Signal.) *There are seven days in a week.*
- When you name the days of the week, what day do you start with? (Signal.) *Sunday.*
- Everybody, say the seven days of the week. Get ready. (Signal.) *Sunday, Monday, Tuesday, Wednesday, Thursday, Friday, Saturday.*
2. Next fact. How many seasons are in a year? (Signal.) *Four.*
- Everybody, say that fact. Get ready. (Signal.) *There are four seasons in a year.*
- When you name the seasons, which season do you start with? (Signal.) *Winter.*
- Your turn. Name the four seasons of the year. Get ready. (Signal.) *Winter, spring, summer, fall.*
3. (Repeat step 2 until firm.)
4. Listen: There are 12 months in a year. How many months are in a year? (Signal.) *12.*
- Say the fact about the months in a year. Get ready. (Signal.) *There are 12 months in a year.*

EXERCISE 4   Classification

Tools

1. I'll tell you the rule for tools: If it's made to help you do work, it's a tool. Say the rule. Get ready. (Signal.) *If it's made to help you do work, it's a tool.*
- Again. Say the rule. Get ready. (Signal.) *If it's made to help you do work, it's a tool.*
2. (Repeat step 1 until firm.)
3. A hammer is made to help you do work. So what do you know about a hammer? (Signal.) *It's a tool.*
- A dresser is not made to help you do work. So what do you know about a dresser? (Signal.) *It's not a tool.*
- A saw is made to help you do work. So what do you know about a saw? (Signal.) *It's a tool.*
- A glass is not made to help you do work. So what do you know about a glass? (Signal.) *It's not a tool.*
4. I'll name some things. You tell me if they are tools.
- Listen: a log. Tell me. Tool or not a tool? (Signal.) *Not a tool.*
- Listen: a bike. Tell me. (Signal.) *Not a tool.*
- Listen: a wrench. Tell me. (Signal.) *Tool.*
- Listen: a jar. Tell me. (Signal.) *Not a tool.*
- Listen: a screwdriver. Tell me. (Signal.) *Tool.*
- Listen: a ladder. Tell me. (Signal.) *Tool.*
- Listen: a wrench. Tell me. (Signal.) *Tool.*

EXERCISE 5   Opposites

1. If something is getting colder, it's not getting hotter. If something is getting hotter, what else do you know about it? (Signal.) *It's not getting colder.*
- If something is getting fatter, what else do you know about it? (Signal.) *It's not getting skinnier.*
- If something is getting longer, what else do you know about it? (Signal.) *It's not getting shorter.*
- If something is getting older, what else do you know about it? (Signal.) *It's not getting younger.*
- If something is getting bigger, what else do you know about it? (Signal.) *It's not getting smaller.*
2. (Repeat step 1 until firm.)

3. Listen: I'm thinking of a snake that is getting longer. What else do you know about it? (Signal.) *It's not getting shorter.*

- Listen: I'm thinking of a man who is getting older. What else do you know about him? (Signal.) *He is not getting younger.*
- Listen: I'm thinking of a leaf that is getting wetter. What else do you know about it? (Signal.) *It's not getting drier.*
- Listen: I'm thinking of a bottle that is getting hotter. What else do you know about it? (Signal.) *It's not getting colder.*

4. (Repeat step 3 until firm.)

EXERCISE 6 Calendar

1. (Present calendar. Point to month.) What month is it now? (Signal.)
- The calendar shows days of the week. (Point to Sunday column.) What day of the week does the first column show? (Signal.) *Sunday.*
- (Point to Monday column.) What day does the next column show? (Signal.) *Monday.*
- (Point to Tuesday column.) What day does the next column show? (Signal.) *Tuesday.*

2. I'll touch columns. You tell me the day of the week for the number.
- (Touch a number for Sunday.) What day? (Signal.) *Sunday.*
- (Touch another number for Sunday.) What day? (Signal.) *Sunday.*
- (Touch a number for Monday.) What day? (Signal.) *Monday.*
- (Touch another number for Monday.) What day? (Signal.) *Monday.*
- (Touch a number for Tuesday.) What day? (Signal.) *Tuesday.*
- (Touch a number for Monday.) What day? (Signal.) *Monday.*
- (Touch a number for Tuesday.) What day? (Signal.) *Tuesday.*
- (Touch a number for Wednesday.) What day? (Signal.) *Wednesday.*
- (Touch a number for Thursday.) What day? (Signal.) *Thursday.*
- (Touch a number for Friday.) What day? (Signal.) *Friday.*
- (Touch a number for Saturday.) What day? (Signal.) *Saturday.*

3. (Repeat step 2 until firm.)
4. I'll show you the number for today.
- (Touch number. Say date: day, month, number; e.g.: Today is **Thurs**day, September 16th.)

- Your turn. Say the date. (Signal.)
5. (Repeat step 4 until firm.)

EXERCISE 7 Sweetie And The Birdbath

Storytelling

1. Everybody, I'm going to read you a story. Listen to the things that happen in the story because you're going to have to fix up a picture that shows part of the story.
2. This is a story about a mean cat named Sweetie and the adventure he had with a birdbath. The story starts before there was a birdbath. Listen:

A woman named Bonnie loved birds. One day she noticed some birds cleaning themselves by splashing in a puddle on the sidewalk. She said, "Those birds shouldn't have to splash in a puddle to get clean. They need a birdbath." That was a good idea.

- Listen: What did Bonnie see that gave her the idea that the birds needed a birdbath? (Call on a child. Idea: *Bonnie saw the birds splashing in a puddle*.)

The more Bonnie thought about getting a birdbath the more she liked the idea. "I will get a birdbath big enough for all the birds that want to take a bath."

So Bonnie went to the pet store and looked at birdbaths. She picked out the biggest birdbath they had.

- Listen: Where did Bonnie go to get a birdbath? (Call on a child.) *To the pet store.*
- Which birdbath did she pick out? (Call on a child. Idea: *The biggest one they had*.)

The next day, a truck delivered the birdbath. Bonnie set it up in her backyard and soon some birds saw it. They called to their friends and the first thing you know all kinds of birds were splashing in the birdbath—red birds, yellow birds, spotted birds and little brown birds.

- See if you can get a picture in your mind of that birdbath with lots of birds in it.
- What color are the birds in the birdbath? (Call on a child. Idea: *Red, yellow, brown and spotted*.)

- What are those birds doing? (Call on a child. Idea: *Splashing in the birdbath*.)

A big yellow cat lived in the house next to Bonnie's house. That cat's name was Sweetie, but that cat was anything but sweet. Sweetie loved to chase birds. When Sweetie saw all the birds in Bonnie's birdbath, Sweetie said to himself, "Yum, yum. Look at all those little birds. I'm going to sneak over to that birdbath, jump up before they know I'm around, and grab a couple of birds. Yum, yum."

- Listen to Sweetie's plan again: "I'm going to sneak over to that birdbath, jump up before they know I'm around, and grab a couple of birds. Yum, yum."
- Tell me the things that Sweetie plans to do. (Call on a child. Idea: *He plans to sneak over to the birdbath, jump up, and grab some birds*.)

So Sweetie crouched down and went through a hole in the fence. Then Sweetie snuck through some bushes that were near the birdbath—closer, closer and closer until he was almost underneath the birdbath.

- Listen: How did Sweetie get into Bonnie's yard? (Call on a child. Idea: *He went through a hole in the fence*.)
- After Sweetie snuck through the hole in the fence, what did Sweetie do? (Call on a child. Idea: *He snuck through the bushes*.)
- Why didn't Sweetie just walk right up to the birdbath? (Call on a child. Ideas: *He didn't want the birds to see him; The birds would have flown away*.)
- So Sweetie snuck through the bushes until he was almost underneath the birdbath.

Sweetie heard some chirping and fluttering, so he crouched down and waited—very still, without moving anything but the tip of his tail, which moved back and forth.

- Listen: What made Sweetie crouch down and become very still? (Call on a child. Idea: *He heard chirping and fluttering*.)

- I bet you wonder why those birds started fluttering and chirping. You're going to find out.

Well, Sweetie couldn't see what was happening in the birdbath because Sweetie was in the bushes. But all that fluttering and chirping came about because a huge eagle decided to take a bath in the birdbath. So the eagle swooped down. And as soon as the other birds saw this huge eagle, with its great beak and its huge claws, they took off— fluttering and chirping.

- Listen: What made all the fluttering and chirping? (Call on a child. Idea: *The little birds started fluttering and chirping when the big eagle swooped down*.)
- Everybody, did Sweetie see the eagle? (Signal.) *No.*
- Why not? (Call on a child. Idea: *Because he was hiding in the bushes*.)

Sweetie didn't know it, but there wasn't a group of little birds in that bath anymore. There was one huge bird— about three times as big as Sweetie.

- Listen: What did Sweetie **think** was in the birdbath? (Call on a child. Idea: *Little birds*.)
- Everybody, what was **really** in the birdbath? (Signal.) *The eagle.*
- I think Sweetie is in for a big surprise.

Things were quiet now, so Sweetie got ready to leap up to the edge of the birdbath and grab a couple of tiny birds. Sweetie crouched down and with a great leap, shot out of the bushes and landed on the edge of the birdbath. He landed with his claws out, grabbing at the first thing he saw. He grabbed the eagle, and before Sweetie knew what was happening, that eagle grabbed him. The eagle picked Sweetie up and slammed him down into the middle of the birdbath. Splash!

- Listen: Sweetie jumped out of the bushes and landed on the edge of the birdbath. What did Sweetie do next? (Call on a child. Idea: *He grabbed at the eagle*.)

- What did the eagle do to Sweetie? (Call on a child. Idea: *Slammed Sweetie into the birdbath*.)
- I'll bet Sweetie was surprised to find himself slammed into the water.

Sweetie hated water, and he was all wet. He put his ears back, and shot out of that birdbath so fast he looked like a wet, yellow blur. He darted across the yard and through the hole in the fence. Then he just sat there with his mouth open and his eyes very wide.

- Everybody, when Sweetie went back to his yard, did he sneak through the bushes? (Signal.) *No.*
- What did he do? (Call on a child. Idea: *He ran across the yard and through the hole in the fence.*)

"What happened?" Sweetie said to himself. One second he was grabbing at something and the next second he was getting slammed into the birdbath.

While Sweetie was trying to figure out what happened, he wasn't looking at the birdbath. He didn't see the eagle. That eagle finished bathing and took off. As soon as the eagle left, all the little birds returned to the birdbath.

So when Sweetie finally peeked through the hole in the fence, he didn't see the eagle. He saw a bunch of little birds, twittering and splashing around in the water.

- Everybody, **before** Sweetie snuck over to the birdbath, what did he see in the birdbath? (Signal.) *Little birds.*
- Everybody, now, when he was all wet, what did he see in the birdbath? (Signal.) *Little birds.*
- So he never saw the eagle when he looked through the hole in the fence.

Sweetie looked and looked at those birds for a long time. Then he said to himself, "From here those birds look pretty small and helpless. But when you get close to them, they are really big and strong. I don't think I'll go near that birdbath again."

- Poor Sweetie has the wrong idea about what happened.
- Listen once more to what Sweetie said to himself: "From here those birds look pretty small and helpless. But when you get close to them, they are really big and strong. I don't think I'll go near that birdbath again."
- What kind of bird did he **think** threw him into the birdbath? (Call on a child. Idea: *A little bird*.)
- Those are the only birds Sweetie ever saw from his side of the fence—those little guys. And he's afraid to go near them because he thinks they're big and strong.

So now Bonnie is happy because her birdbath always has a lot of birds in it. The birds are happy because they can meet all their friends and have a nice bath whenever they want. Sweetie is the only one who is not all that happy. He looks at the birds in Bonnie's yard a lot, but he never goes over there, and he spends a lot of time trying to figure out how those birds could look so small but be so big and strong.

EXERCISE 8 **Story Details**

1. Everybody, open your workbook to Lesson 3. Write your name on the top of the page. ✔

2. Find the picture of Sweetie. ✔
- Here's a picture of something that happened in the story.
- What's Sweetie doing in this picture? (Call on a child. Idea: *Grabbing the eagle*.)
- Everybody, is Sweetie all wet yet? (Signal.) *No.*
- What's going to happen right **after** this picture is over? (Call on a child. Idea: *Sweetie will get slammed into the birdbath*.)
- Everybody, does that eagle look happy? (Signal.) *No.*
3. Look in the trees. There are 10 birds in the trees. See if you can find all of them and color them the right colors. Who remembers what colors they are? (Call on a child. Idea: *Red, yellow, brown and spotted*.)
4. Color the birds. Then color the rest of the picture. Everybody, what color is Sweetie? (Signal.) *Yellow.*
- That eagle is brown and white. The brown parts are a little darker, but they are not brown yet. You'll have to color them brown.

EXERCISE 9   Coloring Rules

1. Everybody, find the next page in your workbook. (Hold up a workbook.) Your page should look just like mine. ✔
2. Touch the first part of your page. (Point to the first half of the page.) You should be touching this part of your page. ✔
3. Find a truck. ✔
4. Here's a coloring rule for this picture. Listen: Make every car red. What's the rule? (Signal.) *Make every car red.*
- (Repeat step 4 until firm.)
5. Make a red mark on one of the cars to show what you do. ✔
6. Here's another coloring rule for this picture. Listen: Make every truck blue. What's the rule? (Signal.) *Make every truck blue.*
- (Repeat step 6 until firm.)

7. Make a blue mark on one of the trucks to show what you do. ✔
8. Some trucks have parts missing. What parts? (Signal.) *The wheels.* Yes, the wheels.
- You'll have to follow the dots with your pencil to make these wheels before you color them.
9. Here's the last coloring rule. Listen: Make the road any color you want. What's the rule? (Signal.) *Make the road any color you want.*
10. Pick a color and make a mark on the road. ✔
- What's the rule for your road? (Call on individual children. Idea: *Make the road _____*.)

EXERCISE 10   Classification

1. (Hold up workbook. Point to second half.) Find the dog. ✔
2. Here's the coloring rule for this picture. Color the vehicles brown. What's the rule? (Signal.) *Color the vehicles brown.*
- (Repeat step 2 until firm.)
3. Mark one of the vehicles brown. ✔
4. Here's another coloring rule for this picture. Color the furniture yellow. What's the rule? (Signal.) *Color the furniture yellow.*
- (Repeat step 4 until firm.)
5. Mark one piece of furniture yellow. ✔
- Here's one more thing to do. Part of the wagon is missing. What part is missing? (Signal.) *The body.* Yes, the body.
- Before you color the wagon, follow the dots with your pencil to make the body.
6. Remember—the marks show you what color to make the vehicles and the furniture.

Independent Work Summary

- Remember—the marks show you what color to make some things in your workbook.

LESSON 4

Objectives

- Identify objects in subclasses and classes. (Exercise 1)
- Follow directions and identify statements that tell "where." (Exercise 2)
- Name the days of the week, the seasons, **and name the first four months of the year.** (Exercise 3)
- **Identify classes.** (Exercise 4)
- Answer questions by generating sentences using opposites. (Exercise 5)
- Identify days and dates on a calendar. (Exercise 6)
- **Listen to and answer questions about a familiar story.** (Exercise 7)
- Make a picture consistent with the details of the story. (Exercise 8)
- **Follow coloring rules involving parts of a whole.** (Exercise 9)
- Follow coloring rules involving specific objects. (Exercise 10)

EXERCISE 1 Classification

Living Things

1. What's the big class name for fruits and vegetables and trees and grass? (Signal.) *Plants.*
- What's the big class name for cows and bugs and other living things that move? (Signal.) *Animals.*
- Listen: Both plants and animals are in a very large class. What's the class that has both plants and animals in it? (Signal.) *Living things.*
- If it's a living thing, it's either a plant or an animal.

2. I'll name some things. You tell me if they are plants or animals. Listen: broccoli. Is that a living thing? (Signal.) *Yes.*
- What kind of living thing? (Signal.) *Plant.*
- Listen: beans. Are they living things? (Signal.) *Yes.*
- What kind of living things? (Signal.) *Plants.*
- Listen: roosters. Are they living things? (Signal.) *Yes.*
- What kind of living things? (Signal.) *Animals.*
- Listen: ants. Are they living things? (Signal.) *Yes.*
- What kind of living things? (Signal.) *Animals.*
- Listen: mushrooms. Are they living things? (Signal.) *Yes.*
- What kind of living things? (Signal.) *Plants.*
- Listen: alligators. Are they living things? (Signal.) *Yes.*
- What kind of living things? (Signal.) *Animals.*

3. Remember, if it's a living thing, it's either a plant or an animal.

4. Get ready to tell me more than one class name.
- Carrots. Are they living things? (Signal.) *Yes.*
- What kind of living things? (Signal.) *Plants.*
- Are they fruits or vegetables? (Signal.) *Vegetables.*
- Listen: cherries. Are they living things? (Signal.) *Yes.*
- What kind of living things? (Signal.) *Plants.*
- Are they fruits or vegetables? (Signal.) *Fruits.*

5. (Repeat step 4 until firm.)

EXERCISE 2 Where

1. Everybody, hold your hand next to your wrist. Get ready. (Signal.) (Wait.) ✔
- Where is your hand? (Signal.) *Next to my wrist.*
- Say the whole thing about where your hand is. Get ready. (Signal.) *My hand is next to my wrist.*
- Say the words in the statement that tell where. Get ready. (Signal.) *Next to my wrist.*
- Hands down.

2. Listen to this statement: My hand is in front of my nose. Does that statement tell where? (Signal.) *Yes.*
- Everybody, say the words in that statement that tell where. Get ready. (Signal.) *In front of my nose.*

3. Listen to this statement: The car drove under the bridge. Does that statement tell where? (Signal.) *Yes.*
- Say the words in the statement that tell where. Get ready. (Signal.) *Under the bridge.*
- Listen: The girls were swimming near the dock. Does that statement tell where? (Signal.) *Yes.*

- Say the words in the statement that tell where. Get ready. (Signal.) *Near the dock.*
- Listen: The cat and the dog were playing with a ball. Does the statement tell where? (Signal.) *No.*
- That statement does not tell where.
- Listen: Her cat was climbing in the tree. Does that statement tell where? (Signal.) *Yes.*
- Say the words in the statement that tell where. Get ready. (Signal.) *In the tree.*
- Listen: Her cat was hungry. Does that statement tell where? (Signal.) *No.*
- That statement does not tell where.
- Listen: His dog was barking in the basement. Does that statement tell where? (Signal.) *Yes.*
- Say the words in the statement that tell where. Get ready. (Signal.) *In the basement.*
4. Remember, a statement tells where if it has words that tell where.

EXERCISE 3   Calendar Facts

1. You learned calendar facts. Everybody, how many days are in a week? (Signal.) *Seven.*
- Say the fact. Get ready. (Signal.) *There are seven days in a week.*
- When you name the days of the week, what day do you start with? (Signal.) *Sunday.*
- Everybody, say the seven days of the week. Get ready. (Signal.) *Sunday, Monday, Tuesday, Wednesday, Thursday, Friday, Saturday.*
- How many seasons are in a year? (Signal.) *Four.*
- Everybody, say that fact. Get ready. (Signal.) *There are four seasons in a year.*
- When you name the seasons, which season do you start with? (Signal.) *Winter.*
- Your turn: Name the four seasons of the year. Get ready. (Signal.) *Winter, spring, summer, fall.*
2. (Repeat step 1 until firm.)
3. How many months are in a year? (Signal.) *12.*
- Say the fact about the months in a year. Get ready. (Signal.) *There are 12 months in a year.*
- I'll say the first four months of the year: January, February, March, April.
- Everybody, say the first four months. Get ready. (Signal.) *January, February, March, April.*
4. (Repeat step 3 until firm.)

EXERCISE 4   Classification

1. If it's made to help you do work, what class of object is it? (Signal.) *Tool.*
- If it holds things, what class of object is it? (Signal.) *Container.*
- If it's made to take you places, what class of object is it? (Signal.) *Vehicle.*
- If it's made to help you do work, it's a tool. Say the rule. Get ready. (Signal.) *If it's made to help you do work, it's a tool.*
- Again. Say the rule. Get ready. (Signal.) *If it's made to help you do work, it's a tool.*
2. (Repeat step 1 until firm.)
3. I'll name some objects. Tell me a class these objects are in. Listen: hammer, saw, ladder, screwdriver. Everybody, what class? (Signal.) *Tools.*
- Listen: cup, glass, bag, bottle. Everybody, what class? (Signal.) *Containers.*
- Listen: dog, rabbit, cow, mouse, mosquito. Everybody, what class? (Signal.) *Animals.*
- Listen: carrots, grass, bushes, trees. Everybody, what class? (Signal.) *Plants.*
- Listen: bicycles, cars, trucks, motorboats. Everybody, what class? (Signal.) *Vehicles.*
4. I'm going to name a class. See how many objects you can name in that class.
- Listen: tools. (Call on individual children to name objects in that class.)
- New class: containers. (Call on individual children to name objects in that class.)
- New class: vehicles. (Call on individual children to name objects in that class.)

EXERCISE 5   Opposites

1. If something is getting longer, what else do you know about it? (Signal.) *It's not getting shorter.*
- If something is getting colder, what else do you know about it? (Signal.) *It's not getting hotter.*
- If something is getting hotter, what else do you know about it? (Signal.) *It's not getting colder.*
- If something is getting smaller, what else do you know about it? (Signal.) *It's not getting bigger.*
- If something is getting bigger, what else do you know about it? (Signal.) *It's not getting smaller.*
2. (Repeat step 1 until firm.)

3. Listen: I'm thinking of a stove that is getting hotter. What else do you know about it? (Signal.) *It's not getting colder.*
• Listen: I'm thinking of a puddle that is getting bigger. What else do you know about it? (Signal.) *It's not getting smaller.*
• Listen: I'm thinking of a line that is getting longer. What else do you know about it? (Signal.) *It's not getting shorter.*
4. (Repeat step 3 until firm.)

EXERCISE 6 Calendar

(Signal.) *Sunday.*
• (Touch a number for Tuesday.) What day? (Signal.) *Tuesday.*
• (Touch a number for Monday.) What day? (Signal.) *Monday.*
• (Touch a number for Wednesday.) What day? (Signal.) *Wednesday.*
• (Touch a number for Thursday.) What day? (Signal.) *Thursday.*
• (Touch a number for Friday.) What day? (Signal.) *Friday.*
• (Touch a number for Saturday.) What day? (Signal.) *Saturday.*
3. (Repeat step 2 until firm.)
4. I'll show you the number for today. (Touch number.) What's the number for today? (Signal.)
• What's the day of the week? (Signal.)
• What's the month? (Signal.)
• Your turn. Say today's date. Get ready. (Signal.)
5. (Repeat step 4 until firm.)

EXERCISE 7 Paul Paints Plums

Storytelling

• Everybody, I'm going to tell you the story about Paul and the purple paint again. Listen carefully because when I'm done, you'll fix up a new picture that shows part of the story.

Paul loved to paint. One day, Paul was on the porch painting a picture of purple plums. He said, "Painting pictures of purple plums on the porch is perfect."

But as he was painting, he dripped some purple paint on the floor of the porch. "Oh, pooh," he said. "Puddles of purple paint are on the porch, but I can fix it."

So he got a great big brush and started to paint the whole floor of the porch purple. But just when he was almost finished, he backed into his painting and the painting fell against the window. It didn't break the window, but it got purple paint on the window pane.

"Whoa," Paul said. "Now there are patches of purple paint on the pane. But I can fix it."

He tried wiping the purple paint from the pane, but that didn't work. At last Paul said, "I fixed the floor of the porch, and I can fix that pane the same way." So he said, "A purple pane may look perfectly pleasing." And he painted the whole window pane purple.

But just as he was painting the last corner of the pane, some purple paint dripped on the wall.

"Wow," Paul said, "perhaps purple paint would look perfect on the wall." So you know what he did next. He painted the whole wall purple. And just as he was finishing up the last corner of the wall, his brother came out of the house. As his brother walked onto the porch, he rubbed against the wall and got a great smear of purple paint on his pants. Paul's brother tried to wipe the purple paint from his pants, but he just smeared the paint.

"I'm a mess," his brother said.

"So you are," Paul agreed. Then he smiled at his brother and said, "But brother, don't worry. I can fix it." And he did just that.

WORKBOOK

EXERCISE 8 Story Details

1. Everybody, open your workbook to Lesson 4. Write your name on the top of the page. Find the picture of Paul. ✔
- Here's a picture of something Paul did in the story. Everybody, what's Paul doing in this picture? (Signal.) *Painting the wall purple.*
- Everybody, who else is on the porch? (Signal.) *Paul's brother.*
- You can see the patch of purple paint on his pants. I see a couple of drops of purple paint on that top stair. I wonder how Paul will fix that stair. What do you think? (Call on a child. Idea: *Paint the stair purple.*)
- I sure hope that cat doesn't get too close to the paint. Who do you think that cat is? (Call on a child. Idea: *Sweetie.*)
2. Get a purple crayon and put a little purple mark on everything that is **already** purple. Don't put a purple mark on anything that Paul hasn't painted purple yet. Raise your hand when you're finished.
(Observe children and give feedback.)
- Name the things you marked with purple. (Call on several children. Praise children who name the plums, the floor of the porch, the whole window, the wall and the smear on the pants.)

3. Your turn: Fix up the picture so that all these things are purple—the plums, the floor of the porch, the whole window, the smear on Paul's brother's pants, and most of the wall. Later, you can color the other parts of the picture any color you wish.

EXERCISE 9 Part-Whole

1. Everybody, find the next page in your workbook. (Hold up a workbook.) Your page should look just like mine. ✔
2. Touch the first part of your page. (Point to the first half of the page.) You should be touching this part of your page. ✔
3. Find the picture of the pencil. Here's a coloring rule for the pencil. Listen: Color the eraser green. What's the rule? (Signal.) *Color the eraser green.*
- Mark the eraser. ✔
4. Here's another coloring rule for the pencil. Listen: Color the shaft blue. What's the rule? (Signal.) *Color the shaft blue.*
- Mark the shaft. ✔
5. Part of the pencil is missing. What part is missing? (Signal.) *The point.* Yes, the point.
- Before you color the pencil, you're going to follow the dots with your pencil to make the point.
6. Here's the coloring rule for the point. Listen: Color the point yellow. What's the rule? (Signal.) *Color the point yellow.*
- Mark the point. ✔

EXERCISE 10 Coloring Rules

1. (Hold up workbook. Point to second half.) Find the flowers. ✔
2. Here's a coloring rule for this picture. Listen: Make every bottle yellow. What's the rule? (Signal.) *Make every bottle yellow.*
- (Repeat step 2 until firm.)
3. Make a yellow mark on one of the bottles to show what you do. ✔

4. Here's another coloring rule for this picture. Listen: Make every hammer purple. What's the rule? (Signal.) *Make every hammer purple.*

- (Repeat step 4 until firm.)

5. Make a purple mark on one of the hammers to show what you do. ✔

6. Some hammers have a part missing. What part? (Signal.) *The handle.* Yes, the handle.

- You'll follow the dots with your pencil to make these handles before you color the hammers.

7. Here's the last coloring rule. Listen: Make all the flowers any color you want. What's the rule? (Signal.) *Make all the flowers any color you want.*

8. Pick a color and make a mark on one of the flowers. ✔

- What's the rule for your flowers? (Call on individual children. Idea: *Make all the flowers _____.*)

9. Remember—the marks show you what color to make the bottles, hammers, and flowers.

Independent Work Summary

- Remember—the marks show you what color to make some things on the workbook. You can color the other things on the workbook any color you want.

Objectives

- **Follow directions, make statements and answer questions involving "and" and "or."** (Exercise 1)
- Identify classes. (Exercise 2)
- Identify statements that tell "where" and **"when."** (Exercise 3)
- Name the days of the week, the seasons, **and name the first eight months of the year.** (Exercise 4)
- Answer questions by generating sentences using opposites. (Exercise 5)
- **Given a calendar, identify the day and date for "yesterday"** and "today." (Exercise 6)
- Listen to a familiar story. (Exercise 7)
- **Answer questions about a familiar story and make a picture consistent with the details of the story.** (Exercise 8)
- Follow coloring rules involving parts of a whole. (Exercise 9)
- Follow coloring rules involving class. (Exercise 10)

EXERCISE 1   Actions

1. Let's play some action games. Everybody, you're going to hold up your foot **and** touch your ears at the same time. Get ready. (Signal.) ✔
- What are you doing? (Signal.) *Holding up my foot and touching my ears.*
2. Say the whole thing. Get ready. (Signal.) *I am holding up my foot and touching my ears.*
- (Repeat step 2 until firm.)
3. Everybody, you're going to touch your chin and hold up your **feet.** Get ready. (Signal.) ✔
- What are you doing? (Signal.) *Touching my chin and holding up my feet.*
4. Say the whole thing. Get ready. (Signal.) *I am touching my chin and holding up my feet.*
- (Repeat step 3 until firm.)
5. Here's another game. I'm going to do something. See if you can figure out what I'm going to do.
6. Listen: I'm going to shake my head or shake my foot or wave. What am I going to do? (Signal.) *Shake your head or shake your foot or wave.*
7. (Repeat step 6 until firm.)

8. Yes, I'm going to shake my head or shake my foot or wave. Am I going to wave? (Signal.) *Maybe.*
- Am I going to shake my foot? (Signal.) *Maybe.*
- Am I going to shake my arm? (Signal.) *No.*
- Am I going to shake my head? (Signal.) *Maybe.*
9. Here I go. (Shake your head.)
- Did I shake my head? (Signal.) *Yes.*
- Did I wave? (Signal.) *No.*
- Did I shake my foot? (Signal.) *No.*
10. (Repeat steps 8 and 9 until firm.)

EXERCISE 2   Classification

Clothing

1. I'll tell you the rule for clothing: If it's something you can wear, it's clothing. Say the rule. Get ready. (Signal.) *If it's something you can wear, it's clothing.*
- Again. Say the rule. Get ready. (Signal.) *If it's something you can wear, it's clothing.*
2. (Repeat step 1 until firm.)
3. A coat is something you can wear. So what do you know about a coat? (Signal.) *It's clothing.*
- A tree is not something you wear. So what do you know about a tree? (Signal.) *It's not clothing.*
4. I'll name some things. Tell me clothing or not clothing.
- Listen: shoes. Tell me. Clothing or not clothing. (Signal.) *Clothing.*

- Listen: hat. Tell me. (Signal.) *Clothing.*
- Listen: dog. Tell me. (Signal.) *Not clothing.*
- Listen: glasses. Tell me. (Signal.) *Clothing.*
- Listen: blue jeans. Tell me. (Signal.) *Clothing.*

5. (Call on individual children to name some articles of clothing.)

6. Listen: If it's made to help you do work, what class of object is it? (Signal.) *Tool.*
- If it holds things, what class of object is it? (Signal.) *Container.*
- If it's made to take you places, what class of object is it? (Signal.) *Vehicle.*
- If it's made to help you do work, it's a tool. Say the rule. Get ready. (Signal.) *If it's made to help you do work, it's a tool.*
- Again. Say the rule. (Signal.) *If it's made to help you do work, it's a tool.*

7. (Repeat step 6 until firm.)

8. I'll name some objects. Tell me a class these objects are in. Listen: wrench, saw, drill. Everybody, what class? (Signal.) *Tools.*
- Listen: hat, shoes, shorts. Everybody, what class? (Signal.) *Clothing.*
- Listen: frog, beetle, mouse, mosquito, fly. Everybody, what class? (Signal.) *Animals.*
- Listen: trucks, bicycles, cars, trains. Everybody, what class? (Signal.) *Vehicles.*

9. I'm going to name a class. See how many objects you can name in that class. Listen: tools. (Call on individual children to name objects in that class.)
- New class: containers. (Call on individual children to name objects in that class.)
- New class: clothing. (Call on individual children to name objects in that class.)

EXERCISE 3   Where—When

1. Everybody, put your hands on your hips. Get ready. (Signal.) (Wait.) ✔
- Where are your hands? (Signal.) *On my hips.*
- Say the whole thing about where your hands are. Get ready. (Signal.) *My hands are on my hips.*
- Listen to this statement: My hands are on my hips.
- Everybody, say the words in that statement that tell where. Get ready. (Signal.) *On my hips.*

2. Hold your hands in back of your head. (Signal.) (Wait.) ✔
- Where are your hands? (Signal.) *In back of my head.*
- Say the whole thing about where your hands are. Get ready. (Signal.) *My hands are in back of my head.*
- Listen: My hands are in back of my head.
- Everybody, say the words in that statement that tell where. Get ready. (Signal.) *In back of my head.*
- Hands down.

3. Listen: Some statements tell **when.** Here are parts that tell when: yesterday, tomorrow, right now, in a minute, before school, at lunchtime.
- Here's a **statement** that tells when: We work very hard in the morning. Listen: **When** do we work hard? (Signal.) *In the morning.*
- Say the statement. Get ready. (Signal.) *We work very hard in the morning.*
- Say the words in the statement that tell when. Get ready. (Signal.) *In the morning.*

4. New statement: We take a break at lunch time. Listen: When do we take a break? (Signal.) *At lunch time.*
- Say the statement. Get ready. (Signal.) *We take a break at lunch time.*
- Say the words in that statement that tell when. Get ready. (Signal.) *At lunch time.*

5. New statement: The baby cried at four in the morning. Listen: When did the baby cry? (Signal.) *At four in the morning.*
- Say the statement. Get ready. (Signal.) *The baby cried at four in the morning.*
- Say the words in that statement that tell when. Get ready. (Signal.) *At four in the morning.*

6. New statement: I do a lot of things before school begins.
- Say the statement. Get ready. (Signal.) *I do a lot of things before school begins.*
- Say the words in that statement that tell when. Get ready. (Signal.) *Before school begins.*

EXERCISE 4   Calendar Facts

1. You learned calendar facts. Everybody, how many days are in a week? (Signal.) *Seven.*
   - Say the fact. Get ready. (Signal.) *There are seven days in a week.*
   - When you name the days of the week, what day do you start with? (Signal.) *Sunday.*
   - Everybody, say the seven days of the week. Get ready. (Signal.) *Sunday, Monday, Tuesday, Wednesday, Thursday, Friday, Saturday.*
   - How many seasons are in a year? (Signal.) *Four.*
   - Everybody, say that fact. Get ready. (Signal.) *There are four seasons in a year.*
   - When you name the seasons, which season do you start with? (Signal.) *Winter.*
   - Your turn: Name the four seasons of the year. Get ready. (Signal.) *Winter, spring, summer, fall.*
2. (Repeat step 1 until firm.)
3. How many months are in a year? (Signal.) *12.*
   - Say the fact about the months in a year. Get ready. (Signal.) *There are 12 months in a year.*
   - Your turn. Say the first four months. Get ready. (Signal.) *January, February, March, April.*
4. (Repeat step 3 until firm.)
5. Here are the next four months: May, June, July, August.
   - Your turn. Say the next four months. Get ready. (Signal.) *May, June, July, August.*
6. (Repeat step 5 until firm.)
7. Listen to the first eight months: January, February, March, April, (pause) May, June, July, August.
   - Everybody, say the first eight months. Get ready. (Signal.) *January, February, March, April, May, June, July, August.*
8. (Repeat step 7 until firm.)

EXERCISE 5   Opposites
Review

1. We're going to play a word game.
2. Listen: I'm thinking about water that is cold. It's cold. So what do you know about it? (Signal.) *It's not hot.*
   - Listen: I'm thinking about a line that is long. It's long. So what do you know about it? (Signal.) *It's not short.*
   - Listen: I'm thinking about a shirt that is wet. It's wet. So what do you know about it? (Signal.) *It's not dry.*
3. (Repeat step 2 until firm.)

EXERCISE 6   Calendar

1. (Present calendar.) First you'll tell me about the days of the week. Then you'll tell me about the dates.
2. Tell me the day of the week it was yesterday. Get ready. (Signal.)
   - Tell me the day of the week it is today. Get ready. (Signal.)
   - Now the dates. Everybody, tell me yesterday's date. Get ready. (Signal.)
   - Tell me today's date. Get ready. (Signal.)
3. (Repeat step 2 until firm.)

EXERCISE 7   Cindy The Squid
Storytelling

- Everybody, I'm going to tell you the story about Cindy the squid again. Listen carefully because when I'm done, you'll fix up a new picture that shows part of the story.

Cindy was a squid who lived among the rocks with schools of little yellow fish and schools of little green fish. Cindy liked these fish, but she didn't like the sharks because when they came to the rocks, they were looking for something to eat. Those sharks loved to eat yellow fish and green fish.

One day a huge shark came to the rocks. The yellow fish darted off this way and that way. The green fish darted off this way and that way. But Cindy the squid didn't move. She said to herself, "I've had enough of these sharks. It is time to teach this shark a lesson."

So she moved right in front of a big rock and started to wave her little tentacles at the shark. "Here I am, you bag of teeth. Come and get me."

The shark looked at Cindy. "Come on," Cindy said. "Look at these tasty tentacles. Yum, yum. Come and get me, tooth face."

The shark was mad. He said to himself, "I'm going to eat that squirmy thing before it can move." And with all the speed and all the strength the shark had, he shot forward through the water, right at Cindy.

But, aha. Cindy had a trick. She sometimes used that trick to entertain the yellow fish and the green fish. She could squirt out a cloud of black ink so thick that you couldn't see anything.

And when the shark was so close to Cindy that all Cindy could see were two rows of huge teeth, Cindy squirted out the biggest cloud of ink she had ever squirted. Then she ducked to one side just as that great shark charged full speed right into the rock.

Bonk. The shark was knocked goofy. That shark was so goofy he didn't know who he was or where he was. When the ink started to clear, the shark looked at Cindy and asked, "Who am I?"

Cindy said, "Why, you are a little yellow fish, of course."

"Oh, yeah," the shark said. "A little yellow fish."

"Well," Cindy said, "you'd better join the other yellow fish."

"Okay," the shark said. And he did just that.

So if you ever go to the place where Cindy lives, you'll see something very strange. You'll see a squid that entertains yellow fish and green fish. But one of the yellow fish looks a little bit different than the others.

EXERCISE 8   Story Details

1. Everybody, open your workbook to Lesson 5. Write your name at the top of the page. ✔
   Find the picture of Cindy the squid and the shark. ✔
- What's Cindy the squid doing in this story? (Call on a child. Ideas: *Floating in front of a rock* or *Making the shark angry*.)
- How does that big shark feel? (Call on a child. Idea: *Angry*.)
- What's that shark going to do right **after** this picture is over? (Call on a child. Idea: *Swim fast toward Cindy and slam his head into the rock*.)
- What's Cindy going to do? (Call on a child. Idea: *Squirt out black ink and move to one side*.)
- Everybody, touch the rock that shark is going to bonk his head on. ✔
- Look at the picture. There are different groups of fish. One group has yellow fish in it. That's the group at the bottom.
- Everybody, what color are the fish in the other group? (Signal.) *Green.*
- Everybody, what color is that big mean shark? (Signal.) *Gray.*
2. Your turn: Color all the things in the picture. You can make Cindy any color you want. Why can you make her any color? (Call on a child. Idea: *Squids can change colors*.)

EXERCISE 9   Part—Whole

1. Everybody, find the next page in your workbook. (Hold up a workbook.) Your page should look just like mine. ✔
2. Touch the first part of your page. (Point to the first half of the page.) You should be touching this part of your page. ✔
- Find the umbrella. ✔
3. Here's a coloring rule for the umbrella. Listen: Color the handle red. What's the rule? (Signal.) *Color the handle red.*
- Mark the handle. ✔
4. Here's another coloring rule for the umbrella. Listen: Color the covering green. What's the rule? (Signal.) *Color the covering green.*
- Mark the covering. ✔
5. Part of the umbrella is missing. What part is missing? (Signal.) *The frame.* Yes, the frame.
- Before you color the umbrella, you're going to follow the dots with your pencil to make the frame.
6. Here's the coloring rule for the frame. Listen: Color the frame blue. What's the rule? (Signal.) *Color the frame blue.*
- Mark the frame. ✔
7. Remember—the marks show you what color to make the parts. Later you can color the other objects on your paper any color you want.

EXERCISE 10   Classification

1. (Hold up your workbook. Point to second half.)
2. Here's a coloring rule for this picture. Color the buildings black. What's the rule? (Signal.) *Color the buildings black.*
- (Repeat step 2 until firm.)
3. Mark one of the buildings black. ✔
4. Here's another coloring rule for this picture. Color the containers yellow. What's the rule? (Signal.) *Color the containers yellow.*
- (Repeat step 4 until firm.)
5. Mark one of the containers yellow. ✔
6. Here's one more thing to do. Part of the house is missing. What part is missing? (Signal.) *The windows.* Yes, the windows.
- Before you color the house, follow the dots with your pencil to make the windows.
7. Remember—the marks show you what color to make the buildings and the containers.

Independent Work Summary

- Remember—the marks show you what color to make some things on the workbook. You can color the other things on the workbook any color you want.

Objectives

- Identify classes. (Exercise 1)
- Identify statements that tell "where." (Exercise 2)
- Name the days of the week and the seasons and name the first eight months of the year. (Exercise 3)
- Identify statements that tell "when" and where, and **discriminate between the statements that tell "when" and those that tell "where."** (Exercise 4)
- Identify objects in subclasses and classes (Exercise 5)
- Answer questions by generating sentences using opposites. (Exercise 6)
- Given a calendar, identify the day and date for "yesterday" and "today," and name the days of the week. (Exercise 7)
- Listen to a familiar story. (Exercise 8)
- **Answer questions about sequence in a familiar story** and make a picture consistent with the details of the story. (Exercise 9)

EXERCISE 1   Classification

1. I'm going to name some objects. Tell me a class these objects are in. (Accept all reasonable responses, but then suggest the response given.)
2. Listen: bottle, jug, cup, suitcase. Everybody, what class? (Signal.) *Containers.* Yes, containers.
   - Listen: apple, egg, bread, meat, milk, pie. Everybody, what class? (Signal.) *Food.* Yes, food.
   - Listen: saw, hammer, pliers, scissors, screwdriver. Everybody, what class? (Signal.) *Tools.* Yes, tools.
3. (Repeat step 2 until firm.)
4. I'm going to name a class. See how many objects you can name in that class.
   - Listen: containers. (Call on individual children. Accept all reasonable responses.)
5. I'm going to name another class. See how many objects you can name in that class.
   - Listen: food. (Call on individual children. Accept all reasonable responses.)
6. I'm going to name another class. See how many objects you can name in that class.
   - Listen: tools. (Call on individual children. Accept all reasonable responses.)

EXERCISE 2   Where

1. Here are some statements.
2. Listen: The cup was broken.
   - Does that statement tell **where** the cup was? (Signal.) *No.*
   - Listen: The cup was red.
   - Does that statement tell **where** the cup was? (Signal.) *No.*
   - Listen: The cup was under the rug.
   - Does that statement tell **where** the cup was? (Signal.) *Yes.*
   - Listen: The cup was old.
   - Does that statement tell **where** the cup was? (Signal.) *No.*
   - Listen: The cup was in the sink.
   - Does that statement tell **where** the cup was? (Signal.) *Yes.*
   - Listen: The cup was in back of the chair.
   - Does that statement tell **where** the cup was? (Signal.) *Yes.*
   - Listen: The cup was dirty.
   - Does that statement tell **where** the cup was? (Signal.) *No.*
   - Listen: The cup was broken.
   - Does that statement tell **where** the cup was? (Signal.) *No.*
3. (Repeat step 2 until firm.)

EXERCISE 3 Calendar Facts

1. You learned calendar facts.
- Everybody, how many days are in a week? (Signal.) *Seven.*
- Say the fact. Get ready. (Signal.) *There are seven days in a week.*
- Everybody, say the seven days of the week. Get ready. (Signal.) *Sunday, Monday, Tuesday, Wednesday, Thursday, Friday, Saturday.*
- Everybody, how many seasons are in a year? (Signal.) *Four.*
- Everybody, say that fact. Get ready. (Signal.) *There are four seasons in a year.*
- Your turn. Name the four seasons of the year. Get ready. (Signal.) *Winter, spring, summer, fall.*
2. (Repeat step 1 until firm.)
3. How many months are in a year? (Signal.) *12.*
- Say the fact about the months in a year. Get ready. (Signal.) *There are 12 months in a year.*
- Listen to the first eight months: January, February, March, April, **(pause)** May, June, July, August.
- Your turn. Say the first eight months. Get ready. (Signal.) *January, February, March, April, May, June, July, August.*
4. (Repeat step 3 until firm.)

EXERCISE 4 Where—When

1. Listen: Some statements tell **when.** Here are parts that tell when: yesterday evening, tomorrow morning, later on, while we ate, during school, in the afternoon, before lunch time.

2. Here's a statement that tells when: We watched a movie last week.
- Listen: When did we watch a movie? (Signal.) *Last week.*
- Say that statement. Get ready. (Signal.) *We watched a movie last week.*
- Say the words in the statement that tell when. Get ready. (Signal.) *Last week.*
3. New statement: Tomorrow we will go on a trip. When will we go on a trip? (Signal.) *Tomorrow.*
- Say the statement. Get ready. (Signal.) *Tomorrow we will go on a trip.*
- Say the word in that statement that tells when. Get ready. (Signal.) *Tomorrow.*
4. New statement: The crickets chirped after the sun went down. When did the crickets chirp? (Signal.) *After the sun went down.*
- Say the statement. Get ready. (Signal.) *The crickets chirped after the sun went down.*
- Say the words in that statement that tell when. Get ready. (Signal.) *After the sun went down.*
5. New statement: I will meet her at noon on Friday.
- Say the statement. Get ready. (Signal.) *I will meet her at noon on Friday.*
- Say the words in that statement that tell when. Get ready. (Signal.) *At noon on Friday.*
   Yes, at noon on Friday.
6. (Repeat steps 2 through 5 until firm.)
7. I'll say statements. Some will tell **when,** and some will tell **where.**
- Listen: She walked under the bridge. Does that tell when she walked or where she walked? (Signal.) *Where she walked.*
- Where did she walk? (Signal.) *Under the bridge.*
8. Listen: She walked to school. Does that tell when she walked or where she walked? (Signal.) *Where she walked.*
- Where did she walk? (Signal.) *To school.*
9. Listen: She walked for two hours. Does that tell when she walked or where she walked? (Signal.) *When she walked.*
- When did she walk? (Signal.) *For two hours.*
10. Listen: She walked near the river. Does that tell when she walked or where she walked? (Signal.) *Where she walked.*
- Where did she walk? (Signal.) *Near the river.*

11. Listen: She walked before she ate dinner. Does that tell when she walked or where she walked? (Signal.) *When she walked.*
  - When did she walk? (Signal.) *Before she ate dinner.*

EXERCISE 5 Classification

Living Things

1. What's the big class name for fruits and vegetables and trees and grass? (Signal.) *Plants.*
  - What's the big class name for cows and bugs and other living things that move? (Signal.) *Animals.*
  - Listen: Both plants and animals are in a very large class. What's the class that has both plants and animals in it? (Signal.) *Living things.*
  - If it's a living thing, it's either a plant or an animal.
2. I'll name some living things. You tell me if they are plants or animals.
  - Listen: alligators. Are they living things? (Signal.) *Yes.*
  - What kind of living things? (Signal.) *Animals.*
  - Listen: beans. Are they living things? (Signal.) *Yes.*
  - What kind of living things? (Signal.) *Plants.*
  - Listen: roosters. Are they living things? (Signal.) *Yes.*
  - What kind of living things? (Signal.) *Animals.*
  - Listen: flowers. Are they living things? (Signal.) *Yes.*
  - What kind of living things? (Signal.) *Plants.*
  - Listen: ants. Are they living things? (Signal.) *Yes.*
  - What kind of living things? (Signal.) *Animals.*
  - Listen: broccoli. Is that a living thing? (Signal.) *Yes.*
  - What kind of living thing? (Signal.) *Plant.*
3. Remember, if it's a living thing, it's either a plant or an animal.

4. Get ready to tell me more than one class name.
  - Listen: cherries. Are they living things? (Signal.) *Yes.*
  - Are they plants or animals? (Signal.) *Plants.*
  - Are they fruits or vegetables? (Signal.) *Fruits.*
  - Carrots. Are they living things? (Signal.) *Yes.*
  - Are they plants or animals? (Signal.) *Plants.*
  - Are they fruits or vegetables? (Signal.) *Vegetables.*
5. (Repeat step 4 until firm.)

EXERCISE 6 Opposites

Review

1. We're going to play a word game.
2. Listen: I'm thinking of a cat who is fat. It's fat. So what do you know about it? (Signal.) *It's not skinny.*
  - Listen: I'm thinking of monsters that are not young. They're not young. So what do you know about them? (Signal.) *They're old.*
  - Listen: I'm thinking about a bridge that is not dry. It's not dry. So what do you know about it? (Signal.) *It's wet.*
3. (Repeat step 2 until firm.)

EXERCISE 7 Calendar

1. (Present calendar.)
  - First you'll tell me about the days of the week. Then you'll tell me about the dates.
2. Tell me the day of the week it was yesterday. Get ready. (Signal.)
  - Tell me the day of the week it is today. Get ready. (Signal.)
  - Now the dates. Everybody, tell me yesterday's date. Get ready. (Signal.)
  - Tell me today's date. Get ready. (Signal.)
3. (Repeat step 2 until firm.)

EXERCISE 8 Sweetie and the Birdbath

Storytelling

  - Everybody, I'm going to tell you the story about Sweetie and the birdbath again. Listen carefully because when I'm done, you'll fix up a new picture that shows part of the story.

A woman named Bonnie loved birds. One day she noticed some birds cleaning themselves by splashing in a puddle on the sidewalk. She said, "Those birds shouldn't have to splash in a puddle to get clean. They need a birdbath." That was a good idea. The more Bonnie thought about getting a birdbath the more she liked the idea. "I will get a birdbath big enough for all the birds that want to take a bath."

So Bonnie went to the pet store and looked at birdbaths. She picked out the biggest birdbath they had.

The next day, a truck delivered the birdbath. Bonnie set it up in her backyard and soon some birds saw it. They called to their friends and the first thing you know all kinds of birds were splashing in the birdbath—red birds, yellow birds, spotted birds and little brown birds.

A big yellow cat lived in the house next to Bonnie's house. That cat's name was Sweetie, but that cat was anything but sweet. Sweetie loved to chase birds. When Sweetie saw all the birds in Bonnie's birdbath, Sweetie said to himself, "Yum, yum. Look at all those little birds. I'm going to sneak over to that birdbath, jump up before they know I'm around, and grab a couple of birds. Yum, yum."

So Sweetie crouched down and went through a hole in the fence. Then Sweetie snuck through some bushes that were near the birdbath—closer, closer and closer until he was almost underneath the birdbath. Sweetie heard some chirping and fluttering, so he crouched down and waited—very still, without moving anything but the tip of his tail, which moved back and forth.

Well, Sweetie couldn't see what was happening in the birdbath because Sweetie was in the bushes. But all that fluttering and chirping came about because a huge eagle decided to take a bath in the birdbath. So the eagle swooped down. And as soon as the other birds saw this huge eagle, with its great beak and its huge claws, they took off— fluttering and chirping.

Sweetie didn't know it, but there wasn't a group of little birds in that bath anymore. There was one huge bird— about three times as big as Sweetie.

Things were quiet now, so Sweetie got ready to leap up to the edge of the birdbath and grab a couple of tiny birds. Sweetie crouched down and with a great leap, shot out of the bushes and landed on the edge of the birdbath. He landed with his claws out, grabbing at the first thing he saw. He grabbed the eagle, and before Sweetie knew what was happening, that eagle grabbed him. The eagle picked Sweetie up and slammed him down into the middle of the birdbath. Splash!

Sweetie hated water, and he was all wet. He put his ears back, and shot out of that birdbath so fast he looked like a wet, yellow blur. He darted across the yard and through the hole in the fence. Then he just sat there with his mouth open and his eyes very wide.

"What happened?" Sweetie said to himself. One second he was grabbing at something and the next second he was getting slammed into the birdbath.

While Sweetie was trying to figure out what happened, he wasn't looking at the birdbath. He didn't see the eagle. That eagle finished bathing and took off. As soon as the eagle left, all the little birds returned to the birdbath.

So when Sweetie finally peeked through the hole in the fence, he didn't see the eagle. He saw a bunch of little birds, twittering and splashing around in the water.

Sweetie looked and looked at those birds for a long time. Then he said to himself, "From here those birds look pretty small and helpless. But when you get close to them, they are really big and strong. I don't think I'll go near that birdbath again."

So now Bonnie is happy because her birdbath always has a lot of birds in it. The birds are happy because they can meet all their friends and have a nice bath whenever they want. Sweetie is the only one who is not all that happy. He looks at the birds in Bonnie's yard a lot, but he never goes over there, and he spends a lot of time trying to figure out how those birds could look so small but be so big and strong.

WORKBOOK

EXERCISE 9 Story Details

1. Everybody, open your workbook to Lesson 6. Write your name on the top of the page. ✔
- What did the eagle do just **before** this picture? (Call on a child. Idea: *Slammed Sweetie into the birdbath*.)
  That's why Sweetie is all wet and looks so confused.
- What did Sweetie do just **before** this picture? (Call on a child. Idea: *Darted across the yard and through the hole in the fence*.)
- Everybody, is Sweetie in his yard or Bonnie's yard? (Signal.) *His yard.*
- What's happening in Bonnie's yard? (Call on a child. Idea: *The eagle is taking off and the little birds are returning to the birdbath*.)
- Everybody, can Sweetie see what's happening? (Signal.) *No.*
- What is Sweetie thinking about in the picture? (Call on a child. Idea: *He's trying to figure out how those birds could look so small, but be so big and strong*.)
- What will Sweetie see when he finally looks through the hole in the fence? (Call on a child. Idea: *The little birds splashing in the birdbath*.)
2. Later you can color the picture. Remember what colors to make Sweetie and the eagle. See how many birds you can find.

Objectives

- Identify statements that tell "where." (Exercise 1)
- Identify statements that tell "when" and discriminate between statements that tell "when" and those that tell "where." (Exercise 2)
- **Identify common nouns given simple definitions.** (Exercise 3)
- Name the days of the week, the seasons and **the twelve months of the year.** (Exercise 4)
- Answer questions by generating sentences using opposites. (Exercise 5)
- Given a calendar, identify the day and date for "yesterday" and "today." (Exercise 6)
- **Relate a sequence of actions of a story character to a picture with numbers (1,2,3,4) identifying where each action occurred.** (Exercise 7)
- Follow coloring rules involving parts of a whole. (Exercise 8)
- Follow coloring rules involving class and parts of a whole. (Exercise 9)

EXERCISE 1 Where

1. Here are some statements.
2. Listen: The girl is playing jump rope. Does that statement tell **where** the girl is? (Signal.) *No.*
- Listen: The girl is reading a book. Does that statement tell **where** the girl is? (Signal.) *No.*
- Listen: The girl is in front of the truck. Does that statement tell **where** the girl is? (Signal.) *Yes.*
- Listen: The girl is between her mother and father. Does that statement tell **where** the girl is? (Signal.) *Yes.*
- Listen: The girl is eating breakfast. Does that statement tell **where** the girl is? (Signal.) *No.*
- Listen: The girl is drinking milk. Does that statement tell **where** the girl is? (Signal.) *No.*
- Listen: The girl is next to the car. Does that statement tell **where** the girl is? (Signal.) *Yes.*
- Listen: The girl brushed her teeth this morning. Does that statement tell **where** the girl is? (Signal.) *No.*
- Listen: The girl is in the swimming pool. Does that statement tell **where** the girl is? (Signal.) *Yes.*
- Listen: The girl is washing her face. Does that statement tell **where** the girl is? (Signal.) *No.*
3. (Repeat step 2 until firm.)

EXERCISE 2 Where-When

1. Here's a statement that tells when: They slept well during the night.
- Say the statement. Get ready. (Signal.) *They slept well during the night.*
- Say the words in the statement that tell when. Get ready. (Signal.) *During the night.*
2. New statement: After recess we had a fire drill.
- Say that statement. Get ready. (Signal.) *After recess we had a fire drill.*
- Say the words in the statement that tell when. Get ready. (Signal.) *After recess.*
3. New statement: The baby slept all night long.
- Say that statement. Get ready. (Signal.) *The baby slept all night long.*
- Say the words in the statement that tell when. Get ready. (Signal.) *All night long.*
4. New statement: At nine in the morning, Donna left home.
- Say that statement. Get ready. (Signal.) *At nine in the morning, Donna left home.*
- Say the words in the statement that tell when. Get ready. (Signal.) *At nine in the morning.*
5. New statement: On Saturday I do a lot of things.
- Say that statement. Get ready. (Signal.) *On Saturday I do a lot of things.*
- Say the words in the statement that tell when. Get ready. (Signal.) *On Saturday.*
6. (Repeat steps 1 through 5 until firm.)
7. I'll say statements. Some will tell **when.** Some will tell **where.**

- Listen: The boat sailed under the bridge. Does that statement tell where or tell when? (Signal.) *Where.*
- Say the words that tell where. Get ready. (Signal.) *Under the bridge.*
8. Listen: The boat sailed in the evening. Does that statement tell where or tell when? (Signal.) *When.*
- Say the words that tell when. Get ready. (Signal.) *In the evening.*
9. Listen: The boat sailed near the shore. Does that statement tell where or tell when? (Signal.) *Where.*
- Say the words that tell where. Get ready. (Signal.) *Near the shore.*
10. Listen: The boat sailed for five days. Does that statement tell where or tell when? (Signal.) *When.*
- Say the words that tell when. Get ready. (Signal.) *For five days.*
11. Listen: The boat sailed during a terrible storm. Does that statement tell where or tell when? (Signal.) *When.*
- Say the words that tell when. Get ready. (Signal.) *During a terrible storm.*
12. Listen: The boat sailed over large waves. Does that statement tell where or tell when? (Signal.) *Where.*
- Say the words that tell where. Get ready. (Signal.) *Over large waves.*

EXERCISE 3   Common Information

1. Let's see how much information you remember from kindergarten.
2. What do we call a place where food is grown? (Signal.) *A farm.*
- What do we call a person who fixes teeth? (Signal.) *A dentist.*
- What do we call a person who puts out fires? (Signal.) *A firefighter.*
- What do we call a person who teaches children? (Signal.) *A teacher.*
3. (Repeat step 2 until firm.)

4. What do we call a person who puts out fires? (Signal.) *A firefighter.*
- Say the whole thing about a firefighter. Get ready. (Signal.) *A firefighter is a person who puts out fires.*
- What do we call a person who teaches children? (Signal.) *A teacher.*
- Say the whole thing about a teacher. Get ready. (Signal.) *A teacher is a person who teaches children.*
- What do we call a person who fixes teeth? (Signal.) *A dentist.*
- Say the whole thing about a dentist. Get ready. (Signal.) *A dentist is a person who fixes teeth.*
- What do we call a place where food is grown? (Signal.) *A farm.*
- Say the whole thing about a farm. Get ready. (Signal.) *A farm is a place where food is grown.*
5. (Repeat step 4 until firm.)

EXERCISE 4   Calendar Facts

1. You learned calendar facts.
- Everybody, how many days are in a week? (Signal.) *Seven.*
- Say the fact. Get ready. (Signal.) *There are seven days in a week.*
- When you name the days of the week, what day do you start with? (Signal.) *Sunday.*
- Everybody, say the seven days of the week. Get ready. (Signal.) *Sunday, Monday, Tuesday, Wednesday, Thursday, Friday, Saturday.*
- Everybody, how many seasons are in a year? (Signal.) *Four.*
- Everybody, say that fact. Get ready. (Signal.) *There are four seasons in a year.*
- Your turn. Name the four seasons of the year. Get ready. (Signal.) *Winter, spring, summer, fall.*
2. (Repeat step 1 until firm.)
3. How many months are in a year? (Signal.) *12.*
- Say the fact about the months in a year. Get ready. (Signal.) *There are 12 months in a year.*

4. Everybody, say the months through August. Get ready. (Signal.) *January, February, March, April, May, June, July, August.*
• (Repeat step 4 until firm.)
5. Here are the last four months: September, October, November, December.
• Everybody, say the last four months. Get ready. (Signal.) *September, October, November, December.*
6. (Repeat step 5 until firm.)
7. Start with January and say all twelve months with me. Get ready. *January, February, March, April, May, June, July, August, September, October, November, December.*
8. Your turn. Start with January and say all twelve months. Get ready. (Signal.) *January, February, March, April, May, June, July, August, September, October, November, December.*
9. (Repeat step 8 until firm.)

EXERCISE 5 Opposites
Review
1. We're going to play a word game.
2. Listen: I'm thinking about a bed that is big. So what do you know about it? (Signal.) *It's not small.*
• Listen: I'm thinking of turtles that are old. So what do you know about them? (Signal.) *They're not young.*
• Listen: I'm thinking about a hill that is small. So what do you know about it? (Signal.) *It's not big.*
3. (Repeat step 2 until firm.)

EXERCISE 6 Calendar
1. (Present calendar.)
• First you'll tell me about the days of the week. Then you'll tell me about the dates.
2. Tell me the day of the week it was yesterday. Get ready. (Signal.)
• Tell me the day of the week it is today. Get ready. (Signal.)
• Now the dates. Everybody, tell me yesterday's date. Get ready. (Signal.)
• Tell me today's date. Get ready. (Signal.)
3. (Repeat step 2 until firm.)

EXERCISE 7 Rita
Sequencing

1. Everybody, open your workbook to Lesson 7. Write your name at the top of the page. ✔
• I'm going to tell you a story about a girl named Rita. You're going to touch the circles I tell you about. Then I'll see who can tell the story to me.
• Listen: Rita is trying to get across the stream without getting wet. So here's what she does first: She backs up.
• Everybody, what does she do first? (Signal.) *Backs up.*
2. One of the circles shows where she goes when she backs up. Touch the circle that shows where she is when she backs up. ✔
• Everybody, what number is in that circle? (Signal.) *One.*
• That's what Rita does first.
3. After Rita backs up, she runs to the bank of the stream.
• Everybody, what does she do? (Signal.) *Runs to the bank of the stream.*
• Touch the circle that shows where she is when she's at the bank of the stream. ✔
• Everybody, what number is in that circle? (Signal.) *Two.*
4. Let's go back to the beginning. First Rita backs up. Touch the circle. ✔
• Then Rita runs to the bank. Touch the circle. ✔
• Now Rita jumps and lands on the big rock in the middle of the stream.
• Everybody, where does she land? (Signal.) *On the big rock.*
• Touch the circle that shows where she lands. ✔
• Everybody, what number is in that circle? (Signal.) *Three.*

Lesson 7 **39**

5. Then Rita jumps from the big rock and lands on the **other** bank of the stream. She lands on the **other** bank of the stream.
- Everybody, where does she land? (Signal.) *On the other bank of the stream.*
- Touch the circle that shows where she lands. ✔
- Everybody, what number is in that circle? (Signal.) *Four.*
6. I'll say the whole thing. Touch the right circles.
- **First,** Rita backs up. What number is in the circle? (Signal.) *One.*
- **Next,** Rita runs to the bank. What number is in the circle? (Signal.) *Two.*
- **Next,** Rita jumps and lands on the big rock. What number is in the circle? (Signal.) *Three.*
- **Next,** Rita jumps from the big rock and lands on the other bank of the stream. What number is in the circle? (Signal.) *Four.*
7. Let's see who can tell the story without making any mistakes. Remember, you have to tell what Rita did at each number.
- (Call on a child:) You tell the story. Everybody else, touch the numbers and make sure that (child's name) tells the right thing for each number.
  (Praise child for telling what happened at each circle. Repeat with several children.)
8. Everybody, I'm going to ask you some hard questions about Rita.
- Touch the circle that shows Rita on the rock. ✔
- Everybody, what number is in the circle you're touching? (Signal.) *Three.*
- Now touch the circle that shows where Rita went just **after** she was on the rock. ✔
- Everybody, what number is in the circle you're touching? (Signal.) *Four.*
- Now touch the circle that shows where Rita was when she backed up. ✔
- Everybody, what number is in the circle you're touching? (Signal.) *One.*
- Now touch the circle that shows where Rita went just **after** she backed up. ✔
- Everybody, what number is in the circle you're touching? (Signal.) *Two.*
9. Later you can color the picture of Rita.

EXERCISE 8 Part-Whole

1. Everybody, find the next page in your workbook. (Hold up a workbook.) Your page should look just like mine. ✔
2. Touch the first part of your page. (Point to the first half of the page.) You should be touching this part of your page. ✔
3. Here's a coloring rule for the wagon. Listen: Color the body blue. What's the rule? (Signal.) *Color the body blue.*
- Mark the body. ✔
4. Here's another coloring rule for the wagon. Listen: Color the frame purple. What's the rule? (Signal.) *Color the frame purple.*
- Mark the frame. ✔
5. Here's another coloring rule for the wagon. Listen: Color the wheels green. What's the rule? (Signal.) *Color the wheels green.*
- Mark the wheels. ✔
6. Part of the wagon is missing. What part is missing? (Signal.) *The handle.*
- Yes, the handle. Before you color the wagon, you're going to follow the dots and make the handle.
7. And here's the coloring rule for the handle. Listen: Color the handle black. What's the rule? (Signal.) *Color the handle black.*
- Mark the handle. ✔

EXERCISE 9 Classification

1. (Hold up your workbook. Point to second half.) Find the truck. ✔
2. Here's a coloring rule for this picture. Color the vehicles yellow. What's the rule? (Signal.) *Color the vehicles yellow.*
   • (Repeat step 2 until firm.)
3. Mark one of the vehicles yellow. ✔
4. Here's another coloring rule for this picture. Color the tools orange. What's the rule? (Signal.) *Color the tools orange.*
   • (Repeat step 4 until firm.)
5. Mark one of the tools orange. ✔
6. Here's one more thing to do. Part of the broom is missing. What part is missing? (Call on a child.) *The bristles.*
   • Yes, bristles. Before you color the broom, follow the dots and make the bristles.
7. Remember—the marks show you what color to make the vehicles and the tools. You can color the other things any color you want.

LESSON 8

Objectives

- **Follow directions involving if-then and discriminate between same and different actions.** (Exercise 1)
- Discriminate between statements that tell "when," "where" or **"neither."** (Exercise 2)
- **Answer questions about previously learned calendar facts.** (Exercise 3)
- **Name ways that two common objects are the same and/or different.** (Exercise 4)
- Identify classes **and name objects in those classes.** (Exercise 5)
- Given a calendar, identify the day and date for "yesterday" and "today." (Exercise 6)
- **Answer questions about the events in a familiar story.** (Exercise 7)
- Relate a sequence of actions of a story character to a picture with numbers showing where various actions occurred. (Exercise 8)
- Follow coloring rules involving class. (Exercise 9)
- Follow coloring rules involving specific objects. (Exercise 10)

EXERCISE 1 Actions

1. We're going to learn a rule and play some games.
2. Listen to this rule: **If the teacher touches the floor, say "yes."**
   - Listen again. **If the teacher touches the floor, say "yes."**
   - Everybody, say the rule. Get ready. (Signal.) *If the teacher touches the floor, say yes.*
3. (Repeat step 2 until firm.)
4. Tell me, what are you going to say if I touch the floor? (Signal.) *Yes.*
   - Are you going to say **yes** if I touch the floor? (Signal.) *Yes.*
   - Are you going to say **yes** if I touch my head? (Signal.) *No.*
   - Are you going to say **yes** if I say "Touch the floor"? (Signal.) *No.*
5. Now we're going to play the game.
6. Let's see if I can fool you. Get ready. (Pause.) (Touch your head.) (Signal.) (The children should not say anything.)
   - Get ready. (Pause.) (Touch the floor.) (Signal.) *Yes.*
   - See if I can fool you this time. Get ready. (Pause.) **Yes.** (Signal.) (The children should not say anything.)
   - Get ready. (Pause.) (Touch the floor.) (Signal.) (Children say *yes*.)
7. (Repeat step 6 until firm.)
   - That's the end of the game.
8. Here's our next action game. Get ready.
9. Everybody, point to the floor. (Signal.) ✔
   - Good. Stop pointing to the floor.

10. Now tell me if I do the same thing you did or something different.
    - Watch me. (Point to the floor.) Did I do the same thing or something different? (Signal.) *The same thing.*
    - Watch me. (Point to the ceiling.) Did I do the same thing or something different? (Signal.) *Something different.*
    - Watch me. (Point to the floor.) Did I do the same thing or something different? (Signal.) *The same thing.*
11. (Repeat step 10 until firm.)

EXERCISE 2 Where-When

1. I'll say statements. Some will tell when. Some will tell where. Some will tell neither when nor where. For each statement, you'll say **when, where,** or **neither.**
2. Listen: We rode our bikes very fast. Tell me: when, where, or neither. (Signal.) *Neither.*
   - Listen: We rode our bikes on a dirt road. Tell me: when, where, or neither. (Signal.) *Where.*
   - Say the words that tell where. Get ready. (Signal.) *On a dirt road.*
   - Listen: We rode our bikes through large puddles. Tell me: when, where, or neither. (Signal.) *Where.*
   - Say the words that tell where. Get ready. (Signal.) *Through large puddles.*
   - Listen: We rode our bikes and stopped three times. Tell me: when, where, or neither. (Signal.) *Neither.*
   - Listen: We rode our bikes yesterday morning. Tell me: when, where, or neither. (Signal.) *When.*

- Say the words that tell when. Get ready. (Signal.) *Yesterday morning.*
- Listen: We rode our bikes before it started to rain. Tell me: when, where, or neither. (Signal.) *When.*
- Say the words that tell when. Get ready. (Signal.) *Before it started to rain.*
- Listen: We rode our bikes through a tunnel. Tell me: when, where, or neither. (Signal.) *Where.*
- Say the words that tell where. Get ready. (Signal.) *Through a tunnel.*

EXERCISE 3 Calendar Facts

1. We're going to talk about days and months.
- Everybody, how many days are in a week? (Signal.) *Seven.*
- Say the fact. Get ready. (Signal.) *There are seven days in a week.*
- Everybody, say the seven days of the week. Get ready. (Signal.) *Sunday, Monday, Tuesday, Wednesday, Thursday, Friday, Saturday.*
2. Everybody, how many months are in a year? (Signal.) *12.*
- Say the fact about the months in a year. Get ready. (Signal.) *There are 12 months in a year.*
3. Name the months of the year through December. Get ready. (Signal.) *January, February, March, April, May, June, July, August, September, October, November, December.*
4. (Repeat step 3 until firm.)
5. Everybody, how many seasons are in a year? (Signal.) *Four.*
- Say the seasons of the year. Get ready. (Signal.) *Winter, spring, summer, fall.*
6. (Repeat step 5 until firm.)

EXERCISE 4 Same-Different

1. We're going to tell how things are the same and how they are different.
- Listen: a bird and an airplane. See if you can think of some ways they are the same. (Call on individual children. Accept reasonable responses such as: *They both fly.*)
2. My turn. I'm going to name some ways they are **different.**
- Listen: A bird is an animal, but an airplane is not an animal. Everybody, say that. Get ready. (Signal.) *A bird is an animal, but an airplane is not an animal.*

- That's one way they are different.
- Listen: A bird has eyes, but an airplane does not have eyes. Everybody, say that. Get ready. (Signal.) *A bird has eyes, but an airplane does not have eyes.*
- That's another way they are different.
3. Now it's your turn.
- Name a way that a bird and an airplane are different. (Call on individual children. For appropriate responses, say:) Everybody, say that. Get ready. (Signal.)

EXERCISE 5 Classification

1. I'm going to name some objects. Tell me a class these objects are in. (Accept all reasonable responses, but then suggest the response given.)
2. Listen: cat, lion, mouse, dog, squirrel. Everybody, what class? (Signal.) *Animals.* Yes, animals.
- Listen: chair, sofa, bed, lamp, rug, cabinet. Everybody, what class? (Signal.) *Furniture.* Yes, furniture.
- Listen: fire station, house, grocery store, school. Everybody, what class? (Signal.) *Buildings.* Yes, buildings.
3. (Repeat step 2 until firm.)
4. I'm going to name a class. See how many objects you can name in that class. Listen: animals. (Call on individual children. Accept all reasonable responses.)
- I'm going to name another class. See how many objects you can name in that class. Listen: furniture. (Call on individual children. Accept all reasonable responses for large and small furniture: *bed, dresser, table, rug, lamp, couch,* and so on.)
- I'm going to name another class. See how many objects you can name in that class. Listen: buildings. (Call on individual children. Accept all reasonable responses.)

EXERCISE 6 Calendar

1. (Present calendar.)
2. Tell me the day of the week it was yesterday. Get ready. (Signal.)
- Tell me the day of the week it is today. Get ready. (Signal.)
- Now the dates.
- Everybody, tell me yesterday's date. Get ready. (Signal.)
- Tell me today's date. Get ready. (Signal.)
3. (Repeat step 2 until firm.)

EXERCISE 7   Sweetie And The Birdbath

Story Review

1. Everybody, let's see how well you remember the story about Sweetie and the birdbath. I'll stop when I'm reading the story. See if you can tell me what happens next in the story.

> A woman named Bonnie loved birds. One day she noticed some birds cleaning themselves by splashing in a puddle on the sidewalk. She said, "Those birds shouldn't have to splash in a puddle to get clean. They need a birdbath." That was a good idea. The more Bonnie thought about getting a birdbath the more she liked the idea. "I will get a birdbath big enough for all the birds that want to take a bath."
>
> So Bonnie went to . . .

- Where did she go? (Call on a child. Idea: *To the pet store to get a birdbath*.)
- Let's see if you are right.

> So Bonnie went to the pet store and looked at birdbaths. She picked out the biggest birdbath they had.
>
> The next day, a truck delivered the birdbath. Bonnie set it up in her backyard and soon some birds saw it. They called to their friends, and the first thing you know all kinds of birds were doing something.

- What were they doing? (Call on a child. Idea: *Splashing in the birdbath*.)
- Let's see if you are right.

> The birds called to their friends and the first thing you know all kinds of birds were splashing in the birdbath—red birds, yellow birds, spotted birds and little brown birds.
>
> A big yellow cat lived in the house next to Bonnie's house. That cat's name was Sweetie, but that cat was anything but sweet. Sweetie loved to chase birds.

> When Sweetie saw all the birds in Bonnie's birdbath, Sweetie said to himself, "Yum, yum. Look at all those little birds. I'm going to sneak over to that birdbath, jump up before they know I'm around, and grab a couple of birds. Yum, yum."
>
> So Sweetie crouched down and went through a hole in the fence. Then Sweetie snuck through some . . .

- What did Sweetie sneak through? (Call on a child. Idea: *Through some bushes*.)
- Let's see if you are right.

> Sweetie snuck through some bushes that were near the birdbath—closer, closer and closer until he was almost underneath the birdbath. Sweetie heard some chirping and fluttering, so he crouched down and waited—very still, without moving anything but the tip of his tail, which moved back and forth.
>
> Well, Sweetie couldn't see what was happening in the birdbath because Sweetie was in the bushes. But all that fluttering and chirping came about because something happened.

- What was that? (Call on a child. Idea: *The eagle got in the birdbath*.)
- Let's see if you are right.

> All that fluttering and chirping came about because a huge eagle decided to take a bath in the birdbath. So the eagle swooped down. And as soon as the other birds saw this huge eagle, with its great beak and its huge claws, they took off—fluttering and chirping. Sweetie didn't know it, but there wasn't a group of little birds in that bath anymore. There was one huge bird—about three times as big as Sweetie.
>
> Things were quiet now. So Sweetie got ready to do something.

- What did he plan to do? (Call on a child. Idea: *Leap into the birdbath and grab some birds*.)

- Let's see if you are right.

Sweetie got ready to leap up to the edge of the birdbath and grab a couple of tiny birds. Sweetie crouched down and with a great leap, shot out of the bushes and landed on the edge of the birdbath. He landed with his claws out, grabbing at the first thing he saw. He grabbed something.

- Tell me what he grabbed and what happened next. (Call on a child. Idea: *Sweetie grabbed the eagle, and the eagle slammed Sweetie into the birdbath.*)
- Let's see if you are right.

Sweetie grabbed the eagle, and before Sweetie knew what was happening, that eagle grabbed him. The eagle picked Sweetie up and slammed him down into the middle of the birdbath. Splash!

Sweetie hated water, and he was all wet. He put his ears back and did something.

- What did he do? (Call on a child. Idea: *He ran back to his own yard.*)
- Let's see if you are right.

Sweetie put his ears back and shot out of that birdbath so fast he looked like a wet yellow blur. He darted across the yard and through the hole in the fence. Then he just sat there with his mouth open and his eyes very wide.

"What happened?" Sweetie said to himself. One second he was grabbing at something and the next second he was getting slammed into the birdbath.

While Sweetie was trying to figure out what happened . . . something was happening in the next yard.

- What was happening? (Call on a child. Idea: *The eagle was taking off and the little birds were returning to the birdbath.*)
- Let's see if you are right.

The eagle finished bathing and took off. As soon as the eagle left, all the little birds returned to the birdbath.

So when Sweetie finally peeked through the hole in the fence, he didn't see the eagle. He saw a bunch of little birds, twittering and splashing around in the water.

Sweetie looked and looked at those birds for a long time. Then he said to himself, "From here those birds look pretty small and helpless. But when you get close to them, they are really . . . "

- What? (Signal.) *Big and strong.*
- So how often is Sweetie going to go over to that birdbath? (Call on a child. Idea: *Never again.*)
- Let's see if you are right.

Sweetie said to himself, "From here those birds look pretty small and helpless. But when you get close to them, they are really big and strong. I don't think I'll go near that birdbath again."

So now Bonnie is happy because her birdbath always has a lot of birds in it. The birds are happy because they can meet all their friends and have a nice bath whenever they want. The only one who is not all that happy is . . .

- Who? (Signal.) *Sweetie.*
- Why isn't Sweetie happy? (Call on a child. Accept reasonable ideas.)
- Right.

Sweetie is the only one who is not all that happy. He looks at the birds in Bonnie's yard a lot, but he never goes over there, and he spends a lot of time trying to figure out . . . something.

- What is that? (Call on a child. Idea: *How those birds could look so small but be so big and strong.*)
- Yes.

Sweetie spends a lot of time trying to figure out how those birds could look so small but be so big and strong.

2. Raise your hand if you knew the right answers to all the questions about this story. ✔
   - You did a really great job of remembering the story.

WORKBOOK

EXERCISE 8   Sequencing

Rita

1. Everybody, open your workbook to Lesson 8. Write your name at the top of the page. ✔
2. I'm going to tell another story about Rita. But you're going to help me finish the story. The numbers show what happened in this story.
3. Rita is trying to get across the stream again without getting wet. We'll see if she did it the right way.
   - Rita did five things to get across the stream. The **first** thing she did is shown by the circle with a 1 in it. The **next** thing she did is shown by the circle with a 2 in it. The **next** thing she did is shown by the circle with what number in it? (Signal.) *Three.*
   - The **next** thing she did is shown by the circle with what number in it? (Signal.) *Four.*
   - The **last** thing she did is shown by the circle with what number in it? (Signal.) *Five.*
4. Everybody, touch Rita. ✔
   - That's where we start.
   - Touch the circle that shows what she did **first.** ✔
   - Everybody, what number is in that circle? (Signal.) *One.*

- That number shows what Rita did first. What did she do? (Signal.) *Backed up.*
5. Touch the circle with the **next** number. ✔
   - Everybody, what number is in that circle? (Signal.) *Two.*
   - Circle 2 shows what Rita did **after** she backed up. What did she do? (Signal.) *Ran back to the bank of the stream.*
6. Touch the circle with the **next** number. ✔
   - Everybody, what number is in that circle? (Signal.) *Three.*
   - Circle 3 shows what Rita did **after** she ran to the bank of the stream. What did she do? (Call on a child. Idea: *Jumped to the little rock*.)
7. Touch the circle with the **next** number. ✔
   - Everybody, what number is in that circle? (Signal.) *Four.*
   - Circle 4 shows where Rita went just **after** she jumped to the little rock. Where did she go? (Signal.) *Into the water.*
   - Oh, dear. I guess she didn't make it across the stream without getting wet.
8. Touch the circle with the **next** number. ✔
   - Everybody, what number is in that circle? (Signal.) *Five.*
   - Circle 5 shows what Rita did **after** she fell kaplunk in the water. What did she do? (Call on a child. Idea: *Waded to the other bank of the stream*.)
   - Was Rita wet or dry when she finally got to number 5? (Signal.) *Wet.*
9. Let's see who can tell the story without making any mistakes. Remember, you have to tell what Rita did at each number.
   - (Call on a child:) You tell the story. Everybody else, touch the numbers and make sure that (child's name) tells the right thing for each number.
   (Praise child for telling what happened at each circle. Repeat with several children.)
10. Everybody, touch the circle that shows Rita in the water. ✔
    - Everybody, what number is in that circle? (Signal.) *Four.*
    - Now touch the circle that shows where Rita was just **before** she fell in the water. ✔
    - Everybody, what number is in the circle you're touching? (Signal.) *Three.*
    - Where was she when she was at circle 3? (Call on a child. Idea: *On a little rock in the middle of the stream*.)

- Here's a hard one. Touch the circle that shows Rita just **after** she fell into the water. ✔
- Everybody, what number is in the circle you're touching? (Signal.) *Five.*
- Where was Rita when she was at circle 5? (Call on a child. Idea: *On the other bank of the stream*.)
- How do you think she felt? (Call on a child. Accept reasonable responses.)
- How wet do you think she was? (Call on a child. Accept reasonable responses.)

EXERCISE 9   Classification

1. Everybody, find the next page in your workbook. (Hold up a workbook.) Your page should look just like mine. ✔
2. Touch the first part of the page. (Point to the first half of the page.) You should be touching this part of your page. ✔
3. Find the bed. ✔
4. Here's a coloring rule for this picture. Color the animals brown. What's the rule? (Signal.) *Color the animals brown.*
- (Repeat step 4 until firm.)
5. Mark one of the animals brown. ✔

6. Here's another coloring rule for this picture. Color the furniture orange. What's the rule? (Signal.) *Color the furniture orange.*
- (Repeat step 6 until firm.)
7. Mark one piece of furniture. ✔
8. Here's one more thing to do. Part of the table is missing. What part is missing? (Signal.) *The legs.*
- Before you color the table, follow the dots with your pencil to make the legs.

EXERCISE 10   Coloring Rules

1. (Hold up your workbook. Point to second half.) Find the front porch. ✔
2. Here's a coloring rule for this picture. Listen: Make every flower yellow. What's the rule? (Signal.) *Make every flower yellow.*
- (Repeat step 2 until firm.)
3. Make a yellow mark on one of the flowers. ✔
4. Here's another coloring rule for this picture. Listen: Make every dog black. What's the rule? (Signal.) *Make every dog black.*
- (Repeat step 4 until firm.)
5. Make a mark on one of the dogs. ✔
6. Some chairs have parts missing. What parts? (Signal.) *The legs.*
- Yes, the legs. You'll have to follow the dots and make the legs before you color them.
7. Here's the last coloring rule. Listen: Make all the chairs any color you want. What's the rule? (Signal.) *Make all the chairs any color you want.*
8. Pick a color and make a mark on one of the chairs. ✔
- What's the rule for your chairs? (Call on individual children. Idea: *Make all the chairs _____*.)
9. Remember—the marks show you what color to make the objects.

Objectives

- Follow directions involving if-then, and discriminate between same and different actions. (Exercise 1)
- Identify classes and name members of those classes. (Exercise 2)
- Identify statements that tell "when" and "where" **and generate statements that tell "when" and "where."** (Exercise 3)
- Answer questions by generating sentences using opposites. (Exercise 4)
- Answer questions about previously learned calendar facts. (Exercise 5)
- Name ways that two common objects are the same and/or different. (Exercise 6)
- **Answer questions involving absurdity of function.** (Exercise 7)
- Given a calendar, identify the day and date for "yesterday" and "today." (Exercise 8)
- Answer questions about the events in a familiar story. (Exercise 9)
- Relate a sequence of actions of a story character to a picture with numbers showing where various actions occurred, and fix a picture to make it consistent with the story. (Exercise 10)
- Follow coloring rules involving parts of a whole. (Exercise 11)
- Follow coloring rules involving class. (Exercise 12)

EXERCISE 1 Actions

1. Everybody, touch both your ears. Get ready. (Signal.) ✔
- Good. Stop touching your ears. ✔
2. Now tell me if I do the same thing you did or something different.
- Watch me. (Touch one ear.) Did I do the same thing or something different? (Signal.) *Something different.*
- Watch me. (Touch both ears.) Did I do the same thing or something different? (Signal.) *The same thing.*
- Watch me. (Touch both ears.) Did I do the same thing or something different? (Signal.) *The same thing.*
3. (Repeat step 2 until firm.)
4. Now we're going to learn a rule and play a game.
5. Listen to this rule: If the teacher says **one** or says **two,** hold up your hand.
- Listen again: If the teacher says **one** or says **two,** hold up your hand.
- Everybody, say the rule. (Signal.) *If the teacher says **one** or says **two,** hold up your hand.*
6. (Repeat step 5 until firm.)
7. Tell me, what are you going to do if I say **one** or say **two?** (Signal.) *Hold up my hand.*
- Are you going to hold up your hand if I hold up my hand? (Signal.) *No.*
- Are you going to hold up your hand if I say **three?** (Signal.) *No.*
- Are you going to hold up your hand if I say **one?** (Signal.) *Yes.*
8. Let's see if I can fool you. Get ready. (Pause.) **Two.** (Signal.) (The children should hold up their hands.)
- See if I can fool you. Get ready. (Pause.) **Now.** (Signal.) (The children should not do anything.)
- See if I can fool you this time. Get ready. (Pause.) **One.** (Signal.) (The children should hold up their hands.)
9. (Repeat step 8 until firm.)

EXERCISE 2 Classification

1. I'm going to name some objects. Tell me a class these objects are in. (Accept all reasonable responses, but then suggest the response given.)
2. Listen: truck, car, train, motorcycle, boat. Everybody, what class? (Signal.) *Vehicles.* Yes, vehicles.
- Listen: hammer, shovel, pliers, saw, hoe. Everybody, what class? (Signal.) *Tools.* Yes, tools.
- Listen: cake, rice, beans, milk, bread. Everybody, what class? (Signal.) *Food.* Yes, food.
3. (Repeat step 2 until firm.)

4. I'm going to name a class. See how many objects you can name in that class. Listen: vehicles. (Call on individual children. Accept all reasonable responses.)
- I'm going to name another class. See how many objects you can name in that class. Listen: tools. (Call on individual children. Accept all reasonable responses.)
- I'm going to name another class. See how many objects you can name in that class. Listen: food. (Call on individual children. Accept all reasonable responses.)

EXERCISE 3 When-Where

1. I'm going to say statements about the bell. Some tell when, some don't tell when.
2. Listen: The bell rang at 4 o'clock.
- Say that statement. Get ready. (Signal.) *The bell rang at 4 o'clock.*
- Does that statement tell **when?** (Signal.) *Yes.*
3. Listen: The bell rang yesterday.
- Say that statement. Get ready. (Signal.) *The bell rang yesterday.*
- Does that statement tell **when?** (Signal.) *Yes.*
4. Listen: The bell was loud.
- Say that statement. Get ready. (Signal.) *The bell was loud.*
- Does that statement tell **when?** (Signal.) *No.*
5. (Repeat steps 2–4 until firm.)
6. I'll say some more statements. You'll tell me about when and where.
7. Listen: The bell was on top of a building.
- Say that statement. Get ready. (Signal.) *The bell was on top of a building.*
- Does that statement tell **when?** (Signal.) *No.*
- Does that statement tell **where?** (Signal.) *Yes.*
8. Listen: The bell was very old. Say that statement. Get ready. (Signal.) *The bell was very old.*
- Does that statement tell **when?** (Signal.) *No.*
- Does that statement tell **where?** (Signal.) *No.*
9. (Repeat steps 7 and 8 until firm.)
10. Your turn.
- Make up a statement about the bell that tells **when.** (Call on individual children. Praise good statements.)

- Make up a statement about the bell that tells **where.** (Call on individual children. Praise good statements.)

EXERCISE 4 Opposites

1. We're going to play a word game.
2. Listen: I'm thinking about a canoe that is long. It's long. So what else do you know about it? (Signal.) *It's not short.*
- Listen: I'm thinking of an elephant that is old. It's old. So what else do you know about it? (Signal.) *It's not young.*
- Listen: I'm thinking about drinks that are cold. They're cold. So what else do you know about them? (Signal.) *They're not hot.*
3. (Repeat step 2 until firm.)

EXERCISE 5 Calendar Facts

1. We're going to talk about days and months.
- Everybody, how many days are in a week? (Signal.) *Seven.*
- Say the fact. Get ready. (Signal.) *There are seven days in a week.*
- Everybody, say the days of the week. Get ready. (Signal.) *Sunday, Monday, Tuesday, Wednesday, Thursday, Friday, Saturday.*
2. How many months are in a year? (Signal.) *12.*
- Say the fact. Get ready. (Signal.) *There are 12 months in a year.*
3. Name the months of the year through December. Get ready. (Signal.) *January, February, March, April, May, June, July, August, September, October, November, December.*
4. (Repeat step 3 until firm.)
5. Everybody, how many seasons are in a year? (Signal.) *Four.*
- Say the seasons of the year. Get ready. (Signal.) *Winter, spring, summer, fall.*
6. (Repeat step 5 until firm.)

EXERCISE 6 Same-Different

1. We're going to tell how things are the same and how they are different.
- Listen: a paper bag and a suitcase. See if you can think of some ways they are the same. (Call on individual children. Accept reasonable responses such as: *They are both containers.*)

2. My turn. I'm going to name some ways they are different.

- Listen: A paper bag is made of paper, but a suitcase is not made of paper. Everybody, say that. Get ready. (Signal.) *A paper bag is made of paper, but a suitcase is not made of paper.*

- That's one way they are different.

- Listen: A paper bag can be used for garbage, but a suitcase isn't for garbage. Everybody, say that. (Signal.) *A paper bag can be used for garbage, but a suitcase isn't for garbage.*

- That's another way they are different.

3. Now it's your turn.

4. Name a way that a paper bag and a suitcase are different. (Call on a child. If the child gives an appropriate response, say:) Everybody, say that. Get ready. (Signal.)

5. Name another way that a paper bag and a suitcase are different. (Call on another child. If the child gives an appropriate response, say:) Everybody, say that. Get ready. (Signal.)

6. (Repeat step 5 until all children who have raised their hands have responded.)

7. Here's another one. Listen: a glove and a hat. Think of them. See if you can name two ways they are the same. (Call on individual children. Have the group repeat each correct answer. Then say:) You told me how a glove and a hat are . . . (Signal.) *the same.*

8. Listen: a glove and a hat. Think of them. See if you can name two ways they are different. (Call on individual children. Have the group repeat each correct answer. Then say:) You told me how a glove and a hat are . . . (Signal.) *different.*

EXERCISE 7   **Absurdity**

1. Listen: Things that are very silly are **absurd.** What's another word for very silly? (Signal.) *Absurd.*

2. Why do we need hats? (Call on a child. Praise good answers such as: *to protect our heads; to keep our heads warm.*)

3. Why do we need shoes? (Call on a child. Praise good answers such as: *to protect our feet; to keep our feet warm.*)

4. Would you wear a hat on your arm? (Signal.) *No.*
   That would be absurd.

- Would you wear a hat on your head? (Signal.) *Yes.*

- Would you use a hat to hammer a nail? (Signal.) *No.*
   That would be absurd.

5. Remember, things that are very silly are **absurd.**

EXERCISE 8   **Calendar**

1. (Present calendar.)

- First you'll tell me about the days of the week. Then you'll tell me about the dates.

2. Tell me the day of the week it was yesterday. Get ready. (Signal.)

- Tell me the day of the week it is today. Get ready. (Signal.)

- Now the dates. Everybody, tell me yesterday's date. Get ready. (Signal.)

- Tell me today's date. Get ready. (Signal.)

3. (Repeat step 2 until firm.)

EXERCISE 9   **Cindy The Squid**

Story Review

1. Everybody, let's see how well you remember the story about Cindy the squid. I'll stop when I'm reading the story. See if you can tell me what happens next in the story.

Cindy was a squid who lived among the rocks with schools of little yellow fish and schools of little green fish. Cindy liked these fish, but she didn't like the sharks because when they came to the rocks, they were looking for something to eat. Those sharks loved to eat yellow fish and green fish.

One day a huge shark came to the rocks.

- Listen: What did the yellow fish and green fish do? (Call on a child. Idea: *Swam away.*)

- Everybody, who didn't move at all? (Signal.) *Cindy.*

- Let's see if you are right.

The yellow fish darted off this way and that way. The green fish darted off this way and that way. But Cindy the squid didn't move. She said to herself, "I've had enough of these sharks. It is time to teach this shark a lesson."

So she moved right in front of a big rock and started to wave her little tentacles at the shark. "Here I am, you bag of teeth. Come and get me."

The shark looked at Cindy. "Come on," Cindy said. "Look at these tasty tentacles. Yum, yum. Come and get me, tooth face."

The shark was mad. He said to himself, "I'm going to eat that squirmy thing before it can move."

- Listen: What did the shark do next? (Call on a child. Idea: *Swam fast at Cindy*.)
- Let's see if you are right.

And with all the speed and all the strength the shark had, he shot forward through the water, right at Cindy.

But, aha. Cindy had a trick.

- Listen: What trick did Cindy do? (Call on a child. Idea: *Squirted out a cloud of black ink*.)
- Why would that trick fool the shark? (Call on a child. Idea: *The shark wouldn't be able to see*.)
- Let's see if you are right.

Cindy had a trick. She sometimes used that trick to entertain the yellow fish and the green fish. She could squirt out a cloud of black ink so thick that you couldn't see anything.

And when the shark was so close to Cindy that all Cindy could see were two rows of huge teeth, Cindy squirted out the biggest cloud of ink she had ever squirted.

- Then Cindy did something else. What was that? (Call on a child. Idea: *Moved to the side*.)
- Let's see if you are right about what Cindy did.

Then Cindy ducked to one side just as that great shark charged full speed right into the rock.

Bonk.

- What was that sound? (Call on a child. Idea: *It was the sound of the shark hitting its head*.)
- What happened to the shark when he got bonked? (Call on a child. Idea: *He couldn't remember who he was*.)
- Let's see if you are right.

The shark was knocked goofy. That shark was so goofy he didn't know who he was or where he was. When the ink started to clear, the shark looked at Cindy and asked . . . a question.

- What did the shark ask? (Signal.) *Who am I?*
- And what did Cindy tell the shark? (Call on a child. Idea: *Cindy told the shark that he was a little yellow fish*.)
- Let's see if you are right.

When the ink started to clear, the shark looked at Cindy and asked, "Who am I?"

Cindy said, "Why, you are a little yellow fish, of course." "Oh, yeah," the shark said.

"A little yellow fish."

- What is Cindy going to tell the shark to do next? (Call on a child. Idea: *Cindy will tell the shark to swim with the yellow fish*.)
- Let's see if you are right.

"Well," Cindy said, "you'd better join the other yellow fish."

"Okay," the shark said. And he did just that.

So if you ever go to the place where Cindy lives, you'll see something very strange. You'll see a squid that entertains yellow fish and green fish. But one of the yellow fish looks a little bit different than the others.

- We know who that different-looking fish is, don't we?
2. Raise your hand if you knew the right answers to all the questions about this story. ✔
- You really did a great job of remembering the story.

WORKBOOK

EXERCISE 10   Sequence Story

Sweetie And The Birdbath

1. Everybody, open your workbook to Lesson 9. Write your name at the top of the page.
2. The picture shows Sweetie and the birdbath. The numbers show what Sweetie did first, what he did next and so forth. Listen:

   Sweetie saw the little birds in the birdbath and said, "Yum, yum. I'm going to grab a couple of little birds."
   So the first thing he did was to sneak up to number 1 in the picture.

3. Everybody touch number 1. ✔
- Where is Sweetie when he's at number 1? (Call on a child. Idea: *Near the hole in the fence*.)

   After Sweetie snuck through the hole in the fence, he darted over to number 2.

4. Everybody, touch number 2. ✔
- Where is he when he's at number 2? (Call on a child. Idea: *In the bushes near the fence*.)

   He was in the bushes that were closest to the fence.
   Then he snuck to number 3.

5. Everybody, touch number 3. ✔
- Where is he when he's at number 3? (Call on a child. Idea: *Still in the bushes—closer to the birdbath*.)

   Then he snuck to number 4.

6. Everybody, touch number 4. ✔
- Where is he when he's at number 4? (Call on a child. Idea: *In the bushes closest to the birdbath*.) Yes.

   Now Sweetie was in the part of the bushes. That was as close to the birdbath as he could get. He was under the bushes so he couldn't see what was happening in the birdbath, but he heard a lot of fluttering and chirping. He didn't know why the birds were making all that noise.

- Why were they making all that noise? (Call on a child. Idea: *A big eagle had landed in the birdbath*.) Yes.

   A big eagle had landed in the birdbath, but Sweetie didn't know that.

- Then Sweetie made a great leap to number 5.
7. Everybody, touch number 5. ✔
- Where is Sweetie when he's at number 5? (Call on a child. Idea: *On the edge of the birdbath*.)

   Sweetie was on the edge of the birdbath and he grabbed the first thing he saw.

- Uh-oh. The picture doesn't show what was in the birdbath. The birdbath is empty.
- Everybody, what was in the birdbath when Sweetie was at number 5? (Signal.) *A big eagle.*
- And what did that eagle do when Sweetie grabbed him? (Call on a child. Idea: *Threw Sweetie in the water*.)

   Then Sweetie moved very fast. He went to number 6.

8. Everybody, touch number 6. ✔
- Where is Sweetie when he's at number 6? (Call on a child. Ideas: *On the other side of the fence* or *In his own yard*.)

   Sweetie was back in his own yard now. He was all wet, and he was trying to figure out something.

- What was he trying to figure out? (Call on a child. Idea: *How those small and helpless birds could be so big and strong*.)

52   *Lesson 9*

9. Everybody, when Sweetie went from number 5 to number 6, did he sneak through the bushes? (Signal.) *No.*

• Your turn: Draw a line from number 5 to number 6 to show the path that Sweetie took. Go right through the hole in the fence. ✔

10. Listen: The numbers in the story tell what Sweetie did first, what he did next and so on.

• Who can touch the numbers and tell all the things that happened in the story? Start with number 1 and tell the whole story.

11. Tell what happened at each number. (Call on a child:) You tell the story. Don't say the numbers. Just tell what happened at each number. Everybody else, follow along and see if (child's name) tells what happened for each number.
(Praise child for a story that tells the sequence of things that Sweetie did.)
(To correct omissions:)
   a. Uh-oh. You missed something. Who knows what was missed?
   b. (Call on another child.)
   (Repeat step 11, calling on another child.)

12. Later you can fix up the picture to show what was in the birdbath when Sweetie was at number 5.

• Everybody, touch number 5. ✔
When Sweetie was there, what was in the birdbath? (Signal.) *A big eagle.*

• There's a picture of an eagle in the corner. You can draw that eagle in the birdbath and then color the whole picture.

• Everybody, what color are you going to make Sweetie? (Signal.) *Yellow.*

EXERCISE 11   Part-Whole

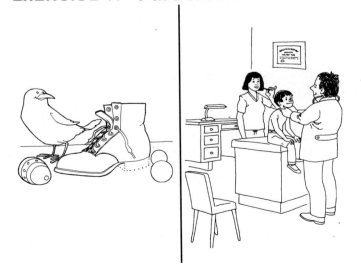

1. Everybody, find the next page in your workbook. (Hold up a workbook.) Your page should look just like mine. ✔

2. Touch the first part of your page. (Point to the first half of the page.) You should be touching this part of your page. ✔

3. Find the big shoe. ✔

4. Here's a coloring rule for the shoe. Listen: Color the sole yellow. What's the rule? (Signal.) *Color the sole yellow.*

• Mark the sole. ✔

5. Here's another coloring rule for the shoe. Listen: Color the laces black. What's the rule? (Signal.) *Color the laces black.*

• Mark the laces. ✔

6. Here's another coloring rule for the shoe. Listen: Color the top brown. What's the rule? (Signal.) *Color the top brown.*

• Mark the top. ✔

7. Part of the shoe is missing. What part is missing? (Signal.) *The heel.*

• Yes, the heel. Before you color the shoe, you're going to follow the dots and make the heel.

8. Here's the coloring rule for the heel. Listen: Color the heel green. What's the rule? (Signal.) *Color the heel green.*

• Mark the heel. ✔

EXERCISE 12   Location

1. (Hold up your workbook. Point to second half.)

• Everybody, what place do you see in this picture? (Signal.) *A doctor's office.*

2. Here's a coloring rule for this picture. Listen: Color the uniforms blue. What's the rule? (Signal.) *Color the uniforms blue.*

• (Repeat step 2 until firm.)

3. Put a mark on one of the uniforms. ✔

4. Here's another coloring rule for this picture. Listen: Color the furniture green. What's the rule? (Signal.) *Color the furniture green.*

• (Repeat step 4 until firm.)

5. Put a green mark on one piece of furniture. ✔

6. Remember—the marks show you what color to make the uniforms and the furniture. You can color the other objects any color you want.

LESSON 10

Objectives

- **Generate a complete sentence to describe an action,** and follow directions involving if-then. (Exercise 1)
- Identify classes and name members of those classes. (Exercise 2)
- Answer questions by generating sentences using opposites. (Exercise 3)
- Answer questions about previously learned calendar facts. (Exercise 4)
- Name ways that two common objects are the same and/or different. (Exercise 5)
- Given a calendar, identify the day and date for "yesterday" and "today." (Exercise 6)
- Answer questions about the events in a familiar story. (Exercise 7)
- Follow coloring rules involving class. (Exercise 8)
- Follow coloring rules involving class. (Exercise 9)

EXERCISE 1   Actions

1. It's time for some actions.
2. Everybody, you're going to hold up your hands and stand up. Get ready. (Signal.) ✔
- What are you doing? (Signal.) *Holding up my hands and standing up.*
3. Say the whole thing. Get ready. (Signal.) *I am holding up my hands and standing up.*
4. (Repeat step 3 until firm.)
5. Everybody, you're going to sit down and hold up your feet. Get ready. (Signal.) ✔
- What are you doing? (Signal.) *Sitting down and holding up my feet.*
6. Say the whole thing. Get ready. (Signal.) *I am sitting down and holding up my feet.*
7. (Repeat step 6 until firm.)
8. Feet down. Now we're going to learn a rule and play a game.
9. Listen to this rule: If I touch my ear **and** touch my knee, wave.
- Listen again: If I touch my ear **and** touch my knee, wave.
- Everybody, say the rule. Get ready. (Signal.) *If you touch your ear **and** touch your knee, wave.*
10. Tell me, what are you going to do if I touch my ear **and** touch my knee? (Signal.) *Wave.*
- Are you going to wave if I touch my ear? (Signal.) *No.*
- Are you going to wave if I wave? (Signal.) *No.*
- Are you going to wave if I touch my ear **and** touch my knee? (Signal.) *Yes.*

11. Let's see if I can fool you. Get ready. (Wave.) (Signal.) (The children should not do anything.)
- Let's see if I can fool you. Get ready. (Touch your ear and your knee.) (Signal.) (The children should wave.)
- Let's see if I can fool you. Get ready. (Touch your knee.) (Signal.) (The children should not do anything.)
12. (Repeat step 11 until firm.)

EXERCISE 2   Classification

1. I'm going to name some objects. Tell me a class these objects are in. One of the classes is vegetables, so be careful. (Accept all reasonable responses, but then suggest the response given.)
2. Listen: ant, ladybug, monkey, wasp. Everybody, what class? (Signal.) *Animals.* Yes, animals.
- Listen: rug, table, chair, lamp, bed. Everybody, what class? (Signal.) *Furniture.* Yes, furniture.
- Listen: train, bicycle, bus, truck, car. Everybody, what class? (Signal.) *Vehicles.* Yes, vehicles.
- Listen: celery, cabbage, carrots, lettuce. Everybody, what class? (Signal.) *Vegetables.* Yes, vegetables.
- Listen: flowers, trees, celery, cabbage, bushes. Everybody, what class? (Signal.) *Plants.* Yes, plants.
3. (Repeat step 2 until firm.)

4. I'm going to name a class. See how many objects you can name in that class.
- Listen: vegetables. (Call on individual children. Accept all reasonable responses.)
- I'm going to name another class. See how many objects you can name in that class. Listen: furniture. (Call on individual children. Accept all reasonable responses.)
- I'm going to name another class. See how many objects you can name in that class. Listen: plants. (Call on individual children. Accept all reasonable responses.)

EXERCISE 3   Opposites

Review

1. We're going to play a word game.
2. Listen: I'm thinking of rabbits that are not hot. They're not hot. So what else do you know about them? (Signal.) *They're cold.*
- Listen: I'm thinking of a chicken that is not wet. It's not wet. So what else do you know about it? (Signal.) *It's dry.*
- Listen: I'm thinking about a basket that is not small. It's not small. So what else do you know about it? (Signal.) *It's big.*
3. (Repeat step 2 until firm.)

EXERCISE 4   Calendar Facts

1. Everybody, how many days are in a week? (Signal.) *Seven.*
- Say the fact. Get ready. (Signal.) *There are seven days in a week.*
- Everybody, say the days of the week. Get ready. (Signal.) *Sunday, Monday, Tuesday, Wednesday, Thursday, Friday, Saturday.*
2. How many months are in a year? (Signal.) *12.*
- Say the fact. Get ready. (Signal.) *There are 12 months in a year.*
3. Name the months of the year through December. Get ready. (Signal.) *January, February, March, April, May, June, July, August, September, October, November, December.*
4. (Repeat step 3 until firm.)
5. Everybody, how many seasons are in a year? (Signal.) *Four.*
- Say the seasons of the year. Get ready. (Signal.) *Winter, spring, summer, fall.*
6. (Repeat step 5 until firm.)

EXERCISE 5   Same-Different

1. We're going to talk about how things are the same and how they are different.
2. Listen: a bird and an airplane. See if you can name two ways they are the same. (Call on individual children. Have the group repeat each correct answer. Then say:) You told me how a bird and an airplane are . . . (Signal.) *the same.*
- Listen: a bird and an airplane. See if you can name two ways they are different. (Call on individual children. Have the group repeat each correct answer. Then say:) You told me how a bird and an airplane are . . . (Signal.) *different.*
3. Here's another one.
- Listen: a chair and a table. See if you can name two ways they are the same. (Call on individual children. Have the group repeat each correct answer. Then say:) You told me how a chair and a table are . . . (Signal.) *the same.*
- Listen: a chair and a table. See if you can name two ways they are different. (Call on individual children. Have the group repeat each correct answer. Then say:) You told me how a chair and a table are . . . (Signal.) *different.*

EXERCISE 6   Calendar

1. (Present calendar.)
- First you'll tell me about the days of the week. Then you'll tell me about the dates.
2. Tell me the day of the week it was yesterday. Get ready. (Signal.)
- Tell me the day of the week it is today. Get ready. (Signal.)
- Now the dates. Everybody, tell me yesterday's date. Get ready. (Signal.)
- Tell me today's date. Get ready. (Signal.)
3. (Repeat step 2 until firm.)

EXERCISE 7   Paul Paints Plums

Story Review

1. Everybody, let's see how well you remember the story about Paul and the purple paint. I'll stop when I'm reading the story. See if you can tell me what happens next in the story.

Paul loved to paint. One day, Paul was on the porch painting a picture of purple plums. He said, "Painting pictures of purple plums on the porch is perfect."

But as he was painting, he dripped some purple paint on the floor of the porch. "Oh, pooh," he said. "Puddles of purple paint are on the porch, but I can fix it."

So he got a great big brush and started to paint the whole floor of the porch purple. But just when he was almost finished, something happened.

- Raise your hand if you know what happened. (Call on several children. Praise idea: *Paul backed into the painting and it fell against the window.*)
- Let's see if you are right.

Just when Paul was almost finished painting the porch, he backed into his painting and the painting fell against the window. It didn't break the window, but it got purple paint on the window pane.

"Whoa," Paul said. "Now there are patches of purple paint on the pane. But I can fix it."

He tried wiping the purple paint from the pane, but that didn't work. At last Paul said, "I fixed the floor of the porch and I can fix that pane the same way." He said, "A purple pane may look perfectly pleasing." And he painted the whole window pane purple.

But just as he was painting the last corner of the pane, something happened.

- Raise your hand if you know what happened. (Call on several children. Praise idea: *Purple paint dripped on the wall.*)
- Let's see if you are right.

Just as Paul was painting the last corner of the pane, some purple paint dripped on the wall.

"Wow," Paul said, "perhaps purple paint would look perfect on the wall." So you know what he did next.

He painted the whole wall purple. And just as he was finishing up the last corner of the wall, something happened.

- Raise your hand if you know what happened. (Call on several children. Praise idea: *Paul's brother came out and got a smear of purple paint on his pants*.)
- Let's see if you are right.

Just as Paul was painting the last corner of the wall, his brother came out of the house. As his brother walked onto the porch, he rubbed against the wall and got a great smear of purple paint on his pants. Paul's brother tried to wipe the purple paint from his pants, but he just smeared the paint.

"I'm a mess," his brother said.

"So you are," Paul agreed. Then he smiled at his brother and said something.

- Raise your hand if you remember what Paul told his brother. (Call on several children. Praise responses such as: *But brother, don't worry. I can fix it*.)
- Let's see if you're right.

Paul smiled at his brother and said, "But brother, don't worry. I can fix it." And he did just that.

2. Raise your hand if you knew the right answers to all the questions about this story. ✔
- You really did a great job of remembering the story.

EXERCISE 8   Coloring Rules

1. Everybody, open your workbook to Lesson 10. (Hold up workbook.) Write your name at the top of the page. ✔
2. Find the tiger. ✔
3. Here's a coloring rule for this picture. Listen: Make every hat orange. What's the rule? (Signal.) *Make every hat orange.*
   • (Repeat step 2 until firm.)
4. Make an orange mark on one of the hats. ✔
5. Here's another coloring rule for this picture. Listen: Make every shoe brown. What's the rule? (Signal.) *Make every shoe brown.*
   • (Repeat step 5 until firm.)
6. Make a brown mark on one of the shoes. ✔
7. Some shoes have parts missing. What parts? (Signal.) *The heels.*
   • Yes, the heels. You'll have to follow the dots and make the heels before you color them.
8. Here's the last coloring rule. Listen: Make all the gloves any color you want. What's the rule? (Signal.) *Make all the gloves any color you want.*

9. Pick a color and make a mark on one of the gloves. ✔
   • What's the rule for your gloves? (Call on individual children. Idea: *Make all gloves _____.*)

EXERCISE 9   Location

1. (Hold up your workbook. Point to the second half.)
2. Everybody, what place do you see in this picture? (Signal.) *A farm.*
3. Here's a coloring rule for this picture. Listen: Color some of the farm animals black and color some of the farm animals brown. What's the rule? (Signal.) *Color some of the farm animals black and color some of the farm animals brown.*
   • (Repeat step 3 until firm.)
4. Put a brown mark on **one** farm animal and a black mark on **another** farm animal. ✔
5. Here's another coloring rule for this picture. Listen: Color the buildings red. What's the rule? (Signal.) *Color the buildings red.*
   • (Repeat step 5 until firm.)
6. Put a red mark on one building. ✔
7. There's one more thing to do. One building has a missing part. What building is that? (Signal.) *The barn.* Yes, the barn.
   • What part of the barn is missing? (Signal.) *The roof.*
   • Yes, the roof. Before you color the barn, follow the dots and make the roof.
8. Remember—the marks show you what color to make the animals and the buildings. You can color the other objects any color you want.

LESSON 11

Objectives

- Generate a complete sentence to describe an action and follow directions involving if-then. (Exercise 1)
- Identify classes and name members of those classes. (Exercise 2)
- Identify statements that tell "where" and generate statements that tell "where" **and statements that tell "where something is not."** (Exercise 3)
- Answer questions by generating sentences using opposites. (Exercise 4)
- Answer questions about previously learned calendar facts. (Exercise 5)
- Name ways that two common objects are the same and/or different. (Exercise 6)
- Given a calendar, identify the day and date for "yesterday" and "today." (Exercise 7)
- **Relate a familiar story grammar to a picture that indicates the sequence of events for a new story. (Exercise 8)**
- Follow coloring rules involving class. (Exercises 9 & 10)

EXERCISE 1   Actions

1. It's time for some actions.
2. Everybody, you're going to touch your chair and touch your head. Get ready. (Signal.) ✔
   - What are you doing? (Signal.) *Touching my chair and touching my head.*
3. Say the whole thing. Get ready. (Signal.) *I am touching my chair and touching my head.*
4. (Repeat step 3 until firm.)
5. Everybody, you're going to stand up and point to the ceiling. Get ready. (Signal.) ✔
   - What are you doing? (Signal.) *Standing up and pointing to the ceiling.*
6. Say the whole thing. Get ready. (Signal.) *I am standing up and pointing to the ceiling.*
7. (Repeat step 6 until firm.)
8. Sit down. Now we're going to learn a rule and play a game.
9. Listen to this rule: If I touch my nose **or** stamp my foot, say **stop.**
   - Listen again: If I touch my nose **or** stamp my foot, say **stop.**
   - Everybody, say the rule. Get ready. (Signal.) *If you touch your nose **or** stamp your foot, say **stop.***
10. (Repeat step 9 until firm.)
11. Tell me, what are you going to say if I touch my nose **or** stamp my foot? (Signal.) *Stop.*
   - Are you going to say **stop** if I stamp my foot? (Signal.) *Yes.*
   - Are you going to say **stop** if I touch my nose? (Signal.) *Yes.*
   - Are you going to say **stop** if I touch my knee? (Signal.) *No.*

12. Let's see if I can fool you. Get ready. **Stop.** (Signal.) (The children should not do anything.)
   - Let's see if I can fool you. Get ready. (Touch your chin.) (Signal.) (The children should not do anything.)
   - Let's see if I can fool you. Get ready. (Stamp your foot.) (Signal.) (Children say *stop.*)
13. (Repeat step 12 until firm.)

EXERCISE 2   Classification

1. I'm going to name some objects. Tell me a class these objects are in. (Accept all reasonable responses, but then suggest the response given.)
2. Listen: house, school, police station. Everybody, what class? (Signal.) *Buildings.* Yes, buildings.
   - Listen: cup, bottle, box, suitcase, bag. Everybody, what class? (Signal.) *Containers.* Yes, containers.
   - Listen: lamp, stool, rug, table, sofa. Everybody, what class? (Signal.) *Furniture.* Yes, furniture.
3. (Repeat step 2 until firm.)
4. I'm going to name a class. See how many objects you can name in that class. Listen: vegetables. (Call on individual children. Accept all reasonable responses.)
   - I'm going to name another class. See how many objects you can name in that class. Listen: containers. (Call on individual children. Accept all reasonable responses.)

- I'm going to name another class. See how many objects you can name in that class. Listen: furniture. (Call on individual children. Accept all reasonable responses.)

EXERCISE 3   Where

1. I'm going to say statements. Some of these statements tell where the cup is. Some of these statements don't tell where the cup is.
2. Listen: The cup is in the sink. Say the statement. Get ready. (Signal.) *The cup is in the sink.*
- Does that statement tell where the cup is? (Signal.) *Yes.*
- Where is the cup? (Signal.) *In the sink.*
3. Listen: The cup is dirty. Say the statement. Get ready. (Signal.) *The cup is dirty.*
- Does that statement tell where the cup is? (Signal.) *No.*
4. Listen: The cup is red. Say the statement. Get ready. (Signal.) *The cup is red.*
- Does that statement tell where the cup is? (Signal.) *No.*
5. (Repeat steps 2 through 4 until firm.)
6. Now it's your turn to make up statements.
- Make up a statement that tells **where** the cup is. (Call on individual children. Praise good statements.)
- Make up a statement that does **not** tell where the cup is. (Call on individual children. Praise good statements.)

EXERCISE 4   Opposites

Review

1. We're going to play a word game.
2. Listen: I'm thinking about a horse that is skinny. It's skinny. So what else do you know about it? (Signal.) *It's not fat.*
- Listen: I'm thinking of pigs that are not old. They're not old. So what else do you know about them? (Signal.) *They're young.*
- Listen: I'm thinking about an alligator that is not long. It's not long. So what else do you know about it? (Signal.) *It's short.*
- Listen: I'm thinking about a ladder that is not tall. It's not tall. So what else do you know about it? (Signal.) *It's short.*
3. (Repeat step 2 until firm.)

EXERCISE 5   Calendar Facts

1. Everybody, how many months are in a year? (Signal.) *12.*
- Say the fact. Get ready. (Signal.) *There are 12 months in a year.*
2. Name the months of the year through December. Get ready. (Signal.) *January, February, March, April, May, June, July, August, September, October, November, December.*
3. (Repeat step 2 until firm.)
4. How many days are in a week? (Signal.) *Seven.*
- Say the fact. Get ready. (Signal.) *There are seven days in a week.*
5. Everybody, say the days of the week. Get ready. (Signal.) *Sunday, Monday, Tuesday, Wednesday, Thursday, Friday, Saturday.*
6. (Repeat step 5 until firm.)
7. Everybody, how many seasons are in a year? (Signal.) *Four.*
- Say the seasons of the year. Get ready. (Signal.) *Winter, spring, summer, fall.*
8. (Repeat step 7 until firm.)

EXERCISE 6   Same-Different

1. We're going to talk about how things are the same and how they are different.
2. Listen: a train and a bus. See if you can name two ways they are the same. (Call on individual children. Have the group repeat each correct answer. Then say:) You told me how a train and a bus are . . . (Signal.) *the same.*
- Listen: a train and a bus. See if you can name two ways they are different. (Call on individual children. Have the group repeat each correct answer. Then say:) You told me how a train and a bus are . . . (Signal.) *different.*
3. Here's another one.
- Listen: a bathtub and a swimming pool. See if you can name two ways they are the same. (Call on individual children. Have the group repeat each correct answer. Then say:) You told me how a bathtub and a swimming pool are . . . (Signal.) *the same.*

- Listen: a bathtub and a swimming pool. See if you can name two ways they are different. (Call on individual children. Have the group repeat each correct answer. Then say:) You told me how a bathtub and a swimming pool are . . . (Signal.) *different.*

EXERCISE 7   Calendar

1. (Present calendar.) First you'll tell me about the days of the week. Then you'll tell me about the dates.
2. Tell me the day of the week it was yesterday. Get ready. (Signal.)
- Tell me the day of the week it is today. Get ready. (Signal.)
- Now the dates. Everybody, tell me yesterday's date. Get ready. (Signal.)
- Tell me today's date. Get ready. (Signal.)
3. (Repeat step 2 until firm.)

WORKBOOK

EXERCISE 8   Sequence Story

Paul Paints a Pot Pink

1. Everybody, open your workbook to Lesson 11. Write your name at the top of the page. ✔
2. The picture shows a different story about Paul. He's painting again. I'll bet you wonder what color he's painting things. The numbers show what Paul painted first, what he painted next and so forth. Listen:

Paul decided to paint something pink. He said, "Pink would be perfect." So he started painting the thing that has a number 1 on it in the picture.

3. Everybody, touch number 1. ✔
- What did Paul paint first? (Signal.) *A pot.*

Paul started to paint the pot pink, when suddenly something happened.

- What do you think happened? (Call on a child. Idea: *Some pink paint spilled on something.*)
4. Everybody, touch number 2. ✔
- What did some of the pink paint plop onto? (Signal.) *A puzzle.*

So Paul said, "Perhaps a pink puzzle would look pretty." So he painted the puzzle pink. But just as he was painting the last part of the puzzle, something happened.

- What do you think happened? (Call on a child. Idea: *Some pink paint spilled on something.*)
5. Everybody, touch number 3. ✔
- What did some of the pink paint plop onto? (Signal.) *A piggy bank.*

Some pink paint got on the piggy bank. Paul said, "That piggy bank looks poor. But I can fix it up." And he did just that.

- What do you think he did? (Call on a child. Idea: *He painted the piggy bank pink.*)

Paul thought he was finished, but when he started to leave the room, he passed number 4 and something happened.

- What do you think happened? (Call on a child. Idea: *Some pink paint spilled on something.*)
6. Everybody, touch number 4. ✔
- What is the name of the thing at number 4? (Signal.) *A pillow.*
- And what do you think Paul did to fix up the pillow? (Call on a child. Idea: *Painted the pillow pink.*)

7. Oh, my. The last circle is on that dog's tail. That dog is a poodle. Everybody, what kind of dog? (Signal.) *A poodle.*

• There's no number in that circle and I hate to think of what must have happened at that circle. I'll let **you** figure that out.

8. Here's how you tell the whole story: You tell what color Paul was painting and what happened for each number. At the end of your story, you may want to tell about that circle that doesn't have a number in it. Who can touch the numbers and tell all the things that happened in the story? Don't say the numbers. Just tell the story.

9. (Call on a child:) You tell the story. Everybody else, follow along and see if (child's name) tells what happened for each number. (Praise child for a story that tells the sequence of things that were painted.)

• (To correct omissions, say:)
   a. Uh-oh. You missed something. Who knows what was missed?
   b. (Call on another child.)
      (Repeat step 9, calling on another child.)

10. Later you can fix up the picture so it shows the things Paul painted pink. I don't know what you're going to do with that poodle.

EXERCISE 9 Classification

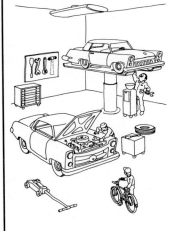

1. Everybody, find the next page in your workbook. (**Hold up a workbook.**) Your page should look just like mine. ✔

2. Touch the first part of the page. (**Point to the first half of the page.**) You should be touching this part of your page.

3. Find the raccoon. ✔

4. Here's a coloring rule for this picture. Color the tools blue. What's the rule? (Signal.) *Color the tools blue.*

• (Repeat step 4 until firm.)

5. Mark one of the tools blue. ✔

6. Here's another coloring rule for this picture. Color the clothing red. What's the rule? (Signal.) *Color the clothing red.*

• (Repeat step 6 until firm.)

7. Mark one piece of clothing red. ✔

8. Here's one more thing to do. Part of the coat is missing. What part is missing? (Signal.) *The sleeve.*

• Before you color the coat, follow the dots and make the sleeve.

EXERCISE 10 Location

1. (Hold up your workbook. Point to second half.)

2. Everybody, tell me what place you see in this picture. Get ready. (Signal.) *A garage.*

3. Here's a coloring rule for this picture. Listen: Color all tools black. What's the rule? (Signal.) *Color all tools black.*

• (Repeat step 3 until firm.)

4. So put a black mark on one tool. ✔

5. Here's another coloring rule for this picture. Listen: Color all vehicles red. What's the rule? (Signal.) *Color all vehicles red.*

• (Repeat step 5 until firm.)

6. So put a red mark on one vehicle. ✔

7. There's one more thing to do. One tool has a missing part. What tool is that? (Signal.) *The hammer.* Yes, the hammer.

• What part of the hammer is missing? (Signal.) *The handle.* Yes, the handle.

• Before you color the hammer, follow the dots and make the handle.

8. Remember—the marks show you what color to make the tools and the vehicles. You can color the other objects any color you want.

LESSON 12

Objectives

- **Label actions, and follow directions involving "all," "some" and "none," and** generate complete sentences to describe an action and answer questions involving "or." (Exercise 1)
- Identify classes and name members of those classes. (Exercise 2)
- Identify statements that tell "where" and generate statements that tell "where" and statements that tell "where something is not." (Exercise 3)
- Answer questions by generating sentences using opposites. (Exercise 4)
- Answer questions about previously learned calendar facts. (Exercise 5)
- Name ways that two common objects are the same and/or different. (Exercise 6)
- Given a calendar, identify the day and date for "yesterday" and "today." (Exercise 7)
- Answer questions about a new story. (Exercise 8)
- Make a picture consistent with the details of the story. (Exercise 9)
- Follow coloring rules involving parts of a whole. (Exercise 10)
- Follow coloring rules involving class. (Exercise 11)

EXERCISE 1   Actions

1. Watch me. Tell if I hold up **all of my fingers** or **some of my fingers** or **none of my fingers.**

2. (Hold up ten fingers.) Is this all of my fingers or some of my fingers or none of my fingers? (Signal.) *All of your fingers.*

- (Hold up two fists.) Is this all of my fingers or some of my fingers or none of my fingers? (Signal.) *None of your fingers.*

- (Hold up three fingers.) Is this all of my fingers or some of my fingers or none of my fingers? (Signal.) *Some of your fingers.*

3. Now it's your turn. Everybody, hold up none of your fingers. Get ready. (Signal.) ✔

- What are you holding up? (Signal.) *None of my fingers.*

- Say the whole thing. Get ready. (Signal.) *I am holding up none of my fingers.*

4. Everybody, hold up all of your fingers. (Signal.) ✔

- What are you holding up? (Signal.) *All of my fingers.*

- Say the whole thing. Get ready. (Signal.) *I am holding up all of my fingers.*

5. (Repeat steps 3 and 4 until firm.)

6. Let's try another game. I'm going to do something. See if you can figure out what I'm going to do.

7. Listen: I'm going to stamp my foot or stamp my feet or stand up. What am I going to do? (Signal.) *Stamp your foot or stamp your feet or stand up.*

8. (Repeat step 7 until firm.)

9. Yes, I'm going to stamp my foot or stamp my feet or stand up. Am I going to stand up? (Signal.) *Maybe.*

- Am I going to stamp my feet? (Signal.) *Maybe.*

- Am I going to stamp my foot? (Signal.) *Maybe.*

- Am I going to sing? (Signal.) *No.*

10. I'm going to stamp my foot or stamp my feet or stand up. What am I going to do? (Signal.) *Stamp your foot or stamp your feet or stand up.*

11. Here I go. (Stamp both feet.) Did I stand up? (Signal.) *No.*

- Did I stamp my feet? (Signal.) *Yes.*

- Did I sit down? (Signal.) *No.*

12. What did I do? (Signal.) *Stamped your feet.*

- Say the whole thing. Get ready. (Signal.) *You stamped your feet.*

13. (Repeat step 12 until firm.)

14. (Repeat steps 11 through 13 until firm.)

EXERCISE 2   Classification

1. I'm going to name some objects. Tell me a class these objects are in. (Accept all reasonable responses, but then suggest the response given.)

2. Listen: spaghetti, beans, ice cream, salad. Everybody, what class? (Signal.) *Food.* Yes, food.
- Listen: school, garage, house, restaurant. Everybody, what class? (Signal.) *Buildings.* Yes, buildings.
- Listen: ax, hoe, hammer, screwdriver, shovel. Everybody, what class? (Signal.) *Tools.* Yes, tools.
3. (Repeat step 2 until firm.)
4. I'm going to name a class. See how many objects you can name in that class. Listen: food. (Call on individual children. Accept all reasonable responses.)
- I'm going to name another class. See how many objects you can name in that class. Listen: buildings. (Call on individual children. Accept all reasonable responses.)
- I'm going to name another class. See how many objects you can name in that class. Listen: tools. (Call on individual children. Accept all reasonable responses.)

EXERCISE 3 Where

1. I'm going to say statements. Some of these statements tell where the bicycle is. Some of these statements don't tell where the bicycle is.
2. Listen: The bicycle is in the street. Say the statement. Get ready. (Signal.) *The bicycle is in the street.*
- Does that statement tell where the bicycle is? (Signal.) *Yes.*
- Where is the bicycle? (Signal.) *In the street.*
3. Listen: The bicycle is wet. Say the statement. Get ready. (Signal.) *The bicycle is wet.*
- Does that statement tell where the bicycle is? (Signal.) *No.*
4. (Repeat steps 2 and 3 until firm.)
5. Now it's your turn to make up statements. Make up a statement that tells **where** the bicycle is. (Call on individual children. Praise good statements.)
- Make up a statement that does **not** tell where the bicycle is. (Call on individual children. Praise good statements.)

EXERCISE 4 Opposites

Review

1. We're going to play a word game.
2. Listen: I'm thinking about trees that are not wet. They're not wet. So what else do you know about them? (Signal.) *They're dry.*
- Listen: I'm thinking of a rabbit that is fat. It's fat. So what else do you know about it? (Signal.) *It's not skinny.*
- Listen: I'm thinking of a woman who is not old. She's not old. So what else do you know about her? (Signal.) *She's young.*
- Listen: I'm thinking about a log that is long. It's long. So what else do you know about it? (Signal.) *It's not short.*
3. (Repeat step 2 until firm.)

EXERCISE 5 Calendar Facts

1. Everybody, how many days are in a week? (Signal.) *Seven.*
- Say the fact. Get ready. (Signal.) *There are seven days in a week.*
- Everybody, say the days of the week. Get ready. (Signal.) *Sunday, Monday, Tuesday, Wednesday, Thursday, Friday, Saturday.*
2. How many months are in a year? (Signal.) *12.*
- Say the fact. Get ready. (Signal.) *There are 12 months in a year.*
3. Name the months of the year through December. Get ready. (Signal.) *January, February, March, April, May, June, July, August, September, October, November, December.*
4. (Repeat step 3 until firm.)
5. Everybody, how many seasons are in a year? (Signal.) *Four.*
- Say the seasons of the year. Get ready. (Signal.) *Winter, spring, summer, fall.*
6. (Repeat step 5 until firm.)

EXERCISE 6 Same-Different

1. We're going to talk about how things are the same and how they are different.
2. Listen: a chair and a table. See if you can name two ways they are the same. (Call on individual children. Have the group repeat each correct answer. Then say:) You told me how a chair and a table are . . . (Signal.) *the same.*

- Listen: a chair and a table. See if you can name two ways they are different. (Call on individual children. Have the group repeat each correct answer. Then say:) You told me how a chair and a table are . . . (Signal.) *different.*

3. Here's another one. Listen: ice cream and snow. See if you can name two ways they are the same. (Call on individual children. Have the group repeat each correct answer. Then say:) You told me how ice cream and snow are . . . (Signal.) *the same.*

- Listen: ice cream and snow. See if you can name two ways they are different. (Call on individual children. Have the group repeat each correct answer. Then say:) You told me how ice cream and snow are . . . (Signal.) *different.*

EXERCISE 7 Calendar

1. (Present calendar.) First you'll tell me about the days of the week. Then you'll tell me about the dates.

2. Tell me the day of the week it was yesterday. Get ready. (Signal.)

- Tell me the day of the week it is today. Get ready. (Signal.)

- Now the dates. Everybody, tell me yesterday's date. Get ready. (Signal.)

- Tell me today's date. Get ready. (Signal.)

3. (Repeat step 2 until firm.)

EXERCISE 8 The Bragging Rats Race

Storytelling

- Everybody, I'm going to read you a story. Listen to the things that happen in the story because you're going to have to fix up a picture that shows part of the story. This is a story about some rats. Listen:

A bunch of rats lived near a pond that was on a farm. The rats got along well, except for two of them. The other rats called these two the bragging rats because they were always bragging, quarreling and arguing about something.

One day they'd argue about who could eat the most. Another day they'd squabble and quarrel over who was the best looking. Neither one of them was very good looking. One was a big gray rat with the longest tail you've ever seen on a rat. The other one wasn't big, but he had the biggest, yellowest teeth you ever saw.

- Listen to the last part again and get a picture in your mind of those rats.

One was a big gray rat with the longest tail you've ever seen on a rat. The other one wasn't big, but he had the biggest, yellowest teeth you ever saw.

- What was unusual about the big gray rat? (Call on a child. Idea: *It had the longest tail you've ever seen on a rat.*)
- What was unusual about the other rat? (Call on a child. Idea: *It had the biggest, yellowest teeth you ever saw.*)
- What are some of the things these two would argue about? (Call on a child. Ideas: *Who was the best looking; who could eat the most.*)

The other rats in the bunch didn't pay much attention to the bragging and quarreling until the two rats started bragging about who was the fastest rat in the whole bunch. This quarrel went on for days, and the other rats got pretty sick of listening to the rats shout and yell and brag about how fast they were.

- Listen: What were the two bragging rats arguing about? (Call on a child. Idea: *Who was the fastest rat.*)

On the third day of their quarrel, they almost got into a fight. The rat with the yellow teeth was saying, "I'm so fast that I could run circles around you while you ran as fast as you could."

The big rat said, "Oh, yeah? Well, I could run circles around your circles. That's how fast I am."

- Are these rats kind of silly? (Call on a child. Accept reasonable responses.)

The two rats continued yelling at each other until a wise old rat said, "Stop! We are tired of listening to all this shouting and yelling and bragging. There is a way to find out who is the fastest rat on this farm."

- How could they find out who was the fastest? (Call on a child. Idea: *Have a race.*)

The wise old rat continued, "We will have a race for any rat that wants to race. Everybody will line up, run down the path to the pond, then run back. The first rat to get back is the winner. And then we'll have no more arguing about which rat is the fastest."

- Get a picture in your mind of how they're going to run. They'll start at the starting line, run down the path to the pond, turn around at the pond and run all the way back to the starting line. The wise old rat said there would be no more arguing about who could run the fastest.
- Why wouldn't there be any more arguing about which rat was the fastest? (Call on a child. Idea: *Because the race would prove who was the fastest.*)

The rats agreed, and early the next morning they were lined up, ready for the big race. Six rats entered the race. The bragging rats were lined up right next to each other, making mean faces and mumbling about how fast they were going to run.

The rats put their noses close to the ground, ready to take off like a flash. "Everybody, steady," the wise old rat said. "Everybody, ready. Go!" The rats took off toward the pond. The big gray rat got ahead of the others, with the yellow-toothed rat right behind him. But just before they got to the pond, the yellow-toothed rat stepped on the long tail of the gray rat, and both rats tumbled over and over in a cloud of dust.

- Listen: Why did the two rats start tumbling? (Call on a child. Idea: *Because the yellow-toothed rat stepped on the long tail of the gray rat.*)

- Where were they when this accident took place? (Call on a child. Idea: *Almost to the pond.*)
- I wonder if something bad is going to happen. Let's see.

The two bragging rats tumbled down the dusty path and right into the pond.

The other rats finished the race. The winner was a little black rat. It was hard for her to finish the race because she was laughing so hard over the bragging rats who were still splashing and sputtering around in the pond.

After the race, all the other rats went back to the pond. The bragging rats were still splashing and sputtering. The wise old rat said to them, "So now we know who the fastest runner on this farm is. It's neither one of you, so we will have no more arguments from either of you about who can run the fastest!"

- Listen: Who won the race? (Call on a child. Idea: *A little black rat.*)
- Do you think the bragging rats will stop arguing about who is the fastest? (Call on a child. Accept reasonable responses.)
- Let's see.

The bragging rats looked at each other. Then the rat with yellow teeth suddenly smiled and said, "I may not be the fastest **runner** in this bunch, but there is no rat in the world that can **swim** as fast as I can."

"Oh, yeah?" said the gray rat.

"I can swim so fast that I could go all the way across the pond without even getting my fur wet."

The wise old rat and the other rats just walked away from the pond, slowly shaking their heads.

- Why do you think they were shaking their heads? (Call on a child. Idea: *The race didn't settle anything.*)
- I don't think these bragging rats will ever stop bragging and arguing.

EXERCISE 9   Story Details

The Bragging Rats

1. Everybody, open your workbook to Lesson 12. Write your name at the top of the page. ✔

2. This picture shows something that happened in the story. Where are the bragging rats? (Call on a child. Idea: *In the pond.*)

• Everybody, do those rats look very happy? (Signal.) *No.*

• Is the race still going on when this picture takes place? (Signal.) *No.*

• How do you know the race is over? (Call on a child. Idea: *All the other rats are laughing at the bragging rats in the pond.*)

• See if you can find the rat that ended up winning the race. Remember, that's a little black rat. ✔

• See if you can find the wise old rat. That's the oldest-looking rat in the picture. ✔

3. Everybody, take out a yellow crayon and a gray crayon. ✔

• Listen: Put a little yellow mark on the teeth of the rat that had yellow teeth. Then put a little gray mark on the other bragging rat. Later you can color this picture.

EXERCISE 10   Part-Whole

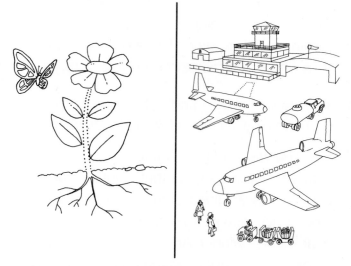

1. Everybody, find the next page in your workbook. (Hold up a workbook.) Your page should look just like mine. ✔

2. Touch the first part of your page. (Point to the first half of the page.) You should be touching this part of your page. ✔

3. Find the flower. ✔

4. Here's a coloring rule for the flower. Listen: Color the petals red. What's the rule? (Signal.) *Color the petals red.*

• Mark the petals. ✔

5. Here's another coloring rule for the flower. Listen: Color the roots brown. What's the rule? (Signal.) *Color the roots brown.*

• Mark the roots. ✔

6. Here's another coloring rule for the flower. Listen: Color the leaves green. What's the rule? (Signal.) *Color the leaves green.*

• Mark the leaves. ✔

7. Part of the flower is missing. What part is missing? (Signal.) *The stem.* Yes, the stem.

• Before you color the flower, you're going to follow the dots and make the stem.

8. Here's the coloring rule for the stem. Listen: Color the stem orange. What's the rule? (Signal.) *Color the stem orange.*

• Mark the stem. ✔

EXERCISE 11 Location

1. (Hold up your workbook. Point to second half.)
2. Everybody, what place do you see in this picture? (Signal.) *An airport.*
3. Here's a coloring rule for this picture. Listen: Color all vehicles yellow. What's the rule? (Signal.) *Color all vehicles yellow.*
   - (Repeat step 3 until firm.)
4. So put a yellow mark on one vehicle. ✔
5. Here's another coloring rule. Listen: Color all buildings green. What's the rule? (Signal.) *Color all buildings green.*
   - (Repeat step 5 until firm.)

6. So put a green mark on one building. ✔
7. There's one more thing to do. One vehicle has a missing part. What vehicle is that? (Signal.) *An airplane.* Yes, one of the airplanes.
   - What part of the airplane is missing? (Signal.) *A wing.* Yes, a wing.
   - Before you color the airplane, follow the dots and make a wing.
8. Remember—the marks show you what color to make the vehicles and the buildings. You can color the other objects any color you want.

Objectives

- Label actions, follow directions involving "all," "some" and "none," and generate complete sentences to describe an action. (Exercise 1)
- Identify classes and name members of those classes. (Exercise 2)
- Answer questions by generating sentences using opposites. (Exercise 3)
- **Generate an absurd sequence for a common activity.** (Exercise 4)
- Name ways that two common objects are the same and/or different (Exercise 5)
- Answer questions about previously learned calendar facts. (Exercise 6)
- Given a calendar, identify the day and date for "yesterday" and "today." (Exercise 7)
- **Write numbers to show the sequence of events, tell a story based on familiar story grammar,** and color a picture to make it consistent with the story. (Exercise 8)
- Follow coloring rules involving parts of a whole. (Exercise 9)
- Follow coloring rules involving class. (Exercise 10)

EXERCISE 1 Actions

1. Watch me. Tell me if I hold up all of my fingers or some of my fingers or none of my fingers. (Hold up two fists.) Is this all of my fingers or some of my fingers or none of my fingers? (Signal.) *None of your fingers.*

- (Hold up eight fingers.) Is this all of my fingers or some of my fingers or none of my fingers? (Signal.) *Some of your fingers.*

- (Hold up ten fingers.) Is this all of my fingers or some of my fingers or none of my fingers? (Signal.) *All of your fingers.*

2. Now it's your turn. Everybody, hold up some of your fingers. Get ready. (Signal.) ✔

- What are you holding up? (Signal.) *Some of my fingers.*

- Say the whole thing. Get ready. (Signal.) *I am holding up some of my fingers.*

- Everybody, hold up none of your fingers. Get ready. (Signal.) ✔

- What are you holding up? (Signal.) *None of my fingers.*

- Say the whole thing. Get ready. (Signal.) *I am holding up none of my fingers.*

3. (Repeat step 2 until firm.)

EXERCISE 2 Classification

1. I'm going to name some objects. Tell me a class these objects are in. (Accept all reasonable responses, but then suggest the response given.)

2. Listen: glass, suitcase, purse, box, bottle. Everybody, what class? (Signal.) *Containers.* Yes, containers.

- Listen: plane, train, bus, car, boat. Everybody, what class? (Signal.) *Vehicles.* Yes, vehicles.

- Listen: saw, rake, screwdriver, pliers, ax. Everybody, what class? (Signal.) *Tools.* Yes, tools.

- Listen: bread, burgers, butter, beans. Everybody, what class? (Signal.) *Food.* Yes, food.

3. (Repeat step 2 until firm.)

4. I'm going to name a class. See how many objects you can name in that class. Listen: containers. (Call on individual children. Accept all reasonable responses.)

- I'm going to name another class. See how many objects you can name in that class. Listen: vehicles. (Call on individual children. Accept all reasonable responses.)

- I'm going to name another class. See how many objects you can name in that class. Listen: tools. (Call on individual children. Accept all reasonable responses.)

EXERCISE 3 Opposites

Review

1. We're going to play a word game.
2. Listen: I'm thinking of an alligator that is not young. It's not young. So what else do you know about it? (Signal.) *It's old.*
   - Listen: I'm thinking about umbrellas that are not dry. They're not dry. So what else do you know about them? (Signal.) *They're wet.*
   - Listen: I'm thinking of a lizard that is fat. It's fat. So what else do you know about it? (Signal.) *It's not skinny.*
   - Listen: I'm thinking about a tree that is not tall. It's not tall. So what else do you know about it? (Signal.) *It's short.*
3. (Repeat step 2 until firm.)

EXERCISE 4 Absurdity

1. Let's say that you wanted to take a bath. Name some things you would have to do. (Call on several children. Praise good answers such as: *take off your clothes; run water in the bathtub; get in the bathtub.*)
2. Here are four things you would have to do to take a bath. Listen: (Hold up one finger.) Fill the tub with water.
   - (Hold up two fingers.) Make sure you have soap and a towel.
   - (Hold up three fingers.) Take off your clothes.
   - (Hold up four fingers.) Get in the tub.
3. Your turn. Name four things you would have to do. (Hold up one finger.) *Fill the tub with water.*
   - (Hold up two fingers.) *Make sure you have soap and a towel.*
   - (Hold up three fingers.) *Take off your clothes.*
   - (Hold up four fingers.) *Get in the tub.*
4. (Repeat step 3 until firm.)
5. I can name an absurd order. Listen: (Hold up one finger.) Fill the tub.
   - (Hold up two fingers.) Take off your clothes.

- (Hold up three fingers.) Get in the tub.
- (Hold up four fingers.) Make sure you have soap and a towel.
6. There's an order that is even more absurd. Who can name the four things in a very absurd order? (Call on a child. Accept reasonable responses.)
   - Everybody, here's an absurd order: (Hold up one finger.) Fill the tub.
   - (Hold up two fingers.) Get in the tub.
   - (Hold up three fingers.) Make sure you have soap and a towel.
   - (Hold up four fingers.) Take your clothes off.
   - Why is that order absurd? (Call on a child. Idea: *Because you would be getting in the tub with your clothes on, so when you take them off they will be soaking wet.*)

EXERCISE 5 Same—Different

1. We're going to talk about how things are the same and how they are different.
2. Listen: a fish and a boat. See if you can name two ways they are the same. (Call on individual children. Have the group repeat each correct answer. Then say:) You told me how a fish and a boat are . . . (Signal.) *the same.*
   - Listen: a fish and a boat. See if you can name two ways they are different. (Call on individual children. Have the group repeat each correct answer. Then say:) You told me how a fish and a boat are . . . (Signal.) *different.*
3. Here's another one. Listen: a chalkboard and paper. See if you can name two ways they are the same. (Call on individual children. Have the group repeat each correct answer. Then say:) You told me how a chalkboard and paper are . . . (Signal.) *the same.*
   - Listen: a chalkboard and paper. See if you can name two ways they are different. (Call on individual children. Have the group repeat each correct answer. Then say:) You told me how a chalkboard and paper are . . . (Signal.) *different.*

EXERCISE 6   Calendar Facts

1. We're going to talk about days and months. Everybody, how many months are in a year? (Signal.) *12.*
- Say the fact. Get ready. (Signal.) *There are 12 months in a year.*
2. Name the months of the year through December. Get ready. (Signal.) *January, February, March, April, May, June, July, August, September, October, November, December.*
3. (Repeat step 2 until firm.)
4. How many days are in a week? (Signal.) *Seven.*
- Say the fact. Get ready. (Signal.) *There are seven days in a week.*
5. Everybody, say the days of the week. Get ready. (Signal.) *Sunday, Monday, Tuesday, Wednesday, Thursday, Friday, Saturday.*
6. (Repeat step 5 until firm.)
7. Everybody, how many seasons are in a year? (Signal.) *Four.*
- Say the seasons of the year. Get ready. (Signal.) *Winter, spring, summer, fall.*
8. (Repeat step 7 until firm.)

EXERCISE 7   Calendar

1. (Present calendar.) First you'll tell me about the days of the week. Then you'll tell me about the dates.
2. Tell me the day of the week it was yesterday. Get ready. (Signal.)
- Tell me the day of the week it is today. Get ready. (Signal.)
- Now the dates. Everybody, tell me yesterday's date. Get ready. (Signal.)
- Tell me today's date. Get ready. (Signal.)
3. (Repeat step 2 until firm.)

EXERCISE 8   Sequence Story

Paul Paints a Purple Parrot

1. Everybody, open your workbook to Lesson 13. Write your name at the top of the page. ✔
2. Paul is painting again.
   I'll tell you a story about Paul two times. The first time I tell it, you'll touch the things that Paul paints. The second time I tell it, you'll write numbers in the circles.
3. The picture shows where Paul was at the beginning of the story. Where is Paul? (Call on a child. Idea: *At his desk in his room.*)
- Here's the story:

> Paul was in his room painting a picture of a purple parrot.

- Everybody, touch the circle on the picture of the parrot. ✔

> Paul painted every part of the parrot purple, but just when he finished, some purple paint plopped onto his pencil.

- Everybody, touch the circle on the pencil. ✔

> Paul looked at the part of his pencil that was purple and said, "I'll fix up that pencil." So he did.

- What do you think he did? (Call on a child. Idea: *Painted the whole pencil purple.*)
- Right.

He painted the whole pencil purple, but just as he was finishing up, he noticed purple paint on his pajama pants.

- Everybody, touch the circle on Paul's pajama pants. ✔

Paul said, "Oh, pooh. The purple part of these pajamas looks poor. But I can fix up these pajama pants." So he did just that.

- What did he do? (Call on a child. Idea: *Painted his pajama pants purple.*)

And just as he was almost finished painting his pajama pants purple, he noticed some purple paint in the palm of his hand.

- Listen: The palm of your hand is the inside, not the back, of your hand. Everybody, touch the palm of your hand. ✔
- Everybody, touch the circle on Paul's palm. ✔

Paul said, "Part of my palm is purple. I can fix that." So he did.

- What do you think he did? (Call on a child. Idea: *Painted his palm purple.*)
4. That's the story about Paul. Now I'll tell it one more time and you'll write the numbers in the circles. Then I'll call on a couple of children to tell the whole story.
- Listen: What was the first thing Paul painted in this story? (Call on a child. Idea: *A picture of a parrot.*)
- Everybody, touch the circle on the picture of the parrot. ✔
- Write a number **one** in that circle. Raise your hand when you're finished. (Observe children and give feedback.)
5. Listen:

When Paul was just finishing painting the parrot purple, some purple paint plopped onto his pencil.

- Everybody, touch the circle on the pencil. ✔
- What number goes in that circle? (Signal.) *Two.*

- Write a number **two** in that circle. Raise your hand when you're finished. (Observe children and give feedback.)
6. Listen:

Paul painted the whole pencil purple. Just as he was finishing up, he noticed purple paint on his pajama pants.

- Everybody, touch the circle on Paul's pajama pants. ✔
- Think big. Everybody, what number goes in that circle? (Signal.) *Three.*
- Write a number **three** in that circle. Raise your hand when you're finished. (Observe children and give feedback.)
7. Listen:

Paul painted his pajama pants purple. But just when he was almost done, he noticed some purple paint in the palm of his hand.

- Everybody, touch the circle on Paul's palm. ✔
- Think big. Everybody, what number goes in that circle? (Signal.) *Four.*
- Write a number **four** in that circle. Raise your hand when you're finished. (Observe children and give feedback.)
8. Now you have numbers that tell about the things that Paul did in this story. Who can tell the whole story? Remember, you have to tell where Paul was at the beginning and what he did for each number. Don't say the numbers. Just tell what he did first, what he did next and so on.
9. (Call on a child:) You tell the story. Everybody else, follow along and see if (child's name) tells what happened for each number. (Praise child for a story that tells the sequence of things that were painted.) (To correct omissions, say:)
   a. Uh-oh. You missed something. Who knows what was missed?
   b. (Call on another child.)
   (Repeat step 9, calling on another child.)
10. Later you can color all the things that Paul painted purple in this story. You can color the things he didn't paint any color you wish.

EXERCISE 9 Part—Whole

1. Everybody, find the next page in your workbook. **(Hold up a workbook.)** Your page should look just like mine. ✔
2. Touch the first part of your page. **(Point to the first half of the page.)** You should be touching this part of your page. ✔
3. Find the boy. ✔
4. Here's a coloring rule for the boy's head. Listen: Color the hair orange. What's the rule? (Signal.) *Color the hair orange.*
- Mark the hair. ✔
5. Here's another coloring rule for the head. Listen: Color the nose brown. What's the rule? (Signal.) *Color the nose brown.*
- Mark the nose. ✔
6. Here's another coloring rule for the head. Listen: Color the eyes blue. What's the rule? (Signal.) *Color the eyes blue.*
- Mark the eyes. ✔
7. Here's another coloring rule for the head. Listen: Color the ear yellow. What's the rule? (Signal.) *Color the ear yellow.*
- Mark the ear. ✔

8. Part of the head is missing. What part is missing? (Signal.) *The mouth.*
- Yes, the mouth. Before you color the head, you're going to follow the dots and make the mouth.
9. Here's the coloring rule for the mouth. Listen: Color the mouth red. What's the rule? (Signal.) *Color the mouth red.*
- Mark the mouth. ✔

EXERCISE 10 Classification

1. (Hold up your workbook. Point to second half.) Find the bears. ✔
2. Here's a coloring rule for this picture. Color the containers orange. What's the rule? (Signal.) *Color the containers orange.*
- (Repeat step 2 until firm.)
3. Mark one of the containers orange. ✔
4. Here's another coloring rule for this picture. Color the vehicles red. What's the rule? (Signal.) *Color the vehicles red.*
- (Repeat step 4 until firm.)
5. Mark one of the vehicles red. ✔
6. Here's one more thing to do. Part of the cup is missing. What part is missing? (Signal.) *The handle.*
- Before you color the cup, follow the dots with your pencil to make the handle.
7. Remember—the marks show you what color to make the containers and vehicles.

Objectives

- Follow directions involving if-then and discriminate between same and different actions. (Exercise 1)
- Answer questions about previously learned calendar facts. (Exercise 2)
- **Listen to and retell a sequence of events then correct sequencing errors when the sequence is given out of order.** (Exercise 3)
- Name ways that two common objects are the same and/or different. (Exercise 4)
- **Identify true and false statements involving common objects.** (Exercise 5)
- Discriminate between statements that tell "when," "where" or "neither." (Exercise 6)
- Write numbers to show the sequence of events, tell a story based on familiar story grammar and color a picture to make it consistent with the story. (Exercise 7)
- Follow coloring rules involving class. (Exercises 8 & 9)

EXERCISE 1 Actions

1. Here's our first action game.
2. Listen: I'm going to touch my ear or touch my nose or clap. What am I going to do? (Signal.) *Touch your ear or touch your nose or clap.*
3. (Repeat step 2 until firm.)
4. Yes, I'm going touch my ear or touch my nose or clap. Am I going to touch my nose? (Signal.) *Maybe.*
   - Am I going to touch my knee? (Signal.) *No.*
   - Am I going to touch my ear? (Signal.) *Maybe.*
   - Am I going to clap? (Signal.) *Maybe.*
5. I'm going to touch my ear or touch my nose or clap. What am I going to do? (Signal.) *Touch your ear or touch your nose or clap.*
6. Here I go. (Touch your nose.) What did I do? (Signal.) *Touched your nose.*
   - Say the whole thing. Get ready. (Signal.) *You touched your nose.*
7. (Repeat step 6 until firm.)
8. (Repeat steps 5 through 7 until firm.)
9. Here's our last action game.

10. Everybody, clap your hands one time. Get ready. (Signal.) ✔
11. Now tell me if I do the same thing you did or something different. Watch me. (Stamp your foot.) Did I do the same thing or something different? (Signal.) *Something different.*
    - Watch me. (Touch your head.) Did I do the same thing or something different? (Signal.) *Something different.*
    - Watch me. (Clap your hands one time.) Did I do the same thing or something different? (Signal.) *The same thing.*
12. (Repeat steps 10 and 11 until firm.)

EXERCISE 2 Calendar Facts

1. We're going to talk about the days and months. Everybody, how many days are in a week? (Signal.) *Seven.*
   - Say the fact. Get ready. (Signal.) *There are seven days in a week.*
2. Everybody, say the days of the week. Get ready. (Signal.) *Sunday, Monday, Tuesday, Wednesday, Thursday, Friday, Saturday.*
3. How many months are in a year? (Signal.) *12.*
   - Say the fact. Get ready. (Signal.) *There are 12 months in a year.*
4. Name the months of the year through December. Get ready. (Signal.) *January, February, March, April, May, June, July, August, September, October, November, December.*

5. Everybody, how many seasons are in a year? (Signal.) *Four.*
- Say the seasons of the year. Get ready. (Signal.) *Winter, spring, summer, fall.*

EXERCISE 3   Sequence

1. I'll tell you four things that happened. Listen: First, the man put on ice skates.
- Next, the man went out on the ice.
- Next, the man skated.
- Last, the ice cracked.
2. Listen again. First, the man put on ice skates.
- Next, the man went out on the ice.
- Next, the man skated.
- Last, the ice cracked.
3. Tell me the four things that happened. What happened first? (Signal.) *The man put on ice skates.*
- What happened next? (Signal.) *The man went out on the ice.*
- What happened next? (Signal.) *The man skated.*
- What happened last? (Signal.) *The ice cracked.*
- (Repeat step 3 until firm.)
4. I'll say the four things, but I'm going to make mistakes. As soon as you hear a mistake, say **stop,** then tell me the right thing that happened.
- Listen: First, the man put on skates. Next, the man skated. (Children say *stop.*)
- What happened just after the man put on ice skates? (Signal.) *He went out on the ice.*
5. Listen again. First, the man put on ice skates. Next, the man went out on the ice. Next, the ice cracked. (Children say *stop.*)
- What happened just after the man went out on the ice? (Signal.) *The man skated.*
6. Everybody, say all four things in the right order. Get ready. (Signal.) *First, the man put on skates. Next, the man went out on the ice. Next, the man skated. Last, the ice cracked.*

EXERCISE 4   Same—Different

1. We're going to talk about how things are the same and how they are different.

2. Listen: a bathtub and a swimming pool. See if you can name two ways they are the same. (Call on individual children. Have the group repeat each correct answer. Then say:) You told me how a bathtub and a swimming pool are . . . (Signal.) *the same.*
- Listen: a bathtub and a swimming pool. See if you can name two ways they are different. (Call on individual children. Have the group repeat each correct answer. Then say:) You told me how a bathtub and a swimming pool are . . . (Signal.) *different.*
3. Here's another one. Listen: ice cream and snow. See if you can name two ways they are the same. (Call on individual children. Have the group repeat each correct answer. Then say:) You told me how ice cream and snow are . . . (Signal.) *the same.*
- Listen: ice cream and snow. See if you can name two ways they are different. (Call on individual children. Have the group repeat each correct answer. Then say:) You told me how ice cream and snow are . . . (Signal.) *different.*

EXERCISE 5   True—False

1. I'm going to make statements about a truck. Say **yes** if I make a statement that is right. Say **no** if I make a statement that is not right. What are you going to say if I make a statement that is right? (Signal.) *Yes.*
- What are you going to say if I make a statement that is not right? (Signal.) *No.*
2. Listen: A truck is good to eat. Is that right? (Signal.) *No.*
- Listen: A truck can carry things. Is that right? (Signal.) *Yes.*
- Listen: A truck is a piece of furniture. Is that right? (Signal.) *No.*
- Listen: A truck has hands. Is that right? (Signal.) *No.*
- Listen: A truck has wheels. Is that right? (Signal.) *Yes.*
3. Listen again. This time say **true** if I make a statement that is right. Say **false** if I make a statement that is not right. What are you going to say if I make a statement that is right? (Signal.) *True.*
- What are you going to say if I make a statement that is not right? (Signal.) *False.*

4. Listen: A truck is good to eat. Is that true or false? (Signal.) *False.*
- Listen: A truck can carry things. Is that true or false? (Signal.) *True.*
- Listen: A truck is a piece of furniture. Is that true or false? (Signal.) *False.*
- Listen: A truck has hands. Is that true or false? (Signal.) *False.*
- Listen: A truck has wheels. Is that true or false? (Signal.) *True.*
5. (Repeat step 4 until firm.)

EXERCISE 6   When—Where—Neither

1. I'll say statements. Some will tell when. Some will tell where. Some will tell neither when or where. For each statement, you'll say when, where, or neither.
2. Listen: The train stopped outside River City. Tell me: When, where, or neither. Get ready. (Signal.) *Where.*
- Say the words that tell where. Get ready. (Signal.) *Outside River City.*
3. Listen: After recess we had a fire drill. Tell me: When, where, or neither. Get ready. (Signal.) *When.*
- Say the words that tell when. Get ready. (Signal.) *After recess.*
4. Listen: At nine in the morning. Donna left home. Tell me: When, where, or neither. Get ready. (Signal.) *When.*
- Say the words that tell when. Get ready. (Signal.) *At nine in the morning.*
5. Listen: We walked very slowly and carefully. Tell me: When, where, or neither. Get ready. (Signal.) *Neither.*
6. Listen: We rode our bikes and stopped three times. Tell me: When, where, or neither. Get ready. (Signal.) *Neither.*
7. Listen: We rode our bikes during the thunderstorm. Tell me: When, where, or neither. Get ready. (Signal.) *When.*
- Say the words that tell when. Get ready. (Signal.) *During the thunderstorm.*
8. Listen: After we got home from school, we rode our bikes. Tell me: When, where, or neither. Get ready. (Signal.) *When.*
- Say the words that tell when. Get ready. (Signal.) *After we got home from school.*

EXERCISE 7   Sequence Story

Sweetie And The Snapping Turtle

1. Everybody, open your workbook to Lesson 14. Write your name at the top of the page. ✔
2. I'll tell a new story about Sweetie. The first time I tell it, you'll touch the places where Sweetie went. The second time I tell it, you'll write the numbers.

Sweetie went for a walk one day, looking for something to catch. He came to a little row of bushes. He saw a fish pond on the other side of the bushes, and he saw a little goldfish jump out of the pond and splash down again. "Yum, yum," Sweetie said. "I love goldfish. Yum, yum." So Sweetie jumped over the little row of bushes.

- Everybody, touch the circle on the other side of the little row of bushes. ✔

Then Sweetie snuck along the bushes until he came to a row of flowers, and he snuck through the flowers.

- Everybody, touch the circle that shows where Sweetie is now. ✔

Then he dashed over to a large bush.

- Everybody, touch the circle where Sweetie is now. ✔

Sweetie darted from the bush and hid under a bench that was right next to the fish pond.

- Everybody, touch the circle that shows where Sweetie is now. ✔

> Then Sweetie took a great leap and landed on the rocks that were on the edge of the fish pond.

- Everybody, touch the circle that shows where Sweetie is now. ✔

> Sweetie grabbed the first thing that moved underwater, but it wasn't a goldfish. Sweetie **thought** it was a goldfish, but it was really a huge turtle. That huge turtle didn't like to be grabbed, so it grabbed Sweetie and tossed him into the fish pond. Splash! Sweetie was all wet again.

- Everybody, touch the circle that shows where Sweetie is now. ✔

> Then Sweetie dashed out of the pond. He went across that yard like a shot and jumped over the row of small bushes.

- Everybody, touch the circle that shows where Sweetie is now. ✔
- Draw a line from the fish pond to the circle that shows where he went when he was all wet. Be careful. Make sure you draw a line to the circle that's on the **other** side of the small bushes.

> After a while, Sweetie looked over the bushes at the fish pond. All he could see were little goldfish jumping out of the water. And Sweetie got the wrong idea again. He looked at those little goldfish and he said to himself, "From here, those goldfish don't look very mean or strong, but let me tell you, those things can really bite."

3. That's the story about Sweetie. Now I'll tell it one more time and you'll write the numbers. Then I'll call on a couple of children to tell the whole story.

- Listen: What was the first thing Sweetie did in this picture? (Call on a child. Idea: *Jumped over the row of small bushes.*)
- Everybody, touch the circle near the bushes. Remember, Sweetie's on the turtle's side of the bushes. ✔
- Write a number **one** in that circle. Raise your hand when you're finished. (Observe children and give feedback.)

4. Listen:

> Sweetie snuck along the bushes until he came to a row of flowers, and he snuck through the flowers.

- Everybody, touch the circle. ✔
- What number goes in that circle? (Signal.) *Two.*
- Write a number **two** in that circle. Raise your hand when you're finished. (Observe children and give feedback.)

5. Listen:

> After Sweetie snuck through the flowers, he dashed over to a large bush.

- Everybody, touch the circle. ✔
- Think big. What number goes in that circle? (Signal.) *Three.*
- Write a number **three** in that circle. Raise your hand when you're finished. (Observe children and give feedback.)

6. Listen:

> Sweetie darted from the large bush and hid under a bench that was right next to the fish pond.

- Everybody, touch the circle. ✔
- Think big. What number goes in that circle? (Signal.) *Four.*
- Write a number **four** in that circle. Raise your hand when you're finished. (Observe children and give feedback.)

7. Listen:

> After Sweetie hid under the bench, he took a great leap and landed on the rocks that were on the edge of the fish pond.

- Everybody, touch the circle. ✔
- Think big. What number goes in that circle? (Signal.) *Five.*

- Write a number **five** in that circle. Raise your hand when you're finished. (Observe children and give feedback.)

8. Listen:

   > After Sweetie landed on the rocks that were on the edge of the fish pond, he grabbed the turtle and the turtle tossed him into the fish pond.

- Everybody, touch the circle. ✔
- Think big. What number goes in that circle? (Signal.) *Six.*
- Write a number **six** in that circle. Raise your hand when you're finished. (Observe children and give feedback.)

9. Listen:

   > After Sweetie was tossed into the fish pond, he darted across the yard and jumped over the row of bushes.

- Everybody, touch the circle. ✔
- Think big. What number goes in the circle? (Signal.) *Seven.*
- Write a number **seven** in that circle. Raise your hand when you're finished. (Observe children and give feedback.)

10. Now you have numbers that tell about the things that Sweetie did in this story. Who can tell the whole story? Remember, you have to tell where Sweetie was at the beginning and what he did for each number. Don't say the numbers. Just tell the story. Remember to tell what Sweetie said to himself when he was at number seven.

11. (Call on a child:) You tell the story. Everybody else, follow along and see if (child's name) tells what happened for each number. (Praise child for a story that tells the sequence of places where Sweetie went.)

    (To correct omissions, say:)

    a. Uh-oh. You missed something. Who knows what was missed?

    b. (Call on another child.)

    (Repeat step 11, calling on another child.)

12. Poor Sweetie got the wrong idea about that turtle, just like he got the wrong idea about the birds in the birdbath.

- Later you can color all the things in the picture. Remember to color Sweetie the right color. And those goldfish are gold. You can color the other things in the picture any color you wish.

EXERCISE 8 Classification

1. Everybody, turn to the next page in your workbook. (Hold up workbook.) Your page should look just like mine. ✔
2. Touch the first part of your page. (Point to the first half of the page.) You should be touching this part of your page. ✔
3. Find the fruit stand.
4. Here's a coloring rule for this picture. Color the animals orange. What's the rule? (Signal.) *Color the animals orange.*
- (Repeat step 4 until firm.)
5. Mark one of the animals orange. ✔
6. Here's another coloring rule for this picture. Color the food purple. What's the rule? (Signal.) *Color the food purple.*
- (Repeat step 6 until firm.)
7. Mark one of the foods purple. ✔
8. Here's one more thing to do. Parts of the pig are missing. What parts are missing? (Signal.) *Ears.*
- Before you color the pig, follow the dots with your pencil to make the ears.

EXERCISE 9 Location

1. (Hold up your workbook. Point to second half.)
2. What place do you see in this picture? (Signal.) *A playground.*
3. Here's a coloring rule for this picture. Listen: Color the things you play with red. What's the rule? (Signal.) *Color the things you play with red.*
   • (Repeat step 3 until firm.)
4. Put a red mark on one of the things you play with. ✔
5. Here's another coloring rule for this picture. Listen: Color the children's clothes blue. What's the rule? (Signal.) *Color the children's clothes blue.*
   • (Repeat step 5 until firm.)

6. Put a blue mark on one of the children's clothes. ✔
7. There's one more thing to do. One of the things you play with has a missing part. Which object is that? (Signal.) *The bicycle.* Yes, the bicycle.
   • What part of the bicycle is missing? (Signal.) *The wheels.* Yes, the wheels.
   • Before you color the bicycle, follow the dots with your pencil to make the wheels.
8. Remember—the marks show you what color to make the children and the things they play with. You can color the other objects any color you want.

Objectives

- **Generate statements to describe actions using present, past and future tense.** (Exercise 1)
- Identify true and false statements involving common objects. (Exercise 2)
- Answer questions about previously learned calendar facts and **the number of days in a year.** (Exercise 3)
- Given a calendar, identify the day and date for "yesterday" and "today." (Exercise 4)
- Name ways that two common objects are the same and/or different. (Exercise 5)
- Listen to and retell a sequence of events, then correct sequencing errors when the sequence is given out of order. (Exercise 6)
- Answer questions about a familiar story, and make a picture consistent with the details of the story. (Exercises 7 & 8)

EXERCISE 1 Actions

1. It's time for some actions.
2. Everybody, let's stand up. Get ready. (Signal.) (You and children are to stand up.)
- What **are** we doing? (Signal.) *Standing up.*
- What **were** we doing? (Signal.) *Sitting down.*
3. Everybody, we will sit down. What will we do? (Signal.) *Sit down.*
- What **are** we doing? (Signal.) *Standing up.*
- What **will** we do? (Signal.) *Sit down.*
- Say the whole thing about what we will do. Get ready. (Signal.) *We will sit down.*
4. Let's do it. (Signal.) (You and the children are to sit down.)
- Everybody, now what are we doing? (Signal.) *Sitting down.*
- What **were** we doing before we sat down? (Signal.) *Standing up.*
- Say the whole thing about what we were doing. Get ready. (Signal.) *We were standing up.*

EXERCISE 2 True—False

1. I'm going to make statements about a box. Say **yes** if I make a statement that is right. Say **no** if I make a statement that is not right. What are you going to say if I make a statement that is right? (Signal.) *Yes.*
- What are you going to say if I make a statement that is not right? (Signal.) *No.*
2. Listen: A box can hold things. Is that right? (Signal.) *Yes.*
- Listen: A box has wheels. Is that right? (Signal.) *No.*
- Listen: A box grows in the ground. Is that right? (Signal.) *No.*
- Listen: A box has sides and a bottom. Is that right? (Signal.) *Yes.*
- Listen: A box has wings. Is that right? (Signal.) *No.*
3. Listen again. This time say **true** if I make a statement that is right. Say **false** if I make a statement that is not right. What are you going to say if I make a statement that is right? (Signal.) *True.*
- What are you going to say if I make a statement that is not right? (Signal.) *False.*
4. Listen: A box can hold things. Is that true or false? (Signal.) *True.*
- Listen: A box has wheels. Is that true or false? (Signal.) *False.*
- Listen: A box is a container. Is that true or false? (Signal.) *True.*
- Listen: A box is a living thing. Is that true or false? (Signal.) *False.*
- Listen: A box has sides and a bottom. Is that true or false? (Signal.) *True.*
5. (Repeat step 4 until firm.)

EXERCISE 3 Calendar Facts

1. You learned calendar facts. Everybody, how many days are in a week? (Signal.) *Seven.*
- Say the fact. Get ready. (Signal.) *There are seven days in a week.*
- How many months are in a year? (Signal.) *12.*
- Say the fact about the months in a year. Get ready. (Signal.) *There are 12 months in a year.*
- How many seasons are in a year? (Signal.) *Four.*
- Say the fact about the seasons in a year. Get ready. (Signal.) *There are four seasons in a year.*
2. (Repeat step 1 until firm.)
3. Here's a new fact about the number of **days in a year.** Listen: There are 365 days in a year. How many days are in a year? (Signal.) *365.*
- Say the fact. Get ready. (Signal.) *There are 365 days in a year.*
- Again. Say the fact. Get ready. (Signal.) *There are 365 days in a year.*
4. (Repeat step 3 until firm.)
5. Let's do all the facts again. How many months are in a year? (Signal.) *12.*
- Say the fact. Get ready. (Signal.) *There are 12 months in a year.*
- How many seasons are in a year? (Signal.) *Four.*
- Say the fact. Get ready. (Signal.) *There are four seasons in a year.*
- How many days are in a year? (Signal.) *365.*
- Say the fact. Get ready. (Signal.) *There are 365 days in a year.*
6. (Repeat step 5 until firm.)

EXERCISE 4 Calendar

1. (Present calendar.) First you'll tell me about the days of the week. Then you'll tell me about the dates.
2. Tell me the day of the week it was yesterday. Get ready. (Signal.)
- Tell me the day of the week it is today. Get ready. (Signal.)
- Now the dates. Everybody, tell me yesterday's date. Get ready. (Signal.)
- Tell me today's date. Get ready. (Signal.)
3. (Repeat step 2 until firm.)

EXERCISE 5 Same—Different

1. We're going to talk about how things are the same and how they are different.
2. Listen: a fish and a boat. See if you can name two ways they are the same. (Call on individual children. Have the group repeat each correct answer. Then say:) You told me how a fish and a boat are . . . (Signal.) *the same.*
- Listen: a fish and a boat. See if you can name two ways they are different. (Call on individual children. Have the group repeat each correct answer. Then say:) You told me how a fish and a boat are . . . (Signal.) *different.*
3. Here's another one. Listen: a motorcycle and a bicycle. See if you can name two ways they are the same. (Call on individual children. Have the group repeat each correct answer. Then say:) You told me how a motorcycle and a bicycle are . . . (Signal.) *the same.*
- Listen: a motorcycle and a bicycle. See if you can name two ways they are different. (Call on individual children. Have the group repeat each correct answer. Then say:) You told me how a motorcycle and a bicycle are . . . (Signal.) *different.*

EXERCISE 6 Sequence

1. I'll tell you four things that happened. Listen: First, Jean put on her coat.
- Next, she made sure she had her car keys.
- Next, she went into the garage.
- Last, she unlocked the car.
2. Listen again. First, Jean put on her coat.
- Next, she made sure she had her car keys.
- Next, she went into the garage.
- Last, she unlocked the car.
3. Tell me the four things. What happened first? (Signal.) *Jean put on her coat.*
- What happened next? (Signal.) *She made sure she had her car keys.*
- What happened next? (Signal.) *She went into the garage.*
- What happened last? (Signal.) *She unlocked her car.*
- (Repeat step 3 until firm.)

4. I'll say the four things, but I'm going to make mistakes. As soon as you hear a mistake, say **stop,** then tell me the right thing that happened. Listen: First, Jean made sure she had her car keys. (Children say *stop.*)

• What happened first? (Signal.) *Jean put on her coat.*

5. Listen again. First, Jean put on her coat. Next, she made sure she had her car keys. Next, she unlocked the car. (Children say *stop.*)

• What happened just after Jean made sure she had her car keys? (Signal.) *She went into the garage.*

6. Everybody, say all four things in the right order. What happened first? (Signal.) *Jean put on her coat.*

• What happened next? (Signal.) *She made sure she had her car keys.*

• What happened next? (Signal.) *She went into the garage.*

• What happened last? (Signal.) *She unlocked her car.*

EXERCISE 7 The Bragging Rats Race

Storytelling

• Everybody, I'm going to tell you the story about the bragging rats again. You're going to fix up a picture that shows part of the story, so remember the things that happened.

A bunch of rats lived near a pond that was on a farm. The rats got along well, except for two of them. The other rats called these two the bragging rats because they were always bragging, quarreling and arguing about something.

One day they'd argue about who could eat the most. Another day they'd squabble and quarrel over who was the best looking. Neither one of them was very good looking. One was a big gray rat with the longest tail you've ever seen on a rat. The other one wasn't big, but he had the biggest, yellowest teeth you ever saw.

The other rats in the bunch didn't pay much attention to the bragging and quarreling until the two rats started bragging about who was the fastest rat in the whole bunch. This quarrel went on for days, and the other rats got pretty sick of listening to the rats shout and yell and brag about how fast they were.

On the third day of their quarrel, they almost got into a fight. The rat with the yellow teeth was saying, "I'm so fast that I could run circles around you while you ran as fast as you could."

The big gray rat said, "Oh, yeah? Well, I could run circles around your circles. That's how fast I am."

The two rats continued yelling at each other until a wise old rat said, "Stop! We are tired of listening to all this shouting and yelling and bragging. There is a way to find out who is the fastest rat on this farm."

The wise old rat continued, "We will have a race for any rat that wants to race. Everybody will line up, run down the path to the pond, then run back. The first rat to get back is the winner. And then we'll have no more arguing about which rat can run the fastest."

The rats agreed, and early the next morning they were lined up, ready for the big race. Six rats entered the race. The bragging rats were lined up right next to each other, making mean faces and mumbling about how fast they were going to run.

The rats put their noses close to the ground, ready to take off like a flash.

"Everybody, steady," the wise old rat said. "Everybody, ready. Go!"

The rats took off toward the pond. The big gray rat got ahead of the others, with the yellow-toothed rat right behind him. But just before they got to the pond, the yellow-toothed rat stepped on the long tail of the gray rat, and both rats tumbled over and over in a cloud of dust. They tumbled down the dusty path and right into the pond.

The other rats finished the race. The winner was a little black rat. It was hard for her to finish the race because she was laughing so hard over the bragging rats, who were still splashing and sputtering around in the pond.

After the race, all the other rats went back to the pond. The bragging rats were still splashing and sputtering. The wise old rat said to them, "So now we know who the fastest runner on this farm is. It's neither one of you, so we will have no more arguments from either of you about who can run the fastest!"

The bragging rats looked at each other. Then the rat with yellow teeth suddenly smiled and said, "I may not be the fastest **runner** in this bunch, but there is no rat in the world that can **swim** as fast as I can."

"Oh, yeah?" said the gray rat. "I can swim so fast that I could go all the way across this pond without even getting my fur wet."

The wise old rat and the other rats just walked away from the pond, slowly shaking their heads.

EXERCISE 8   Story Details

1. Everybody, open your workbook to Lesson 15. Write your name at the top of the page. ✔
2. This is a picture of the bragging rats. What are the rats doing in this picture? (Call on a child. Accept reasonable responses.)
- Touch the rat with the big teeth. He's the one stepping on the tail of the other bragging rat. ✔
- Everybody, what color are those big teeth? (Signal.) *Yellow.*
- Touch the rat with the long tail. ✔
- Everybody, what color is that rat? (Signal.) *Gray.*
- Touch that little rat running behind the bragging rats. ✔
- That's the rat that ended up winning the race. Everybody, what color is that rat? (Signal.) *Black.*
- Who remembers what happened just **after** this picture? (Call on a child. Idea: *The bragging rats tumbled into the pond.*)
3. Later you'll color the picture. Remember the color of the rat with the long tail and the rat that ended up winning the race.

Materials: You will need a cloth shirt with a collar, sleeves, and plastic buttons for exercise 4. You will need to prepare three circles—plastic, paper, and cloth—for exercise 5. Use a plastic lid approximately 5 inches in diameter. Cut the cloth and paper circles to the same size. You should have a lapboard or a large book on which to put the three circles.

Objectives

- **Generate statements to describe actions using prepositional phrases,** and make statements and answer questions involving "or." (Exercise 1)
- Listen to and retell a sequence of events then correct sequencing errors when the sequence is given out of order. (Exercise 2)
- Name ways that two common objects are the same and/or different. (Exercise 3)
- **Identify parts of a common object and the materials it is made of.** (Exercise 4)
- **Identify common materials.** (Exercise 5)
- Identify true and false statements involving common objects. (Exercise 6)
- Answer questions about previously learned calendar facts. (Exercise 7)
- Given a calendar, identify the day and date for "yesterday" and "today." (Exercise 8)
- Relate a familiar story grammar to a picture that indicates the sequence of events for a new story. (Exercise 9)
- Follow coloring rules involving parts of a whole. (Exercise 10)
- Follow coloring rules involving class. (Exercise 11)

EXERCISE 1 Actions

1. It's time for some actions.
2. Everybody, hold your hand under your chair. Get ready. (Signal.) ✔
- Where are you holding your hand? (Signal.) *Under my chair.*
- Say the whole thing. Get ready. (Signal.) *I am holding my hand under my chair.*
3. Everybody, hold your hand over your chair. Get ready. (Signal.) ✔
- Where are you holding your hand? (Signal.) *Over my chair.*
- Say the whole thing. Get ready. (Signal.) *I am holding my hand over my chair.*
4. Everybody, hold your hand on your chair. Get ready. (Signal.) ✔
- Where are you holding your hand? (Signal.) *On my chair.*
- Say the whole thing. Get ready. (Signal.) *I am holding my hand on my chair.*
5. (Repeat steps 2 through 4 until firm.)
6. Here's another game. I'm going to do something. See if you can figure out what I'm going to do.

7. Listen: I'm going to jump or stamp my foot or sit down. What am I going to do? (Signal.) *Jump or stamp your foot or sit down.*
8. (Repeat step 7 until firm.)
9. Yes, I'm going to jump or stamp my foot or sit down. Am I going to jump? (Signal.) *Maybe.*
- Am I going to sit down? (Signal.) *Maybe.*
- Am I going to run? (Signal.) *No.*
- Am I going to stamp my foot? (Signal.) *Maybe.*
10. (Stand up.) I'm going to jump or stamp my foot or sit down. What am I going to do? (Signal.) *Jump or stamp your foot or sit down.*
11. Here I go. (Stamp your foot.) Did I sit down? (Signal.) *No.*
- Did I jump? (Signal.) *No.*
- Did I stamp my foot? (Signal.) *Yes.*
12. What did I do? (Signal.) *Stamped your foot.*
- Say the whole thing. Get ready. (Signal.) *You stamped your foot.*
13. (Repeat step 12 until everyone can make the statement.)
14. (Repeat steps 10 through 13 until firm.)

EXERCISE 2   Sequence

1. I'll tell you four things that happened. Listen: First, Dave got a can of cat food from the cupboard.
- Next, Dave opened the can.
- Next, he put some cat food in the dish.
- Last, he called the cat.
2. Listen again. First, Dave got a can of cat food from the cupboard.
- Next, Dave opened the can.
- Next, he put some cat food in the dish.
- Last, he called the cat.
3. Tell me the four things. What happened first? (Signal.) *Dave got a can of cat food from the cupboard.*
- What happened next? (Signal.) *Dave opened the can.*
- What happened next? (Signal.) *He put some cat food in the dish.*
- What happened last? (Signal.) *He called the cat.*
- (Repeat step 3 until firm.)
4. I'll say the four things, but I'm going to make mistakes. As soon as you hear a mistake, say **stop,** then tell me the right thing that happened. Listen: First, Dave got a can of cat food from the cupboard. Next, he put some cat food in the dish. (Children say *stop.*)
- What happened after Dave got a can of cat food from the cupboard? (Signal.) *He opened the can.*
- Listen again. First, Dave opened a can. (Children say *stop.*)
- What happened first? (Signal.) *Dave got a can of cat food from the cupboard.*
5. Everybody, say all four things in the right order. What happened first? (Signal.) *Dave got a can of cat food from the cupboard.*
- What happened next? (Signal.) *He opened the can.*
- What happened next? (Signal.) *He put some cat food in the dish.*
- What happened last? (Signal.) *He called the cat.*

EXERCISE 3   Same—Different

1. We're going to talk about how things are the same and how they are different.
2. Listen: a chalkboard and paper. See if you can name two ways they are the same. (Call on individual children. Have the group repeat each correct answer. Then say:) You told me how a chalkboard and paper are . . . (Signal.) *the same.*
- Listen: a chalkboard and paper. See if you can name two ways they are different. (Call on individual children. Have the group repeat each correct answer. Then say:) You told me how a chalkboard and paper are . . . (Signal.) *different.*
3. Here's another one. Listen: scissors and a knife. See if you can name two ways they are the same. (Call on individual children. Have the group repeat each correct answer. Then say:) You told me how scissors and a knife are . . . (Signal.) *the same.*
- Listen: scissors and a knife. See if you can name two ways they are different. (Call on individual children. Have the group repeat each correct answer. Then say:) You told me how scissors and a knife are . . . (Signal.) *different.*

EXERCISE 4   Materials

1. (Present a cloth shirt with a collar, sleeves, and plastic buttons.) A shirt has parts. I'll point to some of the parts and name them.
2. (Point to collar.) This is the collar. What part? (Signal.) *Collar.*
- (Point to sleeves.) These are sleeves. What part? (Signal.) *Sleeves.*
- (Point to buttons.) These are buttons. What part? (Signal.) *Buttons.*
3. Your turn to name the parts. (Point to collar.) What part? (Signal.) *Collar.*
- (Point to sleeves.) What part? (Signal.) *Sleeves.*
- (Point to buttons.) What part? (Signal.) *Buttons.*

4. Here's a fact: This shirt has a collar. Say that fact. Get ready. (Signal.) *This shirt has a collar.*

• Here's another fact: This shirt has buttons. Say that fact. Get ready. (Signal.) *This shirt has buttons.*

• Here's the last fact: This shirt has sleeves. Say that fact. Get ready. (Signal.) *This shirt has sleeves.*

5. (Repeat step 4 until firm.)

6. (Touch a button.) What part am I touching? (Signal.) *A button.*

• Listen: The button is made of plastic. What's it made of? (Signal.) *Plastic.*

• Listen: The rest of the shirt is made of cloth. What's it made of? (Signal.) *Cloth.*

• And what's the button made of? (Signal.) *Plastic.*

• What's the rest of the shirt made of? (Signal.) *Cloth.*

7. (Repeat step 6 until firm.)

EXERCISE 5   Materials

1. (Present the three circles.) We're going to learn what things are made of.

• (Point to the circles.) Everybody, what are these? (Signal.) *Circles.* Yes, circles.

2. (Point to the paper circle.) This circle is made of paper. What is it made of? (Signal.) *Paper.*

• (Point to the cloth circle.) This circle is made of cloth. What is it made of? (Signal.) *Cloth.*

• (Point to the plastic circle.) This circle is made of plastic. What is it made of? (Signal.) *Plastic.*

3. I'll point to each circle. You tell me what it is made of.

4. (Point to the plastic circle.) What is this circle made of? (Signal.) *Plastic.*

• (Point to the cloth circle.) What is this circle made of? (Signal.) *Cloth.*

• (Point to the paper circle.) What is this circle made of? (Signal.) *Paper.*

5. (Repeat step 4 until firm.)

EXERCISE 6   True—False

1. I'm going to make statements about a lion. Say **yes** if I make a statement that is right. Say **no** if I make a statement that is not right. What are you going to say if I make a statement that is right? (Signal.) *Yes.*

• What are you going to say if I make a statement that is not right? (Signal.) *No.*

2. Listen: A lion is a plant. Is that right? (Signal.) *No.*

• Listen: A lion can roar. Is that right? (Signal.) *Yes.*

• Listen: A lion has a tail. Is that right? (Signal.) *Yes.*

• Listen: A lion has four legs. Is that right? (Signal.) *Yes.*

• Listen: A lion has seven legs. Is that right? (Signal.) *No.*

3. You'll listen to my statement and say **true** if I make a statement that is right. Say **false** if I make a statement that is not right.

4. Listen: You keep a lion in the house. Is that true or false? (Signal.) *False.*

• Listen: A lion can roar. Is that true or false? (Signal.) *True.*

• Listen: A lion has two eyes. Is that true or false? (Signal.) *True.*

• Listen: A lion has a tail. Is that true or false? (Signal.) *True.*

• Listen: A lion is a plant. Is that true or false? (Signal.) *False.*

5. (Repeat step 4 until firm.)

EXERCISE 7   Calendar Facts

1. You learned calendar facts. Everybody, how many days are in a week? (Signal.) *Seven.*
- Say the fact. Get ready. (Signal.) *There are seven days in a week.*
- How many months are in a year? (Signal.) *12.*
- Say the fact about the months in a year. Get ready. (Signal.) *There are 12 months in a year.*
- How many seasons are in a year? (Signal.) *Four.*
- Say the fact about the seasons in a year. Get ready. (Signal.) *There are four seasons in a year.*
2. (Repeat step 1 until firm.)
3. You learned a new fact about the number of **days in a year.** Everybody, how many days are in a year? (Signal.) *365.*
- Say the fact. Get ready. (Signal.) *There are 365 days in a year.*
- Again. Say the fact. Get ready. (Signal.) *There are 365 days in a year.*
4. (Repeat step 3 until firm.)
5. Let's do all the facts again. How many months are in a year? (Signal.) *12.*
- Say the fact. Get ready. (Signal.) *There are 12 months in a year.*
- How many seasons are in a year? (Signal.) *Four.*
- Say the fact. Get ready. (Signal.) *There are four seasons in a year.*
- How many days are in a year? (Signal.) *365.*
- Say the fact. Get ready. (Signal.) *There are 365 days in a year.*
6. (Repeat step 5 until firm.)

EXERCISE 8   Calendar

1. (Present calendar.) First you'll tell me about the days of the week. Then you'll tell me about the dates.
2. Tell me the day of the week it was yesterday. Get ready. (Signal.)
- Tell me the day of the week it is today. Get ready. (Signal.)
- Now the dates. Everybody, tell me yesterday's date. Get ready. (Signal.)
- Tell me today's date. Get ready. (Signal.)
3. (Repeat step 2 until firm.)

EXERCISE 9   Sequence Story

The Bragging Rats Have a Breathing Contest

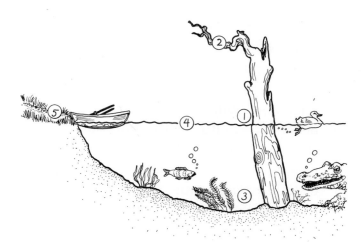

1. Everybody, open your workbook to Lesson 16. Write your name at the top of the page. ✔
2. This picture shows where the bragging rats went to settle another argument they had.

The bragging rats argued for days about who could hold his breath the longest.

- Who knows how to hold their breath? (Call on a child to demonstrate.)
- Yes, when you hold your breath, you don't breathe in and you don't breathe out.

Well, the rats argued and argued about who was the best at holding his breath.

Finally, the wise old rat said, "There's one way to settle this argument so that nobody can cheat and breathe through his nose while he's pretending to hold his breath."

So the wise old rat took the bragging rats to the pond and all three rats got in the boat.

3. Everybody, touch the boat. ✔
- That's where the rats started out. Now touch number 1. ✔
- Where are the rats when they are at number 1? (Call on a child. Idea: *At a dead old tree in the middle of the pond.*)

After they have arrived at the old dead tree, the wise old rat stayed in the boat. He told the bragging rats to go to number 2.

4. Everybody, touch number 2. ✔
- Where is number 2? (Call on a child. Idea: *Up in the tree.*)

Then the wise old rat told them to go to number 3.

5. Everybody, touch number 3. ✔
- Where is number 3? (Call on a child. Idea: *At the bottom of the pond, next to the tree.*)
- Right.

The wise old rat told the bragging rats to dive into the water, go down to the bottom of the pond and hang on to the bottom of the tree. He said, "Stay down there as long as you can. The rat that stays down longer is the winner."

Now here's something you should know about the bragging rats. They could hold their breath for a pretty long time, but they were at the bottom of the pond only a second or two when they both went to number 4 and number 5 the fast way.

6. Everybody, touch number 4. ✔
- Where are they at number 4? (Call on a child. Idea: *At the top of the pond.*)
- Touch number 5. ✔
- Where are they at number 5? (Call on a child. Idea: *At the shore.*)

Those rats went to 4 and 5 just as fast as their little rat bodies could move. And do you know why? Because they saw something underwater, and it wasn't a fish and it wasn't a duck.

- Everybody, what did they see underwater? (Signal.) *An alligator.*

So when they saw the alligator, they shot up to the surface and got out of that pond as fast as they could move.

7. Listen: The numbers in the story tell what the bragging rats did first, what they did next and so on. Who can touch the numbers and tell all the things that happened in the story? Start by telling what the bragging rats were arguing about. Then tell where they went. Then tell what happened at each number, but don't say the numbers. Remember to tell how long they stayed underwater and why they got out of the water the fast way.

8. (Call on a child:) You tell the story. Everybody else, follow along and see if (child's name) tells what happened for each number. (Praise child for a story that tells the sequence of things that the bragging rats did.)
(Repeat step 7, calling on another child.)

9. Draw a picture of the **three** rats sitting in the boat, getting ready for the big breath-holding contest. Later you can color the picture. Color the water blue. Color the other things any color you wish.

EXERCISE 10 Part—Whole

1. Everybody, find the next page in your workbook. (Hold up a workbook.) Your page should look just like mine. ✔
2. Touch the first part of your page. (Point to the first half of the page.) You should be touching this part of your page. ✔
3. Find the chair with rungs. ✔
4. Here's a coloring rule for this chair. Listen: Color the rungs red. What's the rule? (Signal.) *Color the rungs red.*
- Mark the rungs. ✔

5. Here's another coloring rule for this chair. Listen: Color the legs green. What's the rule? (Signal.) *Color the legs green.*
- Mark the legs. ✔
6. Here's another coloring rule for the chair. Listen: Color the back black. What's the rule? (Signal.) *Color the back black.*
- Mark the back. ✔
7. Part of the chair is missing. What part is missing? (Signal.) *The seat.* Yes, the seat.
- Before you color the chair, you're going to follow the dots and make the seat.
8. Here's the coloring rule for the seat. Listen: Color the seat brown. What's the rule? (Signal.) *Color the seat brown.*
- Mark the seat. ✔

EXERCISE 11   Location

1. (Hold up your workbook. Point to second half.)
2. Everybody, what place do you see in this picture? (Signal.) *A dentist's office.*

3. Here's a coloring rule for this picture. Listen: Color the furniture green. What's the rule? (Signal.) *Color the furniture green.*
- (Repeat step 3 until firm.)
4. Make a green mark on one piece of furniture. ✔
5. Here's another coloring rule for this picture. Listen: Color the dentist's tools blue. What's the rule? (Signal.) *Color the dentist's tools blue.*
- (Repeat step 5 until firm.)
6. Make a blue mark on one of the dentist's tools. ✔
7. There's one more thing to do. One piece of furniture has a missing part. What piece of furniture is that? (Signal.) *The cabinet.* Yes, the cabinet.
- Everybody, what part of the cabinet is missing? (Signal.) *The door.* Yes, the door.
- So before you color the cabinet, follow the dots and make the door.
8. Remember—the marks show you what color to make the furniture and the tools. You can color the other objects any color you want.

Materials: You will need the three circles and shirt specified in Lesson 16.

Objectives

- Generate statements to describe actions using present, past and future tense. (Exercise 1)
- Identify statements that tell "when," and generate statements that tell "when" **and statements that tell when something did not occur.** (Exercise 2)
- **Identify and generate absurdities of location.** (Exercise 3)
- Identify common materials. (Exercise 4)
- Identify parts of a common object and the materials it is made of. (Exercise 5)
- Name ways that two common objects are the same and/or different. (Exercise 6)
- Name common opposites. (Exercise 7)
- Listen to and retell a sequence of events, then correct sequencing errors when the sequence is given out of order. (Exercise 8)
- Identify true and false statements involving common objects. (Exercise 9)
- Given a calendar, identify the day and date for "yesterday" and "today." (Exercise 10)
- Relate a familiar story grammar to a picture that indicates the sequence of events for a new story. (Exercise 11)
- **Identify a familiar story character from unique expressions.** (Exercise 12)
- Follow coloring rules involving parts of a whole. (Exercise 13)
- Follow coloring rules involving specific objects. (Exercise 14)

EXERCISE 1 Actions

1. It's time for some actions.
2. Everybody, let's stand up. Get ready. (Signal.) (You and the children are to stand up.)
- What **are** we doing? (Signal.) *Standing up.*
- What **were** we doing? (Signal.) *Sitting down.*
3. Everybody, we will sit down. What will we do? (Signal.) *Sit down.*
- What **are** we doing? (Signal.) *Standing up.*
- What **will** we do? (Signal.) *Sit down.*
- Say the whole thing about what we will do. Get ready. (Signal.) *We will sit down.*
4. Let's do it. (Signal. You and the children sit down.)
- Everybody, what are we doing now? (Signal.) *Sitting down.*
- What **were** we doing before we sat down? (Signal.) *Standing up.*

EXERCISE 2 When

1. Listen: The dog ate bones at 7 o'clock. Say that statement. Get ready. (Signal.) *The dog ate bones at 7 o'clock.*
- Does that statement tell **when** the dog ate bones? (Signal.) *Yes.*
2. Now it's your turn to make up statements.
3. Make up a new statement that tells **when** the dog ate bones. (Call on individual children. Praise good statements.)
4. Make up a statement that does **not** tell when the dog ate bones. (Call on individual children. Praise good statements.)

EXERCISE 3 Absurdity

1. Name some things you would find on a farm. (Call on individual children. Praise good answers. Have the group repeat each good answer. For example:) All right. We find a barn on a farm. Let's all say it. (Signal.) *We find a barn on a farm.*

2. Would you find a skyscraper on a farm? (Signal.) *No.*
- It would be absurd to see a skyscraper on a farm.
- Would you find a tractor on a farm? (Signal.) *Yes.*
- Yes, you would find a tractor on a farm.
- Would you find a field on a farm? (Signal.) *Yes.*
- Yes, you would find a field on a farm.
- Would you find a post office on a farm? (Signal.) *No.*
3. Name something else that would be absurd on a farm. (Call on individual children. Praise good answers.)

EXERCISE 4 Materials

1. (Present the three circles.) We're going to review what things are made of. (Point to the circles.) Everybody, what are these? (Signal.) *Circles.* Yes, circles.
2. (Point to the plastic circle.) This circle is made of plastic. What is it made of? (Signal.) *Plastic.*
- (Point to the paper circle.) This circle is made of paper. What is it made of? (Signal.) *Paper.*
- (Point to the cloth circle.) This circle is made of cloth. What is it made of? (Signal.) *Cloth.*
3. I'll point to each circle. You tell me what it is made of.
4. (Point to the cloth circle.) What is this circle made of? (Signal.) *Cloth.*
- (Point to the plastic circle.) What is this circle made of? (Signal.) *Plastic.*
- (Point to the paper circle.) What is this circle made of? (Signal.) *Paper.*
5. (Repeat step 4 until firm.)

EXERCISE 5 Materials

1. (Present a cloth shirt with a collar, sleeves, and plastic buttons.) We're going to talk about this shirt. Everybody, get ready to name parts of this shirt.

2. (Touch the collar.) What is the name of this part? (Signal.) *Collar.*
- (Touch the sleeves.) What is the name of these parts? (Signal.) *Sleeves.*
- (Touch a button.) What is the name of this part? (Signal.) *Button.*
- What's the button made of? (Signal.) *Plastic.*
- What's the rest of the shirt made of? (Signal.) *Cloth.*
3. (Repeat step 2 until firm.)

EXERCISE 6 Same—Different

1. We're going to talk about how things are the same and how they are different.
2. Listen: a motorcycle and a bicycle. See if you can name two ways they are the same. (Call on individual children. Have the group repeat each correct answer. Then say:) You told me how a motorcycle and a bicycle are . . . (Signal.) *the same.*
- Listen: a motorcycle and a bicycle. See if you can name two ways they are different. (Call on individual children. Have the group repeat each correct answer. Then say:) You told me how a motorcycle and a bicycle are . . . (Signal.) *different.*
3. Here's another one. Listen: a flower and a tree. See if you can name two ways they are the same. (Call on individual children. Have the group repeat each correct answer. Then say:) You told me how a flower and a tree are . . . (Signal.) *the same.*
- Listen: a flower and a tree. See if you can name two ways they are different. (Call on individual children. Have the group repeat each correct answer. Then say:) You told me how a flower and a tree . . . (Signal.) *different.*

EXERCISE 7 Opposites

1. Some words are opposites. Here are opposites: long and short. They are opposites because if something is long, you know it can't be short. You know the opposite of big. What's the opposite of big? (Signal.) *Small.*
- Here's another pair of opposites: big and little. From now on, what will you say for the opposite of big? (Signal.) *Little.*

- Here's another pair of opposites: young and old.
2. Your turn. What are young and old? (Signal.) *Opposites.*
- What are big and little? (Signal.) *Opposites.*
- What are long and short? (Signal.) *Opposites.*
- Who can name another pair of opposites? (Call on individual children. Ideas: *wet and dry; fat and skinny; tall and short; full and empty.*)
3. I'll say words. You tell me the opposite.
- Listen: empty. What's the opposite of empty? (Signal.) *Full.*
- Yes, full is the opposite of . . . (Signal.) *empty.*
- Say the whole thing about full. Get ready. (Signal.) *Full is the opposite of empty.*
- Listen: old. What's the opposite of old? (Signal.) *Young.*
- Say the whole thing about young. Get ready. (Signal.) *Young is the opposite of old.*
- Listen: tall. What's the opposite of tall? (Signal.) *Short.*
- Say the whole thing about short. Get ready. (Signal.) *Short is the opposite of tall.*
4. (Repeat step 3 until firm.)

EXERCISE 8   Sequence

1. I'll tell you four things that happened. Listen: First, Sarah picked up her toothbrush and toothpaste.
- Next, she opened the toothpaste.
- Next, she put toothpaste on her toothbrush.
- Last, she brushed her teeth.
2. Listen again. First, Sarah picked up her toothbrush and toothpaste.
- Next, she opened the toothpaste.
- Next, she put toothpaste on her toothbrush.
- Last, she brushed her teeth.

3. Tell me the four things. What happened first? (Signal.) *Sarah picked up her toothbrush and toothpaste.*
- What happened next? (Signal.) *She opened the toothpaste.*
- What happened next? (Signal.) *She put toothpaste on her toothbrush.*
- What happened last? (Signal.) *She brushed her teeth.*
- (Repeat step 3 until firm.)
4. I'll say the four things, but I'm going to make mistakes. As soon as you hear a mistake, say **stop,** then tell me the right thing that happened. Listen: First, Sarah picked up her toothbrush and toothpaste. Next, she brushed her teeth. (Children say *stop.*)
- What happened after Sarah picked up her toothbrush and toothpaste? (Signal.) *She opened the toothpaste.*
- Listen again. First, Sarah picked up her toothbrush and toothpaste. Next, she put toothpaste on her toothbrush. (Children say *stop.*)
- What happened after Sarah picked up her toothbrush and toothpaste? (Signal.) *She opened the toothpaste.*
5. Everybody, say all four things in the right order. What happened first? (Signal.) *Sarah picked up her toothbrush and toothpaste.*
- What happened next? (Signal.) *She opened the toothpaste.*
- What happened next? (Signal.) *She put toothpaste on her toothbrush.*
- What happened last? (Signal.) *She brushed her teeth.*

EXERCISE 9   True—False

1. I'm going to make statements about a house. Listen: Say **true** if I make a statement that is right. Say **false** if I make a statement that is not right. What are you going to say if I make a statement that is right? (Signal.) *True.*
- What are you going to say if I make a statement that is not right? (Signal.) *False.*

2. Listen: A house can fly. Is that true or false? (Signal.) *False.*
   - Listen: A house has walls. Is that true or false? (Signal.) *True.*
   - Listen: A house has a door. Is that true or false? (Signal.) *True.*
   - Listen: A house has wings. Is that true or false? (Signal.) *False.*
   - Listen: A house can take you places. Is that true or false? (Signal.) *False.*
   - Listen: A house has a roof. Is that true or false? (Signal.) *True.*
3. (Repeat step 2 until firm.)

EXERCISE 10 Calendar

1. (Present calendar.) First you'll tell me about the days of the week. Then you'll tell me about the dates.
2. Tell me the day of the week it was yesterday. Get ready. (Signal.)
   - Tell me the day of the week it is today. Get ready. (Signal.)
   - Now the dates. Everybody, tell me yesterday's date. Get ready. (Signal.)
   - Tell me today's date. Get ready. (Signal.)
3. (Repeat step 2 until firm.)

WORKBOOK

EXERCISE 11 Sequence Story

Paul Paints a Paddle

1. Everybody, open your workbook to Lesson 17. Write your name at the top of the page. ✔

2. Here's a new picture that shows the things that Paul painted pink. You can see that can of paint. It says, "Peony Pink" on it. A peony is a big flower. Some of them are a pretty pink. I'll bet Paul would like those flowers.
3. Everybody, touch number 1. ✔
   - The number 1 shows what Paul painted first. Everybody, what is that? (Signal.) *A paddle.*
   - Yes, Paul was painting the paddle pink because he wanted a pink paddle for paddling with his pals down at Poplar Pond.
4. Touch number 2. ✔
   - The number 2 shows what he painted next. Everybody, what is that? (Signal.) *A purse.*
   - Why do you think Paul painted the purse pink? (Call on a child. Idea: *Because he got some pink paint on it while he was painting the paddle.*)
5. Touch number 3. ✔
   - That's what he painted next. Everybody, what is that? (Signal.) *A plate.*
     Yes, that's a plate.
   - Why do you think he painted the plate pink? (Call on a child. Idea: *Because he got some pink paint on it while he was painting the purse.*)
6. Look at the numbers and say the story to yourself. Then I'll call on several children to see if they can say the whole story to the rest of us. Raise your hand when you're ready to tell the story.
7. (Call on a child:) You tell the story. A really good story would start out by telling that Paul wanted to paddle with his pals on the pond—or something like that. Then tell the color he was painting. Then tell what happened at each number, but don't say the numbers. Everybody else, follow along and see if (child's name) tells what happened for each number.
   (Praise child for a story that tells the sequence of things that were painted.)
   (Repeat step 7, calling on another child.)
8. Later you can color all the things that Paul painted pink in this story. You can color the things he didn't paint any color you wish.
9. A lot of things in this picture have names that begin with **P** and Paul seems to like names that begin with **P**.

- Touch that picture behind Paul. There's a bear in that picture. Does anybody know what kind of bear that is? (Call on a child.) *A polar bear.* Yes, it's a polar bear.
- Look at those two big things on the floor, just behind the can of paint. Everybody, what are those things? (Signal.) *Pumpkins.*
- Look at that thing on Paul's knee. What is that thing called? (Signal.) *A patch.*
- That little horse looking through the window has a special name. What kind of horse is that? (Signal.) *A pony.*
- Some of the things on the table have names that begin with **P.** Who can name any of them? (Call on several children. Ideas: *A pair of pliers, two potatoes, a pretzel, a purse, a plate.*)
- Yes, that tool is a pair of pliers. Those things next to the pliers are potatoes. And there's a big pretzel on the table.
- Look on the floor again. What is that funny thing at the bottom of the picture called? (Signal.) *A puppet.*
- Yes, that's a hand puppet. And it looks like the same kind of bird that is flying outside. That bird is a pelican.
- Touch the lock on the table. Who knows what kind of lock that is? (Call on a child.) *A padlock.*
- If you look in the background, you can see a little lake. What's another name for a little lake? (Signal.) *A pond.*
- And those trees back there may be poplar trees. There sure are a lot of **P** words shown in this picture.

EXERCISE 12   **Extrapolation**

What Characters Say

1. Everybody, let's see how smart you are. I'll say things that some people said. One of those persons was Paul. See if you can pick out the things Paul said.
2. Here's what a person said: "The yellow roses are lovely." Do you think Paul would say that? (Signal.) *No.*

3. Here's what a person said: "The purple petunias are pretty." Do you think Paul would say that? (Signal.) *Yes.*
- (Call on several children:) Why do you think Paul would say, "The purple petunias are pretty"? (Praise ideas: *Paul loves to say words that start with* **P** *or Paul loves purple.*)
4. Here's what a person said: "Polite puppies please people." Do you think Paul would say that? (Signal.) *Yes.*
- (Call on several children:) Why do you think Paul would say, "Polite puppies please people"? (Praise idea: *Paul loves to say words that start with* **P**.)
5. Here's what a person said: "Those little dogs are nice." Do you think Paul would say that? (Signal.) *No.*
6. Your turn: See if you can say something new the way Paul might say it. (Praise precocious pupils.)

EXERCISE 13   **Part—Whole**

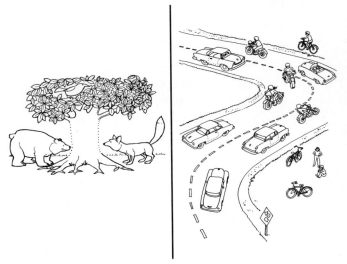

1. Everybody, turn to the next page in your workbook. (Hold up a workbook.) Your page should look just like mine. ✔
2. Touch the first part of your page. (Point to the first half of the page.) You should be touching this part of your page. ✔

3. Find the tree. ✔
4. Here's a coloring rule for the tree. Listen: Color the branches brown. What's the rule? (Signal.) *Color the branches brown*
- Mark the branches. ✔
5. Here's another coloring rule for the tree. Listen: Color the roots red. What's the rule? (Signal.) *Color the roots red.*
- Mark the roots. ✔
6. Here's another coloring rule for the tree. Listen: Color the leaves green. What's the rule? (Signal.) *Color the leaves green.*
- Mark the leaves. ✔
7. Part of the tree is missing. What part is missing? (Signal.) *The trunk.* Yes, the trunk.
- Before you color the tree, you're going to follow the dots and make the trunk.
8. Here's the coloring rule for the trunk. Listen: Color the trunk brown. What's the rule? (Signal.) *Color the trunk brown.*
- Mark the trunk. ✔

EXERCISE 14 Coloring Rules

1. (Hold up a workbook. Point to second half.) Find the road. ✔
2. Here's a coloring rule for this picture. Listen: Make every car orange. What's the rule? (Signal.) *Make every car orange.*
- (Repeat step 2 until firm.)
3. Make an orange mark on one of the cars. ✔

4. Here's another coloring rule for this picture. Listen: Make every motorcycle blue. What's the rule? (Signal.) *Make every motorcycle blue.*
- (Repeat step 4 until firm.)
5. Make a blue mark on one of the motorcycles. ✔
6. Some cars have parts missing. What parts? (Signal.) *The doors.* Yes, the doors.
- You'll have to follow the dots with your pencil to make the doors before you color them.
7. Here's the last coloring rule. Listen: Make all the bicycles any color you want. What's the rule? (Signal.) *Make all the bicycles any color you want.*
8. Pick a color and make a mark on one of the bicycles.
- What's the rule for your bicycles? (Call on individual children. Idea: *Make all the bicycles _____.*)
9. Remember—the marks show you what color to make the vehicles.

Materials: You will need a wooden pencil with an eraser and a point for exercise 2.

Objectives

- Generate statements to describe actions using present and past tense, and answer questions involving "same" or "different" actions. (Exercise 1)
- Identify parts of a common object and the materials it is made of. (Exercise 2)
- Name common opposites. (Exercise 3)
- Identify statements that tell "when," and **generate statements that tell "when" and statements that tell "not when" something occurred.** (Exercise 4)
- **Given two objects, identify whether a statement is true of "only one" or "both" objects.** (Exercise 5)
- Answer questions about previously learned calendar facts. (Exercise 6)
- Listen to and retell a sequence of events, then correct sequencing errors when the sequence is given out of order. (Exercise 7)
- Relate a familiar story grammar to a picture that indicates the sequence of events for a new story. (Exercise 8)
- **Ask questions involving "class" and "parts" to figure out a "mystery" object.** (Exercise 9)
- Follow coloring rules involving class. (Exercise 10)

EXERCISE 1 Actions

1. It's time for some actions.
2. I'm going to call on three children. _____, _____, and _____, point to a window. ✔
- Everybody, what are they doing? (Signal.) *Pointing to a window.*
- Everybody, say the whole thing about what they are doing. Get ready. (Signal.) *They are pointing to a window.*
3. (Say to the three children:) Stop pointing to a window. Now point to a wall. ✔
- Everybody, what are they doing? (Signal.) *Pointing to a wall.*
- Everybody, what **were** they doing? (Signal.) *Pointing to a window.*
- Say the whole thing about what they **were** doing. Get ready. (Signal.) *They were pointing to a window.*
4. (Repeat steps 2 and 3 until firm.)
5. Here's our last action game.

6. Everybody, clap your hands one time. Get ready. (Signal.) ✔
7. Now tell me if I do the same thing you did or something different. Watch me. (Stamp your foot.) Did I do the same thing or something different? (Signal.) *Something different.*
- Watch me. (Touch your head.) Did I do the same thing or something different? (Signal.) *Something different.*
- Watch me. (Clap your hands one time.) Did I do the same thing or something different? (Signal.) *The same thing.*
8. (Repeat steps 6 and 7 until firm.)

EXERCISE 2 Materials

1. (Hold up a pencil.) This is a pencil.
- (Touch the shaft.) This part is the shaft.
- (Touch the eraser.) This part is the eraser.
- (Touch the point.) This part is the point.
2. (Touch the shaft.) What part am I touching? (Signal.) *The shaft.*
- Listen: The shaft is made of wood. What is it made of? (Signal.) *Wood.*
3. (Touch the point.) What part am I touching? (Signal.) *The point.*
- Listen: The point is made of graphite. What's it made of? (Signal.) *Graphite.*

- And what's the shaft made of? (Signal.) *Wood.*
4. (Touch the eraser.) What part am I touching? (Signal.) *The eraser.*
- Listen: The eraser is made of rubber. What's it made of? (Signal.) *Rubber.*
5. And what's the point made of? (Signal.) *Graphite.*
- And what's the shaft made of? (Signal.) *Wood.*
- And what's the eraser made of? (Signal.) *Rubber.*
6. (Repeat step 5 until firm.)

EXERCISE 3   Opposites

1. Some words are opposites. Full and empty are opposites because if something is full, you know it can't be empty.
2. Listen: What's the opposite of full? (Signal.) *Empty.*
- What's the opposite of empty? (Signal.) *Full.*
- Full and empty are opposites. Who can name another pair of opposites? (Call on individual children. Ideas: *wet and dry; fat and skinny; tall and short; young and old; big and little.*)
3. I'll say words. You tell me the opposite. Listen: little. What's the opposite of little? (Signal.) *Big.*
- Say the whole thing about big. Get ready. (Signal.) *Big is the opposite of little.*
- Listen: cold. What's the opposite of cold? (Signal.) *Hot.*
- Say the whole thing about hot. Get ready. (Signal.) *Hot is the opposite of cold.*
- Listen: tall. What's the opposite of tall? (Signal.) *Short.*
- Say the whole thing about short. Get ready. (Signal.) *Short is the opposite of tall.*
- Listen: dry. What's the opposite of dry? (Signal.) *Wet.*
- Say the whole thing about wet. Get ready. (Signal.) *Wet is the opposite of dry.*
4. (Repeat step 3 until firm.)

EXERCISE 4   When

1. Listen: The boy brushed his teeth before dinner. Say that statement. Get ready. (Signal.) *The boy brushed his teeth before dinner.*

- Does that statement tell **when** the boy brushed his teeth? (Signal.) *Yes.*
- Say the words that tell when the boy brushed his teeth. Get ready. (Signal.) *Before dinner.*
2. Now it's your turn to make up statements. Make up a statement that tells **when** the boy brushed his teeth. (Call on individual children. Praise good statements.)
- Make up a statement that does **not** tell when the boy brushed his teeth. (Call on individual children. Praise good statements.)

EXERCISE 5   Only

1. I'm going to make statements that are true. Some of the statements will be true of **only** your eyes. Some statements will be true of **only** your teeth. Some statements will be true of **both** your eyes and your teeth.
2. Listen: You chew food with them. Is that true of only your eyes, only your teeth, or both your eyes and teeth? (Signal.) *Only your teeth.*
- Listen: You see things with them. Is that true of only your eyes, only your teeth, or both your eyes and teeth? (Signal.) *Only your eyes.*
- Listen: They are part of your head. Is that true of only your eyes, only your teeth, or both your eyes and teeth? (Signal.) *Both your eyes and teeth.*
- Listen: They are very hard. Is that true of only your eyes, only your teeth, or both your eyes and teeth? (Signal.) *Only your teeth.*
- Listen: The dentist fixes them when they have a problem. Is that true of only your eyes, only your teeth, or both your eyes and teeth? (Signal.) *Only your teeth.*
- Listen: They hurt if you hit them with a hard object. Is that true of only your eyes, only your teeth, or both your eyes and teeth? (Signal.) *Both your eyes and teeth.*
3. (Repeat step 2 until firm.)

EXERCISE 6 Calendar Facts

1. You learned calendar facts. Everybody, how many days are in a week? (Signal.) *Seven.*
- Say the fact. Get ready. (Signal.) *There are seven days in a week.*
- Say the days of the week. Get ready. (Signal.) *Sunday, Monday, Tuesday, Wednesday, Thursday, Friday, Saturday.*
- How many months are in a year? (Signal.) *12.*
- Say the fact about the months in a year. Get ready. (Signal.) *There are 12 months in a year.*
- Say the months of the year. Get ready. (Signal.) *January, February, March, April, May, June, July, August, September, October, November, December.*
- How many seasons are in a year? (Signal.) *Four.*
- Say the fact about the seasons in a year. Get ready. (Signal.) *There are four seasons in a year.*
- Say the seasons of the year. Get ready. (Signal.) *Winter, spring, summer, fall.*
2. (Repeat step 1 until firm.)
3. How many days are in a year? (Signal.) *365.*
- Say the fact. Get ready. (Signal.) *There are 365 days in a year.*
- Again. Say the fact. Get ready. (Signal.) *There are 365 days in a year.*
4. (Repeat step 3 until firm.)
5. Let's do all the facts again. How many months are in a year? (Signal.) *12.*
- Say the fact. Get ready. (Signal.) *There are 12 months in a year.*
- How many seasons are in a year? (Signal.) *Four.*
- Say the fact. Get ready. (Signal.) *There are four seasons in a year.*
- How many days are in a year? (Signal.) *365.*
- Say the fact. Get ready. (Signal.) *There are 365 days in a year.*
6. (Repeat step 5 until firm.)

EXERCISE 7 Sequence

1. I'll tell you four things that happened. Listen: First, Ben got his shovel.
- Next, he went into the forest.
- Next, he planted a tree.
- Last, he rested.
2. Listen again. First, Ben got his shovel.

- Next, he went into the forest.
- Next, he planted a tree.
- Last, he rested.
3. Tell me the four things. What happened first? (Signal.) *Ben got his shovel.*
- What happened next? (Signal.) *He went into the forest.*
- What happened next? (Signal.) *He planted a tree.*
- What happened last? (Signal.) *He rested.*
- (Repeat step 3 until firm.)
4. I'll say the four things, but I'm going to make mistakes. As soon as you hear a mistake, say **stop,** then tell me the right thing that happened. Listen: First, Ben got his shovel. Next, he rested. (Children say *stop.*)
- What happened after Ben got his shovel? (Signal.) *He went into the forest.*
- Listen again. First, Ben got his shovel. Next, he planted a tree. (Children say *stop.*)
- What happened after Ben got his shovel? (Signal.) *He went into the forest.*
5. Everybody, say all four things in the right order. What happened first? (Signal.) *Ben got his shovel.*
- What happened next? (Signal.) *He went into the forest.*
- What happened next? (Signal.) *He planted a tree.*
- What happened last? (Signal.) *He rested.*

WORKBOOK

EXERCISE 8 Sequence Story

The Bragging Rats Have an Eating Contest

1. Everybody, open your workbook to Lesson 18. Write your name at the top of the page. ✔
2. The picture shows a different story about the bragging rats.

One summer, the bragging rats got into a terrible argument over who could eat the most. They told each other great lies about how many nuts they could eat, how much corn they could eat and how many berries they could eat.

One day, the wise old rat said, "Enough of this arguing. We'll have a contest to see who can eat the most nuts, berries and corn."

He told the bragging rats to gather all the food they could carry and bring it back with them.

3. The picture shows what the rats did. Everybody, touch number 1. ✔
• That's where the rats went first. The picture by number 1 shows what they collected. Everybody, what did they collect first? (Signal.) *Nuts.*

When they had lots of nuts, they went someplace else and collected a different kind of food.

4. Everybody, touch number 2. ✔
• What did they collect at number 2? (Signal.) *Berries.*

When they had lots of berries, they went someplace else and collected a different kind of food.

5. Everybody, touch number 3. ✔
• What kind of food did they collect there? (Signal.) *Corn.*

The rats now had all the food they could carry, so they went to number 4.

6. Everybody, touch number 4. ✔
• Where did they go? (Call on a child. Idea: *To a picnic table.*)
• That's where they had their big eating contest.

That little black rat at the table got into the contest, too. And you'll never guess who won.

• Everybody, who do you think won? (Signal.) *The little black rat.*
• Right.

The little black rat ate circles around the two bragging rats.

• But do you think the bragging rats stopped arguing? (Signal.) *No.*
• Right.

They started arguing about who could eat the most biscuits.

7. Listen: The numbers in the story tell what the bragging rats did first, what they did next and so on. Who can touch the numbers and tell all the things that happened in the story? Start by telling what they were arguing about and what the wise old rat said. Then tell about each number in the picture. Remember, don't say the numbers. Just tell what happened at each number. Remember to tell who won the eating contest.
8. (Call on a child:) You tell the story. Everybody else, follow along and see if (child's name) tells what happened for each number. (Praise child for a story that tells the sequence of things that the bragging rats did.) (Repeat step 7, calling on several children.)
9. Later you can color the picture.

EXERCISE 9 Questioning Skills

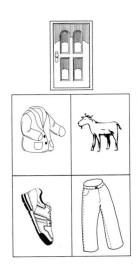

1. Everybody, find the next page in your workbook. (Hold up workbook. Point to first half.) Find the door. ✔
- There is something in back of this door. It's either a coat, a goat, a shoe, or pants. You have to ask two questions to find out what is in back of the door.
2. Here's the first question you're going to ask. What class is it in? Everybody, ask that question. Get ready. (Signal.) *What class is it in?*
- (Repeat step 2 until firm.)
3. Here's the next question. What parts does it have? Everybody, ask that question. Get ready. (Signal.) *What parts does it have?*
- (Repeat step 3 until firm.)
4. Let's see if you can ask both of those questions again. (Hold up one finger.) Everybody, ask the first question. (Signal.) *What class is it in?*
- (Hold up two fingers.) Everybody, ask the next question. (Signal.) *What parts does it have?*
- (Repeat step 4 until firm.)
5. (Hold up one finger.) Everybody, ask the first question again. Get ready. (Signal.) *What class is it in?*

- Here's the answer. It's in the class of clothing. Could it be a coat? (Signal.) *Yes.*
- Could it be a goat? (Signal.) *No.*
- Could it be a shoe? (Signal.) *Yes.*
- Could it be a pants? (Signal.) *Yes.*
6. (Hold up two fingers.) Everybody, now ask the question about the parts. Get ready. (Signal.) *What parts does it have?*
- Here's the answer. A front, a collar, buttons, sleeves, and pockets.
7. Think hard. It's in the class of clothing. And it has a front, a collar, buttons, sleeves, and pockets. Everybody, make a red mark on the clothing in back of the door. ✔
- (Pause.) Everybody, what was in back of the door? (Signal.) *A coat.*

EXERCISE 10 Location

1. (Hold up workbook. Point to second half.)
2. What place do you see in this picture? (Call on a child.) *A city.*
3. Everybody, here's a coloring rule for this picture. Listen: Color all the buildings green. What's the rule? (Signal.) *Color all the buildings green.*
- (Repeat step 3 until firm.)
4. Put a green mark on one building. ✔
5. Here's another coloring rule for this picture. Listen: Color all the vehicles purple. What's the rule? (Signal.) *Color all the vehicles purple.*
- (Repeat step 5 until firm.)
6. Put a purple mark on one vehicle. ✔
7. There's one more thing to do. One of the buildings has a missing part. What building is that? (Signal.) *The shoe store.* Yes, the shoe store.
- What part of the shoe store is missing? (Signal.) *The window.*
- Yes, the window. Before you color the shoe store, follow the dots with your pencil to make the window.

Objectives

- Generate statements to describe actions using present, past and future tense. (Exercise 1)
- Identify parts of a common object and the materials it is made of. (Exercise 2)
- Answer questions by generating sentences using opposites. (Exercise 3)
- Given two objects, identify whether a statement is true of "only one" or "both" objects. (Exercise 4)
- Listen to and retell a sequence of events, then correct sequencing errors when the sequence is given out of order. (Exercise 5)
- Given a calendar, identify the day and date for "yesterday" and "today." (Exercise 6)
- Answer questions about previously learned calendar facts. (Exercise 7)
- Relate a familiar story grammar to a picture that indicates the sequence of events for a new story. (Exercise 8)

EXERCISE 1 Actions

1. It's time for some actions.
2. Everybody, let's stand up. Get ready. (Signal.) (You and the children are to stand up.)
- What **are** we doing? (Signal.) *Standing up.*
- What **were** we doing? (Signal.) *Sitting down.*
3. Everybody, we will sit down. What **will** we do? (Signal.) *Sit down.*
- What **are** we doing? (Signal.) *Standing up.*
- What **will** we do? (Signal.) *Sit down.*
- Say the whole thing about what we **will** do. Get ready. (Signal.) *We will sit down.*
4. Let's do it. (Signal.) (You and the children are to sit down.)
- Everybody, now what **are** we doing? (Signal.) *Sitting down.*
- What **were** we doing before we sat down? (Signal.) *Standing up.*
- Say the whole thing about what we **were** doing. Get ready. (Signal.) *We were standing up.*

EXERCISE 2 Materials

> *Note:* You will need a wooden pencil with an eraser and a point.

1. We're going to talk about this pencil. (Hold up the pencil.)
   Everybody, get ready to name each part of this pencil.

- (Touch the shaft.) This part is the shaft.
- (Touch the eraser.) This part is the eraser.
- (Touch the point.) This part is the point.
2. (Touch the shaft.) What part am I touching? (Signal.) *The shaft.*
- Listen: The shaft is made of wood. What's it made of? (Signal.) *Wood.*
3. (Touch the point.) What part am I touching? (Signal.) *The point.*
- Listen: The point is made of graphite. What's it made of? (Signal.) *Graphite.*
- And what's the shaft made of? (Signal.) *Wood.*
4. (Touch the eraser.) What part am I touching? (Signal.) *The eraser.*
- Listen: The eraser is made of rubber. What's it made of? (Signal.) *Rubber.*
5. And what's the point made of? (Signal.) *Graphite.*
- And what's the shaft made of? (Signal.) *Wood.*
- And what's the eraser made of? (Signal.) *Rubber.*
6. (Repeat step 5 until firm.)

EXERCISE 3 Opposites

1. Get ready to tell me about opposites.
2. I'm thinking of a tree that is opposite of short. So what do you know about the tree? (Signal.) *It's tall.*
- I'm thinking of a tree that is opposite of young. So what do you know about the tree? (Signal.) *It's old.*
- I'm thinking of a tree that is opposite of wet. So what do you know about the tree? (Signal.) *It's dry.*
- I'm thinking of a tree that is opposite of hot. So what do you know about the tree? (Signal.) *It's cold.*
- I'm thinking of a tree that is opposite of big. So what do you know about the tree? (Signal.) *It's little.* Yes, it's little.
3. (Repeat step 2 until firm.)

EXERCISE 4 Only

1. I'm going to make statements that are true. Some of the statements will be true of only your eyes. Some statements will be true of only your nose. Some statements will be true of both your eyes and your nose.
2. Listen: You have two of these things. Is that true of only your eyes, only your nose, or both your eyes and nose? (Signal.) *Only your eyes.*
- Listen: They are part of your head. Is that true of only your eyes, only your nose, or both your eyes and nose? (Signal.) *Both your eyes and nose.*
- Listen: You could use this part to tell if a skunk is around. Is that true of only your eyes, only your nose, or both your eyes and nose? (Signal.) *Both your eyes and nose.*
- Yes, you could see it and you could smell it.
3. (Repeat step 2 until firm.)

EXERCISE 5 Sequence

1. I'll tell you four things that happened. Listen: First, Ryan got a glass from the cupboard.
- Next, he turned on the water.
- Next, he filled the glass with water.
- Last, he drank a glass of water.
2. Listen again. First, Ryan got a glass from the cupboard.
- Next, he turned on the water.
- Next, he filled the glass with water.
- Last, he drank a glass of water.
3. Tell me the four things. What happened first? (Signal.) *Ryan got a glass from the cupboard.*
- What happened next? (Signal.) *He turned on the water.*
- What happened next? (Signal.) *He filled the glass with water.*
- What happened last? (Signal.) *He drank a glass of water.*
- (Repeat step 3 until firm.)
4. I'll say the four things, but I'm going to make mistakes. As soon as you hear a mistake, say **stop,** then tell me the right thing that happened. Listen: First, Ryan got a glass from the cupboard. Next, he filled the glass with water. (Children say *stop.*)
- What happened after Ryan got a glass from the cupboard? (Signal.) *He turned on the water.*
- Listen again. First, he turned on the water. (Children say *stop.*)
- What happened first? (Signal.) *Ryan got a glass from the cupboard.*
5. Everybody, say all four things in the right order. What happened first? (Signal.) *Ryan got a glass from the cupboard.*
- What happened next? (Signal.) *He turned on the water.*
- What happened next? (Signal.) *He filled the glass with water.*
- What happened last? (Signal.) *He drank a glass of water.*

EXERCISE 6 Calendar

1. (Present calendar.) First you'll tell me about the days of the week. Then you'll tell me about the dates.
2. Tell me the day of the week it was yesterday. Get ready. (Signal.)
- Tell me the day of the week it is today. Get ready. (Signal.)
- Now the dates. Everybody, tell me yesterday's date. Get ready. (Signal.)
- Tell me today's date. Get ready. (Signal.)
3. (Repeat step 2 until firm.)

EXERCISE 7 Calendar Facts

1. You learned calendar facts. Everybody, how many days are in a week? (Signal.) *Seven.*
- Say the fact. Get ready. (Signal.) *There are seven days in a week.*
- Say the days of the week. Get ready. (Signal.) *Sunday, Monday, Tuesday, Wednesday, Thursday, Friday, Saturday.*
- How many months are in a year? (Signal.) *12.*
- Say the fact about the months in a year. Get ready. (Signal.) *There are 12 months in a year.*
- Say the months of the year. Get ready. (Signal.) *January, February, March, April, May, June, July, August, September, October, November, December.*
- How many seasons are in a year? (Signal.) *Four.*
- Say the fact about the seasons in a year. Get ready. (Signal.) *There are four seasons in a year.*
- Say the seasons of the year. Get ready. (Signal.) *Winter, spring, summer, fall.*
2. (Repeat step 1 until firm.)
3. How many days are in a year? (Signal.) *365.*
- Say the fact. Get ready. (Signal.) *There are 365 days in a year.*
- Again. Say the fact. Get ready. (Signal.) *There are 365 days in a year.*
4. (Repeat step 3 until firm.)
5. Let's do all the facts again. How many months are in a year? (Signal.) *12.*
- Say the fact. Get ready. (Signal.) *There are 12 months in a year.*
- How many seasons are in a year? (Signal.) *Four.*
- Say the fact. Get ready. (Signal.) *There are four seasons in a year.*
- How many days are in a year? (Signal.) *365.*
- Say the fact. Get ready. (Signal.) *There are 365 days in a year.*
6. (Repeat step 5 until firm.)

EXERCISE 8 Sequence Story

Sweetie And The Red Bow

1. Everybody, open your workbook to Lesson 19. Write your name at the top of the page. ✔
2. This picture shows what happened to Sweetie when he was out in a field hunting for red butterflies. Yum, yum.
3. Everybody, touch number 1. ✔
- Put a red mark on that bow to show the color it should be. ✔
- Listen: Sweetie pounced on that red bow. Why do you think Sweetie pounced on that bow? (Call on a child. Idea: *Sweetie thought it was a red butterfly.*)

So Sweetie pounced on the bow because he thought it was a red butterfly. Sweetie had a good grip on the bow. He said to himself, "This butterfly won't get away."

4. Number 2 shows where Sweetie went next. Everybody, touch number 2. ✔
- Where is Sweetie at number 2? (Call on a child. Idea: *Up in the air.*)
- Why do you think Sweetie was way up in the air? (Call on a child. Idea: *Because the kite carried him up.*)

Sweetie kept hanging on to that bow as tightly as he could. And Sweetie and the kite and the ribbon went to number 2, way up in the air. Then Sweetie went to number 3.

5. Everybody, touch number 3. ✔
- Everybody, where is Sweetie at number 3? (Signal.) *In a tree.*
- Why do you think Sweetie ended up in that big tree? (Call on a child. Idea: *The kite got stuck in the tree and Sweetie was holding on to the bow on the tail of the kite.*)

So when the kite got stuck in the treetop, Sweetie was stuck up in the treetop too. Then Sweetie went slowly to number 4.

6. Everybody, touch number 4. ✔
- Where is Sweetie at number 4? (Call on a child. Idea: *At the bottom of the tree.*)
- How did he get from number 3 to number 4? (Call on a child. Ideas: *He crawled down* or *He climbed down the tree.*)

So Sweetie climbed down that tree slowly. And when he was at the bottom of the tree, he looked up in the tree at this little red bow on the end of the kite tail. He still thought that bow was a little red butterfly. And he said to himself, "From here . . . "

- Well, you tell me what Sweetie said about that butterfly. (Call on a child. Idea: *From here that red butterfly looks pretty small and helpless, but that butterfly is really strong and can really fly.*)

Yes, Sweetie said to himself, "From here that red butterfly looks pretty small and helpless, but that butterfly is really strong and can really fly."

7. Listen: Touch the numbers and say the whole story to yourself. Then we'll see if anybody can tell the whole story. You have to start out by telling what Sweetie thought that bow was and then all the things that happened. Remember to tell what Sweetie said to himself when he was at number 4.
8. (Call on a child:) You tell the story. Everybody else, follow along and see if (child's name) tells what happened for each number. (Praise child for a story that tells the correct sequence of events.)
- (Repeat step 7, calling on another child.)
9. Poor Sweetie got the wrong idea about that bow, just like he got the wrong idea about the birds in the birdbath and the goldfish in the pond.
- Later you can color the picture.

EXERCISE 9 Questioning Skills

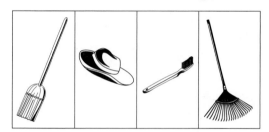

1. (Hold up worksheet. Point to the boxes.) I'm thinking about one of these pictures. It's either a broom, a hat, a toothbrush, or a rake. You'll ask questions to find out what object I'm thinking of.
- Everybody, ask the question about the parts it has. Get ready. (Signal.) *What parts does it have?*
- Everybody, ask a question about where you find it. Get ready. (Signal.) *Where do you find it?*
2. Let's ask those questions again.
3. Everybody, ask the question about the parts it has. Get ready. (Signal.) *What parts does it have?*
- Everybody, ask the question about where you find it. Get ready. (Signal.) *Where do you find it?*
4. (Repeat step 3 until firm.)
5. Ask those questions again, and I'll tell you the answers.

6. Everybody, ask the question about the parts it has. Get ready. (Signal.) *What parts does it have?*
- Here's the answer. A handle and bristles. What parts? (Signal.) *A handle and bristles.*
- Could it be a broom? (Signal.) *Yes.*
- Could it be a hat? (Signal.) *No.*
- Could it be a toothbrush? (Signal.) *Yes.*
- Could it be a rake? (Signal.) *No.*
7. Everybody, ask the question about where you find it. Get ready. (Signal.) *Where do you find it?*
- Here's the answer. In the bathroom. Where do you find it? (Signal.) *In the bathroom.*
8. Everybody, make a yellow mark on the thing I'm thinking of. ✔
- Everybody, what was I thinking of? (Signal.) *A toothbrush.*

EXERCISE 10 Part—Whole

1. (Hold up worksheet. Point to second half.) Find the woman. ✔
2. Here's a coloring rule for the coat. Listen. Color the pockets purple. What's the rule? (Signal.) *Color the pockets purple.*
- Mark the pockets. ✔

3. Here's another coloring rule for the coat. Listen. Color the buttons green. What's the rule? (Signal.) *Color the buttons green.*
- Mark the buttons. ✔
4. Here's another coloring rule for the coat. Listen. Color the front red. What's the rule? (Signal.) *Color the front red.*
- Mark the front. ✔
5. Here's another coloring rule for the coat. Listen. Color the sleeves brown. What's the rule? (Signal.) *Color the sleeves brown.*
- Mark the sleeves. ✔
6. Part of the coat is missing. What part is missing? (Signal.) *The collar.*
- Yes, the collar. Before you color the coat, you're going to follow the dots with your pencil to make the collar.
7. Here's the coloring rule for the collar. Listen. Color the collar orange. What's the rule? (Signal.) *Color the collar orange.*
- Mark the collar. ✔

Materials: You will need a shoe as described in Exercise 2.

Objectives

- Label actions, follow directions involving "all," "some" and "none," **and generate complete sentences to describe an action using past, present and future tense.** (Exercise 1)
- Identify parts of a common object and the materials it is made of. (Exercise 2)
- Identify statements that tell "when," and generate statements that tell "when" and statements that tell "not when" something occurred. (Exercise 3)
- Answer questions by generating sentences using opposites. (Exercise 4)
- Answer questions about previously learned calendar facts. (Exercise 5)
- **Given a complex sentence, answer questions involving "who," "when" and "where."** (Exercise 6)
- Given a calendar, identify the day and date for "yesterday" and "today." (Exercise 7)
- **Generate a story given a picture and numbers identifying story events' sequence.** (Exercise 8)
- **Ask questions involving "use" and "parts" to figure out a "mystery" object.** (Exercise 9)
- Follow coloring rules involving parts of a whole. (Exercise 10)

EXERCISE 1   Actions

1. It's time for some actions.
2. Watch me. Tell me if I hold up all of my fingers or some of my fingers or none of my fingers. (Hold up three fingers.) Is this all of my fingers or some of my fingers or none of my fingers? (Signal.) *Some of your fingers.*
- (Hold up two fists.) Is this all of my fingers or some of my fingers or none of my fingers? (Signal.) *None of your fingers.*
- (Hold up ten fingers.) Is this all of my fingers or some of my fingers or none of my fingers? (Signal.) *All of your fingers.*
3. Now it's your turn.
4. Everybody, hold up none of your fingers. Get ready. (Signal.) ✔
- What are you holding up? (Signal.) *None of my fingers.*
- Say the whole thing. Get ready. (Signal.) *I am holding up none of my fingers.*
5. Everybody, hold up some of your fingers. Get ready. (Signal.) ✔
- What are you holding up? (Signal.) *Some of my fingers.*
- Say the whole thing. Get ready. (Signal.) *I am holding up some of my fingers.*
6. (Repeat steps 4 and 5 until firm.)

7. Here's another action game.
8. (Stand up.) Everybody, I will sit down. Say the whole thing about what I will do. Get ready. (Signal.) *You will sit down.*
- Am I sitting down now? (Signal.) *No.*
- What am I doing now? (Signal.) *Standing up.*
- What will I do? (Signal.) *Sit down.*
9. (Sit down.) What am I doing now? (Signal.) *Sitting down.*
- What was I doing before I sat down? (Signal.) *Standing up.*
- Say the whole thing about what I was doing. (Signal.) *You were standing up.*

EXERCISE 2   Materials

> *Note:* You will need a child wearing shoes with leather tops, rubber heels, and cloth shoelaces. Ask that child to come to the front of class and stand next to you, or use your own shoe.

1. We're going to talk about a shoe.
2. (Touch top.) Listen: The **top** is made of leather. What is the top made of? (Signal.) *Leather.*
- (Touch heel.) Listen: The **heel** is made of rubber. What is the heel made of? (Signal.) *Rubber.*
- (Touch shoelace.) Listen: The **shoelace** is made of cloth. What is the shoelace made of? (Signal.) *Cloth.*
3. (Touch the top of the shoe.) Everybody, what part am I touching? (Signal.) *The top.*
- What is that part made of? (Signal.) *Leather.*
- (Touch the heel.) Everybody, what part am I touching? (Signal.) *The heel.*
- What is that part made of? (Signal.) *Rubber.*
- (Touch the shoelace.) Everybody, what part am I touching? (Signal.) *The shoelace.*
- What is that part made of? (Signal.) *Cloth.*
4. (Repeat steps 2 and 3 until firm.)

EXERCISE 3   When

1. Listen: The girl played basketball at 10 o'clock. Say that statement. Get ready. (Signal.) *The girl played basketball at 10 o'clock.*
- Does that statement tell **when** the girl played basketball? (Signal.) *Yes.*
- When did the girl play basketball? (Signal.) *At 10 o'clock.*
2. Your turn. Make up a statement that tells **when** the girl played basketball. (Call on individual children. Praise good statements.)
- Make up a statement that does **not** tell when the girl played basketball. (Call on individual children. Praise good statements.)

EXERCISE 4   Opposites

1. Get ready to tell me about opposites.
2. I'm thinking of an alligator that is the opposite of dry. So what do you know about it? (Signal.) *It's wet.*
- I'm thinking of an alligator that is the opposite of cold. So what do you know about it? (Signal.) *It's hot.*
- I'm thinking of an alligator that is the opposite of old. So what do you know about it? (Signal.) *It's young.*
- I'm thinking of an alligator that is the opposite of skinny. So what do you know about it? (Signal.) *It's fat.*
- I'm thinking of an alligator that is the opposite of empty. So what do you know about it? (Signal.) *It's full.*
3. (Repeat step 2 until firm.)

EXERCISE 5   Calendar Facts

1. You learned calendar facts. Everybody, how many days are in a week? (Signal.) *Seven.*
- Say the fact. Get ready. (Signal.) *There are seven days in a week.*
- Say the days of the week. Get ready. (Signal.) *Sunday, Monday, Tuesday, Wednesday, Thursday, Friday, Saturday.*
- How many months are in a year? (Signal.) *12.*
- Say the fact about the months in a year. Get ready. (Signal.) *There are 12 months in a year.*
- Say the months of the year. Get ready. (Signal.) *January, February, March, April, May, June, July, August, September, October, November, December.*
- How many seasons are in a year? (Signal.) *Four.*
- Say the fact about the seasons in a year. Get ready. (Signal.) *There are four seasons in a year.*
- Say the seasons of the year. Get ready. (Signal.) *Winter, spring, summer, fall.*
2. (Repeat step 1 until firm.)
3. How many days are in a year? (Signal.) *365.*
- Say the fact. Get ready. (Signal.) *There are 365 days in a year.*
- Again. Say the fact. Get ready. (Signal.) *There are 365 days in a year.*
4. (Repeat step 3 until firm.)

EXERCISE 6 Who-Where-When

1. I'm going to say sentences that answer a lot of questions. You'll answer the questions. Listen: The boys hiked near the river after school.
   - Listen again. The boys hiked near the river after school.
   - Your turn. Say the sentence. Get ready. (Signal.) *The boys hiked near the river after school.*
   - That sentence has words that tell who, words that tell where and words that tell when.
2. Listen: The boys hiked near the river after school. Everybody, say that sentence. Get ready. (Signal.) *The boys hiked near the river after school.*
   - Who hiked? (Signal.) *The boys.*
   - When did the boys hike? (Signal.) *After school.*
   - Where did the boys hike? (Signal.) *Near the river.*
3. Everybody, say the whole sentence. Get ready. (Signal.) *The boys hiked near the river after school.*
   - Which words tell who hiked? (Signal.) *The boys.*
   - Which words tell where they hiked? (Signal.) *Near the river.*
   - Which words tell when they hiked? (Signal.) *After school.*
4. (Repeat steps 2 and 3 until firm.)
5. New statement. Seven mice went in the barn last night. Everybody, say the sentence. Get ready. (Signal.) *Seven mice went in the barn last night.*
   - Who was in the barn? (Signal.) *Seven mice.*
   - Where did the seven mice go? (Signal.) *In the barn.*
   - When did the mice go in the barn? (Signal.) *Last night.*
6. Everybody, say the whole sentence. Get ready. (Signal.) *Seven mice went in the barn last night.*
   - Which words tell who went in the barn? (Signal.) *Seven mice.*
   - Which words tell where they went? (Signal.) *In the barn.*
   - Which words tell when they went in the barn? (Signal.) *Last night.*
7. (Repeat steps 5 and 6 until firm.)

EXERCISE 7 Calendar

1. (Present calendar.) First you'll tell me about the days of the week. Then you'll tell me about the dates.
2. Tell me the day of the week it was yesterday. Get ready. (Signal.)
   - Tell me the day of the week it is today. Get ready. (Signal.)
   - Now the dates. Everybody, tell me yesterday's date. Get ready. (Signal.)
   - Tell me today's date. Get ready. (Signal.)
3. (Repeat step 2 until firm.)

WORKBOOK

EXERCISE 8 Sequence Story

Roger And The Cat

1. Everybody, open your workbook to Lesson 20. Write your name at the top of the page. ✔
2. This picture shows a story about a boy named Roger, but I don't know what that story is. I don't have anything written in my book. Maybe you can help me out. You can see that Roger's jacket is on top of that fence by number 5. That's where his jacket was at the **end** of the story. I don't think Roger would have put his jacket there, so far away and all tangled up. I think he put it at number 1. I'll bet he took it off because it's a warm day. What do you think? (Children respond.)

3. But I can't figure out how that jacket could have moved around. Can you find a clue in the picture that would explain how his jacket moved all the way to that fence? That's a pretty heavy jacket. It would take a pretty strong animal to move it.

• Raise your hand if you can find an animal in the picture strong enough to move Roger's jacket.

• Everybody, what animal did you find? (Signal.) *A cat.*

4. But I wonder **how** the cat moved that jacket, or **why** the cat moved that jacket.

• Who has an idea about where the cat was when Roger put his jacket down? (Call on a child. Idea: *Next to Roger.*)

• I'll bet the cat wasn't very happy getting all tangled up in that jacket.

5. Look at the numbers in the picture and raise your hand when you think you can tell the whole story.

• Remember, you have to tell **why** Roger took his jacket off, what the jacket landed on, and then all the places the jacket went.

• Remember, you also have to tell **why** the jacket is at number 5, but why the cat is not in that jacket.

6. (Call on several children to tell the story. Tell the other children to follow along and raise their hand if something is missed. Praise stories that have these details:
*It was warm so Roger took off his jacket and put it next to him;
he put it on the cat, who got tangled up in it;
the cat took off and climbed the tree;
the cat fell from the tree into the puddle;
the cat ran into the bushes;
the cat jumped up on the fence;
the jacket got caught on the fence and the cat fell out;* and
the cat was wet and confused.)

7. Later you can color the picture.

EXERCISE 9 Questioning Skills

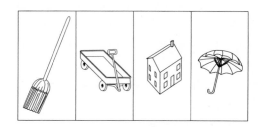

1. (Hold up workbook. Point to boxed pictures.) I'm thinking about one of the pictures. It's either a broom, a wagon, a house, or an umbrella. You'll ask questions to find out which object I'm thinking of. Everybody, ask a question about what you use it for. Get ready. (Signal.) *What do you use it for?*

• Everybody, ask a question about the parts it has. Get ready. (Signal.) *What parts does it have?*

2. Let's ask those questions again.

3. Everybody, ask the question about what you use it for. Get ready. (Signal.) *What do you use it for?*

• Everybody, ask the question about the parts it has. Get ready. (Signal.) *What parts does it have?*

4. (Repeat step 3 until firm.)

5. Ask those questions again, and I'll tell you the answers. Everybody, ask the question about what you use it for. Get ready. (Signal.) *What do you use it for?*
- Here's the answer. To keep the rain off. What is it used for? (Signal.) *To keep the rain off.*
- Everybody, ask the question about the parts it has. Get ready. (Signal.) *What parts does it have?*
- Here's the answer. It has a handle, a frame, and a covering. What parts? (Signal.) *A handle, a frame, and a covering.*
- Could it be a broom? (Signal.) *No.*
- Why not? (Call on a child. Accept reasonable responses.)
- Everybody, could it be a wagon? (Signal.) *No.*
- Why not? (Call on a child. Accept reasonable responses.)
- Everybody, could it be a house? (Signal.) *No.*
- Why not? (Call on a child. Accept reasonable responses.)
- Everybody, could it be an umbrella? (Signal.) *Yes.*
6. Make a purple mark on the thing I'm thinking of. ✔
- Everybody, what object was I thinking of? (Signal.) *An umbrella.*

EXERCISE 10   Part-Whole

1. (Hold up workbook. Point to second half.) Here's a coloring rule for the elephant. Listen: Color the trunk purple. What's the rule? (Signal.) *Color the trunk purple.*
- Mark the trunk. ✔
2. Here's another coloring rule for the elephant. Listen: Color the tail black. What's the rule? (Signal.) *Color the tail black.*
- Mark the tail. ✔
3. Here's another coloring rule for the elephant. Listen: Color the body red. What's the rule? (Signal.) *Color the body red.*
- Mark the body. ✔
4. Here's another coloring rule for the elephant. Listen: Color the head brown. What's the rule? (Signal.) *Color the head brown.*
- Mark the head. ✔
5. Part of the elephant is missing. What part is missing? (Signal.) *The legs.* Yes, the legs.
- Before you color the elephant, you're going to follow the dots and make the legs.
6. Here's the coloring rule for the legs. Listen: Color the legs blue. What's the rule? (Signal.) *Color the legs blue.*
- Mark the legs. ✔

Materials: You will need shirt described in exercise 4.

Objectives

- Generate statements to describe actions using present, past and future tense. (Exercise 1)
- **Identify and generate absurdities of use.** (Exercise 2)
- Given two objects, identify whether a statement is true of "only one" or "both" objects. (Exercise 3)
- Identify parts of a common object and the materials it is made of. (Exercise 4)
- Answer questions by generating sentences using opposites. (Exercise 5)
- **Given classes, order classes by "biggest," "next biggest," and "smallest," answer questions about the classes and given members of a class, identify the class.** (Exercise 6)
- Given a complex sentence, answer questions involving "who," "when," and "where." (Exercise 7)
- Given a calendar, identify the day and date for "yesterday" and "today." (Exercise 8)
- Answer questions about a new story. (Exercise 9)
- Make a picture consistent with the details of the story. (Exercise 10)
- Ask questions involving "use," "parts" and "class" to figure out a "mystery" object. (Exercise 11)
- Follow coloring rules involving parts of a whole. (Exercise 12)

EXERCISE 1 Actions

1. It's time for some actions.
2. Everybody, let's stand up. Get ready. (Signal.) (You and the children stand up.)
- What **are** we doing? (Signal.) *Standing up.*
- What **were** we doing? (Signal.) *Sitting down.*
3. Everybody, we will sit down.
- What **will** we do? (Signal.) *Sit down.*
- What **are** we doing? (Signal.) *Standing up.*
- What **will** we do? (Signal.) *Sit down.*
- Say the whole thing about what we **will** do. Get ready. (Signal.) *We will sit down.*
4. Let's do it. Get ready. (Signal.) (You and the children sit down.)
- Everybody, now what **are** we doing? (Signal.) *Sitting down.*
- What **were** we doing before we sat down? (Signal.) *Standing up.*
- Say the whole thing about what we **were** doing. Get ready. (Signal.) *We were standing up.*

EXERCISE 2 Absurdity

1. It's time for an absurdity. Why do we need brooms? (Call on individual children. Praise good answers such as: *to sweep the floor; to get houses clean.*)
- Why do we need hairbrushes? (Call on individual children. Praise good answers such as: *to get tangles out of our hair; to make our hair look nice.*)
2. Everybody, would you use a broom to sit on? (Signal.) *No.*
- That would be absurd.
- Would you use a broom to wash your clothes? (Signal.) *No.*
- That would be absurd.
- Would you use a broom to sweep a sidewalk? (Signal.) *Yes.*
3. Name something else that would be absurd with a broom. (Call on a child. Accept reasonable responses.)

EXERCISE 3   Only

1. Tell me if each statement I say is true of only the shoe or if it is true of the shoe **and** the shirt.
2. Listen: It is a shoe. Say that statement. Get ready. (Signal.) *It is a shoe.*
• Is that statement true of **only** the shoe? (Signal.) *Yes.*
• What is it true of? (Signal.) *Only the shoe.*
3. (Repeat 2 until firm.)
4. Listen: It has shoelaces. Say that statement. Get ready. (Signal.) *It has shoelaces.*
• Is that statement true of **only** the shoe? (Signal.) *Yes.*
• What is it true of? (Signal.) *Only the shoe.*
5. (Repeat step 4 until firm.)
6. Listen: You buy it at a store. Say that statement. Get ready. (Signal.) *You buy it at a store.*
• Is that statement true of **only** the shoe? (Signal.) *No.*
• What is it true of? (Signal.) *The shoe and the shirt.*
• Yes, that statement is true of the shoe and the shirt.
7. (Repeat step 6 until firm.)
8. (Repeat steps 1 through 7 until firm.)

EXERCISE 4   Materials

> *Note:* You will need a child wearing a cloth shirt with plastic buttons. Ask that child to come to the front of the class and stand next to you.

1. We're going to talk about a shirt.
2. (Touch the front of child's shirt.) Everybody, what part am I touching? (Signal.) *The front.*
• What is that made of? (Signal.) *Cloth.*
3. (Touch a button of the child's shirt.) Everybody, what part am I touching? (Signal.) *A button.*
• What is that part made of? (Signal.) *Plastic.*
4. (Repeat steps 2 and 3 until firm.)

EXERCISE 5   Opposites

1. I'll tell you about some new opposites. Listen: The opposite of fast is slow. What's the opposite of fast? (Signal.) *Slow.*
• What's the opposite of slow? (Signal.) *Fast.*

2. Get ready to tell me about opposites. I'm thinking of a duck that is the opposite of dry. So what do you know about it? (Signal.) *It's wet.*
• I'm thinking of a duck that is the opposite of tall. So what do you know about it? (Signal.) *It's short.*
• I'm thinking of a duck that is the opposite of slow. So what do you know about it? (Signal.) *It's fast.*
• I'm thinking of a duck that is the opposite of cold. So what do you know about it? (Signal.) *It's hot.*
• I'm thinking of a duck that is the opposite of young. So what do you know about it? (Signal.) *It's old.*
• I'm thinking of a duck that is the opposite of skinny. So what do you know about it? (Signal.) *It's fat.*
3. (Repeat step 2 until firm.)

EXERCISE 6   Classification

1. You're going to learn about bigger classes and smaller classes. Here's the rule: The bigger class has more kinds of things in it. Everybody, say that rule. Get ready. (Signal.) *The bigger class has more kinds of things in it.*
2. Listen to these classes: children, girls, baby girls. Everybody, say those three classes. Get ready. (Signal.) *Children, girls, baby girls.*
3. The biggest class is children. It has boys in it. It has girls in it, and it has baby girls in it. What's the biggest class? (Signal.) *Children.*
• Are there girls in that class? (Signal.) *Yes.*
• Are there baby girls in that class? (Signal.) *Yes.*
• Are there boys in that class? (Signal.) *Yes.*
• Say the three classes again. Get ready. (Signal.) *Children, girls, baby girls.*
• Which class is the biggest? (Signal.) *Children.* Yes, the biggest class is children.
4. The next biggest class is girls. It has girls and baby girls in it, but it doesn't have boys in it.

- Say the three classes again. Get ready. (Signal.) *Children, girls, baby girls.*
- Which class is the biggest? (Signal.) *Children.*
- Which class is the next biggest? (Signal.) *Girls.*
- Are there girls in that class? (Signal.) *Yes.*
- Are there baby girls in that class? (Signal.) *Yes.*
- Are there boys in that class? (Signal.) *No.*
5. The smallest class is baby girls. It has only baby girls in it, not older girls or any boys.
6. I'll tell you what is in a class. You tell me which class it is. Listen: This class has boys and girls and baby girls. Which class is that? (Signal.) *Children.*
- Listen: This class has only baby girls in it. What class is that? (Signal.) *Baby girls.*
- Listen: This class has girls and baby girls in it. But it doesn't have any boys in it. Which class is that? (Signal.) *Girls.*
7. (Repeat step 6 until firm.)

EXERCISE 7 Who—Where—When

1. I'm going to say sentences that answer a lot of questions. You'll answer the questions. Listen: Yesterday, a dog chased a rabbit under the house.
- Listen again. Yesterday, a dog chased a rabbit under the house.
- Your turn. Say the sentence. Get ready. (Signal.) *Yesterday, a dog chased a rabbit under the house.*
2. That sentence has words that tell who, words that tell where, and words that tell when. Listen: Yesterday, a dog chased a rabbit under the house.
- Who chased a rabbit? (Signal.) *A dog.*
- A dog chased who? (Signal.) *A rabbit.*
- When did the dog chase the rabbit? (Signal.) *Yesterday.*
- Where did the dog chase the rabbit? (Signal.) *Under the house.*
- Everybody, say the whole sentence. Get ready. (Signal.) *Yesterday, a dog chased a rabbit under the house.*
- Which words tell who? (Signal.) *A dog and a rabbit.*
- Which words tell where? (Signal.) *Under the house.*
- Which word tells when? (Signal.) *Yesterday.*
3. (Repeat step 2 until firm.)

EXERCISE 8 Calendar

1. (Present calendar.)
- First you'll tell me about the days of the week. Then you'll tell me about the dates.
2. Tell me the day of the week it was yesterday. Get ready. (Signal.)
- Tell me the day of the week it is today. Get ready. (Signal.)
- Now the dates.
- Everybody, tell me yesterday's date. Get ready. (Signal.)
- Tell me today's date. Get ready. (Signal.)
3. (Repeat step 2 until firm.)

EXERCISE 9 Clarabelle And The Bluebirds

Storytelling

- Everybody, I'm going to read you a story. Listen to the things that happen in the story because you're going to have to fix up a picture that shows part of the story.

This is a story about a cow named Clarabelle. Clarabelle looked like the other brown-and-white cows on the farm. But Clarabelle was really different. She was always trying to do things that other animals did. In fact, she felt sad about not being a bird or a frog or a child.

- Everybody, what colors was Clarabelle? (Signal.) *Brown and white.*
- How was Clarabelle different from the other brown-and-white cows? (Call on a child. Idea: *She was always trying to do things that other animals did.*)

One day, Clarabelle was looking at the bluebirds that were sitting on a wire that went from the barn to a large pole. Clarabelle said, "I would love to sit on that wire with those bluebirds."

- Everybody, what kind of birds was Clarabelle watching? (Signal.) *Bluebirds.*
- Where were those birds? (Call on a child. Idea: *On a wire that went from the barn to a large pole.*)
- What did Clarabelle think she'd love to do? (Call on a child. Idea: *Sit on the wire with the bluebirds.*)

Some of the other cows heard Clarabelle talking to herself, and they said, "Don't do it, Clarabelle. Remember what happened when you tried to swim like a duck in the duck pond?"

"Yeah," another cow said. "When you jumped **in** the pond, all the water jumped **out** of the pond."

- Listen: Once Clarabelle had tried to be like another animal. Everybody, what kind of animal? (Signal.) *A duck.*
- What happened when Clarabelle tried to swim like a duck in the pond? (Call on a child. Idea: *All the water jumped out of the pond.*)

Another cow said to Clarabelle, "And what about the time you tried to crow like the roosters? That was a real laugh. They were all saying, 'cock-a-doodle-doo.' And you were saying, 'cock-a-doodle-moo.'"

- Everybody, what did the roosters say? (Signal.) *Cock-a-doodle-doo.*
- What did Clarabelle say? (Signal.) *Cock-a-doodle-moo.*

"Ho, ho, ho." All the cows laughed until they had tears in their eyes. "That's not very funny," Clarabelle said. "And if I want to sit on the wire with those bluebirds, you can't stop me."

So Clarabelle went into the barn and up to the window by the wire. While she was getting ready, all the farm animals gathered around. One goat said, "We're in for another great show by Clarabelle."

And so they were. Clarabelle tiptoed out on the wire, but Clarabelle was heavier than one thousand bluebirds, so the wire went down, lower and lower, until it was almost touching the ground.

- Get a picture in your mind of that part of the story. Clarabelle goes from the window in the barn out on the wire. The wire doesn't break, but what does it do? (Call on a child. Idea: *Goes down until it almost touches the ground.*)
- Why does the wire bend down so low? (Call on a child. Idea: *Because Clarabelle is on the wire and she weighs a lot.*)
- Listen to that part again:

Clarabelle tiptoed out on the wire, but Clarabelle was heavier than one thousand bluebirds, so the wire went down, lower and lower, until it was almost touching the ground.

Well, the bluebirds were really angry. One of them said, "What are you doing, you big, fat cow? You've bent our wire almost to the ground."

"Yeah," another bluebird said. "This wire is for bluebirds, not brown-and-white cows."

Meanwhile, the farm animals were laughing and howling and rolling around on the ground. "Look at that," they said, and rolled and laughed some more.

Clarabelle was not happy. She said, "This wire is not as much fun as I thought it would be." Clarabelle looked back up at the barn and said, "Wow, it's going to be hard to walk all the way back up there."

- Listen: To get back into the barn, she'd have to go up, up, up because the wire was bent way down where Clarabelle was.

Then Clarabelle looked down and said, "I'm close to the ground, so maybe it would be easier for me to jump off and land in that haystack."

While she was trying to figure out what to do, all the bluebirds were yelling at her and saying things like, "Well, do something. Get off our wire so we can sit in peace!"

"All right, all right," Clarabelle said. "I'm leaving. Right now."

And with that, she jumped off the wire. Well, when she jumped off, the wire sprang way up into the air. It shot up so fast that it sent the bluebirds way up into the clouds, leaving blue tail feathers fluttering this way and that way.

- Listen: Everybody, how did Clarabelle get off the wire? (Signal.) *She jumped off.*
- What did the wire do as soon as she jumped off? (Call on a child. Idea: *It sprang way up into the air.*)
- That shot the poor little bluebirds all the way up to the clouds. Listen to that part again:

Clarabelle jumped off the wire. Well, when she jumped off, the wire sprang way up into the air. It shot up so fast that it sent the bluebirds way up into the clouds, leaving blue tail feathers fluttering this way and that way.

And the farm animals almost died from laughter. "Did you see that?" a horse said as he rolled around on the ground. "Did you see those birds go flying up to the clouds?"

Everybody laughed except for a bunch of bluebirds and one brown-and-white cow. That cow pouted and kept saying, "It's not **funny.** It's not funny."

But let me tell you: It was, too—**very** funny.

- Everybody, who was that brown-and-white cow that was not very happy? (Signal.) *Clarabelle.*
- Why wasn't Clarabelle happy? (Call on a child. Idea: *Because all the farm animals were laughing at her.*)

EXERCISE 10   Workbook Activity

1. Everybody, open your workbook to Lesson 21. Write your name at the top of the page. ✔
2. This picture took place **after** Clarabelle went out on the wire.
3. Everybody, touch the window in the barn. ✔ That's where Clarabelle started tiptoeing out on the wire.
- What did the wire do when she tiptoed out on it? (Call on a child. Idea: *It bent down almost to the ground.*)
- Yes, it bent down almost to the ground. Then Clarabelle decided to jump off. Everybody, what did she plan to land on? (Signal.) *A haystack.*
- What's Clarabelle doing in this picture? (Call on a child. Idea: *Jumping off the wire into the haystack.*)
- You can see the wire springing up. What are the birds doing? (Call on a child. Idea: *Being shot into the clouds.*)
- Yes, the wire is shooting those bluebirds up to the clouds.
- Look at the other animals.
- Everybody, what are they doing? (Signal.) *Laughing.*
4. Later you can color the picture. Remember what color all the cows are and what color the birds are. That barn should be red.

EXERCISE 11   Questioning Skills

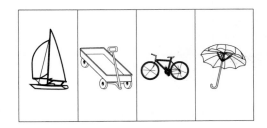

1. (Hold up workbook. Point to boxed pictures.) Find the next page in your workbook. ✔
• I'm thinking about one of the pictures. It's either a boat, a wagon, a bike, or an umbrella. You'll ask questions to find out which object I'm thinking of.
• Everybody, ask a question about the class it is in. Get ready. (Signal.) *What class is it in?*
• Everybody, ask a question about what you use it for. Get ready. (Signal.) *What do you use it for?*
• Everybody, ask a question about the parts it has. Get ready. (Signal.) *What parts does it have?*
2. Let's ask those questions again. Everybody, ask a question about the class it is in. Get ready. (Signal.) *What class is it in?*
3. Everybody, ask the question about what you use it for. Get ready. (Signal.) *What do you use it for?*
• Everybody, ask the question about the parts it has. Get ready. (Signal.) *What parts does it have?*
4. (Repeat step 3 until firm.)
5. Ask those questions again, and I'll tell you the answers.
• Everybody, ask the question about the class it is in. Get ready. (Signal.) *What class is it in?*
• Here's the answer. It's in the class of vehicles. What class is it in? (Signal.) *The class of vehicles.*

6. Everybody, ask the question about what you use it for. Get ready. (Signal.) *What do you use it for?*
• Here's the answer. To carry things. What is it used for? (Signal.) *To carry things.*
7. Everybody, ask the question about the parts it has. Get ready. (Signal.) *What parts does it have?*
• Here's the answer. It has a handle, a body, a frame, and four wheels. What parts? (Signal.) *A handle, a body, a frame, and four wheels.*
8. Make a brown mark on the thing I'm thinking of. ✔
• Everybody, what object was I thinking of? (Signal.) *A wagon.*
• How did you know I wasn't thinking of a boat? (Call on a child. Accept reasonable responses.)
• How did you know I wasn't thinking of a bike? (Call on a child. Accept reasonable responses.)
• How did you know I wasn't thinking of an umbrella? (Call on a child. Accept reasonable responses.)

EXERCISE 12   Part—Whole

1. (Hold up workbook. Point to second half.) Here's a coloring rule for the pencil. Listen: Color the point black. What's the rule? (Signal.) *Color the point black.*
• Mark the point. ✔
2. Here's another coloring rule for the pencil. Listen: Color the shaft yellow. What's the rule? (Signal.) *Color the shaft yellow.*
• Mark the shaft. ✔
3. Part of the pencil is missing. What part is missing? (Signal.) *The eraser.*
• Yes, the eraser. Before you color the pencil, you're going to follow the dots and make the eraser.
4. Here's the coloring rule for the eraser. Listen: Color the eraser brown. What's the rule? (Signal.) *Color the eraser brown.*
• Mark the eraser. ✔

Materials: You will need shoe described in exercise 6.

Objectives

- Follow directions involving "all," "some" and "none," and generate complete sentences to describe actions. (Exercise 1)
- Identify statements that tell "when" and generate statements that tell "when" and statements that tell "not when" something occurred. (Exercise 2)
- Given classes, order classes by "biggest," "next biggest," and "smallest," answer questions about the classes and given a member of a class, identify the class. (Exercise 3)
- Given a calendar, identify the day and date for "yesterday" and "today." (Exercise 4)
- Given two objects, identify whether a statement is true of "only one" or "both" objects. (Exercise 5)
- Identify parts of a common object and the materials it is made of. (Exercise 6)
- Answer questions by generating sentences using opposites. (Exercise 7)
- Listen to a familiar story. (Exercise 8)
- Make a picture consistent with the details of the story. (Exercise 9)
- Ask questions involving "parts" and "class" to figure out a "mystery" object. (Exercise 10)
- Follow coloring rules involving parts of a whole. (Exercise 11)

EXERCISE 1 Actions

1. Everybody, hold up all of your fingers. Get ready. (Signal.) ✔
- What are you holding up? (Signal.) *All of my fingers.*
- Say the whole thing. Get ready. (Signal.) *I am holding up all of my fingers.*
2. Everybody, hold up some of your fingers. Get ready. (Signal.) ✔
- What are you holding up? (Signal.) *Some of my fingers.*
- Say the whole thing. Get ready. (Signal.) *I am holding up some of my fingers.*
3. Everybody, hold up none of your fingers. Get ready. (Signal.) ✔
- What are you holding up? (Signal.) *None of my fingers.*
- Say the whole thing. Get ready. (Signal.) *I am holding up none of my fingers.*

EXERCISE 2 When

1. I'm going to say statements. Some of these statements tell **when** the woman painted a fence. Some of these statements don't tell **when** the woman painted a fence.
2. Listen: The woman painted a fence under the bridge. Say the statement. Get ready. (Signal.) *The woman painted a fence under the bridge.*
- Does that statement tell **when** the woman painted a fence? (Signal.) *No.*
3. Listen: The woman painted a fence at one o'clock.
- Say the statement. Get ready. (Signal.) *The woman painted a fence at one o'clock.*
- Does that statement tell **when** the woman painted a fence? (Signal.) *Yes.*
- When did the woman paint a fence? (Signal.) *At one o'clock.*
4. Listen: The woman painted a fence in the afternoon.

- Say the statement. Get ready. (Signal.) *The woman painted a fence in the afternoon.*
- Does that statement tell **when** the woman painted a fence? (Signal.) *Yes.*
- When did the woman paint a fence? (Signal.) *In the afternoon.*
5. Listen: The woman painted a fence between the tree and the river.
- Say the statement. Get ready. (Signal.) *The woman painted a fence between the tree and the river.*
- Does that statement tell **when** the woman painted a fence? (Signal.) *No.*
6. Listen: The woman painted a fence after driving her car.
- Say the statement. Get ready. (Signal.) *The woman painted a fence after driving her car.*
- Does that statement tell **when** the woman painted a fence? (Signal.) *Yes.*
- When did the woman paint a fence? (Signal.) *After driving her car.*
7. Listen: The woman painted a fence next to the rock.
- Say the statement. Get ready. (Signal.) *The woman painted a fence next to the rock.*
- Does that statement tell **when** the woman painted a fence? (Signal.) *No.*
8. Now it's your turn to make up statements.
- Make up a statement that tells **when** the woman painted a fence. (Call on individual children. Praise good statements.)
- Make up a statement that does **not** tell when the woman painted a fence. (Call on individual children. Praise good statements.)

EXERCISE 3 Classification

1. Remember the rule about bigger classes: The bigger class has more kinds of things in it. Everybody, say that rule. Get ready. (Signal.) *The bigger class has more kinds of things in it.*
- Listen to these classes: girls, children, baby girls. Everybody, say those three classes. Get ready. (Signal.) *Girls, children, baby girls.*
- Which class is the biggest? (Signal.) *Children.*
- Which class is the next biggest? (Signal.) *Girls.*
- Which class is the smallest? (Signal.) *Baby girls.*
2. (Repeat step 1 until firm.)

3. Say the three classes again. Get ready. (Signal.) *Girls, children, baby girls.*
- Which class is the biggest? (Signal.) *Children.*
- Yes, the biggest class is children.
- Listen: The next biggest class is girls. It has girls and baby girls in it, but it doesn't have boys in it.
- Which class is the biggest? (Signal.) *Children.*
- Does it have girls in it? (Signal.) *Yes.*
- Does it have boys in it? (Signal.) *Yes.*
- Which class is the next biggest? (Signal.) *Girls.*
- Does it have girls in it? (Signal.) *Yes.*
- Does it have boys in it? (Signal.) *No.*
- The smallest class is baby girls.
4. I'll tell you what is in a class. You tell me which class it is. Listen: This class has only baby girls in it. Which class is that? (Signal.) *Baby girls.*
- Listen: This class has boys and girls and baby girls. Which class is that? (Signal.) *Children.*
- Listen: This class has girls and baby girls in it. But it doesn't have boys in it. Which class is that? (Signal.) *Girls.*
5. (Repeat step 4 until firm.)
6. Listen: Girls, baby girls, children. Which of those classes has the most kinds of things in it? (Signal.) *Children.*
- So which class is the biggest? (Signal.) *Children.*

EXERCISE 4 Calendar

1. (Present calendar.)
- First you'll tell me about the days of the week. Then you'll tell me about the dates.
2. Tell me the day of the week it was yesterday. Get ready. (Signal.)
- Tell me the day of the week it is today. Get ready. (Signal.)
- Now the dates. Everybody, tell me yesterday's date. Get ready. (Signal.)
- Tell me today's date. Get ready. (Signal.)
3. (Repeat step 2 until firm.)

EXERCISE 5 Only

1. I'm going to make statements that are true. Some of the statements will be true of only your mouth. Some statements will be true of only your nose. Some statements will be true of both your mouth and your nose.
2. Listen: You could use this part to tell if a skunk is around. Is that true of only your mouth, only your nose, or both your mouth and nose? (Signal.) *Only your nose.*
   - Listen: You have one of these things. Is that true of only your mouth, only your nose, or both your mouth and nose? (Signal.) *Both your mouth and nose.*
   - Listen: It is part of your head. Is that true of only your mouth, only your nose, or both your mouth and nose? (Signal.) *Both your mouth and nose.*
   - Listen: You have teeth inside this thing. Is that true of only your mouth, only your nose, or both your mouth and nose? (Signal.) *Only your mouth.*
   - Listen: You can breathe through this part. Is that true of only your mouth, only your nose, or both your mouth and nose? (Signal.) *Both your mouth and nose.*
3. (Repeat step 2 until firm.)

EXERCISE 6 Materials

> *Note:* You will need a child wearing shoes with leather tops, rubber heels, and cloth shoelaces. Ask that child to come to the front of class and stand next to you.

1. We're going to talk about a shoe.
2. (Touch heel.) Everybody, what part am I touching? (Signal.) *The heel.*
   - What is that part made of? (Signal.) *Rubber.*
   - (Touch shoelace.) Everybody, what part am I touching? (Signal.) *The shoelace.*
   - What is that part made of? (Signal.) *Cloth.*
   - (Touch top of shoe.) Everybody, what part am I touching? (Signal.) *The top.*
   - What is that part made of? (Signal.) *Leather.*
3. (Repeat step 2 until firm.)

EXERCISE 7 Opposites

1. You learned a new opposite. What's the opposite of slow? (Signal.) *Fast.*
   - What's the opposite of fast? (Signal.) *Slow.*
2. I'll tell you about some new opposites. Listen: The opposite of happy is sad. What's the opposite of happy? (Signal.) *Sad.*
   - What's the opposite of sad? (Signal.) *Happy.*
3. Get ready to tell me about opposites.
   - I'm thinking of a dog that is the opposite of slow. So what do you know about it? (Signal.) *It's fast.*
   - I'm thinking of a dog that is the opposite of old. So what do you know about it? (Signal.) *It's young.*
   - I'm thinking of a dog that is the opposite of happy. So what do you know about it? (Signal.) *It's sad.*
   - I'm thinking of a dog that is the opposite of cold. So what do you know about it? (Signal.) *It's hot.*
   - I'm thinking of a dog that is the opposite of fat. So what do you know about it? (Signal.) *It's skinny.*
4. (Repeat step 3 until firm.)

EXERCISE 8 Clarabelle And The Bluebirds

Storytelling

- Everybody, I'm going to tell you the story about Clarabelle again. Remember the things that happened, and then you're going to fix up a picture that shows part of the story.

This is a story about a cow named Clarabelle. Clarabelle looked like the other brown-and-white cows on the farm. But Clarabelle was really different. She was always trying to do things that other animals did. In fact, she felt sad about not being a bird or a frog or a child.

One day, Clarabelle was looking at the bluebirds that were sitting on a wire that went from the barn to a large pole. Clarabelle said, "I would love to sit on that wire with those bluebirds."

Some of the other cows heard Clarabelle talking to herself, and they said, "Don't do it, Clarabelle. Remember what happened when you tried to swim like a duck in the duck pond?"

"Yeah," another cow said. "When you jumped **in** the pond, all the water jumped **out** of the pond."

Another cow said to Clarabelle, "And what about the time you tried to crow like the roosters? That was a real laugh. They were all saying, 'cock-a-doodle-doo.' And you were saying, 'cock-a-doodle-moo.'"

"Ho, ho, ho." All the cows laughed until they had tears in their eyes.

"That's not very funny," Clarabelle said. "And if I want to sit on the wire with those bluebirds, you can't stop me."

So Clarabelle went into the barn and up to the window by the wire. While she was getting ready, all the farm animals gathered around. One goat said, "We're in for another great show by Clarabelle."

And so they were. Clarabelle tiptoed out on the wire, but Clarabelle was heavier than one thousand bluebirds, so the wire went down, lower and lower, until it was almost touching the ground.

Well, the bluebirds were really angry. One of them said, "What are you doing, you big, fat cow? You've bent our wire almost to the ground."

"Yeah," another bluebird said. "This wire is for bluebirds, not brown-and-white cows."

Meanwhile, the farm animals were laughing and howling and rolling around on the ground. "Look at that," they said, and rolled and laughed some more.

Clarabelle was not happy. She said, "This wire is not as much fun as I thought it would be." Clarabelle looked back up at the barn and said, "Wow, it's going to be hard to walk all the way back up there."

Then Clarabelle looked down and said, "I'm close to the ground, so maybe it would be easier for me to jump off and land in that haystack."

While she was trying to figure out what to do, all the bluebirds were yelling at her and saying things like, "Well, do something. Get off our wire so we can sit in peace!"

"All right, all right," Clarabelle said "I'm leaving. Right now."

And with that, she jumped off the wire. Well, when she jumped off, the wire sprang way up into the air. It shot up so fast that it sent the bluebirds way up into the clouds, leaving blue tail feathers fluttering this way and that way.

And the farm animals almost died from laughter. "Did you see that?" a horse said as he rolled around on the ground. "Did you see those birds go flying up to the clouds?"

Everybody laughed except for a bunch of bluebirds and one brown-and-white cow. That cow pouted and kept saying, "It's not **funny.** It's not funny."

But let me tell you: It was, too—**very** funny.

WORKBOOK

EXERCISE 9 Workbook Activity

1. Everybody, open your workbook to Lesson 22. Write your name at the top of the page. ✔
2. This picture took place **before** Clarabelle climbed out on the wire. Clarabelle is the cow that's closest to the barn. Clarabelle is wearing a great big bell. That's called a cowbell.
3. Everybody, touch Clarabelle in the picture. ✔
- The cows behind her are trying to tell her something. What are they trying to tell her? (Call on a child. Idea: *Don't do it, Clarabelle.*)
- What is Clarabelle going to do right **after** this picture? (Call on a child. Idea: *Go into the barn and up to the window, then go out on the wire.*)
- Everybody, what colors should all those cows be? (Signal.) *Brown and white.*
- What color should that barn be? (Signal.) *Red.*
- What color should all those birds be? (Signal.) *Blue.*
4. Later you'll color that picture. Remember what colors to use.

EXERCISE 10 Questioning Skills

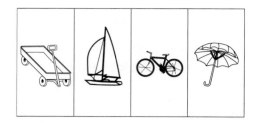

1. (Hold up workbook. Point to boxed pictures.) Find the next page of your workbook. ✔
- I'm thinking about one of the pictures. It's either a wagon, a boat, a bike, or an umbrella. You'll ask questions to find out which object I'm thinking of. Everybody, ask a question about the class it is in. Get ready. (Signal.) *What class is it in?*
- Everybody, ask a question about the parts it has. Get ready. (Signal.) *What parts does it have?*
2. Let's ask those questions again.
3. Everybody, ask a question about the class it is in. Get ready. (Signal.) *What class is it in?*
- Everybody, ask the question about the parts it has. Get ready. (Signal.) *What parts does it have?*
4. (Repeat step 3 until firm.)
5. Ask those questions again, and I'll tell you the answers.
- Everybody, ask the question about the class it is in. Get ready. (Signal.) *What class is it in?*
- Here's the answer. It's in the class of vehicles. What class is it in? (Signal.) *The class of vehicles.*

6. Everybody, ask the question about the parts it has. Get ready. (Signal.) *What parts does it have?*
- Here's the answer. It has wheels, a frame, pedals, and a seat. What parts? (Signal.) *Wheels, a frame, pedals, and a seat.*
7. Make a red mark on the thing I'm thinking of. ✔
- Everybody, what object was I thinking of? (Signal.) *A bicycle.*
- How did you know I wasn't thinking of a wagon? (Call on a child. Accept reasonable responses.)
- How did you know I wasn't thinking of a boat? (Call on a child. Accept reasonable responses.)
- How did you know I wasn't thinking of an umbrella? (Call on a child. Accept reasonable responses.)

EXERCISE 11 Part-Whole

1. (Hold up workbook. Point to second half.) Here's a coloring rule for the flower. Listen: Color the petals red. What's the rule? (Signal.) *Color the petals red.*
- Mark the petals. ✔
2. Here's another coloring rule for the flower. Listen: Color the leaves yellow. What's the rule? (Signal.) *Color the leaves yellow.*
- Mark the leaves. ✔
3. Here's another coloring rule for the flower. Listen: Color the stem green. What's the rule? (Signal.) *Color the stem green.*
- Mark the stem. ✔
4. Part of the flower is missing. What part is missing? (Signal.) *The roots.*
- Yes, the roots. Before you color the flower, you're going to follow the dots with your pencil to make the roots.
5. Here's the coloring rule for the roots. Listen: Color the roots brown. What's the rule? (Signal.) *Color the roots brown.*
- Mark the roots. ✔

LESSON 23

Objectives

- Follow directions for and discriminate between same and different actions. (Exercise 1)
- Given two objects, identify whether a statement is true of "only one" or "both" objects. (Exercise 2)
- Name common opposites and answer questions by generating sentences using opposites. (Exercise 3)
- Identify and generate absurdities of location. (Exercise 4)
- Given classes, order classes by "biggest," "next biggest," and "smallest" and answer questions about the members of the classes. (Exercise 5)
- Answer questions about previously learned calendar facts. (Exercise 6)
- Given a calendar, identify the day and date for "yesterday" and "today." (Exercise 7)
- Write numbers to show the sequence of events and tell the story. (Exercise 8)
- Ask questions involving "use" and "parts" to figure out a "mystery" object. (Exercise 9)
- Follow coloring rules involving class. (Exercise 10)

EXERCISE 1 Actions

1. Let's do some actions.
2. Everybody, smile. Get ready. (Signal.) ✔
- Good. Stop smiling. ✔
3. Now tell me if I do the same thing you did or something different.
- Watch me. (Smile.) Did I do the same thing or something different? (Signal.) *The same thing.*
- Watch me. (Frown.) Did I do the same thing or something different? (Signal.) *Something different.*
- Watch me. (Clap.) Did I do the same thing or something different? (Signal.) *Something different.*
4. (Repeat steps 2 and 3 until firm.)

EXERCISE 2 Only

1. Tell me if each statement I say is true of only a bed or if it is true of a bed **and** a table.
2. Listen: It is furniture. Say that statement. Get ready. (Signal.) *It is furniture.*
- Is that statement true of only a bed? (Signal.) *No.*
- What is it true of? (Signal.) *A bed and a table.*
- Yes, that statement is true of a bed and a table.
3. (Repeat step 2 until firm.)
4. Listen: You lie down on it. Say that statement. Get ready. (Signal.) *You lie down on it.*
- Is that statement true of only a bed? (Signal.) *Yes.*
5. (Repeat step 4 until firm.)

6. Listen: It is made for sleeping. Say that statement. Get ready. (Signal.) *It is made for sleeping.*
- Is that statement true of only a bed? (Signal.) *Yes.*
7. (Repeat step 6 until firm.)
8. Start with the words **it is** and make up a statement that is true of a bed and a dresser. (Call on individual children. Accept reasonable responses.)

EXERCISE 3 Opposites

1. You learned a new opposite. What's the opposite of slow? (Signal.) *Fast.*
- What's the opposite of fast? (Signal.) *Slow.*
- What's the opposite of sad? (Signal.) *Happy.*
- What's the opposite of happy? (Signal.) *Sad.*
2. I'll tell you about some new opposites.
- Listen: The opposite of awake is asleep. What's the opposite of awake? (Signal.) *Asleep.*
- What's the opposite of asleep? (Signal.) *Awake.*
3. Get ready to tell me about opposites.
- I'm thinking of a cow that is the opposite of sad. So what do you know about it? (Signal.) *It's happy.*
- I'm thinking of a cow that is the opposite of fast. So what do you know about it? (Signal.) *It's slow.*

- I'm thinking of a cow that is the opposite of young. So what do you know about it? (Signal.) *It's old.*
- I'm thinking of a cow that is the opposite of awake. So what do you know about it? (Signal.) *It's asleep.*
- I'm thinking of a cow that is the opposite of skinny. So what do you know about it? (Signal.) *It's fat.*

EXERCISE 4 Absurdity

1. Name some things you would find in a kitchen. **(Call on individual children. Praise appropriate observations. Have the group repeat each appropriate observation. For example:** *stove.***)** All right. We find a stove in a kitchen. Let's all say it. (Signal.) *We find a stove in a kitchen.*
2. Would you find a canoe in a kitchen? (Signal.) *No.*
- It would be absurd to see a canoe in a kitchen.
- Would you find a flagpole in a kitchen? (Signal.) *No.*
- That would be absurd.
- Would you find a refrigerator in a kitchen? (Signal.) *Yes.*
  Yes, you find a refrigerator in a kitchen.
- Would you find a camel in a kitchen? (Signal.) *No.*
  That would be absurd.
3. Name something else that would be absurd in a kitchen. **(Call on individual children. Praise appropriate responses.)**

EXERCISE 5 Classification

1. Remember the rule about bigger classes: The bigger class has more kinds of things in it. Everybody, say that rule. Get ready. (Signal.) *The bigger class has more kinds of things in it.*

2. Listen to these classes: cows, living things, animals.
- Everybody, say those three classes. Get ready. (Signal.) *Cows, living things, animals.*
- The biggest class has cows and other animals and plants in it. Raise your hand when you know which of those classes is the biggest. Remember, it has animals and plants in it. ✔
- Everybody, what's the biggest class? (Signal.) *Living things.*
3. The class that is next biggest doesn't have plants in it, but has all the other kinds of living things in it. Which class is that? (Signal.) *Animals.*
- Yes, the biggest class is living things. The next biggest class is animals.
- Which class is the biggest? (Signal.) *Living things.*
- Which class is the next biggest? (Signal.) *Animals.*
- Which class is the smallest? (Signal.) *Cows.*
4. (Repeat steps 2 and 3 until firm.)
5. Here are the classes with the biggest class first: living things, animals, cows.
- Say the three classes in that order. Get ready. (Signal.) *Living things, animals, cows.*
- Which class is the biggest? (Signal.) *Living things.*
- Does it have animals in it? (Signal.) *Yes.*
- Does it have plants in it? (Signal.) *Yes.*
- Which class is the next biggest? (Signal.) *Animals.*
- Does it have animals in it? (Signal.) *Yes.*
- Does it have plants in it? (Signal.) *No.*
- Which class is the smallest? (Signal.) *Cows.*
- What's the only kind of thing that's in that class? (Signal.) *Cows.*
6. I'll tell you what is in a class. You tell me which class it is.
- Listen: This class has all kinds of animals in it, but no plants. Which class is that? (Signal.) *Animals.*
- Listen: This class has cows and all other animals and plants in it. Which class is that? (Signal.) *Living things.*
- Listen: This class has cows in it, but no other kinds of things. Which class is that? (Signal.) *Cows.*
7. (Repeat step 6 until firm.)

8. Listen: cows, animals, living things. Which of those classes has the most kinds of things in it? (Signal.) *Living things.*

• So which class is the biggest? (Signal.) *Living things.*

EXERCISE 6   Calendar Facts

1. You learned calendar facts. Everybody, how many days are in a week? (Signal.) *Seven.*

• Say the fact. Get ready. (Signal.) *There are seven days in a week.*

• Say the days of the week. Get ready. (Signal.) *Sunday, Monday, Tuesday, Wednesday, Thursday, Friday, Saturday.*

• How many months are in a year? (Signal.) *12.*

• Say the fact about the months in a year. Get ready. (Signal.) *There are 12 months in a year.*

• Say the months of the year. Get ready. (Signal.) *January, February, March, April, May, June, July, August, September, October, November, December.*

• How many seasons are in a year? (Signal.) *Four.*

• Say the fact about the seasons in a year. Get ready. (Signal.) *There are four seasons in a year.*

• Say the seasons of the year. Get ready. (Signal.) *Winter, spring, summer, fall.*

2. (Repeat step 1 until firm.)

3. How many days are in a year? (Signal.) *365.*

• Say the fact. Get ready. (Signal.) *There are 365 days in a year.*

• Again. Say the fact. Get ready. (Signal.) *There are 365 days in a year.*

4. (Repeat step 3 until firm.)

5. Let's do all the facts again.

• How many months are in a year? (Signal.) *12.*

• Say the fact. Get ready. (Signal.) *There are 12 months in a year.*

• How many seasons are in a year? (Signal.) *Four.*

• Say the fact. Get ready. (Signal.) *There are four seasons in a year.*

• How many days are in a year? (Signal.) *365.*

• Say the fact. Get ready. (Signal.) *There are 365 days in a year.*

6. (Repeat step 5 until firm.)

EXERCISE 7   Calendar

1. (Present calendar.)

• First you'll tell me about the days of the week. Then you'll tell me about the dates.

2. Tell me the day of the week it was yesterday. Get ready. (Signal.)

• Tell me the day of the week it is today. Get ready. (Signal.)

• Now the dates. Everybody, tell me yesterday's date. Get ready. (Signal.)

• Tell me today's date. Get ready. (Signal.)

3. (Repeat step 2 until firm.)

EXERCISE 8   Sequence Story

Roger And The Bluebird In The Backyard

1. Everybody, open your workbook to Lesson 23. Write your name at the top of the page. ✔

2. I'm going to tell you a story and then you'll tell it to me. Listen:

This is the story of a boy named Roger. Roger had a lot of trouble remembering where he put things. He was always losing his socks, or his mittens or his shoes.

One day, Roger was sitting in the backyard. It was a warm day, so he took off his hat and put it under his chair. He didn't know it, but he put his hat right over a bluebird. Roger didn't know it, but when that bluebird started to move around, his hat started to move around, too.

- Remember, at first, Roger's hat was **under** his chair.

3. Everybody, touch the place where Roger's hat was first. ✔
- Where was his hat first? (Signal.) *Under his chair.*
- Make a **one** in the circle that is **under** Roger's chair to show that this is the **first** place his hat was. Raise your hand when you're finished. (Observe children and give feedback.)

While Roger was looking for his hat, the hat moved **in back of** his chair.

4. Everybody, touch the place where his hat was now. ✔
   Where was his hat now? (Signal.) *In back of his chair.*
- Make a **two** in the circle **in back of** his chair to show that this is where his hat went next. Raise your hand when you're finished.
  (Observe children and give feedback.)
5. Listen to these questions: Everybody, where was Roger's hat **first?** (Signal.) *Under his chair.*
   Where was his hat **next?** (Signal.) *In back of his chair.*

While Roger was looking for his hat, the hat moved **in front of** his foot.

6. Everybody, touch the place where his hat was now. ✔
- Where was his hat now? (Signal.) *In front of his foot.*
- Make a **three** in the circle **in front of** his foot to show that this is where his hat went next. Raise your hand when you're finished. (Observe children and give feedback.)

While Roger was looking for his hat, the hat flew up in the air and landed **on** his knee.

7. Everybody, touch the place where his hat was now. ✔
   Where was his hat now? (Signal.) *On his knee.*

- Make a **four** in the circle. Raise your hand when you're finished.
  (Observe children and give feedback.)

While Roger was looking for his hat, the hat flew up in the air and went **above** his head.

8. Everybody, touch the place where his hat was now. ✔
   Where was his hat now? (Signal.) *Above his head.*
- Make a **five** in the circle. Raise your hand when you're finished.
  (Observe children and give feedback.)

While Roger was looking for his hat, the bird flew out of his hat and the hat fell right **on** Roger's head.

9. Everybody, touch the place where his hat was now. ✔
   Tell me where his hat was now. (Signal.) *On his head.*
- Make a **six** in the circle. Raise your hand when you're finished.
  (Observe children and give feedback.)

While Roger was looking for his hat, his mother came outside. She saw him looking this way and that way, so she said, "Roger, what are you doing?"

He said, "I'm looking for my hat."

She told him where his hat was.

10. Everybody, where was his hat? (Signal.) *On his head.*
- Do you think Roger felt kind of silly when he found out where his hat was? (Signal.) *Yes.*
11. Listen: The numbers in the story tell where Roger's hat was **first,** where it was **next** and so on. Who can touch the numbers and tell all the things that happened in the story? Start by telling us **where** Roger put his hat and **why** it moved from place to place. Then tell what happened at each number, but don't say the numbers. Remember to tell about Roger's mother and what she said at the end of your story.

12. (Call on a child:) You tell the story. Everybody else, follow along and see if (child's name) tells what happened for each number.
(Praise child for a story that tells why Roger's hat moved, where it went and what Roger's mother said.)
(Repeat step 12, calling on another child.)

13. Later you can cut out Roger's hat and put it where it was at the end of the story. Remember to cut along the dotted lines. Then you can color the rest of the picture. Remember the color of that bird.

EXERCISE 9 Questioning Skills

1. (Hold up workbook. Point to boxed pictures.) Find the next page of your workbook. ✔
- I'm thinking about one of the pictures. It's either a chair, a couch, a car, or a table. You'll ask questions to find out which object I'm thinking of.
- Everybody, ask a question about what you use it for. Get ready. (Signal.) *What do you use it for?*
- Everybody, ask a question about the parts it has. Get ready. (Signal.) *What parts does it have?*

2. Let's ask those questions again.

3. Everybody, ask the question about what you use it for. Get ready. (Signal.) *What do you use it for?*
- Everybody, ask the question about the parts it has. Get ready. (Signal.) *What parts does it have?*

4. (Repeat step 3 until firm.)

5. Ask those questions again, and I'll tell you the answers.
- Everybody, ask the question about what you use it for. Get ready. (Signal.) *What do you use it for?*

- Here's the answer. To sit on. What do you use it for? (Signal.) *To sit on.*

6. Everybody, ask the question about the parts it has. Get ready. (Signal.) *What parts does it have?*
- Here's the answer. It has a back, a seat, legs, and rungs. What parts? (Signal.) *A back, a seat, legs, and rungs.*
- Could it be a chair? (Signal.) *Yes.*
- Could it be a couch? (Signal.) *No.* Why not? (Call on a child. Accept reasonable responses.)
- Everybody, could it be a car? (Signal.) *No.* Why not? (Call on a child. Accept reasonable responses.)
- Everybody, could it be a table? (Signal.) *No.* Why not? (Call on a child. Accept reasonable responses.)

7. Make a brown mark on the thing I'm thinking of. ✔
- Everybody, what object was I thinking of? (Signal.) *A chair.*

EXERCISE 10 Location

1. (Hold up workbook. Point to second half.) Everybody, what place do you see in this picture? (Signal.) *A jungle.*

2. Here's a coloring rule for this picture. Listen: Color all the animals brown or black. What's the rule? (Signal.) *Color all the animals brown or black.*
- (Repeat step 2 until firm.)

3. Put a brown mark on **one** animal and a black mark on another animal. ✔

4. Here's another coloring rule for this picture. Listen: Color all the trees orange and green. What's the rule? (Signal.) *Color all the trees orange and green.*
- (Repeat step 4 until firm.)

5. Put an orange and green mark on one tree. ✔

6. There's one more thing to do. One of the animals has a missing part. What animal is that? (Signal.) *The elephant.*
Yes, the elephant.
- What part of the elephant is missing? (Signal.) *The trunk.*
- Yes, the trunk. Before you color the elephant, follow the dots and make the trunk.

Objectives

- Identify parts of a common object and the materials it is made of. (Exercise 1)
- Given a calendar, identify the day and date for "yesterday" and "today." (Exercise 2)
- Given classes, order classes by "biggest," "next biggest," and "smallest" and answer questions about the members of the classes. (Exercise 3)
- Name common opposites and answer questions by generating sentences using opposites. (Exercise 4)
- Given a complex sentence, answer questions involving "who," "when," and "where." (Exercise 5)
- Identify the material of a common object. (Exercise 6)
- Answer questions about a familiar story and relate the story to a picture that has numbers showing where the various events occurred. (Exercise 7)

EXERCISE 1 Materials

> *Note:* You will need a wooden pencil with an eraser and a point.

1. (Touch the eraser.)
- Everybody, what is the name of this part? (Signal.) *The eraser.*
- (Touch the point.)
- Everybody, what is the name of this part? (Signal.) *The point.*
- (Touch the shaft.)
- Everybody, what is the name of this part? (Signal.) *The shaft.*
2. (Repeat step 1 until firm.)
3. (Touch the eraser.)
- What is the name of this part? (Signal.) *The eraser.*
- What is this part made of? (Signal.) *Rubber.*
- (Touch the point.)
- What is the name of this part? (Signal.) *The point.*
- What is this part made of? (Signal.) *Graphite.*
- (Touch the shaft.)
- What is the name of this part? (Signal.) *The shaft.*
- What is this part made of? (Signal.) *Wood.*
4. (Repeat step 3 until firm.)
5. (Ask individual children the following questions. Accept reasonable responses.)
- Why do you think the eraser is made of rubber?
- Why do you think the shaft is made of wood?
- Why do you think the point is made of graphite?

EXERCISE 2 Calendar

1. (Present calendar.)
- First you'll tell me about the days of the week. Then you'll tell me about the dates.
2. Tell me the day of the week it was yesterday. Get ready. (Signal.)
- Tell me the day of the week it is today. Get ready. (Signal.)
- Now the dates.
- Everybody, tell me yesterday's date. Get ready. (Signal.)
- Tell me today's date. Get ready. (Signal.)
3. (Repeat step 2 until firm.)

EXERCISE 3 Classification

1. Remember the rule about bigger classes. What's the rule? (Signal.) *The bigger class has more kinds of things in it.*
- Listen to these classes: trees, living things, plants.
- Everybody, say those three classes. Get ready. (Signal.) *Trees, living things, plants.*
- The biggest class has trees and other plants and animals in it. Raise your hand when you know which of those classes is the biggest. Remember, it has plants and animals in it. ✔
- Everybody, what's the biggest class? (Signal.) *Living things.*
2. The class that is next biggest doesn't have animals in it, but has all the other kinds of living things in it. Which class is that? (Signal.) *Plants.*
- Yes, the biggest class is living things. The next biggest class is plants.

3. Which class is the biggest? (Signal.) *Living things.*
- Which class is the next biggest? (Signal.) *Plants.*
- Which class is smallest? (Signal.) *Trees.*
4. (Repeat step 3 until firm.)
5. Here are the classes with the biggest class first: living things, plants, trees.
- Say the three classes in that order. Get ready. (Signal.) *Living things, plants, trees.*
- Which class is the biggest? (Signal.) *Living things.*
- Does it have animals in it? (Signal.) *Yes.*
- Does it have plants in it? (Signal.) *Yes.*
- Which class is the next biggest? (Signal.) *Plants.*
- Does it have animals in it? (Signal.) *No.*
- Does it have plants in it? (Signal.) *Yes.*
- What's the smallest class? (Signal.) *Trees.*
- What's the only kind of thing that's in that class? (Signal.) *Trees.*
6. I'll tell you what is in a class. You tell me which class it is.
- Listen: This class has all kinds of plants in it, but no animals. Which class is that? (Signal.) *Plants.*
- Listen: This class has trees in it, but no other kinds of things. Which class is that? (Signal.) *Trees.*
- Listen: This class has trees and all other plants and animals in it. Which class is that? (Signal.) *Living things.*
7. Listen: plants, living things, trees. Which of those classes has the most kinds of things in it? (Signal.) *Living things.*
- So which class is the biggest? (Signal.) *Living things.*

EXERCISE 4 Opposites

1. You learned a new opposite. What's the opposite of slow? (Signal.) *Fast.*
- What's the opposite of fast? (Signal.) *Slow.*
- What's the opposite of sad? (Signal.) *Happy.*
- What's the opposite of happy? (Signal.) *Sad.*
- What's the opposite of awake? (Signal.) *Asleep.*
- What's the opposite of asleep? (Signal.) *Awake.*

2. Get ready to tell me about opposites.
- I'm thinking of a cat that is the opposite of slow. So what do you know about it? (Signal.) *It's fast.*
- I'm thinking of a cat that is the opposite of happy. So what do you know about it? (Signal.) *It's sad.*
- I'm thinking of a cat that is the opposite of asleep. So what do you know about it? (Signal.) *It's awake.*
- I'm thinking of a cat that is the opposite of hot. So what do you know about it? (Signal.) *It's cold.*
3. (Repeat step 2 until firm.)

EXERCISE 5 Who—Where—When

1. I'm going to say sentences that answer a lot of questions. You'll answer the questions.
2. Listen: The girls were on the playground just after eleven o'clock.
- Your turn. Say the sentence. Get ready. (Signal.) *The girls were on the playground just after eleven o'clock.*
3. That sentence has words that tell who, words that tell where, and words that tell when.
- Listen: The girls were on the playground just after eleven o'clock.
- Who was on the playground? (Signal.) *The girls.*
- Where were the girls? (Signal.) *On the playground.*
- When were the girls on the playground? (Signal.) *Just after eleven o'clock.*
4. Listen: The girls were on the playground just after eleven o'clock.
- Everybody, say the whole sentence. Get ready. (Signal.) *The girls were on the playground just after eleven o'clock.*
- Which words tell who? (Signal.) *The girls.*
- Which words tell where? (Signal.) *On the playground.*
- Which words tell when? (Signal.) *Just after eleven o'clock.*
5. (Repeat step 4 until firm.)

EXERCISE 6 Materials

1. We're going to talk about your socks.
- Everybody, touch your socks. Get ready. (Signal.) ✔
2. When I call on you, tell me the color of your socks. (Call on three or four children and ask:) What color are your socks? (Praise correct answers.)
3. When I call on you, tell me what your socks are made of. (Call on three or four children and ask:) What are your socks made of? (Accept *cloth, cotton,* and so on.)

WORKBOOK

EXERCISE 7 Sequence Story

Cindy The Squid

1. Everybody, open your workbook to Lesson 24. Write your name at the top of the page. ✔
2. The picture shows Cindy and the shark. The numbers show what the **shark** did first, what he did next and so forth.
3. Everybody, touch the shark. ✔
- That's where the shark starts out.
4. Everybody touch number 1. ✔
- Where is the shark at number 1? (Call on a child. Idea: *In front of Cindy.*)
- Listen: Why did the shark go to number 1? (Call on a child. Idea: *The shark was going to try to eat Cindy.*)
5. Everybody, touch number 2. ✔
- Where is the shark at number 2? (Call on a child. Idea: *At the rock where he hit his head.*)
- It looks like that shark must have gone right through Cindy. Everybody, did that happen? (Signal.) *No.*
- Why not? (Call on a child. Idea: *Cindy made a cloud of black ink and moved to one side.*)
- Why didn't the shark see the rock before he bonked himself? (Call on a child. Idea: *Cindy had squirted out a cloud of black ink.*)
6. Everybody, touch number 3. ✔
- Where is the shark at number 3? (Call on a child. Idea: *The shark is swimming with the yellow fish.*)
- Why would a shark want to swim with those yellow fish? (Call on a child. Idea: *The shark couldn't remember who he was, and Cindy said the shark was a yellow fish.*)
7. Listen: The numbers in the story tell what the shark did first, what he did next and so on. But you have to tell **why** some things happened. You have to tell **why** the shark went to number 1 and **why** the shark didn't go right through Cindy. You have to tell **why** the shark didn't see the rock. And you have to tell **why** that shark went over and swam around with the little yellow fish.
8. Who can touch the numbers and tell all the things that happened in the story? Start by telling **why** the shark went to number 1 and then tell the rest of the story.
9. (Call on a child:) You tell the story. Everybody else, follow along and see if (child's name) tells what happened for each number and why it happened. Raise your hand if you hear a problem. (Praise child for a story that tells the sequence of things that the shark did and why they happened.) (To correct omissions of **why** information, say:)
   a. Uh-oh. You didn't tell **why** _____ . Who knows **why?**
   b. (Call on another child.)
   - (Repeat step 9, calling on another child.)
10. Later you can color the picture. Remember what color the shark is and what color the fish at number 3 should be.

LESSON 25

Objectives

- Ask questions involving "class," and "parts" and **"location"** to figure out a "mystery" object. (Exercise 1)
- Given two objects, identify whether a statement is true of "only one" or "both" objects. (Exercise 2)
- Given a complex sentence, answer questions involving "who," "when," and "where." (Exercise 3)
- Name common opposites and answer questions by generating sentences using opposites. (Exercise 4)
- Given classes, order classes by "biggest," "next biggest," and "smallest." (Exercise 5)
- Given a calendar, identify the day and date for "yesterday" and "today." (Exercise 6)
- Listen to a familiar story. (Exercise 7)
- Make a picture consistent with the details of the story. (Exercise 8)
- Ask questions involving **"material,"** "use" and "parts" to figure out a "mystery" object. (Exercise 9)
- Follow coloring rules involving class. (Exercise 10)

EXERCISE 1 Questioning Skills

1. I'm thinking of an object. You'll ask questions to figure out what that object is. You'll ask these questions:
- What class is it in?
- What parts does it have?
- Where do you find it?
2. Listen to the questions again.
- What class is it in?
- What parts does it have?
- Where do you find it?
3. Everybody, say all three questions.
- Question 1. (Signal.) *What class is it in?*
- Question 2. (Signal.) *What parts does it have?*
- Question 3. (Signal.) *Where do you find it?*
4. Ask question 1. Get ready. (Signal.) *What class is it in?*
- It's in the class of furniture.
5. Ask question 2. Get ready. (Signal.) *What parts does it have?*
- It has a top and drawers.
6. Ask question 3. Get ready. (Signal.) *Where do you find it?*
- You find it in the bedroom.
7. Raise your hand when you know the object. ✔
- Everybody, what object was I thinking of? (Signal.) *A dresser.*
8. (Repeat steps 4 through 7 until firm.)

EXERCISE 2 Only

1. Tell me if each statement I say is true of only a dog or if it is true of a dog **and** a cat.
2. Listen: It says bowwow. Say that statement. Get ready. (Signal.) *It says bowwow.*
- What is it true of? (Signal.) *Only a dog.*
3. Listen: It is an animal. Say that statement. Get ready. (Signal.) *It is an animal.*
- What is it true of? (Signal.) *A dog and a cat.*
- Yes, that statement is true of a dog and a cat.
4. Listen: It is a dog. Say that statement. Get ready. (Signal.) *It is a dog.*
- What is it true of? (Signal.) *Only a dog.*
5. (Repeat steps 2 through 4 until firm.)

EXERCISE 3 Who—Where—When

1. I'm going to say sentences that answer a lot of questions. You'll answer the questions.
2. Listen: Ten fleas got on the dog just before the dog ate.
- Listen again. Ten fleas got on the dog just before the dog ate.
- Your turn. Say the sentence. Get ready. (Signal.) *Ten fleas got on the dog just before the dog ate.*
3. Listen: Ten fleas got on the dog just before the dog ate.
- Who got on the dog? (Signal.) *Ten fleas.*
- When did the fleas get on the dog? (Signal.) *Just before the dog ate.*
- Where did the fleas go? (Signal.) *On the dog.*

4. Listen again. Ten fleas got on the dog just before the dog ate.
- Everybody, say the whole sentence. Get ready. (Signal.) *Ten fleas got on the dog just before the dog ate.*
- Which words tell who got on something? (Signal.) *Ten fleas.*
- Which words tell where they went? (Signal.) *On the dog.*
- Which words tell when they did something? (Signal.) *Just before the dog ate.*
5. (Repeat step 4 until firm.)

EXERCISE 4   Opposites

1. Here's a new pair of opposites: narrow and wide. Something that is narrow is very thin. You may be able to jump across a stream that is narrow. You wouldn't be able to jump across a stream that is wide.
2. What's the opposite of narrow? (Signal.) *Wide.*
- What's the opposite of wide? (Signal.) *Narrow.*
- What's the opposite of slow? (Signal.) *Fast.*
- What's the opposite of fast? (Signal.) *Slow.*
- What's the opposite of sad? (Signal.) *Happy.*
- What's the opposite of happy? (Signal.) *Sad.*
- What's the opposite of awake? (Signal.) *Asleep.*
- What's the opposite of asleep? (Signal.) *Awake.*
3. Get ready to tell me about opposites.
- I'm thinking of a stream that is the opposite of narrow. So what do you know about it? (Signal.) *It's wide.*
- I'm thinking of a road that is the opposite of wide. So what do you know about it? (Signal.) *It's narrow.*
- I'm thinking of runners that are the opposite of slow. So what do you know about them? (Signal.) *They're fast.*
- I'm thinking of a tiger that is the opposite of happy. So what do you know about it? (Signal.) *It's sad.*
- I'm thinking of a cat that is the opposite of awake. So what do you know about it? (Signal.) *It's asleep.*
- I'm thinking of water that is the opposite of hot. So what do you know about it? (Signal.) *It's cold.*
4. (Repeat step 3 until firm.)

EXERCISE 5   Classification

1. Remember the rule about bigger classes. What's the rule? (Signal.) *The bigger class has more kinds of things in it.*
- I'll say classes. You tell me which class is the biggest.
2. Listen to these classes: animals, chickens, farm animals.
- Say those classes. Get ready. (Signal.) *Animals, chickens, farm animals.*
- Which of those classes is the biggest? (Signal.) *Animals.*
3. Listen to these classes: trees, living things, plants.
- Everybody, say those three classes. Get ready. (Signal.) *Trees, living things, plants.*
- Which of those classes is the biggest? (Signal.) *Living things.*
4. Listen to these classes: boys, baby boys, children.
- Everybody, say those three classes. Get ready. (Signal.) *Boys, baby boys, children.*
- Which of those classes is the biggest? (Signal.) *Children.*
5. Listen to these classes: tigers, animals, wild animals.
- Everybody, say those three classes. Get ready. (Signal.) *Tigers, animals, wild animals.*
- Which of those classes is the biggest? (Signal.) *Animals.*
6. Listen to these classes: couches, old couches, furniture.
- Everybody, say those three classes. Get ready. (Signal.) *Couches, old couches, furniture.*
- Which of those classes is the biggest? (Signal.) *Furniture.*
7. Listen to these classes: vehicles, vehicles with wheels, bicycles.
- Everybody, say those three classes. Get ready. (Signal.) *Vehicles, vehicles with wheels, bicycles.*
- Which of those classes is the biggest? (Signal.) *Vehicles.*
8. Listen to these classes: farm animals, animals, pigs.
- Everybody, say those three classes. Get ready. (Signal.) *Farm animals, animals, pigs.*
- Which of those classes is the biggest? (Signal.) *Animals.*
9. (Repeat steps 2 through 8 until firm.)

1. (Present calendar.)
- First you'll tell me about the days of the week. Then you'll tell me about the dates.
2. Tell me the day of the week it was yesterday. Get ready. (Signal.)
- Tell me the day of the week it is today. Get ready. (Signal.)
- Now the dates.
- Everybody, tell me yesterday's date. Get ready. (Signal.)
- Tell me today's date. Get ready. (Signal.)
3. (Repeat step 2 until firm.)

EXERCISE 7   Clarabelle And The Bluebirds

Storytelling

- Everybody, I'm going to read you the story about Clarabelle again. Remember the things that happened and then you're going to fix up a picture that shows part of the story.

This is a story about a cow named Clarabelle. Clarabelle looked like the other brown-and-white cows on the farm. But Clarabelle was really different. She was always trying to do things that other animals did. In fact, she felt sad about not being a bird or a frog or a child.

One day, Clarabelle was looking at the bluebirds that were sitting on a wire that went from the barn to a large pole. Clarabelle said, "I would love to sit on that wire with those bluebirds."

Some of the other cows heard Clarabelle talking to herself, and they said, "Don't do it, Clarabelle. Remember what happened when you tried to swim like a duck in the duck pond?"

"Yeah," another cow said to Clarabelle. "When you jumped **in** the pond, all the water jumped **out** of the pond."

Another cow said to Clarabelle, "And what about the time you tried to crow like the roosters? That was a real laugh. They were all saying, 'cock-a-doodle-doo.' And you were saying, 'cock-a-doodle-moo.'"

"Ho, ho, ho." All the cows laughed until they had tears in their eyes.

"That's not very funny," Clarabelle said. "And if I want to sit on the wire with those bluebirds, you can't stop me."

So Clarabelle went into the barn and up to the window by the wire. While she was getting ready, all the farm animals gathered around. One goat said, "We're in for another great show by Clarabelle."

And so they were. Clarabelle tiptoed out on the wire, but Clarabelle was heavier than one thousand bluebirds, so the wire went down, lower and lower, until it was almost touching the ground.

Well, the bluebirds were really angry. One of them said, "What are you doing, you big, fat cow? You've bent our wire almost to the ground."

"Yeah," another bluebird said. "This wire is for bluebirds, not brown-and-white cows."

Meanwhile, the farm animals were laughing and howling and rolling around on the ground. "Look at that," they said, and rolled and laughed some more.

Clarabelle was not happy. She said, "This wire is not as much fun as I thought it would be." Clarabelle looked back up at the barn and said, "Wow, it's going to be hard to walk all the way back up there."

Then Clarabelle looked down and said, "I'm close to the ground, so maybe it would be easier for me to jump off and land in that haystack."

While she was trying to figure out what to do, all the bluebirds were yelling at her and saying things like, "Well, do something. Get off our wire so we can sit in peace!" "All right, all right," Clarabelle said. "I'm leaving. Right now."

And with that, she jumped off the wire. Well, when she jumped off, the wire sprang way up into the air. It shot up so fast that it sent the bluebirds way up into the clouds, leaving blue tail feathers fluttering this way and that way.

And the farm animals almost died from laughter. "Did you see that?" a horse said as he rolled around on the ground. "Did you see those birds go flying up to the clouds?"

Everybody laughed except for a bunch of bluebirds and for one brown-and-white cow. That cow pouted and kept saying, "It's not **funny.** It's not funny."

But let me tell you: It was too—**very** funny.

WORKBOOK

EXERCISE 8 Workbook Activity

1. Everybody, open your workbook to Lesson 25. Write your name at the top of the page. ✔
2. Here's a picture that shows something that happened in the story.
- What is Clarabelle trying to do? (Call on a child. Idea: *Tiptoe out on the wire with the bluebirds.*)
- Everybody, do those bluebirds look happy? (Signal.) *No.*
- What kind of things do you think they're saying to Clarabelle? (Call on a child. Idea: *Get off our wire.*)

- That wire looks pretty straight and pretty high. What's going to happen to it when Clarabelle gets out in the middle of it? (Call on a child. Idea: *It will bend down almost to the ground.*)
3. Later you'll color the picture. Remember the colors of the cows and of those unhappy birds on the fence.
- Who remembers what color the barn is? (Call on a child.) *Red.*

EXERCISE 9 Questioning Skills

1. Find the next page in your workbook. ✔
- (Hold up workbook. Point to boxed pictures.)
2. I'm thinking about one of the pictures. It's either a cat, a coat, a shirt, or a can. You'll ask questions to find out which object I'm thinking of.
- Everybody, ask a question about what material it is made of. Get ready. (Signal.) *What material is it made of?*
- Everybody, ask a question about the parts it has. Get ready. (Signal.) *What parts does it have?*
- Everybody, ask a question about what you use it for. Get ready. (Signal.) *What do you use it for?*
3. Let's ask those questions again.

4. Everybody, ask a question about what material it is made of. Get ready. (Signal.) *What material is it made of?*

• Everybody, ask a question about the parts it has. Get ready. (Signal.) *What parts does it have?*

• Everybody, ask a question about what you use it for. Get ready. (Signal.) *What do you use it for?*

5. (Repeat step 3 until firm.)

6. Ask those questions again, and I'll tell you the answers.

• Everybody, ask a question about what material it is made of. Get ready. (Signal.) *What material is it made of?*

• Here's the answer. It's made of cloth or leather. What material is it made of? (Signal.) *Cloth or leather.*

7. Everybody, ask the question about the parts it has. Get ready. (Signal.) *What parts does it have?*

• Here's the answer. It has sleeves, a collar, and buttons. What parts? (Signal.) *Sleeves, a collar, and buttons.*

8. Everybody, ask the question about what you use it for. Get ready. (Signal.) *What do you use it for?*

• Here's the answer. To wear when it's cold outside. What is it used for? (Signal.) *To wear when it's cold outside.*

9. Make a black mark on the thing I'm thinking of. ✔

• Everybody, what object was I thinking of? (Signal.) *A coat.*

• How did you know I wasn't thinking of a cat? (Call on a child. Accept reasonable responses.)

• How did you know I wasn't thinking of a shirt? (Call on a child.) *It isn't made of leather.*

• How did you know I wasn't thinking of a can? (Call on a child. Accept reasonable responses.)

EXERCISE 10   Location

1. (Hold up workbook. Point to second half.) Everybody, what place do you see in this picture? (Signal.) *A beach.*

2. Here's a coloring rule for this picture. Listen: Color all the men orange. What's the rule? (Signal.) *Color all the men orange.*

• (Repeat step 2 until firm.)

3. Put an orange mark on one man. ✔

4. Here's another coloring rule for this picture. Listen: Color all the women brown. What's the rule? (Signal.) *Color all the women brown.*

• (Repeat step 4 until firm.)

5. Put a brown mark on one woman. ✔

Objectives

- Given two objects, identify whether a statement is true of "only one" or "both" objects and **generate a statement that is true of both objects.** (Exercise 1)
- Answer questions about previously learned calendar facts. (Exercise 2)
- Given a calendar, identify the day and date for "yesterday" and "today." (Exercise 3)
- Ask questions involving "class," "parts" and "location" to figure out a "mystery" object. (Exercise 4)
- Given classes, order classes by "biggest," "next biggest," and "smallest." (Exercise 5)
- Name common opposites and answer questions by generating sentences using opposites. (Exercise 6)
- Relate a familiar story grammar to a picture that indicates the sequence of events for a new story. (Exercise 7)
- Ask questions involving "class," "use" and "parts" to figure out a "mystery" object. (Exercise 8)
- Follow coloring rules involving parts of a whole. (Exercise 9)

EXERCISE 1 Only

1. I'm going to make statements. Each statement is going to be true of only a boat or only a motorcycle or both a boat and a motorcycle.
2. Listen: It goes on the highway. Say that statement. Get ready. (Signal.) *It goes on the highway.*
- Tell me what that statement is true of. Get ready. (Signal.) *Only a motorcycle.*
3. Listen: It goes in the water. Say that statement. Get ready. (Signal.) *It goes in the water.*
- Tell me what that statement is true of. Get ready. (Signal.) *Only a boat.*
4. Listen: It is a vehicle. Say that statement. Get ready. (Signal.) *It is a vehicle.*
- Tell me what that statement is true of. Get ready. (Signal.) *Both a boat and a motorcycle.*
5. Your turn. Make up a statement that is true of **only** a boat. (Call on individual children. Have the group repeat each reasonable statement. Then ask:) What is that statement true of? (Signal.) *Only a boat.*
6. Your turn. Make up a statement that is true of **only** a motorcycle. (Call on individual children. Have the group repeat each reasonable statement. Then ask:) What is that statement true of? (Signal.) *Only a motorcycle.*

7. Your turn. Make up a statement that is true of **both** a boat and a motorcycle. (Call on individual children. Have the group repeat each reasonable statement. Then ask:) What is that statement true of? (Signal.) *Both a boat and a motorcycle.*

EXERCISE 2 Calendar Facts

1. You learned calendar facts.
2. Everybody, how many days are in a week? (Signal.) *Seven.*
- Say the fact. Get ready. (Signal.) *There are seven days in a week.*
- Say the days of the week. Get ready. (Signal.) *Sunday, Monday, Tuesday, Wednesday, Thursday, Friday, Saturday.*
- How many months are in a year? (Signal.) *12.*
- Say the fact about the months in a year. Get ready. (Signal.) *There are 12 months in a year.*
- Say the months of the year. Get ready. (Signal.) *January, February, March, April, May, June, July, August, September, October, November, December.*
- How many seasons are in a year? (Signal.) *Four.*
- Say the fact about the seasons in a year. Get ready. (Signal.) *There are four seasons in a year.*
- Say the seasons of the year. Get ready. (Signal.) *Winter, spring, summer, fall.*
3. (Repeat step 2 until firm.)

4. How many days are in a year? (Signal.) *365.*
   - Say the fact. Get ready. (Signal.) *There are 365 days in a year.*
   - Again. Say the fact. Get ready. (Signal.) *There are 365 days in a year.*
5. (Repeat step 4 until firm.)
6. Let's do all the facts again.
   - How many months are in a year? (Signal.) *12.*
   - Say the fact. Get ready. (Signal.) *There are 12 months in a year.*
   - How many seasons are in a year? (Signal.) *Four.*
   - Say the fact. Get ready. (Signal.) *There are four seasons in a year.*
   - How many days are in a year? (Signal.) *365.*
   - Say the fact. Get ready. (Signal.) *There are 365 days in a year.*
7. (Repeat step 6 until firm.)

EXERCISE 3 Calendar

1. (Present calendar.)
   - Listen: First, you'll tell me about the days of the week. Then you'll tell me about the dates.
2. Tell me the day of the week it was yesterday. Get ready. (Signal.)
   - Tell me the day of the week it is today. Get ready. (Signal.)
   - Listen: Tell me the day of the week it will be tomorrow. Get ready. (Signal.)
3. Now the dates.
   - Tell me yesterday's date. Get ready. (Signal.)
   - Tell me today's date. Get ready. (Signal.)
   - Tell me tomorrow's date. Get ready. (Signal.)
4. (Repeat steps 2 and 3 until firm.)

EXERCISE 4 Questioning Skills

1. I'm thinking of an object. You'll ask questions to figure out what that object is. You'll ask these questions:
   - What class is it in?
   - What parts does it have?
   - Where do you find it?
2. Listen to the questions again.
   - What class is it in?
   - What parts does it have?
   - Where do you find it?
3. Everybody, say all three questions.
   - Question 1. Get ready. (Signal.) *What class is it in?*
   - Question 2. Get ready. (Signal.) *What parts does it have?*
   - Question 3. Get ready. (Signal.) *Where do you find it?*
4. Ask question 1. Get ready. (Signal.) *What class is it in?*
   - It's in the class of plants.
5. Ask question 2. Get ready. (Signal.) *What parts does it have?*
   - It has bark and leaves and a trunk and branches.
6. Ask question 3. Get ready. (Signal.) *Where do you find it?*
   - You find a lot of them in forests.
7. Raise your hand when you know the object. ✔
   - Everybody, what object was I thinking of? (Signal.) *A tree.*

EXERCISE 5 Classification

1. Remember the rule about bigger classes. What's the rule? (Signal.) *The bigger class has more kinds of things in it.*
- I'll say classes. You tell me which class is the biggest.
2. Listen to these classes: farm animals, animals, chickens.
- Say those classes. Get ready. (Signal.) *Farm animals, animals, chickens.*
- Which of those classes is the biggest? (Signal.) *Animals.*
3. Listen to these classes: men, women, people.
- Everybody, say those three classes. Get ready. (Signal.) *Men, women, people.*
- Which of those classes is the biggest? (Signal.) *People.*
4. Listen to these classes: plants, living things, grass.
- Everybody, say those three classes. Get ready. (Signal.) *Plants, living things, grass.*
- Which of those classes is the biggest? (Signal.) *Living things.*
5. Listen to these classes: wild animals, bears, animals.
- Everybody, say those three classes. Get ready. (Signal.) *Wild animals, bears, animals.*
- Which of those classes is the biggest? (Signal.) *Animals.*
6. Listen to these classes: adults, women, young women.
- Everybody, say those three classes. Get ready. (Signal.) *Adults, women, young women.*
- Which of those classes is the biggest? (Signal.) *Adults.*
7. Listen to these classes: vehicles, boats, sail boats.
- Everybody, say those three classes. Get ready. (Signal.) *Vehicles, boats, sail boats.*
- Which of those classes is the biggest? (Signal.) *Vehicles.*
8. Listen to these classes: farm animals, animals, pigs.
- Everybody, say those three classes. Get ready. (Signal.) *Farm animals, animals, pigs.*
- Which of those classes is the biggest? (Signal.) *Animals.*
9. (Repeat steps 2 through 8 until firm.)

EXERCISE 6 Opposites

1. You learned a new pair of opposites.
- What's the opposite of narrow? (Signal.) *Wide.*
- What's the opposite of wide? (Signal.) *Narrow.*
2. Here's a new pair of opposites: noisy and quiet.
- What's the opposite of noisy? (Signal.) *Quiet.*
- What's the opposite of quiet? (Signal.) *Noisy.*
- What's the opposite of awake? (Signal.) *Asleep.*
- What's the opposite of asleep? (Signal.) *Awake.*
3. Get ready to tell me about opposites.
- I'm thinking of a stream that is the opposite of quiet. So what do you know about it? (Signal.) *It's noisy.*
- I'm thinking of a road that is the opposite of narrow. So what do you know about it? (Signal.) *It's wide.*
- I'm thinking of children who are the opposite of noisy. So what do you know about them? (Signal.) *They're quiet.*
- I'm thinking of a tiger that is the opposite of awake. So what do you know about it? (Signal.) *It's asleep.*
- I'm thinking of a cat that is the opposite of asleep. So what do you know about it? (Signal.) *It's awake.*
4. (Repeat steps 2 and 3 until firm.)

EXERCISE 7   Sequence Story

Roger And The Bluebird At The Park

1. Everybody, open your workbook to Lesson 26. Write your name at the top of the page. ✔
2. This picture shows a different story about Roger and the bluebird in his hat.

Roger was at the park. He was wearing a little black hat today. When Roger sat down on the grass and started eating his candy bar, he put his black hat in the grass, but he put it on top of a bluebird again.

3. Everybody, touch number 1. ✔
- That's where the hat starts out. Where is number 1? (Call on a child. Idea: *Next to Roger's knee.*)
- Everybody, touch number 2. ✔
- That's where the hat goes **next**. Where is number 2? (Call on a child. Idea: *In back of Roger.*)

- Everybody, touch number 3. ✔
- That's where the hat goes **after** it is in back of Roger. Where is number 3? (Call on a child. Idea: *On the branch of a tree.*)
- Everybody, touch number 4. ✔
- That's where the hat goes **after** it is on the branch of a tree. Where is number 4? (Call on a child. Idea: *In the garbage can.*)

After the bluebird left the tree, it flew over the garbage can and a big wind blew the hat right into the garbage can. The bluebird flew away somewhere.

- Does anyone know where it went? (Call on a child. Idea: *To the top of the swing set.*)
4. When Roger finishes eating his candy bar, what should he do with the wrapper? (Call on several children. Idea: *Throw it in the garbage can.*)
- Everybody, when he goes over to that garbage can, what do you think he'll see? (Signal.) *His hat.*
- And what will he say? (Call on several children. Idea: *How did my hat get in there?*)
5. Who can make up the whole story about Roger and his hat? First tell **why** the hat moves around. Then tell where the hat starts out and where it goes. Remember to tell what happens at each number, but don't say the numbers. Everybody, listen carefully to the story and raise your hand if you hear a problem. (Call on several children. Praise stories that describe the sequence.)
6. Later you can color the picture of Roger. You could even draw his little black hat in the garbage can.

EXERCISE 8   Questioning Skills

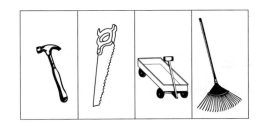

1. Find the next page in your workbook. (Hold up workbook. Point to boxed pictures.) ✔
- I'm thinking about one of the pictures. It's either a hammer, a saw, a wagon, or a rake. You'll ask questions to find out which object I'm thinking of.
- Everybody, ask a question about the class it is in. Get ready. (Signal.) *What class is it in?*
- Everybody, ask a question about the parts it has. Get ready. (Signal.) *What parts does it have?*
- Everybody, ask a question about what you use it for. Get ready. (Signal.) *What do you use it for?*
2. Let's ask those questions again.
3. Everybody, ask a question about the class it is in. Get ready. (Signal.) *What class is it in?*
- Everybody, ask the question about the parts it has. Get ready. (Signal.) *What parts does it have?*
- Everybody, ask the question about what you use it for. Get ready. (Signal.) *What do you use it for?*
4. (Repeat step 3 until firm.)
5. Ask those questions again, and I'll tell you the answers.
- Everybody, ask the question about the class it is in. Get ready. (Signal.) *What class is it in?*
- Here's the answer. It's in the class of tools. What class is it in? (Signal.) *The class of tools.*

6. Everybody, ask the question about the parts it has. Get ready. (Signal.) *What parts does it have?*
- Here's the answer. It has a handle and a head. What parts? (Signal.) *A handle and a head.*
7. Everybody, ask the question about what you use it for. Get ready. (Signal.) *What do you use it for?*
- Here's the answer. You use it to pound nails. What do you use it for? (Signal.) *To pound nails.*
8. Make a red mark on the thing I'm thinking of. ✔
- Everybody, what object was I thinking of? (Signal.) *A hammer.*
- How did you know I wasn't thinking of a saw? (Call on a child. Accept reasonable responses.)
- How did you know I wasn't thinking of a wagon? (Call on a child. Accept reasonable responses.)
- How did you know I wasn't thinking of a rake? (Call on a child. Accept reasonable responses.)

EXERCISE 9   Part—whole

1. (Hold up workbook. Point to second half.) Here's a coloring rule for the sailboat. Listen: Color the hull blue. The hull is the part of the boat below the sail. What's the rule? (Signal.) *Color the hull blue.*
- Mark the hull. ✔
2. Here's another coloring rule for the sailboat. Listen: Color the mast brown. The mast is the pole that holds up the sail. What's the rule? (Signal.) *Color the mast brown.*
- Mark the mast. ✔
3. Part of the sailboat is missing. What part is missing? (Signal.) *The sail.*
- Yes, the sail. Before you color the sailboat, you're going to follow the dots and make the sail.
4. Here's the coloring rule for the sail. Listen: Color the sail red. What's the rule? (Signal.) *Color the sail red.*
- Mark the sail. ✔

LESSON 27

Objectives

- Generate statements to describe actions using present, past and future tense and answer questions involving "or." (Exercise 1)
- Given two objects, identify whether a statement is true of "only one" or "both" objects. (Exercise 2)
- Answer questions about previously learned calendar facts. (Exercise 3)
- Given a complex sentence, answer questions involving "who," "when," "where" and "what." (Exercise 4)
- Ask questions involving "class," "parts" and "location" to figure out a "mystery" object. (Exercise 5)
- Name common opposites and answer questions by generating sentences using opposites. (Exercise 6)
- Given a calendar, identify the day and date for "yesterday" and "today." (Exercise 7)
- Write numbers to show the sequence of events and tell a story based on familiar story grammar. (Exercise 8)
- Ask questions involving "class," "use" and "parts" to figure out a "mystery" object. (Exercise 9)
- Follow coloring rules involving class. (Exercise 10)

EXERCISE 1 Actions

1. It's time for some actions.
2. (Hold your hand over your head.)
- Where am I holding my hand? (Signal.) *Over your head.*
- (Keep your hand over your head.)
3. Listen: I will hold my hand next to my head.
- What am I going to do? (Signal.) *Hold your hand next to your head.*
- Say the whole thing. Get ready. (Signal.) *You will hold your hand next to your head.*
- Am I holding my hand next to my head now? (Signal.) *No.*
- Will I hold my hand next to my head? (Signal.) *Yes.*
- (Hold your hand next to your head.)
- What am I doing now? (Signal.) *Holding your hand next to your head.*
- What was I doing before I held my hand next to my head? (Signal.) *Holding your hand over your head.*
- (Bring your hand down.)
4. Listen: I'm going to clap or point to the desk or point to the chair.
- What am I going to do? (Signal.) *Clap or point to the desk or point to the chair.*
5. (Repeat step 4 until firm.)
6. Yes, I'm going to clap or point to the desk or point to the chair.

- Am I going to clap? (Signal.) *Maybe.*
- Am I going to point to the chair? (Signal.) *Maybe.*
- Am I going to point to the floor? (Signal.) *No.*
- Am I going to point to the desk? (Signal.) *Maybe.*
7. Here I go. (Point to the chair.)
- Did I point to the desk? (Signal.) *No.*
- Did I clap? (Signal.) *No.*
- Did I point to the chair? (Signal.) *Yes.*

EXERCISE 2 Only

1. I'm going to make statements. Each statement is going to be true of only an apple or only a carrot or both an apple **and** a carrot.
2. Listen: It grows on trees. Say that statement. Get ready. (Signal.) *It grows on trees.*
- Tell me what that statement is true of. Get ready. (Signal.) *Only an apple.*
3. Listen: It is orange. Say that statement. Get ready. (Signal.) *It is orange.*
- Tell me what that statement is true of. Get ready. (Signal.) *Only a carrot.*
4. Listen: It is food. Say that statement. Get ready. (Signal.) *It is food.*
- Tell me what that statement is true of. Get ready. (Signal.) *Both an apple and a carrot.*

5. Your turn. Make up a statement that is true of **only** an apple. (Call on individual children. Have the group repeat each reasonable statement. Then ask:) What is that statement true of? (Signal.) *Only an apple.*

6. Your turn. Make up a statement that is true of **only** a carrot. (Call on individual children. Have the group repeat each reasonable statement. Then ask:) What is that statement true of? (Signal.) *Only a carrot.*

7. Your turn. Make up a statement that is true of **both** an apple and a carrot. (Call on individual children. Have the group repeat each reasonable statement. Then ask:) What is that statement true of? (Signal.) *Both an apple and a carrot.*

EXERCISE 3   Calendar Facts

1. How many months are in a year? (Signal.) *12.*
- Say the fact. Get ready. (Signal.) *There are 12 months in a year.*
- How many seasons are in a year? (Signal.) *Four.*
- Say the fact. Get ready. (Signal.) *There are four seasons in a year.*
- How many days are in a year? (Signal.) *365.*
- Say the fact. Get ready. (Signal.) *There are 365 days in a year.*

2. Here's a new fact: There are 52 weeks in a year.
- Everybody, say that fact. Get ready. (Signal.) *There are 52 weeks in a year.*

3. How many months are in a year? (Signal.) *12.*
- How many weeks are in a year? (Signal.) *52.*
- How many days are in a year? (Signal.) *365.*
- How many seasons are in a year? (Signal.) *Four.*

4. Say the seasons of the year. Get ready. (Signal.) *Winter, spring, summer, fall.*
- Say the months of the year. Get ready. (Signal.) *January, February, March, April, May, June, July, August, September, October, November, December.*

5. Last question. How many weeks are in a year? (Signal.) *52.*

EXERCISE 4   Who—where—when—what

1. I'm going to say a sentence that answers questions about who, where, when, and what. You'll answer the questions.

2. Listen: Last night, two birds flew into the nest.
- Listen again. Last night, two birds flew into the nest.
- Your turn. Say the sentence. Get ready. (Signal.) *Last night, two birds flew into the nest.*
- Listen: Who flew into the nest? (Signal.) *Two birds.*
- Listen: What did the birds do? (Signal.) *Flew into the nest.*
- When did the birds do that? (Signal.) *Last night.*
- Where did the birds go? (Signal.) *Into the nest.*

3. Listen again. Last night, two birds flew into the nest.
- Everybody, say the whole sentence. Get ready. (Signal.) *Last night, two birds flew into the nest.*
- Which words tell who? (Signal.) *Two birds.*
- Which word tells what they did? (Signal.) *Flew.*
- Which words tell when? (Signal.) *Last night.*
- Which words tell where? (Signal.) *Into the nest.*

4. (Repeat step 3 until firm.)

EXERCISE 5 Questioning Skills

1. I'm thinking of an object. You'll ask questions to figure out what that object is. You'll ask these questions:
- What class is it in?
- What parts does it have?
- Where do you find it?
2. Listen to the questions again.
- What class is it in?
- What parts does it have?
- Where do you find it?
3. Everybody, say all three questions.
- Question 1. Get ready. (Signal.) *What class is it in?*
- Question 2. Get ready. (Signal.) *What parts does it have?*
- Question 3. Get ready. (Signal.) *Where do you find it?*
4. Ask question 1. Get ready. (Signal.) *What class is it in?*
- It's in the class of vehicles.
5. Ask question 2. Get ready. (Signal.) *What parts does it have?*
- It has a sail and a hull and a mast.
6. Ask question 3. Get ready. (Signal.) *Where do you find it?*
- You find it on the water.
7. Raise your hand when you know the object. ✔
- Everybody, what object was I thinking of? (Signal.) *A sailboat.*
8. (Repeat steps 3 through 7 until firm.)

EXERCISE 6 Opposites

1. You learned a new pair of opposites.
- What's the opposite of quiet? (Signal.) *Noisy.*
- What's the opposite of noisy? (Signal.) *Quiet.*
- What's the opposite of wide? (Signal.) *Narrow.*
- What's the opposite of narrow? (Signal.) *Wide.*
2. I'm thinking of a belt that is the opposite of wide. So what do you know about it? (Signal.) *It's narrow.*
- I'm thinking of children who are the opposite of quiet. So what do you know about them? (Signal.) *They're noisy.*
3. (Repeat steps 1 and 2 until firm.)

4. I'll say a sentence about four kittens. You say the sentence that means the opposite.
- Listen: Four kittens were quiet. Everybody, say that sentence. Get ready. (Signal.) *Four kittens were quiet.*
- Say the sentence about the kittens that means the opposite. Get ready. (Signal.) *Four kittens were noisy.*
5. (Repeat step 4 until firm.)
6. New sentence: Four kittens were awake. Say that sentence. Get ready. (Signal.) *Four kittens were awake.*
- Say the sentence about the kittens that means the opposite. Get ready. (Signal.) *Four kittens were asleep.*
- New sentence: Four kittens were feeling very cold. Say that sentence. Get ready. (Signal.) *Four kittens were feeling very cold.*
- Say the sentence about the kittens that means the opposite. Get ready. (Signal.) *Four kittens were feeling very hot.*
7. (Repeat step 6 until firm.)

EXERCISE 7 Calendar

1. (Present calendar.)
- Listen: First, you'll tell me about the days of the week. Then you'll tell me about the dates.
2. Tell me the day of the week it was yesterday. Get ready. (Signal.)
- Tell me the day of the week it is today. Get ready (Signal.)
- Listen: Tell me the day of the week it will be tomorrow. Get ready. (Signal.)
3. Now the dates.
- Tell me yesterday's date. Get ready. (Signal.)
- Tell me today's date. Get ready. (Signal.)
- Tell me tomorrow's date. Get ready. (Signal.)
4. (Repeat steps 2 and 3 until firm.)

WORKBOOK

EXERCISE 8 Sequence Story

Paul Paints a Pony Pink

1. Everybody, open your workbook to Lesson 27. Write your name at the top of the page. ✔
2. This picture is almost like one you did earlier, but the circles are in different places and there are no numbers in the circles.
3. Touch that big plant that is near Paul. ✔
- That plant is a little palm tree. Everybody, what is it? (Signal.) *A little palm tree.*
- Touch the picture on the wall. ✔
- That picture shows big palm trees and pyramids. Everybody, what kind of trees? (Signal.) *Palm trees.*
- What are the other things in the picture? (Signal.) *Pyramids.*
- Look at the bird cage. That bird inside is a parrot. What kind of bird? (Signal.) *A parrot.*
- And that thing holding up the bird cage is a pole.
- Touch the tablecloth. ✔
- Those dots on the tablecloth are called polka dots. What are they called? (Signal.) *Polka dots.*
- Touch the circle on the poodle. ✔
- That circle is on the poodle's paw.
- What's that thing on the floor next to the poodle's paw? (Signal.) *A pencil.*

- Touch the thing that Paul is painting. ✔
- That is a small horse called a pony. Who knows what color he's painting that pony? (Call on a child. Idea: *Pink.*)
- Yes, Paul is painting the pony pink. He has plenty of pink paint.
4. Listen big: Write number 1 in the circle that is on the pony. That's where the story starts. Raise your hand when you're finished. (Observe children and give feedback.)
- You have to make up the rest of the story and we don't want this story to be like the other one we did.
- (Write on the board:)

2	3	4

You can use these numbers after number 1: **two, three** and **four.** No more. You can put the numbers in **any** of the circles. Then you'll tell us your story. But think about the story before you put the numbers 2, 3 and 4 in the circles. I didn't tell you about all the circles in the picture, so look at the picture carefully. Think about the story, put in your numbers and raise your hand when you're ready to tell your story. Remember, Paul has pink paint. Raise your hand when you're ready. (Observe children and give feedback.)

5. Let's listen to some stories now. When somebody is telling a story, touch each thing the person names and see if the person names four things, starting with the pony.
- (Call on a child:) Tell your story.
- (Look at the storyteller's picture as the child tells the story and make sure the story is consistent with the numbers in the circles. Praise unique stories. Praise parts that are "plausible," particularly those that describe how Paul gets from one circle to the next.)
6. Later you'll color the picture. Remember, the only things you'll color pink are those that have numbered circles on them. So some pictures will look a lot different than other pictures.

Optional Activity

- (After pictures are prepared, tell children to exchange papers.)
Let's see who can tell the story that your neighbor colored. (Call on several children to tell their neighbor's story.)

EXERCISE 9 Questioning Skills

1. Find the next page in your workbook. ✔
    (Hold up workbook. Point to boxed pictures.)
2. I'm thinking about one of the pictures.
    It's either a flower, a tree, a log, or a goat.
    You'll ask questions to find out which
    object I'm thinking of.
    *   Everybody, ask a question about the class it
        is in. Get ready. (Signal.) *What class is it in?*
    *   Everybody, ask a question about the parts
        it has. Get ready. (Signal.) *What parts does
        it have?*
3. Let's ask those questions again.
4. Everybody, ask a question about the class it
    is in. Get ready. (Signal.) *What class is it in?*
    *   Everybody, ask the question about the
        parts it has. Get ready. (Signal.) *What parts
        does it have?*
5. (Repeat step 4 until firm.)
6. Ask those questions again, and I'll tell you
    the answers.
    *   Everybody, ask the question about the
        class it is in. Get ready. (Signal.) *What class
        is it in?*
    *   Here's the answer. It's in the class of
        plants. What class is it in? (Signal.) *The
        class of plants.*

7. Everybody, ask the question about the
    parts it has. Get ready. (Signal.) *What parts
    does it have?*
    *   Here's the answer. It has leaves, roots, and
        a trunk. What parts? (Signal.) *Leaves, roots,
        and a trunk.*
8. Make a red mark on the thing I'm
    thinking of. ✔
    *   Everybody, what object was I thinking of?
        (Signal.) *A tree.*
    *   How did you know I wasn't thinking of a
        log? (Call on a child. Accept reasonable
        responses.)
    *   How did you know I wasn't thinking of a
        flower? (Call on a child.) *It doesn't have
        a trunk.*
    *   How did you know I wasn't thinking of a
        goat? (Call on a child. Accept reasonable
        responses.)

EXERCISE 10 Location

1. (Hold up workbook. Point to second half.)
    Everybody, what place do you see in this
    picture? (Signal.) *A restaurant.*
2. Here's one coloring rule for this picture.
    Listen: Color all the people brown. What's
    the rule? (Signal.) *Color all the people
    brown.*
    *   (Repeat step 2 until firm.)
3. Put a brown mark on one person. ✔
4. Here's another coloring rule for this picture.
    Listen: Color all the furniture red. What's
    the rule? (Signal.) *Color all the furniture red.*
    *   (Repeat step 4 until firm.)
5. Put a red mark on one piece of furniture. ✔
6. There's one more thing to do. One piece
    of furniture has a missing part. What piece
    of furniture is that? (Signal.) *The chair.* Yes,
    the chair.
    *   What part of the chair is missing? (Signal.)
        The back.
    *   Yes, the back. Before you color the chair,
        follow the dots and make the back.

Objectives

- Generate statements to describe actions using present and past tense. (Exercise 1)
- Given a complex sentence, answer questions involving "who," "when," "where" and "what." (Exercise 2)
- Answer questions about previously learned calendar facts. (Exercise 3)
- Name common opposites and answer questions by generating sentences using opposites. (Exercise 4)
- **Given two classes, identify which class is biggest, describe why and name members of the biggest class.** (Exercise 5)
- Given a calendar, identify the day and date for "yesterday" and "today." (Exercise 6)
- Answer questions about a new story. (Exercise 7)
- Answer questions about a picture based on a story and make a picture consistent with the details of a story. (Exercise 8)

EXERCISE 1   Actions

1. Here's an action game.
2. Everybody, hold your hand on your head. Get ready. (Signal.) ✔
- What are you doing? (Signal.) *Holding my hand on my head.*
3. Everybody, hold your hand over your head. Get ready. (Signal.) ✔
- What are you doing? (Signal.) *Holding my hand over my head.*
- Keep holding your hand over your head. ✔
4. What did you do **before** you held your hand over your head? (Signal.) *Held my hand on my head.*
- Yes, you held your hand on your head.
5. Say the whole thing about what you did before you held your hand over your head. Get ready. (Signal.) *I held my hand on my head.*
6. (Repeat step 5 until firm.)
7. What are you doing now? (Signal.) *I am holding my hand over my head.*
- Hands down.

EXERCISE 2   Who—where—when—what

1. I'm going to say a sentence that answers questions about who, where, when, and what. You'll answer the questions.
2. Listen: On Friday evening, three friends will meet in the park.
- Listen again. On Friday evening, three friends will meet in the park.
- Your turn. Say the sentence. Get ready. (Signal.) *On Friday evening, three friends will meet in the park.*
- Listen: Who will meet? (Signal.) *Three friends.*
- Listen: What will the friends do? (Signal.) *Meet in the park.*
- When will they do that? (Signal.) *On Friday evening.*
- Where will they do that? (Signal.) *In the park.*
3. Listen again. On Friday evening, three friends will meet in the park.
- Everybody, say the whole sentence. Get ready. (Signal.) *On Friday evening, three friends will meet in the park.*
- Which words tell who? (Signal.) *Three friends.*
- Which words tell what they will do? (Signal.) *Meet in the park.*
- Which words tell when? (Signal.) *On Friday evening.*
- Which words tell where? (Signal.) *In the park.*
4. (Repeat step 3 until firm.)

EXERCISE 3 Calendar Facts

1. How many months are in a year? (Signal.) *12.*
• Say the fact. Get ready. (Signal.) *There are 12 months in a year.*
• How many seasons are in a year? (Signal.) *Four.*
• Say the fact. Get ready. (Signal.) *There are four seasons in a year.*
• How many days are in a year? (Signal.) *365.*
• Say the fact. Get ready. (Signal.) *There are 365 days in a year.*
2. See if you remember the new fact: How many weeks are in a year? (Signal.) *52.*
• Everybody, say that fact. Get ready. (Signal.) *There are 52 weeks in a year.*
3. Say the seasons of the year. Get ready. (Signal.) *Winter, spring, summer, fall.*
• Say the months of the year. Get ready. (Signal.) *January, February, March, April, May, June, July, August, September, October, November, December.*
4. Last question. How many weeks are in a year? (Signal.) *52.*

EXERCISE 4 Opposites

1. Let's talk about opposites.
• What's the opposite of noisy? (Signal.) *Quiet.*
• What's the opposite of quiet? (Signal.) *Noisy.*
• What's the opposite of wide? (Signal.) *Narrow.*
• What's the opposite of narrow? (Signal.) *Wide.*
2. I'll say a sentence about two trucks. You say the sentence that means the opposite.
• Listen: Two trucks were very, very quiet. Everybody, say that sentence. Get ready. (Signal.) *Two trucks were very, very quiet.*
• Say the sentence about the trucks that means the opposite. Get ready. (Signal.) *Two trucks were very, very noisy.*
3. (Repeat step 2 until firm.)

4. New sentence: Two trucks were wet. Say that sentence. Get ready. (Signal.) *Two trucks were wet.*
• Say the sentence about the trucks that means the opposite. Get ready. (Signal.) *Two trucks were dry.*
• New sentence: Two trucks were on a road that was very narrow. Say that sentence. Get ready. (Signal.) *Two trucks were on a road that was very narrow.*
• Say the sentence that means the opposite. Get ready. (Signal.) *Two trucks were on a road that was very wide.*
• New sentence: Two trucks had fuel tanks that were full. Say that sentence. Get ready. (Signal.) *Two trucks had fuel tanks that were full.*
• Say the sentence that means the opposite. Get ready. (Signal.) *Two trucks had fuel tanks that were empty.*
5. (Repeat step 4 until firm.)

EXERCISE 5 Classification

1. We're going to talk about classes. Remember, the bigger class has more kinds of things in it.
• Tell me which class has more kinds of things in it, the class of ducks or the class of animals. Get ready. (Signal.) *The class of animals.*
• So which class is bigger, the class of ducks or the class of animals? (Signal.) *The class of animals.*

2. Listen: Tell me which class has more kinds of things in it, the class of airplanes or the class of vehicles. Get ready. (Signal.) *The class of vehicles.*

• So which class is bigger, the class of airplanes or the class of vehicles? (Signal.) *The class of vehicles.*

3. Tell me which class has more kinds of things in it, the class of containers or the class of bottles. Get ready. (Signal.) *The class of containers.*

• So which class is bigger, the class of containers or the class of bottles? (Signal.) *The class of containers.*

• Tell me how you know that the class of containers is bigger. Get ready. (Signal.) *The class of containers has more kinds of things in it.*
  Yes, the class of containers has more kinds of things in it.

4. Tell me which class has more kinds of things in it, the class of animals or the class of horses. Get ready. (Signal.) *The class of animals.*

• So which class is bigger, the class of animals or the class of horses? (Signal.) *The class of animals.*

• Are all horses in the class of animals? (Signal.) *Yes.*

• Are there other animals in the class of animals? (Signal.) *Yes.*

• So the class of animals has more kinds of things in it.

5. Suppose we took away all horses from the class of animals. Name some animals that would be left. (Call on individual children. Accept reasonable responses.)

6. (Repeat steps 2 through 5 until firm.)

EXERCISE 6 Calendar

1. (Present calendar.)

• Listen: First, you'll tell me about the days of the week. Then you'll tell me about the dates.

2. Tell me the day of the week it was yesterday. Get ready. (Signal.)

• Tell me the day of the week it is today. Get ready. (Signal.)

• Listen: Tell me the day of the week it will be tomorrow. Get ready. (Signal.)

3. Now the dates.

• Tell me yesterday's date. Get ready. (Signal.)

• Tell me today's date. Get ready. (Signal.)

• Tell me tomorrow's date. Get ready. (Signal.)

4. (Repeat steps 2 and 3 until firm.)

EXERCISE 7 Honey, Andrea And Sweetie

Storytelling

• Everybody, I'm going to read you a story about a dog named Honey, a mouse named Andrea and a yellow cat you already know.

There once was the meanest-looking bulldog you ever saw. She always had a big frown on her face and her lower teeth stuck out. That made her look like she was ready to fight with anybody.

• Who can make a face like that dog? Frown and make your lower teeth stick out. (Praise children who make acceptable faces.)

People were always surprised to find out that this bulldog's name was Honey. The family that owned her gave her that name because she really was as sweet as honey. She loved just about everybody and everything. She loved other dogs. She loved flowers, butterflies and birds. She even loved mice. In fact, she had a favorite mouse—a little gray mouse named Andrea.

- Listen: Why was that mean-looking bulldog named Honey? (Call on a child. Idea: *Because she really was as sweet as honey.*)
- What kind of things did Honey love? (Call on a child. Idea: *Dogs, flowers, butterflies, birds and mice.*)
- Who remembers the name of her favorite mouse? (Call on a child.) *Andrea.*
- Everybody, what color was Andrea? (Signal.) *Gray.*

Honey would sometimes sniff around the dining room, trying to find Andrea. That's where Andrea lived—behind a little hole in the dining room wall. Sometimes Honey would find Andrea, and sometimes she wouldn't, because Andrea was very, very shy.

- Listen: Where did Andrea live? (Call on a child. Idea: *Behind a little hole in the dining room wall.*)
- Why didn't Honey always find her in the dining room? (Call on a child. Idea: *Because Andrea was very, very shy.*)

There was only one thing that Honey didn't like, and that was cats, especially cats that chased birds and butterflies and cats that tried to catch mice.

- I think we may have read about a cat that Honey might not like at all. Everybody, what cat is that? (Signal.) *Sweetie.*

Well, one day Honey was sprawled out on the back porch of her house when a woman came to visit, and that woman had a big yellow cat with her.

- Everybody, who is that big yellow cat? (Signal.) *Sweetie.*

When Honey looked at the cat, she said to herself, "Ugh. I hope that thing doesn't stay around here very long."

The woman and the cat went inside. After a while, Honey got up and stretched and waddled into the kitchen. The woman was sitting at the table, but where was the cat?

Honey found out a moment later. She heard sounds of scurrying and running around in the dining room. So she got up and trotted over to the doorway of the dining room.

- Listen: What do you think was going on in the dining room? (Call on a child. Idea: *Sweetie was chasing Andrea.*)

What Honey saw made her very, very mad. There was poor little Andrea running for her life. And right behind her was that nasty yellow cat, running as fast as he could. The cat and the mouse shot around the room, this way and that way—under the table, across the rug, into the living room and back into the dining room. And all this time, that cat was less than one leap behind Andrea.

The woman who came over with the cat was shouting, "Sweetie, stop chasing that little mouse." But Sweetie didn't stop. Neither did Andrea.

Well, just about the time that Honey decided to take care of this cat, Sweetie and Andrea flew under the table. Sweetie got caught on the tablecloth and pulled it off the table. When Sweetie tried to get untangled, he just got more and more wrapped up in the tablecloth. He wiggled and squirmed and rolled around, but he was all wrapped up in the tablecloth. Only two parts of Sweetie were sticking out. His yellow tail was sticking out of one end of the tablecloth and his whiskers were sticking out of the other end.

Well, while Sweetie was squirming around trying to get free, Honey waddled over and gave Sweetie's tail a little nip—not a great bite, but something hard enough to get Sweetie's attention.

"There," Honey said and waddled back to the kitchen as Sweetie yowled and hissed and rolled around inside that tablecloth.

Finally, Sweetie got free. He looked around the room but he didn't see Andrea, because she was in her mouse hole, and he didn't see Honey, because she was in the kitchen.

So Sweetie shook his head and said to himself, "Gosh, that mouse looked like a frail little thing, but let me tell you: that mouse can really bite hard."

• Uh-oh, poor Sweetie has the wrong idea again. Everybody, did Sweetie **know** who bit him on the tail? (Signal.) *No.*
• Who did Sweetie **think** did that? (Signal.) *Andrea.*
• What really happened? (Call on a child. Idea: *Honey bit Sweetie on the tail.*)
• Sweetie is mixed up again.

EXERCISE 8 **Story Details**

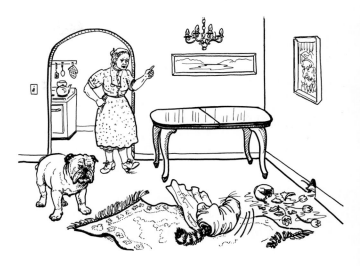

1. Everybody, open your workbook to Lesson 28. Write your name at the top of the page. ✔
2. This picture shows something that happened in the story.
3. Can you find Andrea in this picture? You have to look carefully. Where is she? (Call on a child. Idea: *Going into the hole in the wall.*)
• Where is Sweetie in this picture? (Call on a child. Idea: *In the tablecloth.*)
• Everybody, what are the only parts of Sweetie sticking out? (Signal.) *His tail and whiskers.*
• What's Honey going to do right **after** this picture? (Call on a child. Idea: *Bite Sweetie's tail.*)
• Who is that woman who is shouting at Sweetie? (Call on a child. Idea: *The woman who owns Sweetie.*)
4. You're going to color the picture later. Listen, but don't say anything: Honey is the **same** colors as Clarabelle. See if you remember those colors. Andrea is gray.

EXERCISE 9 **Questioning Skills**

a. (Hold up worksheet. Point to first half.)
- I'm thinking about one of the pictures. It's either a hammer, a broom, a screwdriver, or a saw. You'll ask questions to find out which object I'm thinking of.
- Everybody, ask a question about what material it is made of. Get ready. (Signal.) *What material is it made of?*
- Everybody, ask a question about the parts it has. Get ready. (Signal.) *What parts does it have?*

b. Let's ask those questions again.

c. Everybody, ask a question about what material it is made of. Get ready. (Signal.) *What material is it made of?*
- Everybody, ask a question about the parts it has. Get ready. (Signal.) *What parts does it have?*

d. (Repeat step c until firm.)

e. Ask those questions again, and I'll tell you the answers.
- Everybody, ask the question about what material it is made of. Get ready. (Signal.) *What material is it made of?*
- Here's the answer. Part of it is made of wood and part of it is made of metal. What materials is it made of? (Signal.) *Wood and metal.*

f. Everybody, ask the question about the parts it has. Get ready. (Signal.) What parts does it have?
- Here's the answer. It has a handle and a blade. What parts? (Signal.) *A handle and a blade.*

g. Make a red mark on the thing I'm thinking of. ✔
- Everybody, what object was I thinking of? (Signal.) *A saw.*
- How did you know I wasn't thinking of a hammer? (Call on a child.) *A hammer doesn't have a blade.*
- How did you know I wasn't thinking of a broom? (Call on a child. Accept reasonable responses.)
- How did you know I wasn't thinking of a screwdriver? (Call on a child. Idea: It doesn't cut wood.)

EXERCISE 10 **Classification**

a. (Hold up worksheet. Point to second half.) The box shows two pictures. Some of the things in one picture are shoes. All of the things in the other picture are shoes.

b. Touch the picture where some of the things are shoes. ✔
- Here's the rule about the picture where **some** of the things are shoes. The shoes should be green. What's the rule? (Signal.) *The shoes should be green.*
- Fix up the picture where some of the things are shoes. ✔

c. Here's the rule about the picture where **all** of the things are shoes. The shoes should be yellow or black. What's the rule? (Signal.) *The shoes should be yellow or black.*
- Make a yellow mark on one shoe and a black mark on another shoe. ✔

Objectives

- Generate statements to describe actions using present and past tense. (Exercise 1)
- Answer questions about previously learned calendar facts. (Exercise 2)
- Given two classes, identify which class is biggest, describe why and name members of the biggest class. (Exercise 3)
- Name common opposites, answer questions by generating sentences using opposites and **generate a sentence that means the opposite of a given sentence.** (Exercise 4)
- **Given a sequence, answer questions about the sequence.** (Exercise 5)
- Given two objects, identify whether a statement is true of "only one" or "both" objects. (Exercise 6)
- Given a calendar, identify the day and date for "yesterday" and "today." (Exercise 7)
- Relate a familiar story grammar to a picture that indicates the sequence of events for a new story. (Exercise 8)
- Ask questions involving "class," "use" and "materials" to figure out a "mystery" object. (Exercise 9)
- **Follow coloring rules involving some and all.** (Exercise 10)

EXERCISE 1 Actions

1. Here's an action game.
2. Watch me. (Touch the floor and continue touching it.)
- What am I touching? (Signal.) *The floor.*
3. (Stop touching the floor. Touch your chair and continue touching it.)
- What am I doing now? (Signal.) *Touching your chair.*
- What did I do **before** I touched my chair? (Signal.) *Touched the floor.*
- Yes, I touched the floor.
4. Say the whole thing about what I did before I touched my chair. Get ready. (Signal.) *You touched the floor.*
- What am I doing now? (Signal.) *Touching your chair.*
- Say the whole thing about what I am doing. Get ready. (Signal.) *You are touching your chair.*

EXERCISE 2 Calendar Facts

1. How many months are in a year? (Signal.) *12.*
- Say the fact. Get ready. (Signal.) *There are 12 months in a year.*
- How many seasons are in a year? (Signal.) *Four.*
- Say the fact. Get ready. (Signal.) *There are four seasons in a year.*
- How many days are in a year? (Signal.) *365.*
- Say the fact. Get ready. (Signal.) *There are 365 days in a year.*
- How many weeks are in a year? (Signal.) *52.*
- Everybody, say that fact. Get ready. (Signal.) *There are 52 weeks in a year.*
2. Say the seasons of the year. Get ready. (Signal.) *Winter, spring, summer, fall.*
- Say the months of the year. Get ready. (Signal.) *January, February, March, April, May, June, July, August, September, October, November, December.*

EXERCISE 3   Classification

1. We're going to talk about classes.
2. Tell me which class has more kinds of things in it, the class of bananas or the class of food. Get ready. (Signal.) *The class of food.*
   - So which class is bigger, the class of food or the class of bananas? (Signal.) *The class of food.*
3. Tell me which class has more kinds of things in it, the class of dogs or the class of animals. Get ready. (Signal.) *The class of animals.*
   - So which class is bigger, the class of dogs or the class of animals? (Signal.) *The class of animals.*
4. Tell me which class has more kinds of things in it, the class of boats or the class of vehicles. Get ready. (Signal.) *The class of vehicles.*
   - So which class is bigger, the class of vehicles or the class of boats? (Signal.) *The class of vehicles.*
5. Tell me which class has more kinds of things in it, the class of cups or the class of containers. Get ready. (Signal.) *The class of containers.*
   - So which class is bigger, the class of cups or the class of containers? (Signal.) *The class of containers.*
6. Suppose we took away all cups from the class of containers. Name some containers that would be left. (Call on individual children. Accept appropriate responses.)
   - Yes, there are many kinds of things in the class of containers.
7. (Repeat steps 2 through 6 until firm.)

EXERCISE 4   Opposites

1. You learned new opposites.
   - What's the opposite of slow? (Signal.) *Fast.*
   - What's the opposite of wide? (Signal.) *Narrow.*
   - What's the opposite of quiet? (Signal.) *Noisy.*
   - What's the opposite of noisy? (Signal.) *Quiet.*
2. I'll tell you about a new pair of opposites.
   - Listen: The opposite of difficult is easy.
   - What's the opposite of difficult? (Signal.) *Easy.*
   - What's the opposite of easy? (Signal.) *Difficult.*
   - Listen: The opposite of winning is losing.
   - What's the opposite of winning? (Signal.) *Losing.*
   - What's the opposite of losing? (Signal.) *Winning.*
3. Get ready to tell me about opposites.
   - I'm thinking of a problem that is the opposite of difficult. So what do you know about it? (Signal.) *It's easy.*
   - I'm thinking of a trick that is the opposite of easy. So what do you know about it? (Signal.) *It's difficult.*
4. I'll say sentences. You'll say the sentences that mean the opposite.
5. Listen: The birds were quiet. Everybody, say that sentence. Get ready. (Signal.) *The birds were quiet.*
   - Say the sentence that means the opposite. Get ready. (Signal.) *The birds were noisy.*
6. (Repeat step 5 until firm.)
7. New sentence: The road was narrow. Say that sentence. Get ready. (Signal.) *The road was narrow.*
   - Say the sentence that means the opposite. Get ready. (Signal.) *The road was wide.*
   - New sentence: The bike ride was easy. Say that sentence. Get ready. (Signal.) *The bike ride was easy.*
   - Say the sentence that means the opposite. Get ready. (Signal.) *The bike ride was difficult.*
   - New sentence: The children were awake. Say that sentence. Get ready. (Signal.) *The children were awake.*
   - Say the sentence that means the opposite. Get ready. (Signal.) *The children were asleep.*
   - New sentence: Their team was winning. Say that sentence. Get ready. (Signal.) *Their team was winning.*
   - Say the sentence that means the opposite. Get ready. (Signal.) *Their team was losing.*
8. (Repeat step 7 until firm.)

EXERCISE 5   Sequence

1. Listen:
   - First, Don went to the cupboard.
   - Then, Don got a can of soup.
   - Last, Don opened the can.

2. Listen again.
- First, Don went to the cupboard.
- Then, Don got a can of soup.
- Last, Don opened the can.
3. What did Don do first? (Signal.) *Went to the cupboard.*
- What did Don do next? (Signal.) *Got a can of soup.*
- What did Don do last? (Signal.) *Opened the can.*
4. (Repeat step 3 until firm.)
5. Listen: What did Don do just before he opened the can? (Signal.) *Got a can of soup.*
- What did Don do just before he got the can from the cupboard? (Signal.) *He went to the cupboard.*
6. (Repeat step 5 until firm.)

EXERCISE 6   Only

1. I'm going to make statements. Each statement is going to be true of only a bed or only a dresser or both a bed **and** a dresser.
2. Listen: It has drawers in it. Say that statement. Get ready. (Signal.) *It has drawers in it.*
- Tell me what that statement is true of. Get ready. (Signal.) *Only a dresser.*
3. Listen: You see it in a bedroom. Say that statement. Get ready. (Signal.) *You see it in a bedroom.*
- Tell me what that statement is true of. Get ready. (Signal.) *Both a bed and a dresser.*
4. Listen: It has sheets on it. Say that statement. Get ready. (Signal.) *It has sheets on it.*
- Tell me what that statement is true of. Get ready. (Signal.) *Only a bed.*
5. Your turn. Make up a statement that is true of **only** a bed. (Call on individual children. Have the group repeat each reasonable statement. Then ask:) What is that statement true of? (Signal.) *Only a bed.*
6. Your turn. Make up a statement that is true of **only** a dresser. (Call on individual children. Have the group repeat each reasonable statement. Then ask:) What is that statement true of? (Signal.) *Only a dresser.*
7. Your turn. Make up a statement that is true of **both** a bed and a dresser. (Call on individual children. Have the group repeat each reasonable statement. Then ask:) What is that statement true of? (Signal.) *Both a bed and a dresser.*

EXERCISE 7   Calendar

1. (Present calendar.)
- Listen: First, you'll tell me about the days of the week. Then you'll tell me about the dates.
2. Tell me the day of the week it was yesterday. Get ready. (Signal.)
- Tell me the day of the week it is today. Get ready. (Signal.)
- Listen: Tell me the day of the week it will be tomorrow. Get ready. (Signal.)
3. Now the dates.
- Tell me yesterday's date. Get ready. (Signal.)
- Tell me today's date. Get ready. (Signal.)
- Tell me tomorrow's date. Get ready. (Signal.)
4. (Repeat steps 2 and 3 until firm.)

EXERCISE 8   Sequence Story

Clarabelle And The Bus

1. Everybody, open your workbook to Lesson 29. ✔
- This picture shows another story about Clarabelle. I wonder what Clarabelle is up to in this story. Listen:

Clarabelle watched the children on the farm go to school every day. One day, Clarabelle said, "I'd love to be a student and go to school."

So that's what she decided to do.

It was raining on the morning that she decided to go to school. So she just did what the other children did.

2. Everybody, touch number 1. ✔
- That's the first thing the children did, so that was the first thing Clarabelle did. She put on a yellow raincoat and rain hat.
- Everybody, touch number 2. ✔
- That's a big basket of apples.

After the children put on their yellow raincoats and hats, they went to the basket of apples and each took an apple for their teachers.

So Clarabelle did that too. After she put on her raincoat and hat, she picked a big red apple from the basket.

3. Everybody, touch number 3. ✔
- Where are the children at number 3? (Call on a child. Idea: On the path by the mailbox.)

The children were waiting for the bus by the mailbox. So that's where Clarabelle went after she got her apple. She got in line with the children.

4. Everybody, touch number 4. ✔
- That's where the children get on the school bus. The bus stops right in front of the mailbox and everybody goes in the front door. That's just what Clarabelle did at number 4.

She followed the children and walked in the front door of the bus.

5. Everybody, touch number 5. ✔
- That's where the **back** of the bus is when it stops. That's where the children went, so that's where Clarabelle went after she walked in the front door of the bus.

But something very strange happened to the bus when Clarabelle sat down in the back seat.

- You'll never guess what happened. Does anyone want to take a guess? (Call on a child. Accept reasonable responses.)
6. Everybody, turn your workbook upside-down and you'll see a picture that shows what the bus looked like when Clarabelle sat in the back seat. ✔

Clarabelle was so heavy that the back of the bus went down to the ground and the front wheels went way up in the air.

- And what do you suppose all the children on the bus said to Clarabelle? (Call on a child. Idea: *Get off our bus.*)
- Clarabelle finally got off the bus.
7. Everybody, touch number 6. ✔
- That's where Clarabelle was after she got off the bus. She was crying when she was at number 6. But she wasn't saying "Boo-hoo." What do you think she was saying? (Signal.) *Boo-moo.*
8. Everybody, look at the big picture. ✔
- Remember, the numbers in the story tell what Clarabelle did first, what she did next and so forth. Who can touch the numbers and tell all the things that happened in the story? It's tough because you can't see the bus. Remember, number 4 is the front of the bus. That's where the children and Clarabelle got **on** the bus. Number 5 is where Clarabelle sat down. Who can tell the story? Remember to start out by telling what the children did, then what Clarabelle did.
9. (Call on a child:) You tell the story. Everybody else, follow along and see if (child's name) tells what happened for each number. (Praise child for a story that tells the sequence of things that the children did and that Clarabelle did.)
10. (Repeat step 9, calling on another child.)
11. Before you color the big picture, you're going to cut out the picture of the bus and put it where it belongs in the big picture. Use your scissors and carefully cut along the dotted lines. Then put the bus where it belongs in the big picture. Remember, it goes right where the numbers 4 and 5 are. Later you'll color the picture.

EXERCISE 9   Questioning Skills

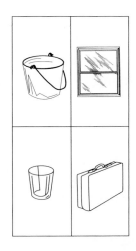 

1. Find the next page in your workbook. ✔
- (Hold up workbook. Point to first half.)
2. I'm thinking about one of the pictures. It's either a pail, a window, a glass, or a suitcase. You'll ask questions to find out which object I'm thinking of.
- Everybody, ask a question about what material it is made of. Get ready. (Signal.) *What material is it made of?*
- Everybody, ask a question about what class it is in. Get ready. (Signal.) *What class is it in?*
- Everybody, ask a question about what you use it for. Get ready. (Signal.) *What do you use it for?*
3. Let's ask those questions again.
4. Everybody, ask a question about what material it is made of. Get ready. (Signal.) *What material is it made of?*
- Everybody, ask a question about what class it is in. Get ready. (Signal.) *What class is it in?*
- Everybody, ask a question about what you use it for. Get ready. (Signal.) *What do you use it for?*
5. (Repeat step 4 until firm.)
6. Ask those questions again, and I'll tell you the answers.
- Everybody, ask the question about what material it is made of. Get ready. (Signal.) *What material is it made of?*
- Here's the answer. It's made of glass. What material is it made of? (Signal.) *Glass.*

7. Everybody, ask a question about what class it is in. Get ready. (Signal.) *What class is it in?*
- Here's the answer. It's in the class of containers. What class? (Signal.) *The class of containers.*
8. Everybody, ask a question about what you use it for. Get ready. (Signal.) *What do you use it for?*
- Here's the answer. To drink out of. What do you use it for? (Signal.) *To drink out of.*
9. Make a blue mark on the thing I'm thinking of. ✔
- Everybody, what object was I thinking of? (Signal.) *A glass.*
- How did you know I wasn't thinking of a pail? (Call on a child. Accept reasonable responses.)
- How did you know I wasn't thinking of a window? (Call on a child. Accept reasonable responses.)
- How did you know I wasn't thinking of a suitcase? (Call on a child. Accept reasonable responses.)

EXERCISE 10   Classification

1. (Hold up workbook. Point to second half.)
- The box shows two pictures. **Some** of the buildings in one picture are houses. **All** of the buildings in the other picture are houses.
2. Touch the picture where **some** of the buildings are houses. ✔
- Here's the rule about the picture where **some** of the buildings are houses. The houses should be orange. What's the rule? (Signal.) *The houses should be orange.*
- Fix up the picture where **some** of the buildings are houses. ✔
3. Here's the rule about the picture where **all** of the buildings are houses. The houses should be blue or black. What's the rule? (Signal.) *The houses should be blue or black.*
- Make a blue mark on one house and a black mark on another house. ✔

LESSON 30

Objectives

- Follow directions for and discriminate between same and different actions. (Exercise 1)
- Identify the material of a common object. (Exercise 2)
- Name common opposites and answer questions by generating sentences using opposites. (Exercise 3)
- Given a calendar, identify the day and date for "today" and "tomorrow" and **one week from today.** (Exercise 4)
- Given two classes, identify which class is biggest, describe why and name members of the biggest class. (Exercise 5)
- Ask questions involving "class," "parts" and "location" to figure out a "mystery" object. (Exercise 6)
- Listen to a familiar story **and answer questions regarding story sequence.** (Exercise 7)
- Ask questions involving "location," "use" and "materials" to figure out a "mystery" object. (Exercise 8)
- Follow coloring rules involving parts of a whole. (Exercise 9)

EXERCISE 1 Actions

1. Here's an action game.
2. Watch me. (Stand up.)
- What am I doing? (Signal.) *Standing up.*
3. My turn. Can I sit down? Sure, I can sit down if I want to. Can I fly across the room? No, I can't fly across the room if I want to.
- Your turn. Can I sit down? (Signal.) *Yes.*
- Can I fly across the room? (Signal.) *No.*
4. Listen carefully. Are you standing up? (Signal.) *No.*
- Say the whole thing. Get ready. (Signal.) *I am not standing up.*
- Can you stand up? (Signal.) *Yes.*
- Say the whole thing. Get ready. (Signal.) *I can stand up.*
- Everybody, stand up. Get ready. (Signal.) ✔
- What are you doing? (Signal.) *Standing up.*
- Say the whole thing. Get ready. (Signal.) *I am standing up.*
- Can you stand up? (Signal.) *Yes.*
- Say the whole thing. Get ready. (Signal.) *I can stand up.*
- Everybody, sit down. ✔
5. (Repeat step 4 until firm. Then say:) Good for you.

6. Here's the next game.
7. Everybody, smile. (Signal.) ✔
- Good. Stop smiling. ✔
8. Now tell me if I do the same thing you did or something different.
- Watch me. (Smile.) Did I do the same thing or something different? (Signal.) *The same thing.*
- Watch me. (Frown.) Did I do the same thing or something different? (Signal.) *Something different.*
- (Sit down.) Watch me. (Stand up.) Did I do the same thing or something different? (Signal.) *Something different.*
9. (Repeat steps 7 and 8 until firm.)

EXERCISE 2   Materials

1. Some things are made of wood. Some things are made of glass. Some things are made of cloth.
2. I'll name things. You tell me what material the things are made of.
- Listen: a shirt. What object? (Signal.) *A shirt.*
  What material is that object made of? (Signal.) *Cloth.*
- Listen: a window. What object? (Signal.) *A window.*
  What material is that object made of? (Signal.) *Glass.*
- Listen: a dresser. What object? (Signal.) *A dresser.*
  What material is that object made of? (Signal.) *Wood.*
- Listen: a rowboat. What object? (Signal.) *A rowboat.*
  What material is that object made of? (Signal.) *Wood.*
- Listen: a pencil. What object? (Signal.) *A pencil.*
  What material is that object made of? (Signal.) *Wood.*
- Listen: a handkerchief. What object? (Signal.) *A handkerchief.*
  What material is that object made of? (Signal.) *Cloth.*
- Listen: a bottle. What object? (Signal.) *A bottle.*
  What material is that object made of? (Signal.) *Glass.*
- Listen: a jar. What object? (Signal.) *A jar.*
  What material is that object made of? (Signal.) *Glass.*
3. (Repeat step 2 until firm.)

EXERCISE 3   Opposites

1. We're going to play a word game.
2. Everybody, think of a rabbit that is not winning. It is doing the opposite of winning. What's it doing? (Signal.) *Losing.*
- So a rabbit that is doing the opposite of winning is . . . (Signal.) *losing.*
3. Everybody, think of a chalkboard that is the opposite of wide. What's the opposite of wide? (Signal.) *Narrow.*
- So a chalkboard that is the opposite of wide is . . . (Signal.) *narrow.*
4. Everybody, think of a table that is the opposite of small. What's the opposite of small? (Signal.) *Big.*
- So a table that is the opposite of small is . . . (Signal.) *big.*
5. Everybody, think of a lion that is the opposite of noisy. What's the opposite of noisy? (Signal.) *Quiet.*
- So a lion that is the opposite of noisy is . . . (Signal.) *quiet.*
6. Everybody, think of a man who is the opposite of short. What's the opposite of short? (Signal.) *Tall.*
- So a man who is the opposite of short is . . . (Signal.) *tall.*
7. (Repeat steps 2 through 6 until firm.)

EXERCISE 4   Calendar

1. (Present calendar.)
- We're going to talk about today, tomorrow, and one week from today.
2. Tell me the day of the week it is today. Get ready. (Signal.)
- Tell me the day of the week it will be tomorrow. Get ready. (Signal.)
- One week from today, it will be the same day it is today. What day is that? (Signal.)
- I'll show you that day on the calendar. **(Touch calendar number that is one week from today.)**
3. Once more. Tell me the day of the week it is today. Get ready. (Signal.)
- Tell me the day of the week it will be tomorrow. Get ready. (Signal.)
- Tell me the day of the week it will be one week from today. Get ready. (Signal.)
4. Tell me tomorrow's date. Get ready. (Signal.)
- Tell me the date it will be one week from today. Get ready. (Signal.)
5. (Repeat steps 2 through 4 until firm.)

EXERCISE 5   Classification

1. We're going to talk about classes.
2. Everybody, tell me which class is bigger, the class of birds or the class of animals. Get ready. (Signal.) *The class of animals.*
- Tell me how you know. Get ready. (Signal.) *The class of animals has more kinds of things in it.*
3. Tell me which class is bigger, the class of containers or the class of bags. Get ready. (Signal.) *The class of containers.*
- Tell me how you know. Get ready. (Signal.) *The class of containers has more kinds of things in it.*
4. Which class is bigger, the class of food or the class of beans? (Signal.) *The class of food.*
- How do you know? (Signal.) *The class of food has more kinds of things in it.*
5. Suppose we took away all beans from the class of food. Name some food that would be left. (Call on individual children. Accept appropriate responses.)
- Yes, there are many kinds of things in the class of food.
6. (Repeat steps 2 through 5 until firm.)

EXERCISE 6   Questioning Skills

1. I'm thinking of an object. You'll ask questions to figure out what that object is. You'll ask these questions:
- What class is it in?
- What parts does it have?
- Where do you find it?
2. Everybody, say all three questions.
- Question 1. Get ready. (Signal.) *What class is it in?*
- Question 2. Get ready. (Signal.) *What parts does it have?*
- Question 3. Get ready. (Signal.) *Where do you find it?*
3. Ask question 1. Get ready. (Signal.) *What class is it in?*
- It's in the class of animals.
4. Ask question 2. Get ready. (Signal.) *What parts does it have?*
- It has fins and teeth.
5. Ask question 3. Get ready. (Signal.) *Where do you find it?*
- You usually find it in the ocean.

6. I'll name some objects. You tell me if each object is one I could be thinking of.
- Listen: killer whale. Could I have been thinking of that object? (Signal.) *Yes.*
- Listen: monkey. Could I have been thinking of that object? (Signal.) *No.*
- Listen: shark. Could I have been thinking of that object? (Signal.) *Yes.*
- Listen: dog. Could I have been thinking of that object? (Signal.) *No.*
7. Name an object I could have been thinking of. (Call on individual children. Accept reasonable responses.)

EXERCISE 7   Clarabelle And The Bluebirds
Review

- Everybody, let's see how well you remember the story about Clarabelle. I'll stop when I'm reading. See if you can tell me what happens next in the story.

Clarabelle looked like the other brown-and-white cows on the farm. But Clarabelle was really different. She was always trying to do things that other animals did. In fact, she felt sad about not being a bird or a frog or a child.

One day, Clarabelle was looking at the bluebirds that were sitting on a wire that went from the barn to a large pole.

- Do you remember what Clarabelle wanted to do? (Call on a child. Idea: *Sit on the wire with the bluebirds.*)

Clarabelle said, "I would love to sit on that wire with those bluebirds."

Some of the other cows heard Clarabelle talking to herself, and they said, "Don't do it, Clarabelle. Remember what happened when you tried to swim like a duck in the duck pond?"

- What happened when she tried to swim like a duck in the pond? (Call on a child. Idea: *All the water jumped out of the pond.*)

"Yeah," another cow said. "When you jumped in the pond, all the water jumped **out** of the pond."

Another cow said to Clarabelle, "And what about the time you tried to crow like the roosters?"

- How good was Clarabelle at crowing like a rooster? (Call on a child. Idea: *Not very good.*)
- Everybody, what did the roosters say? (Signal.) *Cock-a-doodle-doo.*
- And what did Clarabelle say? (Signal.) *Cock-a-doodle-moo.*

"Ho, ho, ho." All the cows laughed until they had tears in their eyes.

"That's not very funny," Clarabelle said. "And if I want to sit on the wire with those bluebirds, you can't stop me."

- So how did Clarabelle get on the wire? (Call on a child. Idea: *She went into the barn and up to the window by the wire. Then she tiptoed out on the wire.*)

So Clarabelle went into the barn and up to the window by the wire. While she was getting ready, all the farm animals gathered around. One goat said, "We're in for another great show by Clarabelle."

And so they were. Clarabelle tiptoed out on the wire.

- Everybody, did the wire break when Clarabelle went out on it? (Signal.) *No.*
- What did the wire do? (Call on a child. Idea: *Bent down almost to the ground.*)
- Why did the wire bend down so far? (Call on a child. Idea: *Because Clarabelle was so heavy.*)

Clarabelle was heavier than one thousand bluebirds, so the wire went down, lower and lower, until it was almost touching the ground.

- How did the bluebirds feel about Clarabelle being on their wire? (Call on a child. Idea: *Really angry.*)
- What kind of things did the bluebirds say? (Call on a child. Idea: *Get off our wire.*)

Yes, the bluebirds were really angry. One of them said, "What are you doing, you big, fat cow? You've bent our wire almost to the ground."

"Yeah," another bluebird said. "This wire is for bluebirds, not brown-and-white cows."

Meanwhile, the farm animals were laughing and howling and rolling around on the ground. "Look at that," they said, and rolled and laughed some more.

Clarabelle was not happy. She said, "This wire is not as much fun as I thought it would be." Clarabelle looked back up at the barn.

- Everybody, did Clarabelle then tiptoe back up to the window? (Signal.) *No.*
- Why not? (Call on a child. Idea: *Because it would be too hard to walk all the way back up to the window.*)
- How did Clarabelle decide to get off the wire? (Call on a child. Idea: *By jumping off and landing in the haystack.*)

Clarabelle looked back up at the barn and said, "Wow, it's going to be hard to walk all the way back up there."

Then Clarabelle looked down and said, "I'm close to the ground, so maybe it would be easier for me to jump off and land in that haystack."

While she was trying to figure out what to do, all the bluebirds were yelling at her and saying things like, "Well, do something. Get off our wire so we can sit in peace!"

"All right, all right," Clarabelle said. "I'm leaving. Right now."

And with that, she jumped off the wire.

- What did the wire do when Clarabelle jumped off? (Call on a child. Idea: *Sprang way up into the air.*)
- What happened to the birds when the wire sprang up? (Call on a child. Idea: *They were sent way up into the clouds.*)
- That's correct.

When Clarabelle jumped off the wire, the wire sprang way up into the air. It shot up so fast that it sent the bluebirds way up into the clouds, leaving blue tail feathers fluttering this way and that way.

And the farm animals almost died from laughter. "Did you see that?" a horse said as he rolled around on the ground. "Did you see those birds go flying up to the clouds?"

- Everybody, who was the only farm animal who was not laughing? (Signal.) *Clarabelle.*

Everybody laughed except for a bunch of bluebirds and for one brown-and-white cow. That cow pouted and kept saying, "It's not **funny.** It's not funny."

- But was it funny? (Signal.) *Yes.*

EXERCISE 8   Questioning Skills

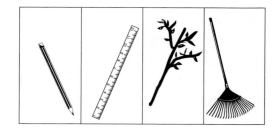

1. Everybody, open your workbook to Lesson 30. Write your name at the top of the page. ✔
2. (Hold up workbook. Point to boxed pictures.)
- I'm thinking about one of the pictures. It's either a pencil, a ruler, a branch, or a rake. You'll ask questions to find out which object I'm thinking of.
- Everybody, ask a question about what material it is made of. Get ready. (Signal.) *What material is it made of?*
- Everybody, ask a question about where you find it. Get ready. (Signal.) *Where do you find it?*
- Everybody, ask a question about what you use it for. Get ready. (Signal.) *What do you use it for?*
3. Let's ask those questions again.
4. Everybody, ask a question about what material it is made of. Get ready. (Signal.) *What material is it made of?*
- Everybody, ask a question about where you find it. Get ready. (Signal.) *Where do you find it?*
- Everybody, ask a question about what you use it for. Get ready. (Signal.) *What do you use it for?*
5. (Repeat step 4 until firm.)

6. Ask those questions again, and I'll tell you the answers.
- Everybody, ask a question about what material it is made of. Get ready. (Signal.) *What material is it made of?*
- Here's the answer. It's made of wood, metal, or plastic. What material is it made of? (Signal.) *Wood, metal, or plastic.*

7. Everybody, ask the question about where you find it. Get ready. (Signal.) *Where do you find it?*
- Here's the answer. You could find it in a desk. Where could you find it? (Signal.) *In a desk.*

8. Everybody, ask the question about what you use it for. Get ready. (Signal.) *What do you use it for?*
- Here's the answer. To measure things. What is it used for? (Signal.) *To measure things.*

9. Make a yellow mark on the thing I'm thinking of. ✔
- Everybody, what object was I thinking of? (Signal.) *A ruler.*
- How did you know I wasn't thinking of a pencil? (Call on a child. Accept reasonable responses.)
- How did you know I wasn't thinking of a branch? (Call on a child. Accept reasonable responses.)
- How did you know I wasn't thinking of a rake? (Call on a child. Accept reasonable responses.)

EXERCISE 9 Part—whole

1. (Hold up workbook. Point to second half.) Here's the coloring rule for the sailboat. Listen: Color the sail red. What's the rule? (Signal.) *Color the sail red.*
- Mark the sail. ✔

2. Here's another coloring rule for the sailboat. Listen: Color the hull blue. What's the rule? (Signal.) *Color the hull blue.*
- Mark the hull. ✔

3. Part of the sailboat is missing. What part is missing? (Signal.) *The mast.*
- Yes, the mast. Before you color the sailboat, you're going to follow the dots with your pencil to make the mast.

4. Here's the coloring rule for the mast. Listen: Color the mast orange. What's the rule? (Signal.) *Color the mast orange.*
- Mark the mast. ✔

Objectives

- Given two classes, identify which class is biggest and describe why. (Exercise 1)
- Name common opposites. (Exercise 2)
- Given a calendar, identify the day and date for "today" and "tomorrow" and one week from today. (Exercise 3)
- Given a complex sentence, answer questions involving "who," "why," "when" and "what." (Exercise 4)
- Given a common noun, name the class. (Exercise 5)
- Answer questions about a familiar story. (Exercise 6)
- **Given a picture from a familiar story, answer literal, inferential and sequence questions and make the picture consistent with the story.** (Exercise 7)
- Ask questions involving "materials," "parts" and "class" to figure out a "mystery" object. (Exercise 8)
- Follow coloring rules involving parts of a whole. (Exercise 9)

EXERCISE 1   Classification

1. We're going to talk about classes.
2. Tell me which class is bigger, the class of pants or the class of clothing. Get ready. (Signal.) *The class of clothing.*
- Tell me how you know. Get ready. (Signal.) *The class of clothing has more kinds of things in it.*
3. (Repeat step 2 until firm.)
4. Tell me which class is bigger, the class of saws or the class of tools. Get ready. (Signal.) *The class of tools.*
- How do you know? (Signal.) *The class of tools has more kinds of things in it.*
5. (Repeat step 4 until firm.)
6. Tell me which class is bigger, the class of animals or the class of horses. Get ready. (Signal.) *The class of animals.*
- How do you know? (Signal.) *The class of animals has more kinds of things in it.*
7. (Repeat step 6 until firm.)

EXERCISE 2   Opposites

1. We're going to play a word game.
2. Everybody, think of a girl who is not winning. She is doing the opposite of winning. What's the opposite of winning? (Signal.) *Losing.*
- So a girl who is doing the opposite of winning is . . . (Signal.) *losing.*
3. Everybody, think of a child who is not noisy. He is the opposite of noisy. What's the opposite of noisy? (Signal.) *Quiet.*
- So a child who is the opposite of noisy is . . . (Signal.) *quiet.*
4. Everybody, think of a cat that is not young. It is the opposite of young. What's the opposite of young? (Signal.) *Old.*
- So a cat that is the opposite of young is . . . (Signal.) *old.*
5. Everybody, think of a man who is not fat. He is the opposite of fat. What's the opposite of fat? (Signal.) *Skinny.*
- So a man who is the opposite of fat is . . . (Signal.) *skinny.*
6. Everybody, think of a rug that is not wide. It is the opposite of wide. What's the opposite of wide? (Signal.) *Narrow.*
- So a rug that is the opposite of wide is . . . (Signal.) *narrow.*
7. (Repeat steps 2 through 6 until firm.)

EXERCISE 3   Calendar

1. (Present calendar.)
• We're going to talk about today, tomorrow, and one week from today.
2. Tell me the day of the week it is today. Get ready. (Signal.)
• Tell me the day of the week it will be tomorrow. Get ready. (Signal.)
• Tell me the day of the week it will be one week from today. Get ready. (Signal.)
3. (Repeat step 2 until firm.)
4. Now the dates.
• Tell me today's date. Get ready. (Signal.)
• (Touch number for today's date.) Here's today's date. Now I'll show you the date that is one week from today.
• (Touch number that is one week from today.) Everybody, say the date that is one week from today. Get ready. (Signal.)
5. Once more.
• Listen: Tell me today's date. Get ready. (Signal.)
• Tell me tomorrow's date. Get ready. (Signal.)
• Tell me the date it will be one week from today. Get ready. (Signal.)
6. (Repeat step 5 until firm.)

EXERCISE 4   Who—When—What—Why

1. I'm going to say a sentence that answers a lot of questions. One of the questions is why.
• Listen: Yesterday, the baby cried because she had a rash.
• Listen again: Yesterday, the baby cried because she had a rash.
• Your turn. Say the sentence. Get ready. (Signal.) *Yesterday, the baby cried because she had a rash.*
2. That sentence has words that tell why. Everybody, why did the baby cry? (Signal.) *Because she had a rash.*
3. Listen: Yesterday, the baby cried because she had a rash.
• Who cried? (Signal.) *The baby.*
• When did the baby cry? (Signal.) *Yesterday.*
• What did the baby do? (Signal.) *Cried.*
• Why did the baby cry? (Signal.) *Because she had a rash.*
4. (Repeat step 3 until firm.)

5. Everybody, say the whole sentence. Get ready. (Signal.) *Yesterday, the baby cried because she had a rash.*
• Which words tell who cried? (Signal.) *The baby.*
• Which word tells when? (Signal.) *Yesterday.*
• Which words tell why? (Signal.) *Because she had a rash.*
6. (Repeat step 5 until firm.)

EXERCISE 5   Classification

1. Listen: fruits and vegetables and trees and grass are in the class of plants. What's the big class name for fruits and vegetables and trees and grass? (Signal.) *Plants.*
• Listen: Another large class has cows and bugs and many other living things that move. That's the class of animals.
2. I'll name some things that are either plants or animals. You tell me the class they're in.
• Listen: dogs. What class? (Signal.) *Animals.*
• Listen: carrots. What class? (Signal.) *Plants.*
• Listen: grass. What class? (Signal.) *Plants.*
• Listen: rabbits. What class? (Signal.) *Animals.*
• Listen: butterflies. What class? (Signal.) *Animals.*
• Listen: trees. What class? (Signal.) *Plants.*
• Listen: turkeys. What class? (Signal.) *Animals.*
3. Who can name some plants we haven't named? (Call on a child. Praise appropriate responses.)
• Who can name some animals we haven't named? (Call on a child. Praise appropriate responses.)

EXERCISE 6   Honey, Andrea And Sweetie

Story Review

- Everybody, I'm going to read you the story about Honey, Andrea and Sweetie again.

There once was the meanest-looking bulldog you ever saw. She always had a big frown on her face and her lower teeth stuck out. That made her look like she was ready to fight with anybody.

People were always surprised to find out . . . something.

- What surprised people about this bulldog? (Call on a child. Idea: *That she was named Honey.*)
- Why were people surprised that Honey was so sweet? (Call on a child. Idea: *Because she looked so mean.*)

Yes, people were always surprised to find out that this bulldog's name was Honey. The family that owned her gave her that name because she really was as sweet as honey. She loved just about everybody and everything.

- Who can remember some of the things she loved? (Call on a child. Idea: *Other dogs, flowers, butterflies, birds and mice.*)
- Everybody, what was the name of the mouse she loved? (Signal.) *Andrea.*
- What color was that mouse? (Signal.) *Gray.* Let's see if you were right.

Honey loved other dogs. She loved flowers, butterflies and birds. She even loved mice. In fact, she had a favorite mouse—a little gray mouse named Andrea.

Honey would sometimes sniff around the dining room, trying to find Andrea. That's where Andrea lived—behind a little hole in the dining room wall. Sometimes Honey would find Andrea, and sometimes she wouldn't.

- Why would Andrea be hiding sometimes? (Call on a child. Idea: *Because Andrea was very shy.*)
Let's see if you were right.

Sometimes Honey would find Andrea and sometimes she wouldn't, because Andrea was very, very shy.

There was only one thing that Honey didn't like.

- Who remembers the one thing that Honey did not like? (Call on a child. Idea: *Cats, especially cats that chased birds, butterflies and mice.*)

Yes, there was only one thing that Honey didn't like, and that was cats, especially cats that chased birds and butterflies and cats that tried to catch mice.

- Why do you think Honey disliked those kinds of cats? (Call on a child. Idea: *Because Honey liked birds, butterflies and mice.*)

Well, one day Honey was sprawled out on the back porch of her house when a woman came to visit and that woman had a big yellow cat with her. (We all know who **that** cat was.)

When Honey looked at the cat, she said to herself, "Ugh. I hope that thing doesn't stay around here very long."

The woman and the cat went inside, and after a while, Honey got up and stretched and waddled into the kitchen. The woman was sitting at the table, but where was the cat?

- Who remembers where that cat was? (Call on a child. Idea: *In the dining room.*)
- And what was Sweetie doing in the dining room? (Call on a child. Idea: *Chasing Andrea.*)

Honey found out where that cat was a moment later. She heard sounds of scurrying and running around in the dining room. So she got up and trotted over to the doorway of the dining room.

What Honey saw made her very, very mad. There was poor little Andrea running for her life.

- And where was Sweetie? (Call on a child. Idea: *Right behind Andrea.*)

Yes, Sweetie was right behind Andrea, running as fast as he could. The cat and the mouse shot around the room, this way and that way—under the table, across the rug, into the living room and back into the dining room. And all this time, that cat was less than one leap behind Andrea.

The woman who came over with the cat was shouting, "Sweetie, stop chasing that little mouse."

- Everybody, did Sweetie stop when the woman told him to? (Signal.) *No.*
- Did Andrea stop? (Signal.) *No.*
 If I were Andrea, I wouldn't stop either, with that big Sweetie right behind me.

Sweetie didn't stop. Neither did Andrea.

Well, just about the time that Honey decided to take care of this cat, Sweetie and Andrea flew under the table.

- Who remembers what happened under the table? (Call on a child. Idea: *Sweetie got caught on the tablecloth and pulled it off. He got tangled up.*)

Sweetie got caught on the tablecloth and pulled it off the table. When Sweetie tried to get untangled, he just got more and more wrapped up in the tablecloth. He wiggled and squirmed and rolled around, but he was all wrapped up in the tablecloth. Only two parts of Sweetie were sticking out. His yellow tail was sticking out of one end of the tablecloth and his whiskers were sticking out of the other end.

Well, while Sweetie was squirming around trying to get free, Honey waddled over and did something.

- What did she do? (Call on a child. Idea: *Gave Sweetie's tail a little nip.*)
- Everybody, did Honey give Sweetie's tail a **great huge** bite? (Signal.) *No.*

- What was Andrea doing while all this was going on? (Call on a child. Idea: *Going into her mouse hole.*)

Well, while Sweetie was squirming around trying to get free, Honey waddled over and gave Sweetie's tail a little nip—not a great bite, but something hard enough to get Sweetie's attention.

"There," Honey said and waddled back to the kitchen, as Sweetie yowled and hissed and rolled around inside that tablecloth.

Finally, Sweetie got free. He looked around the room but he didn't see Andrea.

- Why didn't Sweetie see Andrea? (Call on a child. Idea: *Because she was in the mouse hole.*)
- Why didn't Sweetie see Honey? (Call on a child. Idea: *Because she was in the kitchen.*)
- Here's where Sweetie gets confused again. What did Sweetie **think** happened? (Call on a child. Idea: *That Andrea bit his tail.*)
- Why didn't Sweetie know that **Honey** bit his tail? (Call on a child. Idea: *Because Sweetie was tangled up when Honey bit Sweetie's tail.*)

So Sweetie shook his head and said to himself . . .

- What did he say? (Call on a child. Idea: *That mouse looked like a frail little thing, but let me tell you: that mouse can really bite.*)

Yes, Sweetie shook his head and said to himself, "Gosh, that mouse looked like a frail little thing, but let me tell you: that mouse can **really** bite."

- That Sweetie is always getting the wrong idea about what happened.

EXERCISE 7 Story Details

1. Everybody, open your workbook to Lesson 31. Write your name at the top of the page. ✔
2. Here's another picture from the story.
- Where is Honey in this picture? (Call on a child. Idea: *Lying on the back porch of the house.*)
- Everybody, does this picture take place **before** or **after** the other picture you did for this story? (Signal.) *Before.*
- Right, this is near the beginning of the story, when Sweetie and the woman who owns Sweetie are coming into the house.
- What is Honey thinking in this picture? (Call on a child. Idea: *She is hoping that cat doesn't stay around long.*)
- What do you think Sweetie is thinking? (Call on a child. Accept reasonable ideas.)
3. You're going to color the picture later. Remember what color Honey is and what color Sweetie is.

EXERCISE 8 Questioning Skills

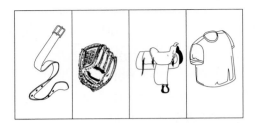

1. Everybody, find the next page in your workbook. ✔
- (Hold up workbook. Point to boxed pictures.)
2. I'm thinking about one of the pictures. It's either a belt, a baseball glove, a saddle, or a T-shirt. You'll ask questions to find out which object I'm thinking of.
- Everybody, ask a question about what material it is made of. Get ready. (Signal.) *What material is it made of?*
- Everybody, ask a question about what class it is in. Get ready. (Signal.) *What class is it in?*
- Everybody, ask a question about what parts it has. Get ready. (Signal.) *What parts does it have?*
3. Let's ask those questions again.
4. Everybody, ask a question about what material it is made of. Get ready. (Signal.) *What material is it made of?*
- Everybody, ask a question about what class is it in. Get ready. (Signal.) *What class is it in?*
- Everybody, ask a question about what parts it has. Get ready. (Signal.) *What parts does it have?*
5. (Repeat step 4 until firm.)

6. Ask those questions again, and I'll tell you the answers.
- Everybody, ask the question about what material it is made of. Get ready. (Signal.) *What material is it made of?*
- Here's the answer. Part of it is leather and part of it is metal. What materials is it made of? (Signal.) *Leather and metal.*
7. Everybody, ask a question about what class is it in. Get ready. (Signal.) *What class is it in?*
- Here's the answer. It is in the class of clothing. What class is it in? (Signal.) *The class of clothing.*
8. Everybody, ask the question about the parts it has. Get ready. (Signal.) *What parts does it have?*
- Here's the answer. It has a buckle and a strap. What parts? (Signal.) *A buckle and a strap.*
9. Make a brown mark on the thing I'm thinking of. ✔
- Everybody, what object was I thinking of? (Signal.) *A belt.*

- How did you know I wasn't thinking of a saddle? (Call on a child. Idea: *A saddle isn't clothing.*)
- How did you know I wasn't thinking of a baseball glove? (Call on a child. Accept reasonable responses.)
- How did you know I wasn't thinking of a T-shirt? (Call on a child. Accept reasonable responses.)

EXERCISE 9   Part—Whole

1. (Hold up workbook. Point to second half.) Here's a coloring rule for the hammer. Listen: Color the head yellow. What's the rule? (Signal.) *Color the head yellow.*
- Mark the head. ✔
2. Part of the hammer is missing. What part is missing? (Signal.) *The handle.*
- Yes, the handle. Before you color the hammer, you're going to follow the dots with your pencil to make the handle.
3. Here's the coloring rule for the handle. Listen: Color the handle black. What's the rule? (Signal.) *Color the handle black.*
- Mark the handle. ✔

LESSON 32

Objectives

- Name classes and subclasses. (Exercise 1)
- Given two classes, identify which class is biggest, describe why and name members of the biggest class. (Exercise 2)
- Given a calendar, identify the day and date for "today" and "tomorrow" and one week from today. (Exercise 3)
- Given a complex sentence, answer questions involving "who," "when" and "why." (Exercise 4)
- Given a common noun, name the class. (Exercise 5)
- Ask questions involving class, material and location to guess a "mystery object." (Exercise 6)
- Relate a familiar story grammar to a picture that indicates the sequence of events for a new story. (Exercise 7)
- **Follow coloring rules involving moving "from" and "to."** (Exercise 8)
- Follow coloring rules involving class. (Exercise 9)

EXERCISE 1   Classification

1. We're going to talk about classes.
2. If we took all cups from the class of containers, would there be any kinds of containers left? (Signal.) *Yes.*
- Name some kinds of containers that would be left. (Call on individual children. Praise appropriate responses.)
3. The class of cups is made of many kinds of cups. I'll name some kinds of cups in the class of cups. Listen: blue cups, red cups, yellow cups.
- You name some kinds of cups in the class of cups. (Call on individual children. Praise reasonable answers, such as: *blue cups, white cups, red cups.*)
4. Think about this. If we took all the yellow cups from the class of cups, would there be any cups left? (Signal.) *Yes.*
- Name some kinds of cups that would be left. (Call on individual children. Praise all acceptable answers: any kind of cup except yellow cups.)
5. Yes, if we took all the yellow cups from the class of cups, there would still be cups left. So which class is bigger, the class of cups or the class of yellow cups? (Signal.) *The class of cups.*
- How do you know? (Signal.) *The class of cups has more kinds of things in it.*
6. Think big. Which class is bigger, the class of containers or the class of cups? (Signal.) *The class of containers.*

- Think big. Which class is bigger, the class of yellow cups or the class of cups? (Signal.) *The class of cups.*

EXERCISE 2   Classification

1. Tell me which class is bigger, the class of containers or the class of drawers. Get ready. (Signal.) *The class of containers.*
- Are all drawers in the class of containers? (Signal.) *Yes.*
- Are there other containers in the class of containers? (Signal.) *Yes.*
- So the class of containers has more kinds of things in it.
2. (Repeat step 1 until firm.)
3. Tell me which class is bigger, the class of schools or the class of buildings. Get ready. (Signal.) *The class of buildings.*
- How do you know? (Signal.) *The class of buildings has more kinds of things in it.*
4. (Repeat step 3 until firm.)
5. Name some things that are in the class of buildings that are not in the class of schools. (Call on individual children. Praise acceptable answers such as: *apartment buildings, churches,* and so on.)
6. Everybody, tell me which class is bigger, the class of vehicles or the class of trucks. Get ready. (Signal.) *The class of vehicles.*
- How do you know? (Signal.) *The class of vehicles has more kinds of things in it.*
7. (Repeat step 6 until firm.)

EXERCISE 3 Calendar

1. (Present calendar.)
- We're going to talk about today, tomorrow, and one week from today.
2. Tell me the day of the week it is today. Get ready. (Signal.)
- Tell me the day of the week it will be tomorrow. Get ready. (Signal.)
- Tell me the day of the week it will be one week from today. Get ready. (Signal.)
3. (Repeat step 2 until firm.)
4. Now the dates.
- Tell me today's date. Get ready. (Signal.)
- (Touch number for today's date.) Here's today's date. Now I'll show you the date that is one week from today.
- (Touch number that is one week from today.) Everybody, say the date that is one week from today. Get ready. (Signal.)
5. Once more.
- Tell me today's date. Get ready. (Signal.)
- Tell me tomorrow's date. Get ready. (Signal.)
- Tell me the date it will be one week from today. Get ready. (Signal.)
6. (Repeat step 5 until firm.)

EXERCISE 4 Who-When-Why

1. I'm going to say a sentence that answers a lot of questions. One of the questions is why.
- Listen: This morning the boys got wet because it rained.
- Your turn. Say the sentence. Get ready. (Signal.) *This morning the boys got wet because it rained.*
2. That sentence has words that tell why. Everybody, why did the boys get wet? (Signal.) *Because it rained.*
3. Listen: This morning the boys got wet because it rained.
- Who got wet? (Signal.) *The boys.*
- When did the boys get wet? (Signal.) *This morning.*
- Why did the boys get wet? (Signal.) *Because it rained.*
4. (Repeat step 3 until firm.)

5. Everybody, say the whole sentence. Get ready. (Signal.) *This morning the boys got wet because it rained.*
- Which words tell who got wet? (Signal.) *The boys.*
- Which words tells when? (Signal.) *This morning.*
- Which words tell why? (Signal.) *Because it rained.*
6. (Repeat step 5 until firm.)

EXERCISE 5 Classification

1. Listen: fruits and vegetables and trees and grass are in a class. What's the class name for fruits and vegetables and trees and grass? (Signal.) *Plants.*
- Listen: Another large class has cows and bugs and other living things that move. What's the name of that class? (Signal.) *Animals.*
2. I'll name some things that are either plants or animals. You tell me the class they're in.
- Listen: fish. What class? (Signal.) *Animals.*
- Listen: mosquitos. What class? (Signal.) *Animals.*
- Listen: bushes. What class? (Signal.) *Plants.*
- Listen: mice. What class? (Signal.) *Animals.*
- Listen: onions. What class? (Signal.) *Plants.*
- Listen: tulips. What class? (Signal.) *Plants.*
- Listen: oak trees. What class? (Signal.) *Plants.*
- Listen: worms. What class? (Signal.) *Animals.*
3. Who can name some plants we haven't named. (Call on a child. Praise appropriate responses.)
- Who can name some animals we haven't named? (Call on a child. Praise appropriate responses.)

EXERCISE 6   Questioning Skills

1. I'm thinking of an object. You'll ask questions to figure out what that object is.
- You'll ask these questions:
- Question 1. What class is it in?
- Question 2. What material is it made of?
- Everybody, say question 2. Get ready. (Signal.) *What material is it made of?*
- Question 3. Where do you find it?
2. Everybody, say all three questions.
Question 1. Get ready. (Signal.) *What class is it in?*
Question 2. Get ready. (Signal.) *What material is it made of?*
Question 3. Get ready. (Signal.) *Where do you find it?*
3. Ask question 1. Get ready. (Signal.) *What class is it in?*
- It's in the class of clothing.
- Ask question 2. Get ready. (Signal.) *What material is it made of?*
- It is usually made of leather.
- Ask question 3. Get ready. (Signal.) *Where do you find it?*
- You usually find it on somebody's foot.
4. Everybody, what object am I thinking of? (Signal.) *A shoe.*
5. I'll name some objects. You tell me if each object is one I could be thinking of.
- Listen: shirt. Could I have been thinking of that object? (Signal.) *No.*
- Why not? (Call on a child. Ideas: *It's not made of leather; you don't wear it on your foot.*)
- Listen: socks. Could I have been thinking of that object? (Signal.) *No.*
- Why not? (Call on a child. Idea: *It's not made of leather.*)
- Listen: gloves. Could I have been thinking of that object? *Signal.) No.*
- Why not? (Call on a child. Idea: *You don't wear it on your foot.*)

EXERCISE 7   Sequence Story

Roger And The Frog

1. Everybody, open your workbook to Lesson 32. Write your name at the top of the page. ✔
2. This picture shows a different story about Roger and his hat. I'll tell the story the right way. Then I'll make mistakes. See if you can find each mistake.

> Roger wanted to take a nap on the grass next to the stream so he took off his hat and put it **next to him.**

3. Everybody, touch number 1. ✔
- That shows where Roger put the hat first.

> Roger didn't know it, but this time there was a **frog** under the hat. While Roger was sleeping, the frog hopped up on the **bench.**

4. Everybody, touch number 2. ✔
- That shows where the hat went after it was next to Roger. Listen:

> Then the frog hopped onto the **log.**

5. Everybody, touch number 3. ✔
- That's where the hat went after it was on the bench.

> Then the frog took a great leap into the **stream.**

6. Everybody, touch number 4. ✔
- That shows where the hat went—right next to that big rock.

The frog went underwater and swam away.

- I don't see that frog in the picture, but I'll bet it's there somewhere if you look hard.
7. Anyhow, Roger's hat floated down the stream to number 5.
- Everybody, touch number 5. ✔

Roger woke up and saw his hat floating down the stream. The hat was still moving and by the time Roger got to it, that hat was already **past** number 5.

8. Listen: Draw an arrow from number 5 to show which way that hat was moving. Raise your hand when you're finished. (Observe children and give feedback.)
- Listen:

When Roger finally reached his hat, it was caught on that **branch** that is in the stream.

9. Raise your hand if your arrow went to that branch. ✔
- Listen: Make a circle by the branch and write the number 6 in that circle. Raise your hand when you're finished. (Observe children and give feedback.)

Well, when Roger finally got his hat from the branch in the stream, he was very confused. He didn't know how his hat got into the stream.

There's an animal in the picture somewhere. And that animal knows how the hat got in the stream. And that's why you might find a great big smile on that animal's face—**if** you can find that animal in the picture.

10. Now I'm going to tell the story the **wrong** way. Follow along. As soon as you hear me make a mistake, don't say anything, just raise your hand. I'm pretty tricky. So you'll have to listen very carefully. Here we go.

Roger went to sleep on a **bench.**

(Praise children who raise their hands.)
- Everybody, where **did** Roger go to sleep? (Signal.) *On the grass.*
11. Let me start over again.

Roger wanted to take a nap on the grass so he took off his hat and put it **next** to him. Roger didn't know it, but there was a **bird** under his hat.

(Praise children who raise their hands.)
- Everybody, what was **really** under Roger's hat? (Signal.) *A frog.*
12. Okay, there was a **frog** under the hat.

The frog hopped onto the log. And . . .

(Praise children who raise their hands.)
- Everybody, where **did** the frog hop? (Signal.) *Onto the bench.*
13. Okay, the frog hopped onto the **bench.**

Then the frog hopped onto the **log.** Then the frog took a great leap into the water and the hat landed where the branch is.

(Praise children who raise their hands.)
- Everybody, where **did** the hat land? (Signal.) *Next to the big rock.*
14. Okay, the frog took a great leap into the stream and the hat landed right **next to the big rock.**

Roger woke up and saw his hat. When Roger got to the hat, it was at number 5.

(Praise children who raise their hands.)
- Everybody, where was the hat when Roger got to it? (Signal.) *At the branch.*

The animal that knows what happened to the hat is in the picture, and that animal is hiding under the bench.

(Praise children who raise their hands.)
- Everybody, where **is** the frog hiding? (Signal.) *Under the log.*

15. Who can tell the whole story the **right** way? Remember, you have to tell where Roger was at the beginning. You have to tell **why** his hat moved around. Then you have to tell all the places the hat went, and tell what Roger did and what the frog did. That's a lot of telling.

16. (Call on a child to tell the story. Instruct other children to follow along and raise their hands if they hear a problem. Repeat with several children. Praise children who tell the story in the correct sequence.)

17. Later you'll color the picture.

EXERCISE 8 From—To

1. Everybody, find the next page in your workbook. ✔
• (Hold up workbook.) Find the black dog. ✔
2. The **black dog** is moving **from** the circle to the triangle. What is the dog moving **from?** (Signal.) *The circle.*
• What is the dog moving **to?** (Signal.) *The triangle.*
3. (Repeat step 2 until firm.)
4. Touch the thing the dog is moving **from.** ✔
• Everybody, what are you touching? (Signal.) *The circle.*
• Touch the thing the dog is moving **to.** ✔ Everybody, what are you touching? (Signal.) *The triangle.*

5. Here's the rule about the thing the dog is moving **to.** It should be yellow. Name the thing you are going to color yellow. Get ready. (Signal.) *The triangle.*
• Make a yellow mark on the thing the dog is moving **to.** (Observe children and give feedback.)
• Here's a rule about the thing the dog is moving **from.** It should be blue. Name the thing you are going to color blue. Get ready. (Signal.) *The circle.*
• Make a blue mark on the thing the dog is moving **from.** (Observe children and give feedback.)
6. Touch the **spotted dog.** ✔
• That dog is moving **from** something to something else. Touch the thing the dog is moving **from.** ✔
• Everybody, what is the dog moving **from?** (Signal.) *The circle.*
• Touch the thing the dog is moving **to.** ✔
• Everybody, what is the dog moving **to?** (Signal.) *The triangle.*
7. The rule is the same for **all** the dogs. The thing the dog is moving **to** should be yellow. Name the thing you are going to color yellow. (Signal.) *The triangle.*
• Make a yellow mark on the thing the spotted dog is moving **to.** (Observe children and give feedback.)
• The thing the dog is moving **from** should be blue. Name the thing you are going to color blue. (Signal.) *The circle.*
• Make a blue mark on the thing the spotted dog is moving **from.** (Observe children and give feedback.)
8. Now make marks for a **white dog.** Make a yellow mark on the thing that dog is moving **to.** ✔
• Make a blue mark on the thing that the dog is moving **from.** ✔
9. Later you'll fix the other white dog.

EXERCISE 9   Location

1. (Hold up workbook. Point to second half.)
2. Everybody, what place do you see in this picture? (Signal.) *A fire station.*
3. Here's a coloring rule for this picture. Listen: Color the vehicle red. What's the rule? (Signal.) *Color the vehicle red.*
4. (Repeat step 3 until firm.)
5. Put a red mark on the vehicle. ✔
6. Here's another coloring rule for this picture. Listen: Color the clothes black. What's the rule? (Signal.) *Color the clothes black.*
7. (Repeat step 6 until firm.)

8. Put a black mark on one piece of clothing. ✔
9. There's one more thing to do. One piece of clothing has a missing part. What piece of clothing is that? (Signal.) *A coat.*
   Yes, a coat.
10. What part of the coat is missing? (Signal.) *The sleeve.*
   • Yes, the sleeve. Before you color the coat, follow the dots and make the sleeve.

LESSON 33

Objectives

- Given a common noun, name the class (Exercise 1)
- Given a complex sentence, answer questions involving "who," "what" and "why." (Exercise 2)
- Ask questions involving class, material and location to guess a "mystery object." (Exercise 3)
- Name classes and subclasses. (Exercise 4)
- Given a calendar, identify the day and date for "today" and "tomorrow" and one week from today. (Exercise 5)
- Answer questions about a new story. (Exercise 6)
- Make a picture consistent with the details of a story **using "beginning" and "end."** (Exercise 7)

EXERCISE 1   Classification

1. What's the big class name for fruits and vegetables, and trees, and grass? (Signal.) *Plants.*
- What's the big class name for cows, and bugs, and other living things that move? (Signal.) *Animals.*
- Both those classes are in the very large class of living things. What's the class that has both plants and animals in it? (Signal.) *Living things.*
2. I'll name some things. You tell me if they are living things or not living things.
- Listen: water. Living thing or not living thing? (Signal.) *Not living thing.*
- Listen: birds. Living things or not living things? (Signal.) *Living things.*
- Are birds plants or animals? (Signal.) *Animals.*
- Listen: carrots. Living things or not living things? (Signal.) *Living things.*
- Are carrots plants or animals? (Signal.) *Plants.*
- Listen: spiders. Living things or not living things? (Signal.) *Living things.*
- What kind of living things? (Signal.) *Animals.*
- Listen: sheep. Living things or not living things? (Signal.) *Living things.*
- What kind of living things? (Signal.) *Animals.*
- Listen: clouds. Living things or not living things? (Signal.) *Not living things.*
- Listen: trees. Living things or not living things? (Signal.) *Living things.*
- What kind of living things? (Signal.) *Plants.*
3. I'll name some things that are either plants or animals. You tell me the class they're in.

- Listen: cow. What class? (Signal.) *Animals.*
- Listen: bees. What class? (Signal.) *Animals.*
- Listen: weeds. What class? (Signal.) *Plants.*
- Listen: fish. What class? (Signal.) *Animals.*
- Listen: lettuce. What class? (Signal.) *Plants.*
- Listen: tulips. What class? (Signal.) *Plants.*
- Listen: apple trees. What class? (Signal.) *Plants.*
- Listen: worms. What class? (Signal.) *Animals.*

EXERCISE 2   Who—What—Why

1. I'm going to say sentences that answer questions. One of the questions is why.
2. Listen: Mr. Wilson stopped the car because it was almost out of gas.
- Say the sentence. Get ready. (Signal.) *Mr. Wilson stopped the car because it was almost out of gas.*
- Who stopped the car? (Signal.) *Mr. Wilson.*
- What did Mr. Wilson do? (Signal.) *Stopped the car.*
- Why did he stop the car? (Signal.) *Because it was almost out of gas.*
3. (Repeat step 2 until firm.)
4. Everybody, say the whole sentence. Get ready. (Signal.) *Mr. Wilson stopped the car because it was almost out of gas.*
- Which words tell who? (Signal.) *Mr. Wilson.*
- Which words tell what he did? (Signal.) *Stopped the car.*
- Which words tell why? (Signal.) *Because it was almost out of gas.*
5. (Repeat step 4 until firm.)

EXERCISE 3   Questioning Skills

1. I'm thinking of an object. You'll ask questions to figure out what that object is.
- You'll ask these questions:
- Question 1. What class is it in?
- Question 2. What material is it made of?
- Question 3. Where do you find it?
2. Everybody, say all three questions.
Question 1. Get ready. (Signal.) *What class is it in?*
Question 2. Get ready. (Signal.) *What material is it made of?*
Question 3. Get ready. (Signal.) *Where do you find it?*
3. Ask question 1. Get ready. (Signal.) *What class is it in?*
- It's in the class of containers.
- Ask question 2. Get ready. (Signal.) *What material is it made of?*
- It is usually made of glass.
- Ask question 3. Get ready. (Signal.) *Where do you find it?*
- You usually find it in the kitchen.
4. Everybody, what object am I thinking of? (Signal.) *A cup.*
5. I'll name some objects. You tell me if each object is one I could be thinking of.
- Listen: bucket. Could I have been thinking of that object? (Signal.) *No.*
- Why not? (Call on a child. Idea: *It's not made of glass.*)
- Listen: window. Could I have been thinking of that object? (Signal.) *No.*
- Why not? (Call on a child. Idea: *It's not a container.*)
- Listen: pan. Could I have been thinking of that object? (Signal.) *No.*
- Why not? (Call on a child. Idea: *It's not made of glass.*)

EXERCISE 4   Classification

1. We're going to talk about classes.
2. If we took all flowers from the class of plants, would there be any kinds of plants left? (Signal.) *Yes.*
- Name some kinds of plants that would be left. (Call on individual children. Praise appropriate responses.)
3. The class of flowers is made up of many kinds of flowers. I'll name some kinds of flowers in the class of flowers. Listen: daisies, tulips, roses.

- You name some kinds of flowers in the class of flowers. (Call on individual children. Praise reasonable answers such as: *bluebonnets, lilies, violets.*)
4. Think about this. If we took all the roses from the class of flowers, would there be any flowers left? (Signal.) *Yes.*
- Name some kinds of flowers that would be left. (Call on individual children. Praise all acceptable answers: that is, any kind of flower except roses.)
5. Yes, if we took all the roses from the class of flowers, there would still be flowers left. So which class is bigger, the class of flowers or the class of roses? (Signal.) *The class of flowers.*
- How do you know? (Signal.) *The class of flowers has more kinds of things in it.*
6. Everybody, think big. Which class is bigger, the class of plants or the class of flowers? (Signal.) *The class of plants.*
- Think big. Which class is bigger, the class of roses or the class of flowers? (Signal.) *The class of flowers.*

EXERCISE 5   Calendar

1. (Present calendar.)
- We're going to talk about today, tomorrow, and one week from today.
2. Tell me the day of the week it is today. Get ready. (Signal.)
- Tell me the day of the week it will be tomorrow. Get ready. (Signal.)
- Tell me the day of the week it will be one week from today. Get ready. (Signal.)
3. (Repeat step 2 until firm.)
4. Now the dates.
- Tell me today's date. Get ready. (Signal.)
- (Touch number for today's date.) Here's today's date. Now I'll show you the date that is one week from today.
- (Touch number that is one week from today.) Everybody, say the date that is one week from today. Get ready. (Signal.)
5. Once more.
- Listen: Tell me today's date. Get ready. (Signal.)
- Tell me tomorrow's date. Get ready. (Signal.)
- Tell me the date it will be one week from today. Get ready. (Signal.)
6. (Repeat step 5 until firm.)

EXERCISE 6   Roxie The Rock Collector

Storytelling

- Everybody, I'm going to read you a story about a girl named Roxie.

> Roxie loved rocks. She loved red rocks and blue rocks and round rocks and flat rocks. She loved striped rocks and spotted rocks and smooth rocks and rough rocks. Every place Roxie went, she'd find some rocks.
>
> Yes, Roxie loved rocks and she hated to throw rocks away. That bothered her mother, because Roxie had rocks in her room, rocks in her closet, rocks in the basement and even rocks in her bed.

- Everybody, what's the name of the girl in this story? (Signal.) *Roxie.*
- What did Roxie love? (Signal.) *Rocks.*
- Who can name some of the kinds of rocks she collected? (Call on several children. Idea: *Red rocks, blue rocks, round rocks, flat rocks, striped rocks, spotted rocks, smooth rocks and rough rocks.*)
- Who can name some of the places Roxie kept her rocks? (Call on a child. Idea: *In her room, in her closet, in the basement and in her bed.*)
- Why wasn't her mother happy about Roxie's rock collection? (Call on a child. Idea: *She didn't like all the rocks everywhere.*)
- Yes, I'll bet that would be a mess with rocks all over the house and even in the bed.

> "This has to stop," Roxie's mother said one day. "This house is turning into one big rock collection. You're going to have to take all the rocks out of the house."
>
> "Where will I put them?" Roxie asked.
>
> "I don't know," her mother said, "but you can't keep them in the house anymore."
>
> Roxie didn't know what to do. If she put her rocks in boxes, she wouldn't be able to see them or hold them or arrange them in pretty piles. She said, "I can't stand rocks in a box."
>
> But she didn't know what she should do.

- Listen: Why didn't Roxie like the idea of putting rocks in boxes? (Call on a child. Idea: *Because she wouldn't be able to see them or hold them or arrange them in pretty piles.*)

> Roxie thought and thought. At last she came up with a wonderful idea. "I'll put my rocks in my tree house."

- What's a tree house? (Call on a child. Idea: *A small house in a tree.*)

The tree house was in the backyard. It was a little shack that Roxie's dad built in a huge tree. "That would be great," Roxie said to herself. "If my rocks are in the tree house, I can look at them whenever I want."

So she started moving rocks. She started early Saturday morning, carrying the big rocks, loading her pockets with rocks, putting rocks in socks and taking them up the ladder to her tree house. She made trip after trip after trip to that tree house.

- Listen: Why did Roxie like the tree house better than boxes for her rocks? (Call on a child. Idea: *Because she could look at them whenever she wanted.*)
- How did she get the rocks to her tree house? (Call on a child. Idea: *She carried the big rocks and put rocks in her pockets and socks.*)
- She had to climb that ladder with each load of rocks. I'll bet she got tired.

By noon, the pile of rocks inside the tree house was as big as a buffalo. By late afternoon, the pile was as big as two buffaloes. But still Roxie came with more rocks, trip after trip after trip.

- Who can stand up and show me how big a buffalo is? (Call on a child. Accept reasonable approximations.)
- So by noon, her pile was that big. Tell me, how big was the pile by late afternoon? (Call on a child. Idea: *As big as two buffaloes.*)
- I hope the floor of that tree house was pretty strong, because that pile of rocks had to be **very** heavy.

Just before supper time, Roxie was in the basement gathering up the last load of rocks when she heard a strange groaning and creaking sound in the backyard.

- Listen: By late afternoon, that pile was as big as two buffaloes. How big do you think it was by supper time? (Call on a child. Accept reasonable responses.)
- And Roxie was still hauling rocks. She heard a strange sound coming from the backyard. Do you have any idea what was making that sound? (Call on a child. Accept reasonable responses.) Let's see.

Roxie went outside and saw what was making the sound. It was the tree house. The floor was sagging down and making groaning sounds and creaking sounds. "Uh-oh," Roxie said. "The floor is starting to give way."

And Roxie was right. All those rocks were so heavy that the floor could not hold them, and as Roxie stood there looking at the tree house with her mouth open, the floor sagged down farther and farther and finally—crash, bang, pow— the floor gave way and all the rocks came tumbling down—red rocks, yellow rocks, striped rocks, spotted rocks, big ones and little ones—all spilling out of the tree house and falling onto the ground.

"Oh, no," Roxie said. "Now I've got to start all over and figure out some other place to keep my rocks."

But just then, her mother came out of the house. She had heard those rocks crash and bang and pow around.

Roxie was just about ready to tell her mother what happened when her mother smiled and said, "Roxie, what a wonderful idea."

Roxie blinked and looked at her mother. Roxie didn't know what her mother was talking about.

- Everybody, where were all the rocks now? (Signal.) *On the ground.*
- Her mother said, "Roxie, what a wonderful idea." Do you think that had anything to do with the rocks? (Signal.) *Yes.*
- We'll see.

"Roxie," her mother said, "that is the most beautiful rock garden I have ever seen. And how clever you were to put it around that tree. You are so smart sometimes." She bent over and gave Roxie a great big kiss.

Roxie blushed and didn't know what to say, but when she looked at that pile of rocks, she had to agree with her mother. It was a beautiful rock garden.

So now Roxie's mother is happy and so is Roxie. Roxie has her rocks where she can look at them whenever she wants—her brown rocks and green rocks, her smooth rocks and rough rocks, and all the rest of them.

And, oh yes. One more thing: Every day Roxie's rock garden gets a little bit bigger. I wonder how big it will get.

- Why do you think that garden gets a little bit bigger every day? (Call on a child. Idea: *Because Roxie is still collecting rocks.*)

EXERCISE 7

1. Everybody, open your workbook to Lesson 33. Write your name at the top of the page. ✔
2. Everybody, did this picture take place at the **beginning** of the story or at the **end?** (Signal.) *At the end.*
- How do you know it took place at the end? Tell me about some things in the picture that let you know it took place at the end. (Call on several children. Ideas: *The tree house floor is broken; The rocks have made a rock garden; Roxie's mother and Roxie are admiring the rock garden together.*)
3. At the end of the story, nobody knows how big that rock garden will get. I'll bet if it gets too big, Roxie's mother will tell her to stop filling the yard with rocks. You can show me how big that rock garden will get by fixing up the picture. You can draw some more rocks. But remember, don't let that rock garden get too big. And keep it pretty.

Objectives

- Name classes and subclasses. (Exercise 1)
- Given two classes, identify which class is biggest, and describe why. (Exercise 2)
- Given a calendar, identify the day and date for "today" and "tomorrow" and one week from today. (Exercise 3)
- Given a complex sentence, answer questions involving "where," "what" and "why." (Exercise 4)
- **Given a sequence of actions, repeat the sequence, recall and carry out the sequence of actions and answer questions about the sequence.** (Exercise 5)
- Answer questions about the events in a familiar story. (Exercise 6)
- Follow coloring rules involving moving "from" and "to." (Exercise 7)
- Follow coloring rules involving parts of a whole. (Exercise 8)

EXERCISE 1 Classification

1. We're going to talk about classes.
2. If we took all cows from the class of animals, would there be any kinds of animals left? (Signal.) *Yes.*
- Name some kinds of animals that would be left. (Call on individual children. Praise appropriate responses.)
3. The class of cows is made of many kinds of cows. I'll name some kinds of cows in the class of cows. Listen: brown cows, spotted cows, black cows.
- Your turn. Name some kinds of cows in the class of cows. (Call on individual children. Praise reasonable answers, such as: *white cows, black cows, tan cows.*)
4. Think about this. If we took all the brown cows from the class of cows, would there be any cows left? (Signal.) *Yes.*
- Name some kinds of cows that would be left. (Call on individual children. Praise all acceptable answers: any kind of cow except brown cows.)
5. Yes, if we took all the brown cows from the class of cows, there would still be cows left. So which class is bigger, the class of cows or the class of brown cows? (Signal.) *The class of cows.*
- How do you know? (Signal.) *The class of cows has more kinds of things in it.*
6. Everybody, think big. Which class is bigger, the class of animals or the class of cows? (Signal.) *The class of animals.*
- Think big. Which class is bigger, the class of cows or the class of brown cows? (Signal.) *The class of cows.*

EXERCISE 2 Classification

1. We're going to talk about classes.
2. Tell me which class is bigger, the class of buildings or the class of houses. Get ready. (Signal.) *The class of buildings.*
- How do you know? (Signal.) *The class of buildings has more kinds of things in it.*
3. (Repeat step 2 until firm.)
4. Everybody, tell me which class is bigger, the class of buses or the class of vehicles. Get ready. (Signal.) *The class of vehicles.*
- How do you know? (Signal.) *The class of vehicles has more kinds of things in it.*
5. (Repeat step 4 until firm.)
6. Everybody, tell me which class is bigger, the class of cats or the class of animals. Get ready. (Signal.) *The class of animals.*
- How do you know? (Call on a child. Idea: *The class of animals has all the cats and has other animals in it.*)
7. (Repeat step 6 until firm.)

EXERCISE 3 Calendar

1. (Present calendar.)
- We're going to talk about today, tomorrow, and one week from today.
2. Tell me the day of the week it is today. Get ready. (Signal.)
- Tell me the day of the week it will be tomorrow. Get ready. (Signal.)
- Tell me the day of the week it will be one week from today. Get ready. (Signal.)
3. (Repeat step 2 until firm.)
4. Now the dates.
- Tell me today's date. Get ready. (Signal.)

- (Touch number for today's date.) Here's today's date. Now I'll show you the date that is one week from today.
- (Touch number that is one week from today.) Everybody, say the date that is one week from today. Get ready. (Signal.)

5. Once more.
- Listen: Tell me today's date. Get ready. (Signal.)
- Tell me tomorrow's date. Get ready. (Signal.)
- Tell me the date it will be one week from today. Get ready. (Signal.)
6. (Repeat step 5 until firm.)

EXERCISE 4   What—Where—Why

1. I'm going to say a sentence that answers questions. One of the questions is why.
2. Listen: The car started to slide on the road because the road was frozen.
- Say the sentence. Get ready. (Signal.) *The car started to slide on the road because the road was frozen.*
- What started to slide? (Signal.) *The car.*
- Where did the car start to slide? (Signal.) *On the road.*
- Why did the car start to slide? (Signal.) *Because the road was frozen.*
3. (Repeat step 2 until firm.)
4. Everybody, say the whole sentence. Get ready. (Signal.) *The car started to slide on the road because the road was frozen.*
- Which words tell what started to slide? (Signal.) *The car.*
- Which words tell what the car did? (Signal.) *Started to slide.*
- Which words tell where? (Signal.) *On the road.*
- Which words tell why? (Signal.) *Because the road was frozen.*
5. (Repeat step 4 until firm.)

EXERCISE 5   Actions

Before/After

1. Listen: First I'll touch my head. Then I'll tap my foot. Then I'll smile.
- What will I do first? (Signal.) *Touch your head.*
- What will I do after I touch my head? (Signal.) *Tap your foot.*
- What will I do last? (Signal.) *Smile.*

2. Listen to the three things again: I'll touch my head, tap my foot, smile.
- Everybody, say those three things I'll do. Get ready. (Signal.) *Touch your head, tap your foot, smile.*
- Say the second thing I'll do. Get ready. (Signal.) *Tap your foot.*
- Listen: I'll do something just **before** I tap my foot. What will I do just before I tap my foot? (Signal.) *Touch your head.*
- I'll do something just after I tap my foot. What will I do after I tap my foot? (Signal.) *Smile.*
3. (Repeat step 2 until firm.)
4. Here I go. (Touch your head, tap your foot, smile.)
5. Your turn. First you'll touch your head. Then you'll tap your foot. Then you'll smile.
- Everybody, do those three actions. Get ready. (Tap 3 times.) (Children touch head, tap foot, smile.)
6. (Repeat step 5 until firm.)
7. Everybody, show me the **second** thing you did. Get ready. (Signal.) (Children tap foot.)
- Show me what you did just **before** you tapped your foot. Get ready. (Signal.) (Children touch head.)
- Show me what you did just **after** you tapped your foot. Get ready. (Signal.) (Children smile.)
8. Listen: After you tapped your foot, you did something. Say the whole thing about what you did **after you tapped your foot.** Get ready. (Signal.) *After I tapped my foot, I smiled.*

EXERCISE 6   Roxie The Rock Collector

Review

- Everybody, I'm going to read you the story about Roxie, the rock collector, again. Listen:

Roxie loved rocks.

- Who remembers some of the rocks she liked? (Call on several children. Idea: *Red, blue, round, flat, striped, spotted, smooth and rough rocks.*)

Roxie loved red rocks and blue rocks and round rocks and flat rocks. She loved striped rocks and spotted rocks and smooth rocks and rough rocks. Every place Roxie went, she'd find some rocks.

Yes, Roxie loved rocks and Roxie hated to throw rocks away. That bothered her mother.

- Listen: Who remembers some of the places Roxie kept her rocks? (Call on several children. Idea: *In her room, closet, basement and bed.*)
- Right.

Roxie had rocks in her room, rocks in her closet, rocks in the basement and even rocks in her bed.

"This has to stop," Roxie's mother said one day. "This house is turning into one big rock collection. You're going to have to take all the rocks out of the house."

"Where will I put them?" Roxie asked.

"I don't know," her mother said, "but you can't keep them in the house anymore."

Roxie didn't know what to do.

- Listen: Roxie didn't want to put them in boxes. Why not? (Call on a child. Idea: *Because then she wouldn't be able to see them or hold them or arrange them.*)
- Right.

If Roxie put her rocks in boxes, she wouldn't be able to see them or hold them or arrange them in pretty piles. She said, "I can't stand rocks in a box."

But she didn't know what she should do.

Roxie thought and thought. At last she came up with a wonderful idea.

- Who remembers her wonderful idea? (Call on a child. Idea: *To put them in her tree house.*)
- Everybody, where was her tree house? (Signal.) *In the backyard.*

- Why did she like the idea of having rocks in her tree house rather than in boxes? (Call on a child. Idea: *So she could look at them whenever she wanted.*)

So Roxie said to herself, "I'll put my rocks in my tree house."

The tree house was in the backyard. It was a little shack that Roxie's dad built in a huge tree. "That would be great," Roxie said to herself. "If my rocks are in the tree house, I can look at them whenever I want."

So she started moving rocks. She started early Saturday morning, carrying the big rocks, loading her pockets with rocks, putting rocks in socks and taking them up the ladder to her tree house. She made trip after trip after trip to that tree house. By noon, the pile of rocks inside the tree house was big.

- Who remembers how big it was by noon? (Call on a child. Idea: *As big as a buffalo.*)
- Right.

By noon the pile of rocks inside the tree house was as big as a buffalo. By late afternoon, the pile was as big as two buffaloes. But still Roxie came with more rocks, trip after trip after trip.

Just before supper time, Roxie was in the basement gathering up the last load of rocks when she heard something.

- What did she hear? (Call on a child. Idea: *A groaning and creaking sound.*)
- What was happening to the tree house? (Call on a child. Idea: *The floor was starting to sag.*)
- Why was the floor giving way? (Call on a child. Idea: *There were too many rocks on it.*)
- It was a good thing Roxie wasn't in that tree house when that floor gave way.

Roxie heard a strange groaning and creaking sound in the backyard. Roxie went outside and saw what was making the sound. It was the tree house. The floor was sagging down and making groaning sounds and creaking sounds. "Uh-oh," Roxie said. "The floor is starting to give way."

And Roxie was right. All those rocks were so heavy that the floor could not hold them, and as Roxie stood there looking at the tree house with her mouth open, the floor sagged down farther and farther and finally—crash, bang, pow.

- What was making all that noise? (Call on a child. Idea: *All the rocks were tumbling down because the floor gave way.*)
- Yes.

The floor gave way and all the rocks came tumbling down—red rocks, yellow rocks, striped rocks and spotted rocks, big ones and little ones—all spilling out of the tree house and falling onto the ground.

"Oh, no," Roxie said. "Now I've got to start all over and figure out some other place to keep my rocks."

But just then, her mother came out of the house. She had heard those rocks crash and bang and pow around.

Roxie was just about ready to tell her mother what happened when her mother smiled and said, "Roxie, what a wonderful idea."

- What did her mother think was Roxie's wonderful idea? (Call on a child. Idea: *To make a rock garden.*)
- Everybody, did her mother think Roxie made that rock garden on purpose? (Signal.) *Yes.*

Roxie blinked and looked at her mother. Roxie didn't know what her mother was talking about.

"Roxie," her mother said, "that is the most beautiful rock garden I have ever seen. And how clever you were to put it around that tree. You are so smart sometimes." She bent over and gave Roxie a great big kiss.

Roxie blushed and didn't know what to say, but when she looked at that pile of rocks, she had to agree with her mother. It was a beautiful rock garden.

So now Roxie's mother is happy and so is Roxie. Roxie has her rocks where she can look at them whenever she wants—her brown rocks and green rocks, her smooth rocks and rough rocks, and all the rest of them.

And, oh yes. One more thing . . .

- Listen: Every day something happens to that rock garden. What's that? (Call on a child. Idea: *It gets bigger.*)
- Why does that rock garden keep growing? (Call on a child. Idea: *Because Roxie keeps collecting rocks.*)
- Yes.

Every day Roxie's rock garden gets a little bit bigger. I wonder how big it will get.

WORKBOOK

EXERCISE 7   From—To

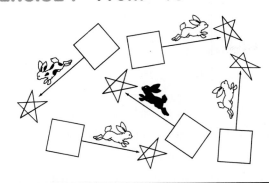

1. Everybody, open your workbook to Lesson 34. Write your name at the top of the page. ✔
   (Hold up workbook. Point to first half.)
2. Find the spotted bunny. ✔
3. The **spotted bunny** is moving **from** the square to the star. What is the bunny moving **from?** (Signal.) *The square.*
   • What is the bunny moving **to?** (Signal.) *The star.*
   • (Repeat step 3 until firm.)
4. Touch the thing the bunny is moving **from.** ✔
   • Everybody, what are you touching? (Signal.) *The square.*
   • Touch the thing the bunny is moving **to.** ✔
   • Everybody, what are you touching? (Signal.) *The star.*
5. Here's the rule about the thing the bunny is moving **to.** It should be red. Name the thing you are going to color red. Get ready. (Signal.) *The star.*
   • Make a red mark on the thing the bunny is moving **to.**
   (Observe children and give feedback.)
   • Here's a rule about the thing the bunny is moving **from.** It should be black. Name the thing you are going to color black. Get ready. (Signal.) *The square.*
   • Make a black mark on the thing the bunny is moving **from.**
   (Observe children and give feedback.)

6. Touch the **black bunny.** ✔
   • That bunny is moving **from** something to something else. Touch the thing the bunny is moving **from.** ✔
   • Everybody, what is the bunny moving **from?** (Signal.) *The square.*
   • Touch the thing the bunny is moving **to.** ✔
   • Everybody, what is the bunny moving **to?** (Signal.) *The star.*
7. The thing the bunny is moving **to** should be red. Name the thing you are going to color red. (Signal.) *The star.*
   • Make a red mark on the thing the bunny is moving **to.**
   (Observe children and give feedback.)
   • The thing the bunny is moving **from** should be black. Name the thing you are going to color black. (Signal.) *The square.*
   • Make a black mark on the thing the bunny is moving **from.**
   (Observe children and give feedback.)
8. Now make marks for a **white bunny.** Make a red mark on the thing that bunny is moving **to.** ✔
   • Make a black mark on the thing that bunny is moving **from.** ✔
9. Later you'll fix the other white bunnies.

EXERCISE 8   Part-Whole

1. (Hold up workbook. Point to second half.) Here's a coloring rule for the umbrella. Listen: Color the handle purple. What's the rule? (Signal.) *Color the handle purple.*
   • Mark the handle. ✔
2. Part of the umbrella is missing. What part is missing? (Signal.) *The covering.*
   • Yes, the covering. Before you color the umbrella you're going to follow the dots and make the covering.
3. Here's the coloring rule for the covering. Listen: Color the covering green. What's the rule? (Signal.) *Color the covering green.*
   • Mark the covering. ✔

LESSON 35

Objectives

- Given a sequence of actions, repeat the sequence, recall and carry out the sequence of actions and answer questions about the sequence. (Exercise 1)
- Given a calendar, identify the day and date for "today" and "tomorrow" and one week from today. (Exercise 2)
- Given a complex sentence, answer questions involving "where," "who" and "why." (Exercise 3)
- Given two classes, identify which class is biggest, and describe why. (Exercise 4)
- Given a common noun, identify the color and material of the object. (Exercise 5)
- Relate a familiar story grammar to a picture that indicates the sequence of events for a new story. (Exercise 6)
- Follow coloring rules involving moving "from" and "to." (Exercise 7)
- Ask questions involving "parts," "use," and "location" to guess a "mystery object." (Exercise 8)

EXERCISE 1   Actions

Before/After

1. Listen: First I'll frown. Then I'll tap my foot. Then I'll clap.
- What will I do first? (Signal.) *Frown.*
- What will I do after I frown? (Signal.) *Tap your foot.*
- What will I do last? (Signal.) *Clap.*
2. Listen to the three things again: I'll frown, tap my foot, clap.
- Everybody, say those three things I'll do. Get ready. (Signal.) *Frown, tap your foot, clap.*
- Say the second thing I'll do. Get ready. (Signal.) *Tap your foot.*
- Listen: I'll do something just **before** I tap my foot. What will I do just before I tap my foot? (Signal.) *Frown.*
- I'll do something just after I tap my foot. What will I do after I tap my foot? (Signal.) *Clap.*
3. (Repeat step 2 until firm.)
4. Here I go. (Frown, tap your foot, clap.)
5. Your turn. First you'll frown. Then you'll tap your foot. Then you'll clap.
- Everybody, do those three actions. Get ready. (Tap 3 times.) (Children frown, tap foot, clap.)
6. (Repeat step 5 until firm.)
7. Everybody, show me the **second** thing you did. Get ready. (Signal.) (Children tap foot.)
- Show me what you did just **before** you tapped your foot. Get ready. (Signal.) (Children frown.)
- Show me what you did just **after** you tapped your foot. Get ready. (Signal.) (Children clap.)

8. Listen: After you tapped your foot, you did something. Say the whole thing about what you did **after you tapped your foot.** Get ready. (Signal.) *After I tapped my foot, I clapped.*

EXERCISE 2   Calendar

1. (Present calendar.)
- We're going to talk about today, tomorrow, and one week from today.
2. Tell me the day of the week it is today. Get ready. (Signal.)
- Tell me the day of the week it will be tomorrow. Get ready. (Signal.)
- Tell me the day of the week it will be one week from today. Get ready. (Signal.)
3. (Repeat step 2 until firm.)
4. Now the dates.
- Tell me today's date. Get ready. (Signal.)
- (Touch number for today's date.) Here's today's date. Now I'll show you the date that is one week from today.
- (Touch number that is one week from today.) Everybody, say the date that is one week from today. Get ready. (Signal.)
5. Once more.
- Listen: Tell me today's date. Get ready. (Signal.)
- Tell me tomorrow's date. Get ready. (Signal.)
- Tell me the date it will be one week from today. Get ready. (Signal.)
6. (Repeat step 5 until firm.)

EXERCISE 3   Who—Where—Why

1. I'm going to say a sentence that answers questions. One of the questions is why.
2. Listen: Those girls ran toward the stream because bees were chasing them.
   - Say the sentence. Get ready. (Signal.) *Those girls ran toward the stream because bees were chasing them.*
   - Who ran? (Signal.) *Those girls.*
   - Where did they run? (Signal.) *Toward the stream.*
   - Why did they run toward the stream? (Signal.) *Because bees were chasing them.*
3. (Repeat step 2 until firm.)
4. Everybody, say the whole sentence. Get ready. (Signal.) *Those girls ran toward the stream because bees were chasing them.*
   - Which words tell who? (Signal.) *Those girls.*
   - Which words tell where? (Signal.) *Toward the stream.*
   - Which words tell why? (Signal.) *Because bees were chasing them.*
5. (Repeat step 4 until firm.)

EXERCISE 4   Classification

1. We're going to talk about classes.
2. Tell me which class is bigger, the class of plants or the class of trees. Get ready. (Signal.) *The class of plants.*
   - How do you know? (Signal.) *The class of plants has more kinds of things in it.*
3. (Repeat step 2 until firm.)
4. Everybody, tell me which class is bigger, the class of containers or the class of buckets. Get ready. (Signal.) *The class of containers.*
   - How do you know? (Signal.) *The class of containers has more kinds of things in it.*
5. (Repeat step 4 until firm.)
6. Everybody, tell me which class is bigger, the class of cows or the class of animals. Get ready. (Signal.) *The class of animals.*
   - How do you know? (Signal.) *The class of animals has more kinds of things in it.*
7. (Repeat step 6 until firm.)

EXERCISE 5   Materials

1. We're going to talk about your socks.
2. Everybody, touch your socks. Get ready. (Signal.) ✔
3. When I call on you, tell me the color of your socks. (Call on three or four children and ask:) What color are your socks? (Praise good answers.)
4. When I call on you, tell me what your socks are made of. (Call on three or four children and ask:) What are your socks made of? (Accept *cloth, cotton,* and so on.)

WORKBOOK

EXERCISE 6   Clarabelle And The Diving Board

Sequence Story

1. Everybody, open your workbook to Lesson 35. Write your name at the top of the page. ✔
2. Here's a picture that shows Clarabelle standing by the pool, looking at a girl.
   - Everybody, what's that girl doing? (Signal.) *Diving.*
     I'll bet Clarabelle is getting some ideas.
3. Everybody, touch number 1. ✔
   - That's where Clarabelle goes first. Where is Clarabelle at number 1? (Call on a child. Idea: *On the diving board.*)
   - I think I know what Clarabelle is doing and why she's doing it.

4. Everybody, touch number 2. ✔
- That shows where Clarabelle went next.
5. Everybody, touch number 3. ✔
- Number 3 is underwater. Uh-oh. Bad trouble. And I'll bet I know just what happened.
6. Everybody, touch number 4. ✔
- Where is Clarabelle at number 4? (Call on a child. Idea: *In the middle of the pool.*)
- If you look at number 5, you'll see where she's going.
- Where is she going? (Call on a child. Idea: *To the ladder.*)
- Right, she wants to climb up that ladder and get out of the pool.
7. Everybody, touch number 5. ✔
- Where is Clarabelle at number 5? (Call on a child. Idea: *At the top of the ladder.*)
- Yes, she's on top of the ladder. But then look where she is next.
8. Everybody, touch number 6. ✔
- She **was** at the **top** of the ladder at number **5.** But where is she at number **6?** (Call on a child. Idea: *Underwater.*)
- What do you think happened to the ladder? (Call on a child. Idea: *It broke.*)
- Right. Clarabelle is so heavy she broke the ladder and landed **back** in the water. I'll bet none of the children in the pool were very happy with Clarabelle by now. She **broke** the **diving board.** Then when she tried to get out of the pool, she **broke** the **ladder.**
9. Look at the numbers and say the whole story to yourself. Raise your hand when you can tell everything that happened. Remember, you have to tell **why.** Tell **why** Clarabelle wanted to go on that diving board: tell **why** she ended up in the water right under the diving board; and tell **why** she ended up in the water right under the ladder.
- (Call on a child to tell the story. Instruct the other children to follow along and raise their hands if they hear a problem. Repeat with several children. Praise stories that follow the sequence and tell why things happened.)
10. Later you'll color the picture.

EXERCISE 7 From—To

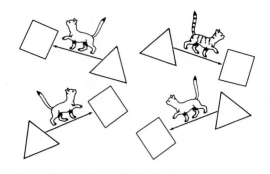

1. Everybody, find the next page in your workbook. Find the striped cat. ✔
2. The **striped cat** is moving **from** the triangle to the square. What is the cat moving **from?** (Signal.) *The triangle.*
- What is the cat moving **to?** (Signal.) *The square.*
3. (Repeat step 2 until firm.)
4. Touch the thing the cat is moving **from.** ✔ Everybody, what are you touching? (Signal.) *The triangle.*
- Touch the thing the cat is moving **to.** ✔ Everybody, what are you touching? (Signal.) *The square.*
5. Here's the rule about the thing the cat is moving **to.** It should be brown. Name the thing you are going to color brown. Get ready. (Signal.) *The square.*
- Make a brown mark on the thing the cat is moving **to.** (Observe children and give feedback.)
- Here's a rule about the thing the cat is moving **from.** It should be purple. Name the thing you are going to color purple. Get ready. (Signal.) *The triangle.*
- Make a purple mark on the thing the cat is moving **from.** (Observe children and give feedback.)
6. Now make marks for the **other cats.** Make a brown mark on the thing those cats are moving **to.** ✔
- Make a purple mark on the thing that those cats are moving **from.** ✔

EXERCISE 8   Questioning Skills

1. (Hold up workbook. Point to boxed pictures.) I'm thinking about one of the pictures. It's either a suitcase, a hammer, a cup, or a pot. You'll ask questions to find out which object I'm thinking of.
- Everybody, ask a question about the parts it has. Get ready. (Signal.) *What parts does it have?*
- Everybody, ask a question about what you use it for. Get ready. (Signal.) *What do you use it for?*
- Everybody, ask a question about where you find it. Get ready. (Signal.) *Where do you find it?*
2. Let's ask those questions again.
3. Everybody, ask the question about the parts it has. Get ready. (Signal.) *What parts does it have?*
- Everybody, ask the question about what you use it for. Get ready. (Signal.) *What do you use it for?*
- Everybody, ask a question about where you find it. Get ready. (Signal.) *Where do you find it?*
4. (Repeat step 3 until firm.)
5. Ask those questions again, and I'll tell you the answers.
- Everybody, ask the question about the parts it has. Get ready. (Signal.) *What parts does it have?*
- Here's the answer. It has a handle and a bowl. What parts? (Signal.) *A handle and a bowl.*

6. Everybody, ask the question about what you use it for. Get ready. (Signal.) *What do you use it for?*
- Here's the answer. To drink from. What do you use it for? (Signal.) *To drink from.*
7. Everybody, ask the question about where you can find it. Get ready. (Signal.) *Where can you find it?*
- Here's the answer. You could find it in a kitchen. Where could you find it? (Signal.) *In a kitchen.*
8. Make a red mark on the thing I'm thinking of. ✔
- Everybody, what object was I thinking of? (Signal.) *A cup.*
- How did you know I wasn't thinking of a pot? (Call on a child. Ideas: *You don't drink from it.*)
- How did you know I wasn't thinking of a hammer? (Call on a child. Accept reasonable responses.)
- How did you know I wasn't thinking of a suitcase? (Call on a child. Accept reasonable responses.)

LESSON 36

Objectives

- Name classes and subclasses. (Exercise 1)
- Given a complex sentence, answer questions involving "who," **"how"** and "why." (Exercise 2)
- Answer questions about previously learned calendar facts. (Exercise 3)
- Given two classes, identify which class is biggest, and describe why. (Exercise 4)
- **Given a material, name common nouns made of that material.** (Exercise 5)
- Given a short statement, generate an expanded sentence that tells "why," "when" or "where." (Exercise 6)
- Given a calendar, identify the day and date for "today" and "tomorrow" and one week from today. (Exercise 7)
- **Given sequenced pictures, retell a familiar story.** (Exercise 8)
- Follow coloring rules involving moving from and to. (Exercise 9)
- Ask questions involving "parts," "use," and "location" to guess a "mystery object." (Exercise 10)

EXERCISE 1 Classification

1. We're going to talk about classes.
2. If we took all shirts from the class of clothing, would there be any kinds of clothing left? (Signal.) *Yes.*

- Name some kinds of clothing that would be left. (Call on individual children. Praise appropriate responses.)

3. The class of shirts is made up of many kinds of shirts. I'll name some kinds of shirts. Listen: striped shirts, flowered shirts, spotted shirts.

- You name some kinds of shirts in the class of shirts. (Call on individual children. Praise reasonable answers, such as: *striped shirts, polka-dot shirts, plaid shirts.*)

4. Think about this. If we took all the striped shirts from the class of shirts, would there be any shirts left? (Signal.) *Yes.*

- Name some kinds of shirts that would be left. (Call on individual children. Praise all acceptable answers: any pattern of shirt except striped shirts.)

5. Yes, if we took all the striped shirts from the class of shirts, there would still be shirts left. So which class is bigger, the class of shirts or the class of striped shirts? (Signal.) *The class of shirts.*

- How do you know? (Signal.) *The class of shirts has more kinds of things in it.*

6. Everybody, think big. Which class is bigger, the class of shirts or the class of clothing? (Signal.) *The class of clothing.*

- Think big. Which class is bigger, the class of shirts or the class of striped shirts? (Signal.) *The class of shirts.*

EXERCISE 2 Who—How—Why

1. Some sentences have words that tell **how** somebody did things.
2. Listen: She ate slowly. How did she eat? (Signal.) *Slowly.*

- Listen: She ate without looking up. How did she eat? (Signal.) *Without looking up.*

3. Listen: The boys slept soundly because they had done a lot of work.

- Say the sentence. Get ready. (Signal.) *The boys slept soundly because they had done a lot of work.*
- How did the boys sleep? (Signal.) *Soundly.*
- Listen again: The boys slept soundly because they had done a lot of work.
- Who slept soundly? (Signal.) *The boys.*
- How did they sleep? (Signal.) *Soundly.*
- Why did they sleep soundly? (Signal.) *Because they had done a lot of work.*

4. (Repeat step 3 until firm.)

5. Everybody, say the whole sentence. Get ready. (Signal.) *The boys slept soundly because they had done a lot of work.*

- Which words tell who? (Signal.) *The boys.*
- Which two words tell what they did? (Signal.) *Slept soundly.*
- Which word tells how they slept? (Signal.) *Soundly.*
- Which words tell why? (Signal.) *Because they had done a lot of work.*

6. (Repeat step 5 until firm.)

EXERCISE 3   Calendar Facts

1. How many months are in a year? (Signal.) *12.*
   - Say the fact. Get ready. (Signal.) *There are 12 months in a year.*
   - How many seasons are in a year? (Signal.) *Four.*
   - Say the fact. Get ready. (Signal.) *There are four seasons in a year.*
   - How many days are in a year? (Signal.) *365.*
   - Say the fact. Get ready. (Signal.) *There are 365 days in a year.*
   - How many weeks are in a year? (Signal.) *52.*
   - Say the fact. Get ready. (Signal.) *There are 52 weeks in a year.*
2. (Repeat step 1 until firm.)
3. Say the seasons of the year. Get ready. (Signal.) *Winter, spring, summer, fall.*
   - Say the months of the year. Get ready. (Signal.) *January, February, March, April, May, June, July, August, September, October, November, December.*

EXERCISE 4   Classification

1. We're going to talk about classes.
2. Tell me which class is bigger, the class of bowls or the class of containers. Get ready. (Signal.) *The class of containers.*
   - How do you know? (Signal.) *The class of containers has more kinds of things in it.*
3. (Repeat step 2 until firm.)
4. Name some things that are in the class of containers that are not in the class of bowls. (Call on individual children. Praise acceptable answers, such as: *buckets, bags,* etc.)
5. Tell me which class is bigger, the class of clothing or the class of coats. Get ready. (Signal.) *The class of clothing.*
   - How do you know? (Signal.) *The class of clothing has more kinds of things in it.*
6. (Repeat step 5 until firm.)
7. Tell me which class is bigger, the class of sandwiches or the class of food. Get ready. (Signal.) *The class of food.*
   - How do you know? (Signal.) *The class of food has more kinds of things in it.*
8. (Repeat step 7 until firm.)

EXERCISE 5   Materials

1. Think of things that are made of leather.
2. Let's see who can name at least three things made of leather. (Call on individual children to name objects made of leather. Each child should name at least three things.)
3. Think of things that are made of metal.
4. Let's see who can name at least three things made of metal. (Call on individual children to name objects made of metal. Each child should name at least three things.)
5. Think of things that are made of concrete.
6. Let's see who can name at least three things made of concrete. (Call on individual children to name objects made of concrete. Each child should name at least three things.)

EXERCISE 6   Why—When—Where

1. We're going to make up statements.
2. Here's the statement we start with: The dog got wet.
   - Say that statement. Get ready. (Signal.) *The dog got wet.*
3. My turn. I'm going to make up a statement that tells **why** the dog got wet. Listen: The dog got wet because it went for a swim. I told you why the dog got wet.
4. Listen: The dog got wet. Your turn. Make up a statement that tells **why** the dog got wet. (Call on one child. If the child's statement is acceptable, have the group repeat it.)
5. Listen: The dog got wet. Make up another statement that tells **why** the dog got wet. (Call on another child. If the child's statement is acceptable, have the group repeat it.)
6. Listen: The dog got wet. Make up statements that tell **when** the dog got wet. (Call on three individual children. Have the group repeat each acceptable statement.)
7. Listen: The dog got wet. Make up statements that tell **where** the dog got wet. (Call on three individual children. Have the group repeat each acceptable statement.)

EXERCISE 7   Calendar

1. (Present calendar.)
- We're going to talk about today, tomorrow, and one week from today.
2. Tell me the day of the week it is today. Get ready. (Signal.)
- Tell me the day of the week it will be tomorrow. Get ready. (Signal.)
- Tell me the day of the week it will be one week from today. Get ready. (Signal.)
3. (Repeat step 2 until firm.)
4. Now the dates.
- Tell me today's date. Get ready. (Signal.)
- (Touch number for today's date.) Here's today's date. Now I'll show you the date that is one week from today.
- (Touch number that is one week from today.) Everybody, say the date that is one week from today. Get ready. (Signal.)
5. Once more.
- Listen: Tell me today's date. Get ready. (Signal.)
- Tell me tomorrow's date. Get ready. (Signal.)
- Tell me the date it will be one week from today. Get ready. (Signal.)
6. (Repeat step 5 until firm.)

WORKBOOK 36

EXERCISE 8   Clarabelle And The Bluebirds

Sequencing

1. Everybody, open your workbook to Lesson 36. Write your name at the top of the page. ✔
- These are pictures that show the first story about Clarabelle. The pictures are in order. That means that the **first** picture shows something that happened at the **beginning** of the story. The **next** picture shows something that happened **next** in the story. The very **last** picture shows something that happened at the **end** of the story.
2. Everybody, touch picture 1. ✔
- What's happening in that picture? (Call on several children. Ideas: *Clarabelle is looking at the bluebirds on the wire* or *Clarabelle is saying she wants to be like the bluebirds.*)
3. Everybody, touch picture 2. ✔
- What's happening in that picture? (Call on several children. Idea: *Clarabelle is starting to tiptoe out on the wire.*)
4. Everybody, touch picture 3. ✔
- What's happening in that picture? (Call on several children. Ideas: *The wire is almost touching the ground* or *The bluebirds are telling Clarabelle to get off the wire.*)
5. Everybody, touch picture 4. ✔
- What's happening in that picture? (Call on several children. Ideas: *Clarabelle is jumping off the wire into the haystack; The birds are being shot up into the air; The other animals are laughing.*)
6. You can use these pictures to tell the **whole** story about Clarabelle and the bluebirds. You have to start out by telling **why** Clarabelle wanted to sit on the wire in the first place. Then tell the things that happened in each picture. Raise your hand if you think you can tell the whole Clarabelle story. Remember, you have to tell the beginning and then tell about each picture.
7. (Call on several children to tell the story. Instruct the other children to follow along and raise their hand if they hear a problem. Praise stories that tell what happens in each picture.)
8. Later you can color the pictures. I know that everybody remembers what colors Clarabelle is, what color the birds are and what color the barn is supposed to be.

EXERCISE 9   From-To

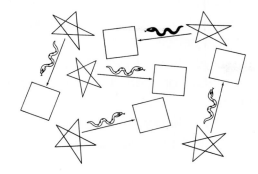

1. Everybody, find the next page in your workbook. Find the black snake. ✔
2. The **black snake** is moving **from** the star to the square. What is the snake moving **from?** (Signal.) *The star.*
• What is the snake moving **to?** (Signal.) *The square.*
3. (Repeat step 2 until firm.)
4. Touch the thing the snake is moving **from.** ✔
• Everybody, what are you touching? (Signal.) *The star.*
• Touch the thing the snake is moving **to.** ✔
• Everybody, what are you touching? (Signal.) *The square.*
5. Here's the rule about the thing the snake is moving **to.** It should be green. Name the thing you are going to color green. Get ready. (Signal.) *The square.*
• Make a green mark on the thing the snake is moving **to.**
(Observe children and give feedback.)
• Here's a rule about the thing the snake is moving **from.** It should be orange. Name the thing you are going to color orange. Get ready. (Signal.) *The star.*
• Make an orange mark on the thing the snake is moving **from.**
(Observe children and give feedback.)
6. Now make marks for the **other snakes.** Make a green mark on the things that the snakes are moving **to.** ✔
• Make an orange mark on the things that the snakes are moving **from.** ✔

EXERCISE 10   Questioning Skills

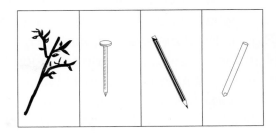

1. (Hold up workbook. Point to boxed pictures.)
• I'm thinking about one of the pictures. It's either a branch, a nail, a pencil, or chalk. You'll ask questions to find out which object I'm thinking of. Everybody, ask a question about what material it is made of. Get ready. (Signal.) *What material is it made of?*
• Everybody, ask a question about the parts it has. Get ready. (Signal.) *What parts does it have?*
• Everybody, ask a question about what you use it for. Get ready. (Signal.) *What do you use it for?*
2. Let's ask those questions again.
3. Everybody, ask a question about what material it is made of. Get ready. (Signal.) *What material is it made of?*
• Everybody, ask a question about the parts it has. Get ready. (Signal.) *What parts does it have?*
• Everybody, ask a question about what you use it for. Get ready. (Signal.) *What do you use it for?*
4. (Repeat step 3 until firm.)

5. Ask those questions again, and I'll tell you the answers. Everybody, ask a question about what material it is made of. Get ready. (Signal.) *What material is it made of?*

- Here's the answer. It's made of wood. What material is it made of? (Signal.) *Wood.*

6. Everybody, ask the question about the parts it has. Get ready. (Signal.) *What parts does it have?*

- Here's the answer. It has a shaft, an eraser, and a point. What parts? (Signal.) *A shaft, an eraser, and a point.*

7. Everybody, ask the question about what you use it for. Get ready. (Signal.) *What do you use it for?*

- Here's the answer. To write with. What is it used for? (Signal.) *To write with.*

8. Make a red mark on the thing I'm thinking of. ✔

- Everybody, what object was I thinking of? (Signal.) *A pencil.*
- How did you know I wasn't thinking of a branch? (Call on a child. Accept reasonable answers.)
- How did you know I wasn't thinking of chalk? (Call on a child. Accept reasonable answers.)
- How did you know I wasn't thinking of a nail? (Call on a child. Accept reasonable answers.)

Objectives

- Generate statements to describe actions using present, past and future tense. (Exercise 1)
- Given actions, answer questions involving moving to and from. (Exercise 2)
- **Given two sentences, identify which gives more information and if it tells "where," "why," or "when."** (Exercise 3)
- Answer questions about previously learned calendar facts. (Exercise 4)
- Name common opposites. (Exercise 5)
- Given a complex sentence, answer questions involving "who," "how," "why," and "where." (Exercise 6)
- Given a calendar, identify the day and date for "today" and "tomorrow" and one week from today. (Exercise 7)
- Retell a familiar story by making a picture consistent with story details. (Exercise 8)

EXERCISE 1 Actions

1. It's time for some actions.
2. Everybody, let's stand up. Get ready. (Signal.) (You and the children are to stand up.)
- What are we doing? (Signal.) *Standing up.*
- What were we doing? (Signal.) *Sitting down.*
3. Everybody, we will sit down. What will we do? (Signal.) *Sit down.*
- What are we doing? (Signal.) *Standing up.*
- What will we do? (Signal.) *Sit down.*
- Say the whole thing about what we will do. Get ready. (Signal.) *We will sit down.*
4. Let's do it. (Signal.) (You and the children are to sit down.)
- Everybody, now what are we doing? (Signal.) *Sitting down.*
- Say the whole thing about what we were doing. Get ready. (Signal.) *We were standing up.*

EXERCISE 2 From—To

1. (Draw a small circle on the chalkboard.)
- Get ready to tell me if I move my finger **from** the circle.

2. (Place your finger to the left of the circle.) Watch. (Move it toward the circle.)
- Did I move from the circle? (Signal.) *No.*
3. (Place your finger inside the circle.) Watch. (Move it straight up from the circle.)
- Did I move from the circle? (Signal.) *Yes.*
4. (Place your finger inside the circle.) Watch. (Move it from the circle to the left.)
- Did I move from the circle? (Signal.) *Yes.*
5. (Place your finger above the circle.) Watch. (Move it straight down to the circle.)
- Did I move from the circle? (Signal.) *No.*
6. (Place your finger inside the circle.) Watch. (Move it from the circle to the right.)
- Did I move from the circle? (Signal.) *Yes.*
7. (Place your finger below the circle.) Watch. (Move it straight up to the circle.)
- Did I move from the circle? (Signal.) *No.*
8. (Repeat steps 2 through 7 until firm.)
9. (Place your finger inside the circle.) Watch. (Move it below the circle.)
- Did I move from the circle? (Signal.) *Yes.*
- How did I move my finger? (Signal.) *From the circle.*
- Say the whole thing about how I moved my finger. Get ready. (Signal.) *You moved your finger from the circle.*
10. (Repeat step 9 until firm.)

EXERCISE 3 Why—When—Where

1. I'm going to say two statements. One statement tells more about what happened.
2. Here's the first statement: The man fixed a car in a garage. Everybody, say that statement. Get ready. (Signal.) *The man fixed a car in a garage.*
   - Here's the second statement: The man fixed a car. Everybody, say that statement. Get ready. (Signal.) *The man fixed a car.*
3. Listen to the statements again. (Hold up one finger.) The man fixed a car in a garage.
   - (Hold up two fingers.) The man fixed a car.
4. Everybody, say the statement that tells more. Get ready. (Signal.) *The man fixed a car in a garage.*
   - That statement tells more than the other statement. Tell me if it tells **where, why,** or **when.** Get ready. (Signal.) *Where.*
   - Where did the man fix a car? (Signal.) *In a garage.*
5. I'm going to say two more statements. One statement tells more about what happened.
6. Here's the first statement: The car didn't work. Everybody, say that statement. Get ready. (Signal.) *The car didn't work.*
   - Here's the second statement: The car didn't work because it had a flat tire. Everybody, say that statement. Get ready. (Signal.) *The car didn't work because it had a flat tire.*
7. Listen to the statements again. (Hold up one finger.) The car didn't work.
   - (Hold up two fingers.) The car didn't work because it had a flat tire.
8. Everybody, say the statement that tells more. Get ready. (Signal.) *The car didn't work because it had a flat tire.*
   - That statement tells more than the other statement. Tell me if it tells **where, why,** or **when.** Get ready. (Signal.) *Why.*
9. Why didn't the car work? (Signal.) *Because it had a flat tire.*

EXERCISE 4 Calendar Facts

1. How many months are in a year? (Signal.) *12.*
   - Say the fact. Get ready. (Signal.) *There are 12 months in a year.*
   - How many seasons are in a year? (Signal.) *Four.*
   - Say the fact. Get ready. (Signal.) *There are four seasons in a year.*
   - How many days are in a year? (Signal.) *365.*
   - Say the fact. Get ready. (Signal.) *There are 365 days in a year.*
   - How many weeks are in a year? (Signal.) *52.*
   - Say the fact. Get ready. (Signal.) *There are 52 weeks in a year.*
2. (Repeat step 1 until firm.)
3. Say the seasons of the year. Get ready. (Signal.) *Winter, spring, summer, fall.*
   - Say the months of the year. Get ready. (Signal.) *January, February, March, April, May, June, July, August, September, October, November, December.*

EXERCISE 5 Opposites

1. We're going to play a word game.
2. Everybody, think of a board that is not wide. It is the opposite of wide. What's the opposite of wide? (Signal.) *Narrow.*
   - So a board that is the opposite of wide is . . . (Signal.) *narrow.*
3. Everybody, think of a car that is not fast. It is the opposite of fast. What's the opposite of fast? (Signal.) *Slow.*
   - So a car that is the opposite of fast is . . . (Signal.) *slow.*
4. Everybody, think of hair that is not long. It is the opposite of long. What's the opposite of long? (Signal.) *Short.*
   - So hair that is the opposite of long is . . . (Signal.) *short.*
5. Everybody, think of a book that is not difficult. It is the opposite of difficult. What's the opposite of difficult? (Signal.) *Easy.*
   - So a book that is the opposite of difficult is . . . (Signal.) *easy.*

EXERCISE 6 Who—How—Why—Where

1. I'm going to say sentences that answer questions. One of the questions is **how.**
2. Listen: At the dinner, they ate slowly because there was a lot of food. How did they eat? (Signal.) *Slowly.*

3. Listen: At the dinner, Tim ate slowly because there was a lot of food. Say that sentence. Get ready. (Signal.) *At the dinner, Tim ate slowly because there was a lot of food.*
   - How did Tim eat? (Signal.) *Slowly.*
4. Listen again. At the dinner, Tim ate slowly because there was a lot of food. Who ate slowly? (Signal.) *Tim.*
   - How did he eat? (Signal.) *Slowly.*
   - Where did he eat slowly? (Signal.) *At the dinner.*
   - Why did he eat slowly? (Signal.) *Because there was a lot of food.*
5. (Repeat step 4 until firm.)
6. Everybody, say the whole sentence. Get ready. (Signal.) *At the dinner, Tim ate slowly because there was a lot of food.*
   - Which word tells who? (Signal.) *Tim.*
   - Which word tells how? (Signal.) *Slowly.*
   - Which words tell where? (Signal.) *At the dinner.*
   - Which words tell why? (Signal.) *Because there was a lot of food.*

EXERCISE 7   Calendar

1. (Present calendar.) We're going to talk about today, tomorrow, and one week from today.
2. Tell me the day of the week it is today. Get ready. (Signal.)
   - Tell me the day of the week it will be tomorrow. Get ready. (Signal.)
   - Tell me the day of the week it will be one week from today. Get ready. (Signal.)
3. (Repeat step 2 until firm.)
4. Now the dates. Tell me today's date. Get ready. (Signal.)
   - (Touch the number for today's date.) Here's today's date. Everybody, tell me the date it will be one week from today. Get ready. (Signal.)
5. Once more. Listen: Tell me today's date. Get ready. (Signal.)
   - Tell me tomorrow's date. Get ready. (Signal.)
   - Tell me the date it will be one week from today. Get ready. (Signal.)
6. (Repeat step 5 until firm.)

EXERCISE 8   Roxie The Rock Collector

Sequencing

1. Everybody, open your workbook to Lesson 37. Write your name at the top of the page. ✔
2. This picture shows a part of the story about Roxie and her rock collection.
3. The numbers in the picture show what happened to Roxie's rocks. But a lot of things went on **before** the rocks ended up at number 4. You have to tell all those things.
   - You have to tell **why.** You have to tell **why** Roxie had to move her rocks. You can see her mother in the picture. That will give you a clue about **why** Roxie had to move her rocks.
   - You have to tell **why** the rocks went from number 3 to 4. If Roxie put just the rocks she's carrying in this picture in the tree house, that floor would **not** creak and groan and finally break. She'd have to put a **lot** of rocks in that tree house before that would happen. So she'd have to keep going from number 1 to 2 to 3—**all day**—before that floor would break.
   - Then when the rocks landed at number 4, they stayed at number 4. You have to tell **why** Roxie didn't have to move them again.
4. So this is a tough story to tell. Raise your hand when you think you can do it. ✔
   - (Call on several children to tell the story. Instruct the other children to follow along and raise their hand if they hear a problem. Praise stories that tell **why** Roxie had to move the rocks, **why** the floor finally broke and **why** Roxie didn't have to move the rocks after they landed at number 4.)
5. Later you can color this picture. You may want to make a rock garden.

LESSON 38

Objectives

- Name classes and subclasses. (Exercise 1)
- Identify statements that tell "when" and "where" and answer "when" and "where" questions. (Exercise 2)
- **Answer classification questions involving "only," and name members of the given class.** (Exercise 3)
- Answer questions about previously learned calendar facts. (Exercise 4)
- **Answer classification questions involving "true", "false" and "only."** (Exercise 5)
- **Given a common noun, generate questions and statements involving class, use, and location.** (Exercise 6)
- Given a calendar, identify the day and date for "today" and "tomorrow" and one week from today. (Exercise 7)
- Answer questions about a new story. (Exercise 8)
- Make a picture consistent with the details of the story. (Exercise 9)
- **Follow coloring rule for involving material.** (Exercise 10)
- Follow coloring rules involving classification using "some" and "all." (Exercise 11)

EXERCISE 1 Classification

1. We're going to talk about classes.
2. If we took all potatoes from the class of food, would there be any kinds of food left? (Signal.) *Yes.*
- Name some kinds of food that would be left. (Call on individual children. Praise appropriate responses.)
3. The class of potatoes is made up of many kinds of potatoes. I'll name some kinds of potatoes in the class of potatoes. Listen: mashed potatoes, boiled potatoes.
- You name some kinds of potatoes in the class of potatoes. (Call on individual children. Praise reasonable answers, such as: *fried potatoes, scalloped potatoes, baked potatoes.*)
4. Think about this. If we took all the mashed potatoes from the class of potatoes, would there be any potatoes left? (Signal.) *Yes.*
- Name some kinds of potatoes that would be left. (Call on individual children. Praise all acceptable answers: any kind of potato except mashed potatoes.)
5. Yes, if we took all the mashed potatoes from the class of potatoes, there would still be potatoes left. So which class is bigger, the class of mashed potatoes or the class of potatoes? (Signal.) *The class of potatoes.*
- How do you know? (Signal.) *The class of potatoes has more kinds of things in it.*

6. Think big. Which class is bigger, the class of potatoes or the class of food? (Signal.) *The class of food.*
- Think big. Which class is bigger, the class of potatoes or the class of mashed potatoes? (Signal.) *The class of potatoes.*

EXERCISE 2 When—Where

1. I'm going to say statements. Some of these statements tell **where** the pig ate corn. Some of these statements tell **when** the pig ate corn.
2. Listen: The pig ate corn on Tuesday. Everybody, say that statement. Get ready. (Signal.) *The pig ate corn on Tuesday.*
- Does the statement tell **where** the pig ate corn or **when** the pig ate corn? (Signal.) *When.*
- When did the pig eat corn? (Signal.) *Tuesday.*
3. Listen: The pig ate in the back of the pigpen. Everybody, say that statement. Get ready. (Signal.) *The pig ate in the back of the pigpen.*
- Does the statement tell **where** the pig ate corn or **when** the pig ate corn? (Signal.) *Where.*
- Where did the pig eat corn? (Signal.) *In the back of the pigpen.*
4. Listen: The pig ate corn last week. Everybody, say that statement. Get ready. (Signal.) *The pig ate corn last week.*

- Does that statement tell **where** the pig ate corn or **when** the pig ate corn? (Signal.) *When.*
- When did the pig eat corn? (Signal.) *Last week.*

5. Listen: The pig ate corn on the farm. Everybody, say that statement. Get ready. (Signal.) *The pig ate corn on the farm.*
- Does that statement tell **where** the pig ate corn or **when** the pig ate corn? (Signal.) *Where.*
- Where did the pig eat corn? (Signal.) *On the farm.*

6. (Repeat steps 2 through 5 until firm.)

EXERCISE 3   Only

1. I'm going to say a statement.
2. Listen: It is food. Say that. Get ready. (Signal.) *It is food.*
- Is that statement true of milk? (Signal.) *Yes.*
- Is that statement true of only milk? (Signal.) *No.*
- Name some other things it's true of. (Call on individual children. Praise all reasonable responses.)

3. Listen: You can work with it. Say that. Get ready. (Signal.) *You can work with it.*
- Is that statement true of milk? (Signal.) *No.*

4. Listen: You can drink it. Say that. Get ready. (Signal.) *You can drink it.*
- Is that statement true of milk? (Signal.) *Yes.*
- Think about this. Is that statement true only of milk? (Signal.) *No.*
- Name some other things it's true of. (Call on individual children. Praise all reasonable responses.)

5. Listen: You can drink it and it comes from cows. Say that. Get ready. (Signal.) *You can drink it and it comes from cows.*
- Is that statement true of milk? (Signal.) *Yes.*
- Think about this. Is that statement true only of milk? (Signal.) *Yes.* Yes, that statement is true of only milk.

EXERCISE 4   Calendar Facts

1. How many months are in a year? (Signal.) *12.*
- Say the fact. Get ready. (Signal.) *There are 12 months in a year.*
- How many seasons are in a year? (Signal.) *Four.*
- Say the fact. Get ready. (Signal.) *There are four seasons in a year.*
- How many days are in a year? (Signal.) *365.*
- Say the fact. Get ready. (Signal.) *There are 365 days in a year.*
- How many weeks are in a year? (Signal.) *52.*
- Say the fact. Get ready. (Signal.) *There are 52 weeks in a year.*

2. (Repeat step 1 until firm.)
3. Say the seasons of the year. Get ready. (Signal.) *Winter, spring, summer, fall.*
- Say the months of the year. Get ready. (Signal.) *January, February, March, April, May, June, July, August, September, October, November, December.*

EXERCISE 5   Only

1. I'm going to say a statement.
2. Listen: It has wheels. Say that. Get ready. (Signal.) *It has wheels.*
- Is that statement true of a bicycle? (Signal.) *Yes.*
- Is that statement true of only a bicycle? (Signal.) *No.*
- Name some other things it's true of. (Call on individual children. Praise all reasonable responses.)

3. Listen: It is good to eat. Say that. Get ready. (Signal.) *It is good to eat.*
- Is that statement true of a bicycle? (Signal.) *No.*

4. Listen: It has handlebars. Say that. Get ready. (Signal.) *It has handlebars.*
- Is that statement true of a bicycle? (Signal.) *Yes.*
- Think about this. Is that statement true only of a bicycle? (Signal.) *No.*
- Name some other things it's true of. (Call on individual children. Praise all reasonable responses.)

5. Listen: You pedal it and it has two wheels. Say that. Get ready. (Signal.) *You pedal it and it has two wheels.*
- Is that statement true of a bicycle? (Signal.) *Yes.*

- Think about this. Is that statement true only of a bicycle? (Signal.) *Yes.* Yes, that statement is true of only a bicycle.

EXERCISE 6   Questioning Skills

1.   Everybody, think about a drinking glass.
- Ask a question about the class it is in. Get ready. (Signal.) *What class is it in?*
- Ask a question about what it's used for. Get ready. (Signal.) *What is it used for?*
- Ask a question about where you find it. Get ready. (Signal.) *Where do you find it?*
2.   (Repeat step 1 until firm.)
3.   Ask a question about the class a drinking glass is in. Get ready. (Signal.) *What class is it in?*
- Tell me the answer. Get ready. (Signal.) *Containers.*
- Let's make a statement about the class a glass is in. Get ready. (Respond with the children.) *A glass is in the class of containers.*
4.   (Repeat step 3 until firm.)
5.   Ask a question about what it's used for. Get ready. (Signal.) *What is it used for?*
- Tell me the answer. Get ready. (Signal.) *Drinking.*
- Let's make a statement about what a glass is used for. Get ready. (Respond with the children.) *A glass is used for drinking.*
6.   (Repeat step 5 until firm.)
7.   Ask a question about where you find it. Get ready. (Signal.) *Where do you find it?*
- Tell me the answer. (Call on individual children. Accept all reasonable responses.)
- Let's say: in the kitchen. Everybody, let's make a statement about where you find a glass. Get ready. (Respond with the children.) *You find a glass in the kitchen.*
8.   (Repeat step 7 until firm.)
9.   Get ready to make those statements again. Don't ask questions. Just make the statements. Say the statement about the class a glass is in. Get ready. (Signal.) *A glass is in the class of containers.*
- Say the statement about what a glass is used for. Get ready. (Signal.) *A glass is used for drinking.*
- Say the statement about where you find a glass. Get ready. (Signal.) *You find a glass in the kitchen.*
10. (Repeat step 9 until firm.)

EXERCISE 7   Calendar

1.   (Present calendar.) We're going to talk about today, tomorrow, and one week from today.
2.   Tell me the day of the week it is today. Get ready. (Signal.)
- Tell me the day of the week it will be tomorrow. Get ready. (Signal.)
- Tell me the day of the week it will be one week from today. Get ready. (Signal.)
3.   (Repeat step 2 until firm.)
4.   Now the dates. Tell me today's date. Get ready. (Signal.)
- (Touch the number for today's date.) Here's today's date. Everybody, tell me the date it will be one week from today. Get ready. (Signal.)
5.   Once more. Listen: Tell me today's date. Get ready. (Signal.)
- Tell me tomorrow's date. Get ready. (Signal.)
- Tell me the date it will be one week from today. Get ready. (Signal.)
6.   (Repeat step 5 until firm.)

EXERCISE 8
Rolla, The Merry-Go-Round Horse
Storytelling

- Everybody, I'm going to read you a story about a merry-go-round and a horse on that merry-go-round named Rolla.

   There once was a wonderful merry-go-round in a park. Everybody loved that merry-go-round. The music would play, and the horses on the merry-go-round would go up and down with children on them.

- See if you can get a picture in your mind of that merry-go-round with the children on it.

   The mothers were happy, the children were happy and even the horses in the merry-go-round were happy—all except Rolla.

- Everybody, which horse was not happy? (Signal.) *Rolla.*
- How many horses do you think were in that merry-go-round? (Call on a child. Accept reasonable responses.)

Each horse in the merry-go-round had a number. There were eight horses and Rolla was horse number eight. She had a big number painted on her—number eight.

- Everybody, how many horses were in the merry-go-round? (Signal.) *Eight.*
- What number was Rolla? (Signal.) *Eight.*

At first, that number didn't bother her, but after a while, she started to think, "Why should I be number **eight?** I would rather be number five or three, or **best** of all, number **one.**"

- Everybody, what number did Rolla like best of all? (Signal.) *Number one.*
- Why do you think she liked number one better than number eight? (Call on a child. Idea: *It's first place.*)

Rolla liked number one best because she thought one was the first-place number. Two was the second-place number. And **eight . . .** eight was the **eighth-place** number. Boo.

Rolla figured that the only way she could change her number was to go faster. If she passed up the horse in front of her, she'd be number seven. If she passed up **all** the other horses, she'd be number **one.**

- How did she think she could get to be number one? (Call on a child. Idea: *Go fast enough to pass up all the other horses.*)

So one day, Rolla started going faster. She went up and down faster and she moved forward faster. But when she went faster, all the other horses had to go faster, too. Even the music had to go faster.

That did not make the mothers or the children very happy. The horses were going up and down so fast that the children could hardly hang on to them. The merry-go-round was turning so fast that the mothers who were standing next to their children had to hang on to poles or they would be thrown off the merry-go-round. And the music sounded terrible. It was going so fast that it

sounded screechy and jumpy. The other horses were not very happy either. "Hey, what are you doing?" they would call to Rolla. "Slow down. When you go fast, we have to go fast."

- Listen: What were some of the problems Rolla created when she started going faster? (Call on several children. Ideas: *The children could hardly hang on to the horses; The mothers had to hang on to poles or they'd get thrown off; All the horses had to go fast; The music was screechy.*)
- Why did the other horses have to go fast when Rolla went fast? (Call on a child. Idea: *They were all fixed in place.*)

But Rolla didn't slow down. The next day she went even faster. She went so fast that nobody would even get on the merry-go-round. "This is not a merry-go-round," one mother said. "It's a rodeo. I'm not bringing my children here anymore."

- Listen: What happens at a rodeo? (Call on a child. Idea: *The horses try to buck the riders off.*)
- Why did one mother say the merry-go-round was like a rodeo? (Call on a child. Idea: *Because the horses were going so fast that the children couldn't hang on to them.*)

And the horses were getting sore and tired from bobbing up and down and racing around like the wind. They kept yelling at Rolla, "Slow down. This is not fun." But all day, she kept trying to pass up the horse in front of her. She didn't succeed. And at the end of the day, she was sore and tired, too. And she was very sad.

"I'm tired of being number eight," she said with a tear in her eye. "But I can't seem to catch the horse in front of me."

"Is that your problem?" horse number one said. "You think that you're in last place just because you're number eight?"

All the horses gave her a big horse laugh. Horse number three said, "The numbers don't mean anything. Every horse **follows** another horse and every horse is right **in front** of another horse."

"Yeah," horse number five said. "The numbers don't mean anything."

"That's easy for **you** to say," Rolla said. "You're number five. But I'm number eight. I'm the last horse on this merry-go-round." She had **another** great big tear in her eye.

The other horses whispered to each other and nodded their heads up and down. They had a plan.

- What do you think their plan is? (Call on a child. Accept reasonable responses.)
- We'll see if you're right.

After a lot of whispering and nodding, horse number two said, "Rolla, if you had a **different** number, would you stop trying to go fast?"

"Of course," she said.

So guess what the other horses did?

- What do you think they did? (Call on a child. Idea: *They gave her another number.*)
- Here's the last part of the story:

If you go to that merry-go-round today, you won't hear any mothers complaining about it being like a rodeo. You won't see children with frightened faces holding on with all their might. You won't hear that screechy, jumpy music. You'll see a happy group of horses going around at a nice slow pace—in time with the music. You'll see children laughing and mothers smiling. You'll also notice that the horses are smiling. And if you look closely, you'll see that one horse has a bigger smile than the other horses. That horse is number **one.** And that horse's name is **Rolla.**

- Listen: Now we know what the plan was. Everybody, what number did the other horses give Rolla? (Signal.) *One.*
- Do you think that the horse that's **now** number eight is unhappy? (Signal.) *No.*

- Why not? (Call on a child. Ideas: *The horses agreed to the plan* or *The horse knows that the numbers don't mean anything.*)

EXERCISE 9   Workbook Activity

1. Everybody, open your workbook to Lesson 38. Write your name at the top of the page. ✔
2. This picture shows a part of the story about Rolla and the merry-go-round. Think big. Did this picture take place on the **first** day or the **second** day Rolla was trying to pass the other horses? (Signal.) *The first day.*
- How do you know it was the **first** day? (Call on a child. Idea: *Because on the second day, nobody would even get on the merry-go-round.*)
3. Why are the horses going so fast in this picture? (Call on a child. Idea: *Because Rolla is going too fast.*)
- How can you tell that they're going very fast? (Call on a child. Ideas: *Two mothers are hanging on to poles, almost falling off; Some kids are screaming; The poles are bent; Everybody is looking on with fright.*)
- How will the merry-go-round look different at the end of the story? (Call on a child. Ideas: *The children will be laughing; The mothers will be smiling; The horses will be smiling.*)
4. Somebody forgot to put the numbers on those horses. But if you look at them, you can find Rolla. She's the spotted horse in the middle of the picture. The other horses are yelling at Rolla. Touch Rolla. ✔

- Put number **eight** in the box for Rolla's number. ✔
- The horse that is right **behind** her is number one. Write **one** in the box for that horse. ✔
- Touch the horse that's right **in front** of Rolla. That's the big white horse with the little kid on it. ✔
- That's the first horse that Rolla would have to pass up. Raise your hand if you know what number that horse is. Everybody, what number? (Signal.) *Seven.*
- Write **seven** on that white horse. Then number the other horses. Remember, Rolla would have to pass up horse seven, then horse six, then horse five . . . and all the way around to horse one, which is the horse right behind her. Raise your hand when you've written numbers on all the horses.

  (Observe children and give feedback.)
5. Later you can color the picture of Rolla and the merry-go-round. See how pretty you can make the merry-go-round and the horses. But remember what color the horse in front of Rolla is.

EXERCISE 10 Materials

 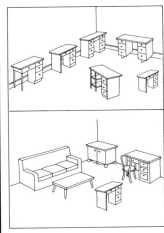

1. Find the next page in your workbook. ✔
- (Hold up workbook. Point to first half.)
2. Here's a coloring rule for this picture. If an object is made of paper, color it green. What's the rule? (Signal.) *If an object is made of paper, color it green.*
3. (Repeat step 2 until firm.)
4. Make a green mark on **one** of the objects made of paper. ✔
5. Here's another coloring rule for this picture. If an object is made of metal, color it black. What's the rule? (Signal.) *If an object is made of metal, color it black.*
6. (Repeat step 5 until firm.)
7. Make a black mark on **one** of the objects made of metal. ✔
8. Here's one more thing to do. Part of the pot is missing. What part is missing? (Signal.) *The handle.*
- Yes, the handle. Before you color the pot, follow the dots with your pencil to make the handle.

EXERCISE 11 Classification

1. (Hold up workbook. Point to second half.) The boxes show two pictures. **Some** of the pieces of furniture in one picture are desks. **All** of the pieces of furniture in the other picture are desks.
2. Touch the picture where **some** of the pieces of furniture are desks. ✔
- Here's the rule about the picture where **some** of the pieces of furniture are desks. The desks should be brown. What's the rule? (Signal.) *The desks should be brown.*
- Mark the desks in the picture where **some** of the pieces of furniture are desks. ✔
3. Here's the rule about the picture where **all** of the pieces of furniture are desks: Color each desk either black or purple. What's the rule? (Signal.) *Color each desk either black or purple.*
- Make a black mark on one desk and a purple mark on another desk. ✔

LESSON 39

Objectives

- Name classes and subclasses. (Exercise 1)
- Answer classification questions involving "true", "false" and "only." (Exercise 2)
- Name common opposites. (Exercise 3)
- Given a calendar, identify the day and date for "today" and "tomorrow" and one week from today. (Exercise 4)
- Relate a familiar story grammar to a picture that indicates the sequence of events for a new story. (Exercise 5)
- **Put on a play to show a new story.** (Exercise 6)
- **Given a picture, identify an object being moved away "from" and the object being moved "to."** (Exercise 7)
- Follow coloring rules involving material. (Exercise 8)

EXERCISE 1 Classification

1. We're going to talk about classes.
2. Everybody, think about classes. Which class is bigger, the class of tools or the class of hammers? (Signal.) *The class of tools.*
   - How do you know? (Signal.) *The class of tools has more kinds of things in it.*
3. (Repeat step 2 until firm.)
4. Everybody, think about classes. Which class is bigger, the class of bushes or the class of plants? (Signal.) *The class of plants.*
   - How do you know? (Signal.) *The class of plants has more kinds of things in it.*
5. (Repeat step 4 until firm.)
6. Everybody, think about classes. Which class is bigger, the class of buildings or the class of gas stations? (Signal.) *The class of buildings.*
   - How do you know? (Signal.) *The class of buildings has more kinds of things in it.*
7. (Repeat step 6 until firm.)
8. Everybody, think about classes. Which class is bigger, the class of clothing or the class of socks? (Signal.) *The class of clothing.*
   - How do you know? (Signal.) *The class of clothing has more kinds of things in it.*
9. (Repeat step 8 until firm.)

10. Everybody, think about classes. Which class is bigger, the class of vehicles or the class of trains? (Signal.) *The class of vehicles.*
    - How do you know? (Signal.) *The class of vehicles has more kinds of things in it.*
11. (Repeat step 10 until firm.)
12. Everybody, think about classes. Which class is bigger, the class of beds or the class of furniture? (Signal.) *The class of furniture.*
    - How do you know? (Signal.) *The class of furniture has more kinds of things in it.*
13. (Repeat step 12 until firm.)

EXERCISE 2 Only

1. I'm going to say a statement.
2. Listen: You need a ticket to get inside. Say that. Get ready. (Signal.) *You need a ticket to get inside.*
   - Is that statement true of a movie theater? (Signal.) *Yes.*
   - Think about this. Is that statement true of only a movie theater? (Signal.) *No.*
   - Name some other things it's true of. (Call on individual children. Praise all reasonable responses.)
3. Listen: You can buy candy bars there. Say that. Get ready. (Signal.) *You can buy candy bars there.*
   - Is that statement true of a movie theater? (Signal.) *Yes.*
   - Think about this. Is that statement true only of a movie theater? (Signal.) *No.*

- Name some other things it's true of. (Call on individual children. Praise all reasonable responses.)

4. Listen: You can drink it. Say that. Get ready. (Signal.) *You can drink it.*

- Is that statement true of a movie theater? (Signal.) *No.*

5. Listen: It has a big screen and lots of seats. Say that. Get ready. (Signal.) *It has a big screen and lots of seats.*

- Is that statement true of a movie theater? (Signal.) *Yes.*

- Think about this. Is that statement true only of a movie theater? (Signal.) *Yes.* Yes, that statement is true of only a movie theater.

EXERCISE 3   Opposites

1. We're going to play a word game.
2. Everybody, think of a test that is the opposite of difficult. What's the opposite of difficult? (Signal.) *Easy.*

- So a test that is the opposite of difficult is . . . (Signal.) *easy.*

3. Everybody, think of a runner who is doing the opposite of losing. What's the opposite of losing? (Signal.) *Winning.*

- So a runner who is doing the opposite of losing is . . . (Signal.) *winning.*

4. Everybody, think of an airplane that is the opposite of slow. What's the opposite of slow? (Signal.) *Fast.*

- So an airplane that is the opposite of slow is . . . (Signal.) *fast.*

5. Everybody, think of a dish that is the opposite of wet. What's the opposite of wet? (Signal.) *Dry.*

- So a dish that is the opposite of wet is . . . (Signal.) *dry.*

6. Everybody, think of a woman who is doing the opposite of laughing. Listen: The opposite of laughing is crying. What's the opposite of laughing? (Signal.) *Crying.*

- So a woman who is doing the opposite of laughing is . . . (Signal.) *crying.*

EXERCISE 4   Calendar

1. (Present calendar.) We're going to talk about today, tomorrow, and one week from today.

2. Tell me the day of the week it is today. Get ready. (Signal.)

- Tell me the day of the week it will be tomorrow. Get ready. (Signal.)

- Tell me the day of the week it will be one week from today. Get ready. (Signal.)

3. (Repeat step 2 until firm.)

4. Now the dates. Tell me today's date. Get ready. (Signal.)

- (Touch the number for today's date.) Here's today's date. Everybody, tell me the date it will be one week from today. Get ready. (Signal.)

5. Once more. Listen: Tell me today's date. Get ready. (Signal.)

- Tell me tomorrow's date. Get ready. (Signal.)

- Tell me the date it will be one week from today. Get ready. (Signal.)

6. (Repeat step 5 until firm.)

WORKBOOK 39

EXERCISE 5   Sequence Story

The Bragging Rats

1. Everybody, open your workbook to Lesson 39. Write your name at the top of the page. ✔

2. This picture shows another story about the bragging rats.

3. Everybody, touch number 1. ✔

- You can see the rats arguing about something. And you can see the wise old rat telling them to do something. I'll bet he's telling them how to settle their argument. He's pointing to number 2.
- Touch number 2. ✔
- That's where the bragging rats go next. That thing is a barbell, a big heavy weight.
- Touch number 3. ✔
- That's the little black rat that won the running race in one story. She also won another contest. Who remembers what contest that was? (Call on a child. Idea: *The eating contest.*)

4. That black rat is going to do something in this story. But I can't read you this story about the bragging rats because somebody forgot to write it down in my book. Listen: Don't say anything. But see if you can figure out what the rats are arguing about and how the wise old rat is telling them to settle their argument. That's what you'll have to tell at number 1. Then you'll tell what the bragging rats did at number 2 to settle the argument. Then you'll have to tell something about number 3 and what that little black rat did.

5. Raise your hand if you think you can tell the whole story. Remember, you have to tell everything that happened at number 1, then at number 2 and then you'll tell about the little black rat.

- (Call on a child to tell the story. Repeat with several children. Praise stories that cover the following ideas at the appropriate number: (1) The rats were arguing about who was the strongest; the wise old rat told them how to settle their argument by lifting the barbell to see who was the strongest; (2) The bragging rats tried to lift the barbell, but neither of them could do it; (3) The little black rat lifted the barbell and won the contest.)

6. Later, you'll color the picture.

EXERCISE 6 Putting On A Play

1. (Use a chalkboard pointer, broom or large chalkboard eraser for a barbell.) Let's act out this story.

- (Identify children to play the parts of the two bragging rats, the wise old rat and the little black rat.)
  (Identify the object that is supposed to be the barbell. Say:) Pretend this is that big heavy barbell.
- (Place the barbell near the group of characters.)

2. We'll start out with the bragging rats arguing. So I want to hear a good argument. I want to hear those bragging rats telling about how strong they are. They don't always tell the truth, do they?

- So they could say things like, "I'm so strong that I could . . ." and then you'll have to tell something amazing.
- After they argue awhile; the wise old rat has to step in and tell them to stop arguing. Then he'll tell them how to settle their argument.
- And the bragging rats will take turns trying to lift the barbell. They'll really do a poor job.
- But then, it's the little black rat's turn. And I'll bet those bragging rats will not be very happy when they see that little black rat lift that heavy weight.

3. Here we go. Are the bragging rats ready to give us a good argument?

- Go. (Prompt each bragging rat to tell a couple of lies. Then prompt the wise old rat to intervene. Praise good acting.)

EXERCISE 7 From-To

1. Everybody, find the next page in your workbook. ✔

- (Hold up workbook. Point to top half.)

2. Each **horse** is moving **from** one thing to another thing. What is each horse moving **from?** (Signal.) *A rectangle.*

• What is each horse moving **to?** (Signal.) *A pencil.*

3. (Repeat step 2 until firm.)

4. Touch the thing a horse is moving **from.** ✔

• Everybody, what are you touching? (Signal.) *A rectangle.*

• Touch the thing a horse is moving **to.** ✔

• Everybody, what are you touching? (Signal.) *A pencil.*

5. Here's the rule about the thing a horse is moving **to.** It should be yellow. Name the thing you are going to color yellow. Get ready. (Signal.) *A pencil.*

• Make a yellow mark on the thing a horse is moving **to.**
(Observe children and give feedback.)

• Here's a rule about the thing a horse is moving **from.** It should be red. Name the thing you are going to color red. Get ready. (Signal.) *A rectangle.*

• Make a red mark on the thing the horse is moving **from.**
(Observe children and give feedback.)

6. Now make marks for the **other** horses. Make a yellow mark on the thing those horses are moving **to.** Make a red mark on the thing those horses are moving **from.**
(Observe children and give feedback.)

EXERCISE 8 **Materials**

1. (Hold up workbook. Point to bottom half.)

2. Here's a coloring rule for this picture. If an object is made of rubber, color it purple. What's the rule? (Signal.) *If an object is made of rubber, color it purple.*

3. (Repeat step 2 until firm.)

4. Make a purple mark on **one** of the objects made of rubber. ✔

5. Here's another coloring rule for this picture. If an object is made of cloth, color it yellow. What's the rule? (Signal.) *If an object is made of cloth, color it yellow.*

6. Make a yellow mark on **one** of the objects made of cloth. ✔

7. Here's one more thing to do. Part of the shirt is missing. What part is missing? (Signal.) *The collar.* Yes, the collar.

• Before you color the shirt, follow the dots and make the collar.

LESSON 40

Objectives

- Name classes and subclasses. (Exercise 1)
- Answer classification questions involving true, false and only. (Exercise 2)
- Given a complex sentence, answer questions involving "who," "what," "how" and "why." (Exercise 3)
- Name common opposites. (Exercise 4)
- **Given a complex sentence, answer questions involving "why" and discriminate between statements that tell "where" and "why."** (Exercise 5)
- Given a calendar, identify the day and date for "today" and "tomorrow" and one week from today. (Exercise 6)
- **Follow coloring rules involving classes and subclasses.** (Exercise 7)
- Given a picture, identify an object being moved away "from" and the object being moved "to." (Exercise 8)
- **Put on a play to show a familiar story.** (Exercise 9)

EXERCISE 1   Classification

1. We're going to talk about classes.
2. If we took all houses from the class of buildings, would there be any kinds of buildings left? (Signal.) *Yes.*
- Name some kinds of buildings that would be left. (Call on individual children. Praise appropriate responses.)
3. The class of houses is made up of many kinds of houses. I'll name some kinds of houses. Listen: brick houses, stucco houses. You name some kinds of houses in the class of houses. (Call on individual children. Praise reasonable answers, such as: *wood houses, brick houses, stucco houses.*)
4. Think about this. If we took all the brick houses from the class of houses, would there be any houses left? (Signal.) *Yes.*
- Name some kinds of houses that would be left. (Call on individual children. Praise all acceptable answers: that is, any kind of material except brick.)
5. Yes, if we took all the brick houses from the class of houses, there would still be houses left. So which class is bigger, the class of brick houses or the class of houses? (Signal.) *The class of houses.*
- How do you know? (Signal.) *The class of houses has more kinds of things in it.*
6. Everybody, think big. Which class is bigger, the class of houses or the class of buildings? (Signal.) *The class of buildings.*

- Think big. Which class is bigger, the class of brick houses or the class of houses? (Signal.) *The class of houses.*

EXERCISE 2   Only

1. I'm going to say a statement.
2. Listen: You can write with it. Say that. Get ready. (Signal.) *You can write with it.*
- Is that statement true of a bathing suit? (Signal.) *No.*
3. Listen: It is made of cloth. Say that. Get ready. (Signal.) *It is made of cloth.*
- Is that statement true of a bathing suit? (Signal.) *Yes.*
- Think about this. Is that statement true of only a bathing suit? (Signal.) *No.*
- Name some other things it's true of. (Call on individual children. Praise all reasonable responses.)
4. Listen: You can wear it. Say that. Get ready. (Signal.) *You can wear it.*
- Is that statement true of a bathing suit? (Signal.) *Yes.*
- Think about this. Is that statement true only of a bathing suit? (Signal.) *No.*
- Name some other things it's true of. (Call on individual children. Praise all reasonable responses.)
5. Listen: It is made for you to wear when you go swimming. Say that. Get ready. (Signal.) *It is made for you to wear when you go swimming.*
- Is that statement true of a bathing suit? (Signal.) *Yes.*

EXERCISE 3 Who—How—Why

1. I'm going to say a sentence that answers questions. One of the questions is **how.**
2. Listen: After the meeting, they walked fast because the street was dark. Say that sentence. Get ready. (Signal.) *After the meeting, they walked fast because the street was dark.*
- When did they walk? (Signal.) *After the meeting.*
- How did they walk? (Signal.) *Fast.*
- Why did they walk fast? (Signal.) *Because the street was dark.*
3. (Repeat step 2 until firm.)
4. Listen to the sentence again: After the meeting, they walked fast because the street was dark. Everybody, say the whole sentence. Get ready. (Signal.) *After the meeting, they walked fast because the street was dark.*
- Which word tells who? (Signal.) *They.*
- Which words tell what they did? (Signal.) *Walked fast.*
- Which word tells how? (Signal.) *Fast.*
- Which words tell why? (Signal.) *Because the street was dark.*
5. (Repeat step 4 until firm.)

EXERCISE 4 Opposites

1. We're going to play a word game.
2. Everybody, think of a whistle that is the opposite of noisy. What's the opposite of noisy? (Signal.) *Quiet.*
- So a whistle that is the opposite of noisy is . . . (Signal.) *quiet.*
3. Everybody, think of a baby who is doing the opposite of crying. What's the opposite of crying? (Signal.) *Laughing.*
- So a baby who is doing the opposite of crying is . . . (Signal.) *laughing.*
4. Everybody, think of a game that is the opposite of difficult. What's the opposite of difficult? (Signal.) *Easy.*
- So a game that is the opposite of difficult is . . . (Signal.) *easy.*
5. Everybody, think of a house that is the opposite of big. What's the opposite of big? (Signal.) *Little.*
- So a house that is the opposite of big is . . . (Signal.) *little.*
6. Everybody, think of a turtle that is the opposite of fast. What's the opposite of fast? (Signal.) *Slow.*
- So a turtle that is the opposite of fast is . . . (Signal.) *slow.*

EXERCISE 5 Why

1. I'm going to say some statements.
- Listen: The man ran. Say that statement. Get ready. (Signal.) *The man ran.*
- Does that statement tell why the man ran? (Signal.) *No.*
2. Listen: The man ran (pause) **because he was in a hurry.**
- Say that statement. Get ready. (Signal.) *The man ran because he was in a hurry.*
- That statement tells why. Everybody, **why** did the man run? (Signal.) *Because he was in a hurry.*
3. I'll say some statements that tell **where** and some statements that tell **why.** See if I can fool you.
4. Listen: The girl laughed in the car. Does that statement tell **where** or **why?** (Signal.) *Where.*
5. Listen: The girl laughed because she saw a dog. Does that statement tell **where** or **why?** (Signal.) *Why.*
6. Listen: The man ate dinner in the kitchen. Does that statement tell **where** or **why?** (Signal.) *Where.*
7. Listen: The man ran to the store. Does that statement tell **where** or **why?** (Signal.) *Where.*
8. (Repeat steps 4 through 7 until firm.)

EXERCISE 6 Calendar

1. (Present calendar.) We're going to talk about today, tomorrow, and one week from today.
2. Tell me the day of the week it is today. Get ready. (Signal.)
- Tell me the day of the week it will be tomorrow. Get ready. (Signal.)
- Tell me the day of the week it will be one week from today. Get ready. (Signal.)
3. (Repeat step 2 until firm.)
4. Now the dates. Tell me today's date. Get ready. (Signal.)

- (Touch the number for today's date.) Here's today's date. Everybody, tell me the date it will be one week from today. Get ready. (Signal.)
5. Once more. Listen: Tell me today's date. Get ready. (Signal.)
- Tell me tomorrow's date. Get ready. (Signal.)
- Tell me the date it will be one week from today. Get ready. (Signal.)
6. (Repeat step 5 until firm.)

WORKBOOK

EXERCISE 7   Classification

1. Everybody, find Lesson 40 in your workbook. Write your name at the top of the page. ✔
2. (Hold up workbook. Point to first half.) The pictures in the boxes show two classes. One class has **one** kind of thing in it, the other class has **more** kinds of things in it.
3. Touch the picture that shows only **one** kind of thing. ✔
- What kind of thing is that in the picture? (Signal.) *Dresses.*
- Touch the picture that shows **more** than one kind of thing. ✔
- That picture shows dresses and other things, too. Everybody, circle the picture that shows **more** kinds of things. ✔
- Everybody, touch the picture that shows only **one** kind of thing. ✔

4. Here's the coloring rule for the picture that shows only one kind of thing. The dresses in that picture should be blue or purple. What colors? (Signal.) *Blue or purple.*
- Make a blue mark on one dress and a purple mark on another dress. ✔
- Everybody, touch the picture that shows **more** than one kind of thing. ✔
- The dresses in the picture that shows **more** than one kind of thing should be green. Mark two dresses in that picture. ✔

EXERCISE 8   From—To

1. (Hold up workbook. Point to second half.) The fish is moving **from** one thing to another thing. What is the fish moving **from?** (Signal.) *The boat.*
- What is the fish moving **to?** (Signal.) *The seal.*
2. (Repeat step 1 until firm.)
3. Touch the thing the fish is moving **from.** ✔ Everybody, what are you touching? (Signal.) *The boat.*
- Touch the thing the fish is moving **to.** ✔
- Everybody, what are you touching? (Signal.) *The seal.*
4. Here's the rule about the thing the fish is moving **to.** It should be black. Name the thing you are going to color black. Get ready. (Signal.) *The seal.*
- Make a black mark on the thing the fish is moving **to.** (Observe children and give feedback.)
- Here's a rule about the thing the fish is moving **from.** It should be red. Name the thing you are going to color red. Get ready. (Signal.) *The boat.*
- Make a red mark on the thing the fish is moving **from.** (Observe children and give feedback.)

EXERCISE 9 Putting On A Play

Bragging Rats Strength Contest

Note: If time permits, repeat the play about the bragging rats' strength contest.

1. Everybody, find the next page in your workbook. ✔
- You've seen this picture before. The picture shows the bragging rats arguing about how strong they are. Let's see if different actors can do a good job of putting on a play for that picture. Who could do a good job of being a bragging rat? (Select two children.)

- Who could be a good wise old rat? (Select a child.)
- Who would like to be the little black rat? (Select a child.)
2. (Identify the object that is to be the barbell. Say:) Remember, this is that big, heavy barbell that the bragging rats will try to lift.
3. We'll start out with the bragging rats arguing. So I want to hear a good argument. I want to hear those bragging rats telling about how strong they are. They don't always tell the truth, do they?
- So they could say things like "I'm so strong that I could . . ." and then you'll have to tell something amazing.
- After they argue awhile, the wise old rat has to step in and tell them to stop arguing. Then he'll tell them how to settle their argument.
- And the bragging rats will take turns trying to lift the barbell. They'll do a poor job.
- But then, it's the little black rat's turn. And I bet those bragging rats will not be very happy when they see that little black rat lift that heavy weight.
4. Here we go. Are the bragging rats ready to give us a good argument?
- Go. (Prompt each bragging rat to tell a couple of lies. Then prompt the wise old rat to intervene. Praise good acting.)

LESSON 41

Objectives

- **Given a common noun, construct a definition by naming the class and saying something true of only that noun.** (Exercise 1)
- **Given an action, answer questions involving movement "from" and "to" and generate statements about the movement.** (Exercise 2)
- **Given a common noun, answer questions involving "can do."** (Exercise 3)
- **Given a common noun, name three classes containing the noun (smallest, bigger, really big).** (Exercise 4)
- Given a calendar, identify the day and date for "today" and "tomorrow" and one week from today. (Exercise 5)
- **Given a common object, answer true/false questions.** (Exercise 6)
- Answer questions about the events in a familiar story. (Exercise 7)
- Given a picture from a familiar story, answer literal, inferential and sequence questions and make the picture consistent with the story. (Exercise 8)
- Follow coloring rules involving classes and subclasses. (Exercise 9)
- Follow coloring rules involving parts of a whole. (Exercise 10)

EXERCISE 1   Definitions

1. We're going to make up a definition for **corn.** First we name a class. Then we say something that is true of only corn. Remember, first we name a class. What do we do first when we make up a definition? (Signal.) *Name a class.*
- Next we say something that is true of only corn.
- What do we do next? (Signal.) *Say something that is true of only corn.*
2. (Repeat step 1 until firm.)
3. Once more. Everybody, what do we do first? (Signal.) *Name a class.*
- What do we do next? (Signal.) *Say something that is true of only corn.*
4. (Repeat step 3 until firm.)
5. Now let's make up a definition. Everybody, what do we do first? (Signal.) *Name a class.*
- Name a class for **corn.** (Call on individual children. Accept reasonable responses but use: *food or plant.*) Yes, corn is a food or corn is a plant.
- We named a class. Now what do we do? (Signal.) *Say something that is true of only corn.*
- Yes, now say something that is true of only corn. (Call on one or two children. Accept all reasonable responses, but use: *It grows on ears.*) Yes, it grows on ears.

6. I'll say the definition for **corn:** Corn is food that grows on ears.
7. Your turn. Say the definition for **corn.** Get ready. (Signal.) *Corn is food that grows on ears.*
- (Repeat step 7 until firm.)
8. We're going to make up a definition for **tree.** Everybody, what do we do first? (Signal.) *Name a class.*
- Name a class for **tree.** Get ready. (Signal.) *Plants.* Yes, a tree is a plant.
- We named a class. Now what do we do? (Signal.) *Say something that is true of only a tree.*
- Yes, now say something that is true of only a tree. (Call on one or two children. Accept all reasonable responses, but use: *It has leaves, branches, and a trunk.*) Yes, it has leaves, branches, and a trunk.
9. Everybody, now say the definition for **tree.** Get ready. (Signal.) *A tree is a plant that has leaves, branches, and a trunk.*
- (Repeat step 9 until firm.)
10. Let's see if you remember these definitions. Everybody, say the definition for **corn.** Get ready. (Signal.) *Corn is food that grows on ears.*
- Everybody, say the definition for **tree.** Get ready. (Signal.) *A tree is a plant that has leaves, branches, and a trunk.*

EXERCISE 2 From—To

1. (Draw a small square on the chalkboard.)
2. Get ready to tell me if I move the chalk **from** the square.
3. (Place the chalk inside the square.) Watch. (Move it straight up from the square.) Did I move from the square? (Signal.) *Yes.*
   - (Place the chalk inside the square.) Watch. (Move it to the left from the square.) Did I move from the square? (Signal.) *Yes.*
   - (Place the chalk below the square.) Watch. (Move it toward the square.) Did I move from the square? (Signal.) *No.*
   - (Place the chalk inside the square.) Watch. (Move it to the right from the square.) Did I move from the square? (Signal.) *Yes.*
   - (Place the chalk to the left of the square.) Watch. (Move it toward the square.) Did I move from the square? (Signal.) *No.*
4. (Repeat step 3 until firm.)
5. (Place the chalk inside the square.) Watch. (Move it to the left from the square.) Did I move from the square? (Signal.) *Yes.*
   - How did I move the chalk? (Signal.) *From the square.*
   - Say the whole thing about how I moved the chalk. Get ready. (Signal.) *You moved the chalk from the square.*
6. (Repeat step 5 until firm.)

EXERCISE 3 Can Do

1. Get ready to answer some questions about a pair of scissors.
2. Can you use a pair of scissors to cut paper? (Signal.) *Yes.*
   - Can you use a pair of scissors to cut string? (Signal.) *Yes.*
   - Can you tear a pair of scissors into little pieces? (Signal.) *No.*
   - Can you drink from a pair of scissors? (Signal.) *No.*
3. (Repeat step 2 until firm.)
4. Here are some more questions about what you can do with a pair of scissors.

5. Can you put a pair of scissors into a box? (Signal.) *Yes.*
   - Can you cook hamburgers with a pair of scissors? (Signal.) *No.*
   - Can you step on a pair of scissors? (Signal.) *Yes.*
   - Can you hide inside a pair of scissors? (Signal.) *No.*
6. (Repeat step 5 until firm.)
7. I'm going to ask you about what a woman can do with a pair of scissors.
8. Can a woman cut paper with a pair of scissors? (Signal.) *Yes.*
   - Say the whole thing about what a woman can do. Get ready. (Signal.) *A woman can cut paper with a pair of scissors.*
   - Can a woman write a letter with a pair of scissors? (Signal.) *No.*
   - Say the whole thing. Get ready. (Signal.) *A woman cannot write a letter with a pair of scissors.*
9. (Repeat step 8 until firm.)

EXERCISE 4 Classification

1. I'm thinking of a glass. I'm going to name some classes a glass is in.
2. (Make a small circle with your hands.) Here's the smallest class: glasses.
   - (Make a wider circle.) Here's the next bigger class: things to drink from.
   - (Make a still wider circle.) Here's a really big class: containers.
3. Which class has the most kinds of things in it, glasses, things to drink from, or containers? (Signal.) *Containers.*
4. Now it's your turn to name some classes a glass is in. (Make a small circle with your hands.)
   What's the smallest class for a glass? (Signal.) *Glasses.*
   - (Make a wider circle.) What's the next bigger class? (Signal.) *Things to drink from.*
   - (Make a still wider circle.) What's a really big class? (Signal.) *Containers.*
5. (Repeat step 4 until firm.)
6. There is one kind of object you would find in all of those classes. Everybody, name the kind of object you would find in all those classes. Get ready. (Signal.) *A glass.*

EXERCISE 5 Calendar

1. (Present calendar.) We're going to talk about today, tomorrow, and one week from today.
2. Tell me the day of the week it is today. Get ready. (Signal.)
   - Tell me the day of the week it will be tomorrow. Get ready. (Signal.)
   - Tell me the day of the week it will be one week from today. Get ready. (Signal.)
3. (Repeat step 2 until firm.)
4. Now the dates. Tell me today's date. Get ready. (Signal.)
   - (Touch the number for today's date.) Here's today's date. Everybody, tell me the date it will be one week from today. Get ready. (Signal.)
5. Once more. Listen: Tell me today's date. Get ready. (Signal.)
   - Tell me tomorrow's date. Get ready. (Signal.)
   - Tell me the date it will be one week from today. Get ready. (Signal.)
6. (Repeat step 5 until firm.)

EXERCISE 6 True—False

1. I'm going to make statements about hammers. You're going to say true or false.
2. Listen: Hammers are good to eat. True or false? (Signal.) *False.*
   - Listen: Hammers have a handle. True or false? (Signal.) *True.*
   - Listen: Hammers have bristles. True or false? (Signal.) *False.*
   - Listen: You can pound nails with hammers. True or false? (Signal.) *True.*
   - Listen: Hammers are tools. True or false? (Signal.) *True.*
3. (Repeat step 2 until firm.)

EXERCISE 7 Rolla, The Merry-Go-Round Horse

Review

- Everybody, I'm going to read you the story about a merry-go-round and a horse again. What was the name of that horse? (Signal.) *Rolla.*

- What number was that horse at the beginning of the story? (Signal.) *Eight.*
- Listen:

There once was a wonderful merry-go-round in a park. Everybody **loved** that merry-go-round. The music would play, and the horses on the merry-go-round would go up and down with children on them.

- Listen: How did the mothers feel about the merry-go-round? (Call on a child. Idea: *They loved it.*)
- How did the children feel about the merry-go-round? (Call on a child. Idea: *They loved it.*)
- Everybody, was there anybody who **wasn't** happy? (Signal.) *Yes.*
- Who was that? (Signal.) *Rolla.*

Right, the mothers were happy, the children were happy and even the horses in the merry-go-round were happy—**all except Rolla.**

Each horse in the merry-go-round had a number. There were eight horses and Rolla was horse number eight. She had a big number painted on her—number eight.

At first that number didn't bother her, but after a while, she started to think, "Why should **I** be number **eight**? I would rather be number five or three, or best of all . . ."

- Everybody, what number? (Signal.) *One.*
- Right, Rolla would like to be number **one** best of all.

Rolla liked number one best because she thought one was the first place number. Two was the second place number. And **eight . . .** eight was the **eighth**-place number. Boo.

- Listen: Rolla didn't like that number. Who remembers the plan she had for getting a different number? (Call on a child. Idea: *To go faster and pass up all the other horses.*) Yes.

Rolla figured that the only way she could change her number was to go faster. If she passed up the horse in front of her, she'd be number seven. If she passed up **all** the other horses, she'd be number **one.**

So one day, Rolla started going faster. She went up and down faster and she moved forward faster.

- When Rolla went faster, what happened to the other horses? (Call on a child. Idea: *They had to go faster.*)
- Why did they have to go faster when Rolla went faster? (Call on a child. Idea: *Because they're all fixed in place.*)
- What did the music do when the horses started going faster and faster? (Call on a child. Idea: *It went faster.*)
- Right.

When Rolla went faster, all the other horses had to go faster too. Even the music had to go faster.

That did not make the mothers or the children very happy.

- Why not? (Call on a child. Idea: *They had to hang on or they would get thrown off.*)
- How did the horses like this high-speed merry-go-round? (Call on a child. Idea: *They didn't like it.*)
- Why didn't they like it? (Call on a child. Idea: *Because they had to go very fast.*)

The horses were going up and down so fast that the children could hardly hang on to them. The merry-go-round was turning so fast that the mothers who were standing next to their children had to hang on to poles or they would be thrown off the merry-go-round. And the music sounded terrible. It was going so fast that it sounded screechy and jumpy. The other horses were not very happy either. "Hey, what are you doing?" they would call to Rolla. "Slow down. When you go fast, we have to go fast."

But Rolla didn't slow down. The next day, she went even faster. She went so fast that nobody would even get on the merry-go-round. "This is not a merry-go-round," one mother said. "It's a rodeo. I'm not bringing my children here anymore."

And the horses were getting sore and tired from bobbing up and down and racing around like the wind. They kept yelling at Rolla, "Slow down. This is not fun." But all day, she kept trying to pass up the horse in front of her. She didn't succeed. And at the end of the day, she was sore and tired, too. And she was very sad.

"I'm tired of being number eight," she said with a tear in her eye. "But I can't seem to catch the horse in front of me."

"Is that your problem?" horse number one said. "You think that you're in last place just because you're number eight?"

All the horses gave her a big horse laugh. Horse number three said, "The numbers don't mean anything. Every horse **follows** another horse and every horse is right **in front** of another horse."

"Yeah," horse number five said. "The numbers don't mean anything."

"That's easy for **you** to say," Rolla said. "You're number five. But I'm number eight. I'm the **last** horse on this merry-go-round." She had **another** great big tear in her eye.

The other horses whispered to each other and nodded their heads up and down. They had a plan.

- And what was that plan? (Call on a child. Idea: *To change numbers and give Rolla number one.*)

After a lot of whispering and nodding, horse number two said, "Rolla, if you had a **different** number, would you stop trying to go fast?"

"Of course," she said.

So guess what the other horses did?

- Well, we **know** what they did.

If you go to that merry-go-round today, you won't hear any mothers complaining about it being like a rodeo. You won't see children with frightened faces holding on with all their might. You won't hear that screechy, jumpy music. You'll see a happy group of horses going around at a nice slow pace—in time with the music. You'll see children laughing and mothers smiling. You'll also notice that the horses are smiling. And if you look closely, you'll see that one horse has a bigger smile than the other horses. That horse is number **one.** And that horse's name is **Rolla.**

WORKBOOK

EXERCISE 8 Workbook Activity

1. Everybody, open your workbook to Lesson 41. Write your name at the top of the page. ✔
- This picture shows a part of the story about Rolla and the merry-go-round. Look at this picture very carefully, especially at the horses. Everybody, did this picture take place **before** Rolla started to run fast or **after** she started to run fast? (Signal.) *After she started to run fast.*
- What clue in the picture lets you know that it took place **after** Rolla started to run fast? (Call on a child. Ideas: *Rolla is happy* or *Rolla is number one.*)

2. This picture is a lot different from the way things looked when Rolla was trying to pass up the other horses. Name some ways that things are different in this picture. Let's see if we can name at least five ways that things are different.
(Call on several children. For each acceptable response, hold up a finger. Praise the class if five or more differences are named. Ideas: *Rolla is number one; All the horses are happy; The mothers and children are happy; The mothers do not have to hold on to the poles; The merry-go-round is going slower.*)
- Everybody, the only horse with a number is Rolla. If she's number one, what's the number of the horse right **behind** her? (Signal.) *Two.*
3. Later you can color this picture. Remember to put numbers on all the horses you can see.

EXERCISE 9 Classification

1. Everybody, find the next page of your workbook. ✔
- (Hold up workbook. Point to first half.) The pictures in the boxes show two classes. One class has **one** kind of thing in it, the other class has **more** kinds of things in it.
2. Touch the picture that shows only **one** kind of thing. ✔
- What kind of thing is that in the picture? (Signal.) *Trees.*
- Touch the picture that shows **more** than one kind of thing. ✔

- That picture shows trees and other things, too. Everybody, circle the picture that shows **more** kinds of things. ✔
3. Here's the coloring rule for the picture that shows **more** kinds of things. The trees in that picture should be green or yellow. What colors? (Signal.) *Green or yellow.*
- Make a green mark on one tree and a yellow mark on another tree. ✔
- Everybody, touch the picture that shows **one** kind of thing. ✔
- The trees in the picture that shows one kind of thing should be green. Mark two trees in that picture. ✔

EXERCISE 10 Part—Whole

1. (Hold up workbook. Point to second half.) Here's a coloring rule for the purse. Listen: Color the side of the purse brown. What's the rule? (Signal.) *Color the side of the purse brown.*
- Mark the side of the purse. ✔
2. Here's another coloring rule for the purse. Listen: Color the front yellow. What's the rule? (Signal.) *Color the front yellow.*
- Mark the front. ✔
3. Part of the purse is missing. What part is missing? (Call on a child. Accept *strap,* but use *handle.*) Yes, the handle.
- Before you color the purse, you're going to follow the dots and make the handle.
4. Here's the coloring rule for the handle. Listen: Color the handle red. What's the rule? (Signal.) *Color the handle red.*
- Mark the handle. ✔

LESSON 42

Objectives

- Generate statements to describe actions using present, past and future tense. (Exercise 1)
- Given a common noun, construct a definition by naming the class and saying something true of only that noun. (Exercise 2)
- Given a common noun, name three classes containing the noun (smallest, next bigger, really big). (Exercise 3)
- Given a calendar, identify the day and date for "today" and "tomorrow" and one week from today. (Exercise 4)
- Given an action, answer questions involving movement "from" and "to" and generate statements about the movement. (Exercise 5)
- **Generate statements involving "can do" and "cannot do."** (Exercise 6)
- Given a common noun, answer questions involving "can do." (Exercise 7)
- Given a common object, answer true/false questions and **generate true/false statements.** (Exercise 8)
- **Collect data on groups and tell whether statements about groups are true or false.** (Exercise 9)

EXERCISE 1 Actions

1. It's time for some actions.
2. Everybody, let's stand up. Get ready. (Signal.) (You and children are to stand up.)
- What are we doing? (Signal.) *Standing up.*
- What were we doing? (Signal.) *Sitting down.*
3. Everybody, we will sit down. What will we do? (Signal.) *Sit down.*
- What are we doing? (Signal.) *Standing up.*
- What will we do? (Signal.) *Sit down.*
- Say the whole thing about what we will do. Get ready. (Signal.) *We will sit down.*
4. Let's do it. (Signal.)
(You and the children are to sit down.)
- Everybody, now what are we doing? (Signal.) *Sitting down.*
- What were we doing before we sat down? (Signal.) *Standing up.*
- Say the whole thing about what we were doing. Get ready. (Signal.) *We were standing up.*

EXERCISE 2 Definitions

1. We're going to make up a definition for **spider.**
2. First we name a class. Then we say something that is true of only a spider. Remember, first we name a class. What do we do first when we make up a definition? (Signal.) *Name a class.*
- Next we say something that is true of only a spider. What do we do next? (Signal.) *Say something that is true of only a spider.*

3. Once more. Everybody, what do we do first? (Signal.) *Name a class.*
- What do we do next? (Signal.) *Say something that is true of only a spider.*
4. (Repeat step 3 until firm.)
5. Now let's make up a definition. Everybody, what do we do first? (Signal.) *Name a class.*
- Name a class for **spider.** (Call on individual children. Accept all reasonable responses, but use: *animals.*) Yes, a spider is an animal.
- We named a class. Now what do we do? (Signal.) *Say something that is true of only a spider.* Yes, now say something that is true of only a spider. (Call on one or two children. Accept all reasonable responses, but use: *It makes a web.*) Yes, it makes a web.
6. Everybody, now say the definition for **spider.** Get ready. (Signal.) *A spider is an animal that makes a web.*
- (Repeat step 6 until firm.)
7. Now we're going to make up a definition for **elephant.** Everybody, what do we do first? (Signal.) *Name a class.*
- Name a class for **elephant.** Get ready. (Signal.) *Animals.* Yes, an elephant is an animal.
- We named a class. Now what do we do? (Signal.) *Say something that is true of only an elephant.*

216   *Lesson 42*

- Yes, now say something that is true of only an elephant. (Call on one or two children. Accept all reasonable responses, but use: *It has a trunk*.) Yes, it has a trunk.
8. Everybody, now say the definition for **elephant.** Get ready. (Signal.) *An elephant is an animal that has a trunk.*
- (Repeat step 8 until firm.)
9. Now let's see if you remember these definitions. Everybody, say the definition for **spider.** Get ready. (Signal.) *A spider is an animal that makes a web.*
- Everybody, say the definition for **elephant.** Get ready. (Signal.) *An elephant is an animal that has a trunk.*

EXERCISE 3 Classification

1. I'm thinking of a frying pan. I'm going to name some classes a frying pan is in.
2. (Make a small circle with your hands.) Here's the smallest class: frying pans.
- (Make a wider circle.) Here's the next bigger class: things you cook in.
- (Make a still wider circle.) Here's a really big class: containers.
3. Which class has the most kinds of things in it, frying pans, things to cook in, or containers? (Signal.) *Containers.*
4. Now it's your turn to name some classes a frying pan is in.
- (Make a small circle with your hands.) What's the smallest class for a frying pan? (Signal.) *Frying pans.*
- (Make a wider circle.) What's the next bigger class? (Signal.) *Things to cook in.*
- (Make a still wider circle.) What's a really big class? (Signal.) *Containers.*
5. (Repeat step 4 until firm.)
6. There is one kind of object you would find in all of those classes. Everybody, name the kind of object you would find in all those classes. Get ready. (Signal.) *A frying pan.*

EXERCISE 4 Calendar

1. (Present calendar.)
- We're going to talk about today, tomorrow, and one week from today.
2. Tell me the day of the week it is today. Get ready. (Signal.)
- Tell me the day of the week it will be tomorrow. Get ready. (Signal.)
- Tell me the day of the week it will be one week from today. Get ready. (Signal.)
3. (Repeat step 2 until firm.)
4. Now the dates. Tell me today's date. Get ready. (Signal.)
- (Touch the number for today's date.) Here's today's date. Everybody, tell me the date it will be one week from today. Get ready. (Signal.)
5. Once more. Listen: Tell me today's date. Get ready. (Signal.)
- Tell me tomorrow's date. Get ready. (Signal.)
- Tell me the date it will be one week from today. Get ready. (Signal.)
6. (Repeat step 5 until firm.)

EXERCISE 5 From—To

1. Get ready for some actions.
2. Everybody, put your finger on your knee. Get ready. (Signal.) ✔
- Where is your finger? (Signal.) *On my knee.*
- Everybody, move your finger from your knee. Get ready. (Signal.) ✔
- How did you move your finger? (Signal.) *From my knee.*
- Say the whole thing about how you moved your finger. Get ready. (Signal.) *I moved my finger from my knee.*
3. (Repeat step 2 until firm.)
4. Here's a new one.
5. Everybody, put your finger on your nose. Get ready. (Signal.) ✔
- Where is your finger? (Signal.) *On my nose.*
- Everybody, move your finger from your nose. Get ready. (Signal.) ✔
- How did you move your finger? (Signal.) *From my nose.*
- Say the whole thing about how you moved your finger. Get ready. (Signal.) *I moved my finger from my nose.*
6. (Repeat step 5 until firm.)

EXERCISE 6   Can Do

1. I'm going to ask questions about a man and a saw.
2. Everybody, can a man drink a saw? (Signal.) *No.*
   Say the statement. Get ready. (Signal.) *A man cannot drink a saw.*
- Everybody, can a man cut with a saw? (Signal.) *Yes.*
- Say the statement. Get ready. (Signal.) *A man can cut with a saw.*
3. (Call on a child.) Your turn. Make up another statement that tells something a man can do with a saw. (After the child makes an acceptable statement, call on the group.) Say that statement about what a man can do with a saw. Get ready. (Signal.) (The group repeats the child's statement.)
4. (Call on another child.) Your turn. Listen: Make up a statement that tells something a man **cannot** do with a saw. (After the child makes an acceptable statement, call on the group.) Say that statement about what a man **cannot** do with a saw. (Signal.) (The group repeats the child's statement.)
5. (Repeat steps 3 and 4, calling on individual children.)

EXERCISE 7   Can Do

1. Get ready to answer some questions about a wagon.
2. Can you ride in a wagon? (Signal.) *Yes.*
- Can you fold a wagon? (Signal.) *No.*
- Can you fly a wagon? (Signal.) *No.*
- Can you put a dog in a wagon? (Signal.) *Yes.*
- Can you pull a wagon? (Signal.) *Yes.*
- Can you write with a wagon? (Signal.) *No.*
- Can you tear a wagon into pieces? (Signal.) *No.*
- Can a wagon hold water? (Signal.) *Yes.*
3. (Repeat step 2 until firm.)
4. Can a boy pull a wagon? (Signal.) *Yes.*
   Say the whole thing about what a boy can do. Get ready. (Signal.) *A boy can pull a wagon.*
- Can a boy fly a wagon? (Signal.) *No.*
- Say the whole thing. Get ready. (Signal.) *A boy cannot fly a wagon.*
5. (Repeat step 4 until firm.)

EXERCISE 8   True—False

1. I'm going to make statements about beds. You'll say true or false.
2. Listen: You put blankets on beds. Is that true or false? (Signal.) *True.*
- Listen: You can sleep on a bed. True or false? (Signal.) *True.*
- Listen: Beds grow in the ground. True or false? (Signal.) *False.*
- Listen: You see a bed in a bedroom. True or false? (Signal.) *True.*
- Listen: Beds are covered with stone. True or false? (Signal.) *False.*
- (Repeat step 2 until firm.)
3. I'm going to say statements. Some of these statements are true and some are false. You tell me about each statement.
4. Cows lay eggs. True or false? (Signal.) *False.*
- Water is dry. True or false? (Signal.) *False.*
- Birds have feathers. True or false? (Signal.) *True.*
- A bottle is a container. True or false? (Signal.) *True.*
- Trees grow in the clouds. True or false? (Signal.) *False.*
5. My turn. I'm going to make up a statement about cows that is true. Listen: Cows sometimes live in barns. That statement is true.
6. Your turn. You make up a statement about cows that is true. (Call on one child. Praise an acceptable answer and have the group repeat it. Then say:) Everyone, that statement is . . . (Signal.) *true.*
7. Make up another statement about cows that is true. (Call on another child. Praise an acceptable answer and have the group repeat it. Then say:) Everyone, that statement is . . . (Signal.) *true.*
8. My turn. I'm going to make up statements about cows that are false. Listen: Cows say **meow.** Cows have feathers. Cows are plants. Those statements are false.
9. Your turn. You make up a statement about cows that is false. (Call on one child. Praise an acceptable answer and have the group repeat it. Then say:) Everyone, that statement is . . . (Signal.) *false.*

10. Make up another statement about cows that is false. (Call on another child. Praise an acceptable answer and have the group repeat it. Then say:) Everyone, that statement is . . . (Signal.) *false.*

WORKBOOK

EXERCISE 9 Data Collection

🐦 R	Red birds	☐
🐦 Y	Yellow birds	☐
🐦 B	Blue birds	☐
	Other animals	☐

1. You've heard a story about a woman named Bonnie who bought a birdbath for her yard.

> One day, Bonnie was talking to her neighbors. Bonnie said, "I always have red birds and yellow birds and blue birds in my yard. But there are always more **red** birds than any other color."
>
> One neighbor said, "No, that's not true. I've looked in your yard many times when I was trying to find Sweetie. And I know for a fact that there are always more **yellow** birds than any other color."
>
> "Not true," another neighbor said. "Every time I've looked in your yard while walking my wonderful dog, Honey, I've always seen more **blue** birds than birds of any other color."

- If the wise old rat heard this conversation, how do you think he'd go about finding the right answer? (Call on a child. Idea: *Count the birds.*) Yes, the smart way is to find out the answer by counting the birds. So **you** can be smart.

2. Everybody, open your workbook to Lesson 42. Write your name at the top of the page. ✔
- The letters on the birds show what color they should be. The letter **R** on a bird shows that the bird should be **red.**
- Your turn: Take out your **red** crayon and put a **red** mark on all the birds that have the letter **R** on them. Don't miss any birds, but do it fast and don't color the whole bird. Just put a red mark on each bird inside the picture that has an **R** on it. Don't color the bird in the big box. Raise your hand when you're finished.
(Observe children and give feedback.)

3. Now look at the box below the picture. You'll see a picture of a bird with an **R** on it.
- Touch that bird. ✔
- Right after that bird are the words **red birds.** Then there's an empty box. Write the number of **red** birds in that box. Count all the red birds in the picture and write that number in the top box. Raise your hand when you're finished.
(Observe children and give feedback.)
- Everybody, what number did you write for the **red** birds? (Signal.) *Ten.*

4. Now do the same thing for the **yellow** birds. Make a **yellow** mark on every bird in the picture that has the letter **Y** on it. The **Y** is for **yellow.** After you make your yellow marks, count the **yellow** birds and write that number in the box for **yellow** birds. Raise your hand when you're finished.
(Observe children and give feedback.)
- Everybody, what number did you write for the **yellow** birds? (Signal.) *Six.*

5. Now do the same thing for the **blue** birds. Make a **blue** mark on every bird in the picture that has the letter **B** on it. The **B** is for **blue.** After you make your blue marks, count the **blue** birds and write that number in the box for **blue** birds. Raise your hand when you're finished.
   (Observe children and give feedback.)
   • Everybody, what number did you write? (Signal.) *Seven.*

6. Get ready to read your numbers one more time. Listen: How many **red** birds are in the picture? (Signal.) *Ten.*
   • How many **yellow** birds are in the picture? (Signal.) *Six.*
   • How many **blue** birds are in the picture? (Signal.) *Seven.*

7. Let's see who was right about the birds in Bonnie's yard. Here's what Bonnie said: "There are always more **red** birds than any other color." Think about it. Is that statement true or false? (Signal.) *True.*
   • One neighbor said, "There are always more **yellow** birds than any other color." Is that statement true or false? (Signal.) *False.*
   • Another neighbor said that there are always more **blue** birds than any other color. Is that statement true or false? (Signal.) *False.*
   • So who was right, Bonnie or one of her neighbors? (Signal.) *Bonnie.*

8. Before we leave this picture, there's one more box to fill out below the picture, but I really don't know what goes in there.
   • Touch the last box below the picture. ✔
   • It says, **other animals.** I guess they want you to write the number of other animals that are in the picture. But I really don't see any. Maybe you do. Look at the picture very carefully. See if you can find any other animals in the picture. Count up any animals that are **not** birds and write that number in the last box. If you don't find any other animals, you can write **zero** in the box. Raise your hand when you have a number in the last box.
   (Observe children and give feedback.)
   • Everybody, what number did you write for **other animals?** (Signal.) *Two.*
   • I guess they were hiding in the picture. I didn't see them.

9. Later, you can color everything in the picture.

Objectives

- **Demonstrate relationship between "or" alternatives and the word "maybe."** (Exercise 1)
- Given a common noun, construct a definition by naming the class and saying something true of only that noun. (Exercise 2)
- Given a calendar, identify the day and date for "today" and "tomorrow" and one week from today. (Exercise 3)
- Given a common object, answer true/false questions and generate true/false statements. (Exercise 4)
- **Generate statements utilizing past, present and future tenses of the verb "to be."** (Exercise 5)
- Given a common noun, name three classes containing the noun (smallest, next bigger, really big). (Exercise 6)
- Answer questions about a new story. (Exercise 7)
- Make a picture consistent with the details of a story. (Exercise 8)
- Follow coloring rules involving classes and subclasses. (Exercise 9)
- Follow coloring rules involving moving "from" and "to". (Exercise 10)

EXERCISE 1 Actions

1. Get ready for some actions.
2. Listen: I'm going to clap or stand up or snap my fingers. What am I going to do? (Signal.) *Clap or stand up or snap your fingers.*
- Yes, I'm going to clap or stand up or snap my fingers.
- Am I going to jump? (Signal.) *No.*
- Am I going to stand up? (Signal.) *Maybe.*
- Am I going to snap my fingers? (Signal.) *Maybe.*
- Am I going to clap? (Signal.) *Maybe.*
3. I'm going to clap or stand up or snap my fingers. What am I going to do? (Signal.) *Clap or stand up or snap your fingers.*
4. Here I go. (Clap.)
- Is that something I said I would do? (Signal.) *Yes.*
- Here I go again. (Touch your head.)
- Is that something I said I would do? (Signal.) *No.*
- What did I say I would do? (Signal.) *Clap or stand up or snap your fingers.*
- Here I go again. (Snap your fingers.)
- Is that something I said I would do? (Signal.) *Yes.*
- Here I go again. (Touch your nose.)
- Is that something I said I would do? (Signal.) *No.*
- What did I say I would do? (Signal.) *Clap or stand up or snap your fingers.*
- Here I go again. (Stand up.)
- Is that something I said I would do? (Signal.) *Yes.*
- (Sit down.)
5. Your turn to clap or stand up or snap your fingers. (Call on individual children. Praise children who do one of the actions.)
6. Everybody, put your hand on your head. Get ready. (Signal.) ✔
- Where is your hand? (Signal.) *On my head.*
7. Everybody, move your hand from your head. Get ready. (Signal.) ✔
- How did you move your hand? (Signal.) *From my head.*
- Say the whole thing about how you moved your hand. Get ready. (Signal.) *I moved my hand from my head.*
8. (Repeat steps 6 and 7 until firm.)
9. Everybody, put your hand on your back. Get ready. (Signal.) ✔
- Where is your hand? (Signal.) *On my back.*
10. Everybody, move your hand from your back. Get ready. (Signal.) ✔
- How did you move your hand? (Signal.) *From my back.*
- Say the whole thing. Get ready. (Signal.) *I moved my hand from my back.*
11. (Repeat steps 9 and 10 until firm.)

EXERCISE 2   Definitions

1. We're going to make up a definition for **bird.**
2. First we name a class. Then we say something that is true of only a bird. Remember, first we name a class. What do we do first when we make up a definition? (Signal.) *Name a class.*
- Next we say something that is true of only a bird. What do we do next? (Signal.) *Say something that is true of only a bird.*
3. Once more. Everybody, what do we do first? (Signal.) *Name a class.*
- What do we do next? (Signal.) *Say something that is true of only a bird.*
4. (Repeat step 3 until firm.)
5. Now let's make up a definition. Everybody, what do we do first? (Signal.) *Name the class.*
- Name a class for **bird.** (Call on individual children. Accept reasonable responses, but use: *animals.*) Yes, a bird is an animal.
6. We named a class. Now what do we do? (Signal.) *Say something that is true of only a bird.*
- Yes, now say something that is true of **only** a **bird.** (Call on one or two children. Accept reasonable responses, but use: *It has feathers.*) Yes, it has feathers.
7. Everybody, now say the definition for **bird.** Get ready. (Signal.) *A bird is an animal that has feathers.*
- (Repeat step 7 until firm.)
8. Now we're going to make up a definition for **hammer.**
9. Everybody, what do we do first? (Signal.) *Name a class.*
- Name a class for **hammer.** Get ready. (Signal.) *Tools.* Yes, a **hammer** is a tool.
10. We named a class. Now what do we do? (Signal.) *Say something that is true of only a hammer.*
- Yes, now say something that is true of only a **hammer.** (Call on one or two children. Accept reasonable responses, but use: *You pound nails with it.*) Yes, you pound nails with it.
11. Everybody, now say the definition for **hammer.** Get ready. (Signal.) *A hammer is a tool you pound nails with.*

12. Now let's see if you remember these definitions.
13. Everybody, say the definition for **bird.** Get ready. (Signal.) *A bird is an animal that has feathers.*
14. Everybody, say the definition for **hammer.** Get ready. (Signal.) *A hammer is a tool you pound nails with.*

EXERCISE 3   Calendar

1. (Present calendar.) We're going to talk about today, tomorrow, and one week from today.
2. Tell me the day of the week it is today. Get ready. (Signal.)
- Tell me the day of the week it will be tomorrow. Get ready. (Signal.)
- Tell me the day of the week it will be one week from today. Get ready. (Signal.)
3. (Repeat step 2 until firm.)
4. Now the dates. Tell me today's date. Get ready. (Signal.)
- Look at the calendar. ✔
- Tell me tomorrow's date. Get ready. (Signal.)
- Tell me the date it will be one week from today. Get ready. (Signal.)
5. Once more. Listen: Tell me today's date. Get ready. (Signal.)
- Tell me tomorrow's date. Get ready. (Signal.)
- Tell me the date it will be one week from today. Get ready. (Signal.)
6. (Repeat step 5 until firm.)

EXERCISE 4   True—False

1. I'm going to say statements. Some of these statements are true and some are false. You tell me about each statement.
2. The sun shines at night. True or false? (Signal.) *False.*
- A car is a vehicle. True or false? (Signal.) *True.*
- There is water in the ocean. True or false? (Signal.) *True.*
- A plant is an animal. True or false? (Signal.) *False.*
- Glasses are made out of wood. True or false. (Signal.) *False.*
3. My turn. I'm going to make up a statement about the sun that is true. Listen: The sun is hot. That statement is true.

4. Your turn. You make up a statement about the sun that is true. (Call on one child. Praise an acceptable answer and have the group repeat it. Then say:) Everyone, that statement is . . . (Signal.) *true.*

5. My turn. I'm going to make up statements about the sun that are false. Listen: The sun is square. The sun has legs. The sun is a vehicle. Those statements are false.

6. Your turn. Make up a statement about the sun that is false. (Call on one child. Praise an acceptable answer and have the group repeat it. Then say:) Everyone, that statement is . . . (Signal.) *false.*

7. Your turn. Make up another statement about the sun that is false. (Call on one child. Praise an acceptable answer and have the group repeat it. Then say:) Everyone, that statement is . . . (Signal.) *false.*

EXERCISE 5   Verb Tense

1. Listen: Tomorrow the cars **will be** on the street. Today the cars **are** on the street. Yesterday the cars **were** on the street.

2. I'll make the statement about the cars tomorrow. Tomorrow the cars will be on the street.
- Your turn. Make the statement about the cars tomorrow. Get ready. (Signal.) *Tomorrow the cars will be on the street.*

3. I'll make the statement about the cars today. Today the cars are on the street.
- Your turn. Make the statement about the cars today. Get ready. (Signal.) *Today the cars are on the street.*

4. I'll make the statement about the cars yesterday. Yesterday the cars were on the street.
- Your turn. Make the statement about the cars yesterday. Get ready. (Signal.) *Yesterday the cars were on the street.*

5. (Repeat steps 2 through 4 until firm.)

6. Listen to these statements.
- Today the car **is** on the street.
- Tomorrow the car **will be** on the street.
- Yesterday the car **was** on the street.

7. Make the statement about the car today. Get ready. (Signal.) *Today the car is on the street.*

8. Make the statement about the car tomorrow. Get ready. (Signal.) *Tomorrow the car will be on the street.*

9. Make the statement about the car yesterday. Get ready. (Signal.) *Yesterday the car was on the street.*

EXERCISE 6   Classification

1. I'm thinking of a cat. I'm going to name some classes a cat is in.

2. (Make a small circle with your hands.) Here's the smallest class: cats.
- (Make a wider circle.) Here's the next bigger class: pets.
- (Make a still wider circle.) Here's the next bigger class: animals.
- (Make an even wider circle.) Here's a really big class: living things.

3. Which class has the most kinds of things in it, cats, pets, animals, or living things? Get ready. (Signal.) *Living things.*

4. Now it's your turn to name some classes a cat is in. (Make a small circle with your hands.) What's the smallest class for a cat? (Signal.) *Cats.*
- (Make a wider circle.) What's the next bigger class? (Signal.) *Pets.*
- (Make a still wider circle.) What's the next bigger class? (Signal.) *Animals.*
- (Make an even wider circle.) What's a really big class? (Signal.) *Living things.*

5. There is one kind of object you would find in all those classes. Everybody, name the kind of object you would find in all those classes. Get ready. (Signal.) *A cat.*

EXERCISE 7   Molly Mix-up And Bleep, Part 1

Storytelling

1. Everybody, I'm going to read you a story about a woman named Molly.

   There once was an inventor named Molly Mix-up. Her last name wasn't really Mix-up, but that's what people called her: Molly Mix-up. She got that name because the things she invented all had the same problem: They didn't work right.

- Everybody, what was the last name that people gave Molly? (Signal.) *Mix-up.*

- Why did they give her that name? (Call on a child. Idea: *Because the things she invented didn't work right.*)
- The story says that she was an inventor. Inventors are very smart people. They make machines and other things that nobody has ever made before. So even though Molly's inventions didn't work right, she must have been pretty smart to invent anything.

Molly once invented an electric can opener. That can opener opened cans. But it also ripped the cans into little pieces.

- What was wrong with the electric can opener she invented? (Call on a child. Idea: *It ripped cans into little pieces.*)
- That would be a problem, wouldn't it?

Molly once invented a toaster that toasted eight slices of bread at the same time. The problem was that it toasted only **one** side of each slice. So you'd get a slice of bread that was toasted on one side, but **not** on the other side.

- Everybody, how many pieces of bread did her toaster toast at the same time? (Signal.) *Eight.*
- What was the problem with the toaster? (Call on a child. Idea: *It only toasted one side of the bread.*)
- That would be a problem, wouldn't it?

Molly Mix-up invented over 50 different things, but they had the same old problem.

- Everybody, what was that problem? (Signal.) *They didn't work right.*

The invention Molly was most proud of was a robot named "Bleep." It took her over seven years to make that robot, and when she was done, that robot could do all kinds of things. Bleep could follow directions. You could tell him to go to the door, and he would say, "Bleep," and then walk to the door. You could tell him to fix breakfast, and he would say, "Bleep," and then fix breakfast. Bleep could even answer the telephone.

- Everybody, what was Molly's proudest invention? (Signal.) *Bleep.*
- How long did it take her to invent Bleep? (Signal.) *Over seven years.*
- Name some things that Bleep could do. (Call on several children. Ideas: *Fix breakfast; Answer the telephone; Follow directions.*)
- Everybody, do you think Bleep was perfect? (Signal.) *No.*
- Why not? (Call on a child. Idea: *All the things that Molly invented had a problem.*)
- Listen:

That robot had the same problem as the other things Molly invented.

The problem with Bleep was that he could answer questions and make statements. But the answers weren't **always** correct and the statements weren't **always** true. You could ask the robot, "What day is today?"

And Bleep would say, "Bleep. Tuesday."

But **maybe** that answer was correct and **maybe** it wasn't. You never knew.

- What was the problem with Bleep? (Call on a child. Idea: *Bleep's answers weren't always correct.*)
- Everybody, were **all** the statements that Bleep made **false?** (Signal.) *No.*
- Were they **all true?** (Signal.) *No.*
- You just never knew whether they were true or false. That would be a problem, wouldn't it?

Sometimes, that robot got Molly in a lot of trouble, because when Bleep talked, he sounded a lot like Molly when she talked. There was one little difference. And if you knew that difference, you could tell right away who was talking.

- I know the difference. Ha, ha. Who else thinks they know the difference? (Call on a child. Idea: *He always said "Bleep" before talking.*)

But sometimes people would not listen carefully and would get fooled, particularly a friend of Molly's named Mrs. Anderson, who didn't hear too well.

- Everybody, who got fooled by Bleep? (Signal.) *Mrs. Anderson.*
- Why did she get fooled? (Call on a child. Idea: *Because she didn't hear too well.*)
- Maybe she didn't hear all those bleeps.

One day, Mrs. Anderson called up Molly. The two women were supposed to meet for lunch. When Mrs. Anderson called, Molly was out in the garage working on a new invention. So who do you think answered the phone?

- Everybody, who? (Signal.) *Bleep.*

Mrs. Anderson said, "Hello Molly. Today's the day we're supposed to meet for lunch."

Bleep said, "Bleep. That is correct."

Mrs. Anderson then said, "Where do you want to meet?"

Bleep said, "Bleep. The corner of 13th and Elm Street."

- Listen: Where did Bleep say the women should meet? (Call on a child. Idea: *The corner of 13th and Elm Street.*)
- Do you **know** if Bleep is saying statements that are true? (Signal.) *No.*
- We just don't know whether they're true or not. I wonder what's on that corner.

Mrs. Anderson said, "I don't know what restaurant is on that corner."

Bleep said, "Bleep. You will like it a lot."

Mrs. Anderson said, "Okay, I'll see you there around noon."

Bleep said, "Bleep. Okay, baby."

Just after Bleep hung up the phone, Molly came in and said, "Were there any calls?"

Bleep said, "Bleep. Yes."

- Everybody, was that the truth? (Signal.) *Yes.*

"Oh," Molly said, "who called?"
Bleep said, "Bleep. Mrs. Anderson."

- Everybody, is that true? (Signal.) *Yes.*

Molly asked, "Did Mrs. Anderson call about lunch?"
Bleep said, "Bleep. Yes."

- Everybody, is that true? (Signal.) *Yes.*

Molly said, "Did **Mrs. Anderson** say where she wanted to eat?"
Bleep said, "Bleep. Yes."

- Everybody, was that statement true? (Signal.) *No.*
- Who **really** said where they should meet for lunch? (Signal.) *Bleep.*

Molly asked, "Where did Mrs. Anderson want to eat?"
"Bleep. The corner of 13th and Elm Street. A wonderful restaurant. You'll love it."
"Thanks," Molly said.

- Listen to the question Molly asked again and listen to Bleep's answer.

Molly asked, "Where did Mrs. Anderson want to eat?"
"Bleep. The corner of 13th and Elm Street."

- Everybody, did Bleep make a true statement? (Signal.) *No.*
- Right, **Mrs. Anderson** didn't want to eat there. **Bleep** is the one who suggested that corner.

After Molly said, "Thanks," Bleep said, "Bleep. Okay, baby."
So Molly went to the address that Bleep had told her. And Mrs. Anderson went to the same address. But you'll have to wait until next time to find out what happened there.

- Oh, what a disappointment. We'll have to wait until next time to see what happens.

2. Well, let's take a vote and see if we can figure out what might happen.

- (Write on the board:)

Yes _____	No _____

- Raise your hand if you think there's a nice restaurant on the corner of 13th and Elm Street. (Count the number of raised hands and write that number, or write 0, in the space after **Yes**.)
- Raise your hand if you don't think there's a nice restaurant on the corner of 13th and Elm Street. (Count the number of raised hands and write that number in the space after **No**.)
- (Call on several children who just raised their hand:) Why don't you think that Bleep directed the women to a nice restaurant? (Idea: *Bleep says too many things that are not true.*)
- We have no way of knowing what's on the corner. But if you had to make a guess, what do you think the women will find on that corner? (Call on several children. Write suggestions on the board and save for the next part of the story.)
- Well, I guess we'll find out next time.

WORKBOOK

EXERCISE 8 Workbook Activity

1. Everybody, open your workbook to Lesson 43. Write your name at the top of the page. ✔
- This picture shows part of the story. But it's a different kind of picture. Bleep is on one side. A woman is on the other side.

2. Everybody, what are they doing in this picture? (Signal.) *Talking on the phone.*
- So who is that woman Bleep is talking to? (Signal.) *Mrs. Anderson.*
- Look. Mrs. Anderson is starting to write something on her pad. It looks like she's written the number 1. Think big. What do you think she's going to write? (Call on a child. Idea: *13th and Elm.*)
- (Write on the board:)

13th and Elm

- I'll bet this is what she'll write on her pad. It says: **13th and Elm.**
- If Mrs. Anderson is writing that address, what is Bleep telling her? (Call on a child. Idea: *Where to meet Molly for lunch.*)
- Where is Molly while this conversation is going on? (Call on a child. Idea: *Out in the garage.*)
- What will happen just after Bleep and Mrs. Anderson finish their conversation? (Call on a child. Idea: *Molly will come inside and ask if there were any calls.*)

3. When you color the picture, you can write the address on Mrs. Anderson's note pad.

EXERCISE 9 Classification

1. Everybody, find the next page in your workbook. ✔
- (Hold up workbook. Point to first half.) The pictures in the boxes show two classes. One class has **one** kind of thing in it, the other class has **more** kinds of things in it.

2. Touch the picture that shows only **one** kind of thing. ✔
- What kind of thing is that in the picture? (Signal.) *Fish.*
- Touch the picture that shows **more** than one kind of thing. ✔
- That picture shows fish and other things, too. Everybody, circle the picture that shows **more** kinds of things. ✔

3. Here's the coloring rule for the picture that shows **more** kinds of things. The fish in that picture should be yellow with black spots. What colors? (Signal.) *Yellow with black spots.*
- Make two marks to show the colors of the fish in that picture. ✔
- Everybody, touch the picture that shows **one** kind of thing. ✔
- The fish in the picture that shows one kind of thing should be brown or green. Mark two fish in that picture. ✔

EXERCISE 10 From—To

1. (Hold up workbook. Point to second half.) The pig is moving **from** one thing **to** another thing. What is the pig moving **from?** (Signal.) *The cow.*
- What is the pig moving **to?** (Signal.) *The sheep.*
2. (Repeat step 1 until firm.)
3. Touch the thing the pig is moving **from.** ✔
- Everybody, what are you touching? (Signal.) *The cow.*
- Touch the thing the pig is moving **to.** ✔
- Everybody, what are you touching? (Signal.) *The sheep.*
4. Here's the rule about the thing the pig is moving **to.** It should be brown. Name the thing you are going to color brown. Get ready. (Signal.) *The sheep.*
- Make a brown mark on the thing the pig is moving **to.**
  (Observe children and give feedback.)
- Here's a rule about the thing the pig is moving **from.** It should be all black. Name the thing you are going to color all black. Get ready. (Signal.) *The cow.*
- Make a black mark on the thing the pig is moving **from.**
  (Observe children and give feedback.)

Objectives

- Follow directions involving if-then. (Exercise 1)
- Given a common noun, name three classes containing the noun (smallest, next bigger, really big). (Exercise 2)
- Given a calendar, identify the day and date for "today" and "tomorrow" and one week from today. (Exercise 3)
- Given an action, answer questions involving movement "from" and "to" and generate statements about the movement. (Exercise 4)
- Given a common noun, answer questions involving "can do." (Exercise 5)
- Given a common object, answer true/false questions and generate true/false statements. (Exercise 6)
- **Answer questions and make predictions about a new story.** (Exercise 7)
- Answer questions about a story and make a picture consistent with the details of the story. (Exercise 8)
- Follow coloring rules involving moving "from" and "to". (Exercise 9)
- Follow coloring rules involving parts of a whole. (Exercise 10)

EXERCISE 1 Actions

1. Here's our first action game.
2. Listen to this rule. If the teacher says **stand up** or says **sit down,** clap. Listen again. If the teacher says **stand up** or says **sit down,** clap. Everybody, say the rule with me. Get ready. (Signal.) *If the teacher says stand up or says sit down, clap.*
   - All by yourselves. Say the rule. Get ready. (Signal.) *If the teacher says stand up or says sit down, clap.*
3. (Repeat step 2 until firm.)
4. What's the rule? (Signal.) *If the teacher says stand up or says sit down, clap.*
   - What are you going to do if the teacher says **stand up** or says **sit down?** (Signal.) *Clap.*
5. Are you going to clap if the teacher says **clap?** (Signal.) *No.*
   - Are you going to clap if the teacher says **sit down?** (Signal.) *Yes.*
   - Are you going to clap if the teacher says **stand up?** (Signal.) *Yes.*
6. Now we're going to play the game.

7. (Stand up.) What's the rule? (Signal.) *If the teacher says stand up or says sit down, clap.*
8. Let's see if I can fool you. (Pause.) (Sit down.) (Signal.) (The children should not do anything.)
9. See if I can fool you. (Pause.) (Clap.) (Signal.) (The children should not do anything.)
10. See if I can fool you this time. (Pause.) **Stand up.** (Signal.) (Every child should clap.)
11. (Repeat steps 7 through 10 until firm. Must be standing before step 8.)

EXERCISE 2 Classification

1. I'm thinking of a goat. I'm going to name some classes a goat is in.
2. (Make a small circle with your hands.) Here's the smallest class: goats.
   - (Make a wider circle.) Here's the next bigger class: farm animals.
   - (Make a still wider circle.) Here's the next bigger class: animals.
   - (Make an even wider circle.) Here's a really big class: living things.
3. Tell me which class has the most kinds of things in it, goats, farm animals, animals, or living things. Get ready. (Signal.) *Living things.*

4. Now it's your turn to name some classes a goat is in.

- (Make a small circle with your hands.) What's the smallest class for a goat? (Signal.) *Goats.*
- (Make a wider circle.) What's the next bigger class? (Signal.) *Farm animals.*
- (Make a still wider circle.) What's the next bigger class? (Signal.) *Animals.*
- (Make an even wider circle.) What's a really big class? (Signal.) *Living things.*

5. There is one kind of object you would find in all those classes. Everybody, name the kind of object you would find in all those classes. Get ready. (Signal.) *A goat.*

EXERCISE 3 Calendar

1. (Present calendar.) We're going to talk about today, tomorrow, and one week from today.
2. Tell me the day of the week it is today. Get ready. (Signal.)
- Tell me the day of the week it will be tomorrow. Get ready. (Signal.)
- Tell me the day of the week it will be one week from today. Get ready. (Signal.)
3. (Repeat step 2 until firm.)
4. Now the dates. Tell me today's date. Get ready. (Signal.)
- Look at the calendar. ✔
- Tell me the date it will be one week from today. Get ready. (Signal.)
5. Once more. Listen: Tell me today's date. Get ready. (Signal.)
- Tell me tomorrow's date. Get ready. (Signal.)
- Tell me the date it will be one week from today. Get ready. (Signal.)
6. (Repeat step 5 until firm.)

EXERCISE 4 From—To

1. (Draw a circle on the chalkboard.)
- Get ready to tell me if I move my finger **from** the circle.
2. (Place your finger above the circle.) Watch. (Move it to the circle.) Did I move from the circle? (Signal.) *No.*
- That's right. I didn't move **from** the circle. I moved **to** the circle. How did I move? (Signal.) *To the circle.*
3. (Place your finger below the circle.) Watch. (Move it to the circle.) Did I move from the circle? (Signal.) *No.*
- That's right. I didn't move **from** the circle. I moved **to** the circle. How did I move? (Signal.) *To the circle.*
4. (Repeat steps 2 and 3 until firm.)
5. Get ready to tell me if I move to the circle or from the circle.
6. (Place your finger to the left of the circle.) Watch. (Move it to the circle.)
- How did I move? (Signal.) *To the circle.*
7. (Place your finger inside the circle.) Watch. (Move it to the left of the circle.)
- How did I move? (Signal.) *From the circle.*
8. (Place your finger to the right of the circle.) Watch. (Move it to the circle.)
- How did I move? (Signal.) *To the circle.*
- Say the whole thing about how I moved my finger. Get ready. (Signal.) *You moved your finger to the circle.*
9. (Place your finger inside the circle.) Watch. (Move it above the circle.)
- How did I move? (Signal.) *From the circle.*
- Say the whole thing about how I moved my finger. Get ready. (Signal.) *You moved your finger from the circle.*
10. (Repeat step 9 until firm.)

EXERCISE 5 Can Do

1. Get ready to answer some questions about a paper bag.
2. Can you drive a car in a paper bag? (Signal.) *No.*
   - Can you carry water in a paper bag? (Signal.) *No.*
   - Can you put trash in a paper bag? (Signal.) *Yes.*
   - Can you carry groceries in a paper bag? (Signal.) *Yes.*
   - Can you wrap a book with a paper bag? (Signal.) *Yes.*
   - Can you chop down a tree with a paper bag? (Signal.) *No.*
   - Can you draw a picture on a paper bag? (Signal.) *Yes.*
   - Can you tear a paper bag? (Signal.) *Yes.*
3. (Repeat step 2 until firm.)
4. Can a man carry groceries in a paper bag? (Signal.) *Yes.*
   - Say the whole thing. Get ready. (Signal.) *A man can carry groceries in a paper bag.*
   - Can a man carry water in a paper bag? (Signal.) *No.*
   - Say the whole thing. Get ready. (Signal.) *A man cannot carry water in a paper bag.*
5. (Repeat step 4 until firm.)

EXERCISE 6 True—False

1. I'm going to say statements. Some of these statements are true and some are false. You tell me about each statement.
2. A house cannot walk. True or false? (Signal.) *True.*
   - A dog is an animal. True or false? (Signal.) *True.*
   - A book is made out of paper. True or false? (Signal.) *True.*
   - A book does not have pages. True or false? (Signal.) *False.*
   - A book does not have a handle. True or false? (Signal.) *True.*
3. (Repeat step 2 until firm.)
4. Your turn. Make up a statement about a book that is true. (Call on three children. Praise each acceptable statement and have the group repeat it. Then say:) Everybody, that statement is . . . (Signal.) *true.*

5. Your turn. Now make up a statement about a book that is false. (Call on three children. Praise each acceptable statement and have the group repeat it. Then say:) Everyone, that statement is . . . (Signal.) *false.*

EXERCISE 7 Molly Mix-up And Bleep, Part 2

Storytelling

1. Last time, I read you the first part of a story about a robot. Everybody, who invented that robot? (Signal.) *Molly Mix-up.*
   - How were all of Molly's inventions the same? (Signal.) *They didn't work right.*
   - What was the name of Molly's robot? (Signal.) *Bleep.*
   - Why do you think that robot got the name Bleep? (Call on a child. Idea: *He always said, "Bleep," before he talked.*)
   - Everybody, when Bleep said things, were they **always** true? (Signal.) *No.*
   - Were they **always** false? (Signal.) *No.* Sometimes the things Bleep said were **true** and sometimes they were **false.**
   - What was the name of the woman who called Molly to make a date for lunch? (Signal.) *Mrs. Anderson.*
   - Did Mrs. Anderson **know** she was talking to Bleep on the phone? (Signal.) *No.*
   - Why not? (Call on a child. Idea: *Because she didn't hear too well.*)
   - Everybody, who did Mrs. Anderson **think** she was talking to? (Signal.) *Molly.*
   - Who came up with a suggestion for a place to eat lunch? (Signal.) *Bleep.*
   - And where was that place? (Call on a child. Idea: *The corner of 13th and Elm.*)
   - When Molly came in, Bleep told her that **Mrs. Anderson** suggested this place for lunch. Everybody, was that true? (Signal.) *No.*
2. Well, here's what happened.

Mrs. Anderson and Molly went in their own cars to meet for lunch. Actually, Molly's car was a big red van that she used to carry around parts. Mrs. Anderson's car was also red, but it was a cute little red sports car. What a surprise the women had when they got to 13th and Elm. The only business on the corner of 13th and Elm was **not** a restaurant or even a market. It was an automobile wrecking yard, where workers take cars apart and then scrunch up what's left with a great scrunching machine.

- Everybody, what was on the corner? (Signal.) *A wrecking yard.*
- What do they do with cars at a wrecking yard? (Call on a child. Idea: *Workers take the cars apart and scrunch them.*)
- Did anybody in our class think there would be a wrecking yard on the corner? (Children respond. Refer to list of ideas on the chalkboard from previous lesson.)
- Who thought that there would **not** be a restaurant on the corner? (Children respond.)
- Let's see how many people said **No.** (Refer to number written next to **No** on the chalkboard from previous lesson.)
- That was a pretty smart guess.

Well, Molly arrived at 13th and Elm first. She didn't see a restaurant so she parked her car in front of the wrecking yard in a parking space that had a sign in front of it—"Drop-off zone."

- Where did Molly park her car? (Call on a child. Idea: *In front of the wrecking yard; in a drop-off zone.*)
- Everybody, what did the sign in front of the parking space say? (Signal.) *Drop-off zone.*
- I wonder what a drop-off zone is. I guess we'll find out.

Molly began to walk around, looking for a restaurant.

When Mrs. Anderson got to the corner of 13th and Elm, she didn't see Molly, so she parked her car in front of the wrecking yard right next to Molly's car—in the drop-off zone.

- Why didn't Mrs. Anderson see Molly when she pulled up? (Call on a child. Idea: *Because Molly was walking around looking for a restaurant.*)
- Where did Mrs. Anderson park? (Call on a child. Ideas: *Right next to Molly; In front of the wrecking yard; In the drop-off zone.*)
- Get a picture in your mind of that place. There are two cars in front of the wrecking yard. What kind of car did Molly drive? (Call on a child. Idea: *A red van.*)
- What kind of car did Mrs. Anderson drive? (Call on a child. Idea: *A cute little red sports car.*)
- The cars were the same color. Everybody, what color was that? (Signal.) *Red.*
- And both those cars were in the drop-off zone. Listen:

Mrs. Anderson didn't see Molly, so she walked around, looking for Molly. She finally found Molly about a block away. She said, "Molly, what a terrible place this is. Where's the restaurant you told me about?"

"**I** didn't tell **you** about a restaurant. **You** told **me** about a restaurant."

"No, no," Mrs. Anderson said. "I remember exactly what you said when I asked you where you wanted to meet. You said, "Bleep. The corner of 13th and Elm Street.""

Molly said to Mrs. Anderson, "Oh, you were talking to Bleep. Let's go back to our cars and find a decent restaurant."

Mrs. Anderson said, "Yes, let's get out of this terrible place."

But it wasn't that easy to get out of that terrible place because when they got back to the wrecking yard, they discovered that their cars were no longer in front of the wrecking yard.

In fact, their cars were no longer cars.

- How could that be possible? How could their cars no longer be cars? (Call on a child. Idea: *Because they had been taken apart or scrunched up.*)

Their cars were piles of parts and pieces. The workers at the wrecking yard were just ready to put what was left of Molly's car in the scrunching machine when the two women realized what had happened to their cars. "Stop, stop," they yelled.

And the workers **did** stop. Mrs. Anderson shouted at them. "How dare you take my beautiful sports car apart!"

One worker said, "Lady, here's the rule about this place: If a car is parked in a drop-off zone, we take it apart. Those two cars were left in the drop-off zone. So we took those two cars apart."

- Listen to what that worker said again:

"If a car is parked in a drop-off zone, we take it apart. Those two cars were left in the drop-off zone. So we took those two cars apart."

- What's the rule about the drop-off zone? (Call on a child. Idea: *If a car is parked in a drop-off zone, it gets taken apart.*)
- Everybody, were any cars parked in the drop-off zone? (Signal.) *Yes.*
- So what did the workers do? (Signal.) *Took them apart.*

"Uh-oh. What will we do?" Mrs. Anderson said.

"I don't know," the worker said. "We only know how to take cars **apart.** We can't put them back together."

The women thought and thought. The workers thought and thought. Finally Molly said, "Well, I'm pretty good at making things. I can tell everybody how to put the cars back together, and if we can all pitch in, we can put those two cars together before suppertime."

- What was Molly's plan? (Call on a child. Idea: *To put the cars back together again.*)
- Everybody, who would tell everybody how to put the cars back together? (Signal.) *Molly.*
- She said she was pretty good at putting things together. Is that statement **entirely** true? (Signal.) *No.*

- Why not? (Call on a child. Idea: *Because something is always wrong with her inventions.*)
- Everybody, do you suppose that there will be a problem with the cars if Molly tells everybody how to put them back together? (Signal.) *Yes.*

The workers said they would help. And so, everybody pitched in. And . . . you'll have to wait until next time to find out what happened.

- It's another one of those stories that stops right in the middle. I wonder if we'll ever find out what happens in this story.
3. Let's take a vote about what we think will happen next time.
- (Write on the board:)

Yes ____	Same ____
No ____	Different ____

- Raise your hand if you think that everybody pitches in and they get the cars put back together **before** suppertime. (Count the number of raised hands and write that number on the board after **Yes.**)
- Raise your hand if you think they will **not** get the cars back together before suppertime. (Count the number of raised hands and write that number on the board after **No.**)
- Raise your hand if you think the cars will be put back together just the way they were **before** the workers took them apart. (Count the number of raised hands and write that number on the board after **Same.**)
- Raise your hand if you think the cars will be **different** than they were before. (Count the number of raised hands and write that number on the board after **Different.**)
- (Call on a child with hand raised:) How do you think the cars might be different? (Praise a response that expresses the idea: *The parts of the cars will be mixed up.*)
4. Next time we'll find out who was right. (Save numbers on board for next lesson.)

WORKBOOK

EXERCISE 8 Workbook Activity

1. Everybody, open your workbook to Lesson 44. Write your name at the top of the page. ✔
2. This picture shows something that happened in the story.
3. What's the address of the place in the picture? (Signal.) *13th and Elm Street.*
- What are the workers doing in the background? (Signal.) *Taking apart cars.*
- What is this kind of place called? (Signal.) *A wrecking yard.*
- How many cars are in front of the place? (Signal.) *Two.*
- Who does that van belong to? (Signal.) *Molly.*
- Where is Molly? (Call on a child. Idea: *Looking for a restaurant.*)
- Everybody, what do those signs in front of the cars say? (Signal.) *Drop-off zone.*
- What is Mrs. Anderson doing? (Call on a child. Idea: *Parking her car.*)
- What's she going to do next? (Call on a child. Idea: *Look for Molly.*)
- What will the workers do while she's looking for Molly? (Call on a child. Idea: *Take the cars apart.*)
- Oh, gracious. That pretty little sports car is going to be nothing but pieces.

- Near the end of the story, Molly and Mrs. Anderson come back just as the workers are getting ready to scrunch what was left of their cars. Can you find the scrunching machine in this picture? It's scrunching up what's left of somebody's car right now.
4. Later you can color the picture. Everybody, what color should the cars be? (Signal.) *Red.*
- Remember that when you color the picture.

EXERCISE 9 From—To

1. Everybody, find the next page in your workbook. ✔
- (Hold up workbook.) Find the cheese. ✔
- The mouse is moving **from** one thing **to** another thing. What is the mouse moving **from?** (Signal.) *The cheese.*
- What is the mouse moving **to?** (Signal.) *The flower.*
2. (Repeat step 1 until firm.)
3. Touch the thing the mouse is moving **from.** ✔
- Everybody, what are you touching? (Signal.) *The cheese.*
- Touch the thing the mouse is moving **to.** ✔
- Everybody, what are you touching? (Signal.) *The flower.*

4. Here's the rule about the thing the mouse is moving **to.** It should be blue. Name the thing you are going to color blue. Get ready. (Signal.) *The flower.*

- Make a blue mark on the thing the mouse is moving **to.**
(Observe children and give feedback.)

- Here's a rule about the thing the mouse is moving **from.** It should be yellow. Name the thing you are going to color yellow. Get ready. (Signal.) *The cheese.*

- Make a yellow mark on the thing the mouse is moving **from.**
(Observe children and give feedback.)

EXERCISE 10 Part—Whole

1. (Hold up workbook. Point to the rake.) Here's a coloring rule for the rake. Listen: Color the handle black. What's the rule? (Signal.) *Color the handle black.*
- Mark the handle. ✔
2. Part of the rake is missing. What part is missing? (Signal.) *The prongs.*
- Yes, the prongs. Before you color the rake, you're going to follow the dots with your pencil to make the prongs.

3. Here's the coloring rule for the prongs. Listen: Color the prongs orange. What's the rule? (Signal.) *Color the prongs orange.*
- Mark the prongs. ✔
4. (Hold up workbook. Point to the house.) Here's a coloring rule for the house. Listen: Color the roof yellow. What's the rule? (Signal.) *Color the roof yellow.*
- Mark the roof. ✔
5. Here's another coloring rule for the house. Listen: Color the door orange. What's the rule? (Signal.) *Color the door orange.*
- Mark the door. ✔
6. Here's another coloring rule for the house. Listen: Color the walls black. What's the rule? (Signal.) *Color the walls black.*
- Mark the walls. ✔
7. Part of the house is missing. What part is missing? (Signal.) *The window.*
- Yes, the window. Before you color the house, you're going to follow the dots with your pencil to make the window.
8. Here's the coloring rule for the window. Listen: Color the window purple. What's the rule? (Signal.) *Color the window purple.*
- Mark the window. ✔

Objectives

- Follow directions involving if-then. (Exercise 1)
- Given a common noun, answer questions involving "can do." (Exercise 2)
- **Listen to a short story and answer questions involving "who," "when," "why," "where" and "what".** (Exercise 3)
- Given a calendar, identify the day and date for "today" and "tomorrow" and one week from today. (Exercise 4)
- Given a common noun, name three classes containing the noun. (Exercise 5)
- **Given a common noun, name things that "can" and "cannot" be done with the noun.** (Exercise 6)
- Given a common object, answer true/false questions. (Exercise 7)
- Answer questions about a new story. (Exercise 8)
- Answer questions about a story and make a picture consistent with the details of the story. (Exercise 9)
- **Follow coloring rules involving "all" and "some."** (Exercise 10)
- Follow coloring rules involving class. (Exercise 11)

EXERCISE 1 Actions

1. We're going to learn a rule and play a game.
2. Listen to this rule. If the teacher waves or says **stop,** say **go.** Everybody, say the rule with me. Get ready. (Signal.) *If the teacher waves or says **stop,** say **go.***
3. (Repeat step 2 until firm.)
4. What's the rule? (Signal.) *If the teacher waves or says **stop,** say **go.***
- What are you going to say if the teacher waves or says **stop?** (Signal.) *Go.*
5. Are you going to say **go** if the teacher waves? (Signal.) *Yes.*
- Are you going to say **go** if the teacher says **go?** (Signal.) *No.*
- Are you going to say **go** if the teacher says **stop?** (Signal.) *Yes.*
6. Now we're going to play the game.
7. What's the rule? (Signal.) *If the teacher waves or says **stop,** say **go.***
8. Let's see if I can fool you. (Pause.) **Stop.** (Signal.) (Every child should say *go.*)
9. See if I can fool you. (Pause.) (Wave.) (Signal.) (Every child should say *go.*)
10. See if I can fool you this time. (Pause.) (Clap.) (Signal.) (The children should not do anything.)
11. (Repeat steps 8 through 10 until firm.)

EXERCISE 2 Can Do

1. Get ready to answer some questions about an envelope.
2. What are you going to answer questions about? (Signal.) *An envelope.*
3. Can you carry lemonade in an envelope? (Signal.) *No.*
- Can you fold an envelope? (Signal.) *Yes.*
- Can you write a shopping list on an envelope? (Signal.) *Yes.*
- Can you put a letter in an envelope? (Signal.) *Yes.*
4. (Repeat step 3 until firm.)
5. Here are some more questions about what you can do with an envelope. Can you pound a nail with an envelope? (Signal.) *No.*
- Can you hide an elephant in an envelope? (Signal.) *No.*
- Can you tear an envelope? (Signal.) *Yes.*
- Can you use an envelope to cut your fingernails? (Signal.) *No.*
6. (Repeat step 5 until firm.)

7. Listen: Can a woman put a letter in an envelope? (Signal.) *Yes.*
   - Say the whole thing. Get ready. (Signal.) *A woman can put a letter in an envelope.*
   - Can a woman hide an elephant in an envelope? (Signal.) *No.*
   - Say the whole thing. Get ready. (Signal.) *A woman cannot hide an elephant in an envelope.*
8. (Repeat step 7 until firm.)

EXERCISE 3   Who—What—When—Where—Why

1. Listen to this story.
2. The man woke up early in the morning. He was very sleepy, so he drank some coffee. After he drank the coffee, he went to work in his garage.
3. (Repeat step 2.)
4. Tell who woke up. Get ready. (Signal.) *The man.*
   - Tell when the man woke up. Get ready. (Signal.) *Early in the morning.*
   - Tell why the man drank some coffee. Get ready. (Signal.) *Because he was very sleepy.*
   - Tell me what the man did after he drank the coffee. Get ready. (Signal.) *Went to work.*
   - Tell where the man went to work. Get ready. (Signal.) *In his garage.*
5. (Repeat step 4 until firm.)

EXERCISE 4   Calendar

1. (Present calendar:) We're going to talk about today, tomorrow, and one week from today.
2. Tell me the day of the week it is today. Get ready. (Signal.)
   - Tell me the day of the week it will be tomorrow. Get ready. (Signal.)
   - Tell me the day of the week it will be one week from today. Get ready. (Signal.)
3. (Repeat step 2 until firm.)
4. Now the dates. Tell me today's date. Get ready. (Signal.)
   - Look at the calendar. ✔
   - Tell me the date it will be one week from today. Get ready. (Signal.)
5. Once more.
   - Listen: Tell me today's date. Get ready. (Signal.)
   - Tell me tomorrow's date. Get ready. (Signal.)
   - Tell me the date it will be one week from today. Get ready. (Signal.)
6. (Repeat step 5 until firm.)

EXERCISE 5   Classification

1. I'm thinking of an oak tree. I'm going to name some classes an oak tree is in.
2. (Make a small circle with your hands.) Here's the smallest class: oak trees.
   - (Make a wider circle.) Here's the next bigger class: trees.
   - (Make a still wider circle.) Here's the next bigger class: plants.
   - (Make an even wider circle.) Here's a really big class: living things.
3. Tell me which class has the most kinds of things in it, oak trees, trees, plants, or living things. Get ready. (Signal.) *Living things.*
4. Now it's your turn to name some classes an oak tree is in. (Make a small circle with your hands.) What's the smallest class for an oak tree? (Signal.) *Oak trees.*
   - (Make a wider circle.) What's the next bigger class? (Signal.) *Trees.*
   - (Make a still wider circle.) What's the next bigger class? (Signal.) *Plants.*
   - (Make an even wider circle.) What's a really big class? (Signal.) *Living things.*
5. There is one kind of object you would find in all those classes. Everybody, name the kind of object you would find in all those classes. Get ready. (Signal.) *An oak tree.*

EXERCISE 6 Can Do

1. Everybody, I'm going to call on individual children to name things we can do with a book.

2. (Call on a child.) What's one thing we can do with a book? (After the child gives a correct response, call on the group.) Let's all say the whole thing. Get ready. (Signal.) (The group repeats the child's response until firm.)

3. (Call on another child.) What's another thing we can do with a book? (After the child gives a correct response, call on the group.) Let's all name those things we can do with a book.
   - What's the first thing? (Hold up one finger.) (The group repeats the first response.)
   - What's the second thing? (Hold up two fingers.) (The group repeats the second response until firm.)

4. (Call on another child.) What's another thing we can do with a book? (After the child gives a correct response, call on the group.) Let's all name those things we can do with a book.
   - What's the first thing? (Hold up one finger.) (The group repeats the first response.)
   - What's the second thing? (Hold up two fingers.) (The group repeats the second response.)
   - What's the third thing? (Hold up three fingers.) (The group repeats the third response.)

5. Now I'm going to call on individual children to name things we can**not** do with a book.

6. (Call on a child.) What's one thing we cannot do with a book? (After the child gives a correct response, call on the group.) Let's all say the whole thing. (Signal.) (The group repeats the child's response until firm.)

7. (Call on another child.) What's another thing we cannot do with a book? (After the child gives a correct response, call on the group.) Let's all name those things we cannot do with a book.
   - What's the first thing? (Hold up one finger.) (The group repeats the first response.)

   - What's the second thing? (Hold up two fingers.) (The group repeats the second response until firm.)

8. (Call on another child.) What's another thing we cannot do with a book? (After the child gives a correct response, call on the group.) Let's all name those things we cannot do with a book.
   - What's the first thing? (Hold up one finger.) (The group repeats the first response.)
   - What's the second thing? (Hold up two fingers.) (The group repeats the second response.)
   - What's the third thing? (Hold up three fingers.) (The group repeats the third response.)

EXERCISE 7 True—False

1. I'm going to say statements. Some of these statements are true and some are false. You tell me about each statement.

2. You use scissors to write with. True or false? (Signal.) *False.*
   - A nurse does not work in a hospital. True or false? (Signal.) *False.*
   - Scissors are made out of glass. True or false? (Signal.) *False.*
   - People eat vehicles. True or false? (Signal.) *False.*
   - Scissors do not have wheels. True or false? (Signal.) *True.*

3. (Repeat step 2 until firm.)

4. Your turn. Make up a statement about scissors that is true. (Call on three children. Praise each acceptable statement and have the group repeat it. Then say:) Everyone, that statement is . . . (Signal.) *true.*

5. Your turn. Now make up a statement about scissors that is false. (Call on three children. Praise each acceptable statement and have the group repeat it. Then say:) Everyone, that statement is . . . (Signal.) *false.*

EXERCISE 8   Molly Mix-up And Bleep, Part 3

Storytelling

1. In the last two lessons, we've heard a story about a robot. But we still haven't finished that story. Who is that robot? (Signal.) *Bleep.* Yes, Bleep.

- And Bleep said something that made great big problems for Molly and Mrs. Anderson. What did Bleep say to create all those problems? (Call on a child. Idea: *That the two women should meet for lunch at the corner of 13th and Elm Street.*)

2. In the last part of the story, Molly and Mrs. Anderson went to an address. Everybody, what address was that? (Signal.) *13th and Elm.*

- Molly and Mrs. Anderson thought there would be a restaurant there. Everybody, what was **really** on the corner of 13th and Elm? (Signal.) *A wrecking yard.*
- Who got there first? (Signal.) *Molly.*
- What kind of vehicle did Molly drive? (Signal.) *A van.*
- Molly parked her van in a bad place. What place was that? (Signal.) *A drop-off zone.*
- Why wasn't that a good place to park? (Call on a child. Idea: *Because the workers take apart cars that are parked there.*)

3. Here's the first part of the rule about the drop-off zone: If a car is parked in the drop-off zone . . .

- What's the second part of the rule? (Signal.) *The workers take it apart.*
- Everybody, say the whole rule about the drop-off zone. (Signal.) *If a car is parked in the drop-off zone, the workers take it apart.* I guess Molly found that out later.

4. Mrs. Anderson also parked in a bad place. Where did she park? (Signal.) *In the drop-off zone.*

- What kind of car did she drive? (Signal.) *A sports car.*
- Both those cars were the same in some way. How were they the same? (Signal.) *They were both red.*
- What did both the women do after they parked? (Call on a child. Idea: *They walked around looking for the restaurant.*)

- They met about a block away and then walked back to the wrecking yard. Then where were they going to go? (Call on a child. Idea: *To find a decent restaurant.*)
- Why weren't they able to drive to a restaurant? (Call on a child. Idea: *Because the workers had taken apart their cars.*)
- What were the workers getting ready to do when Molly and Mrs. Anderson came back to the yard? (Call on a child. Idea: *Put what was left of Molly's car in the scrunching machine.*)
- Everybody, did the workers end up scrunching what was left of Molly's car? (Signal.) *No.*
- Who came up with an idea about how to put the cars back together? (Signal.) *Molly.*
- That sounds like a great idea, but there was one problem with the things that Molly made. I wonder if she'll have that same problem putting the cars together.

5. Here's what happened.

Molly and Mrs. Anderson and the workers started gathering up parts and pieces—wheels and engines and rods and doors and seats and steering wheels. Molly was in charge and she told everybody what parts and pieces to put where.

And by suppertime, there were two cars, but those cars had a **very** serious problem. That problem probably wouldn't have happened if one of the cars was yellow and the other one was red, or even if one was red and one was pink or purple. But **both** cars were red. And Molly wasn't always sure which doors went with which car or which fenders went with which car.

So when the cars were finally put together, there was not a red **van** and a red **sports car.** There were two cars, but each of them was part van and part sports car.

- Listen: Why wouldn't Molly have had a problem if one car was pink and one was red? (Call on a child. Idea: *Because she'd know which pieces went with which vehicle.*)

- Everybody, when the cars were put back together again, was there a red **sports car** and a red **van?** (Signal.) *No.*
- What was there? (Call on a child. Idea: *Two cars that were part-van and part-sports car.*)
- Can you get a picture in your mind of those two funny looking vehicles?

Mrs. Anderson said, "Ugh. What happened to my beautiful sports car? All I see are two ugly red things."

The workers were laughing pretty hard, but one of them managed to say, "Yeah, those things look pretty ugly."

The only one who disagreed was Molly. She said, "Well, I think they look kind of cute."

- I wonder what **you** would think of them.

The women didn't know what else to do, so Molly drove one of those red things home and Mrs. Anderson drove the other red thing home.

When Mrs. Anderson got home, she went inside and cried and cried.

And when Molly got home, she looked at the red thing she was driving and finally said to herself, "They are right. This thing **is** ugly."

- Everybody, what did Mrs. Anderson do when she got home? (Signal.) *Cried and cried.*
- Why did she cry and cry? (Call on a child. Idea: *Because her sports car was ruined.*)
- What did Molly think after she got home with her red thing? (Call on a child. Idea: *That it was ugly.*)

Then Molly went inside. Bleep met her at the door and said, "Bleep. Did you enjoy lunch at the corner of 13th and Elm?"

Molly looked at Bleep a long time. Here's what Molly **thought** about doing. She thought about taking Bleep to a place she'd been to before and dropping off Bleep in a zone that she knew about.

- Everybody, what zone did Molly think about? (Signal.) *The drop-off zone.*
- What would happen to Bleep if somebody left Bleep in the drop-off zone? (Call on a child. Idea: *Bleep would get taken apart.*)
- Why was Molly thinking about having Bleep taken apart? (Call on a child. Idea: *She was mad at Bleep.*)

After Molly thought about it some more, she came up with another plan. She got a set of wrenches and a screwdriver and said to Bleep, "I'm going to make some changes in you so you won't say, 'bleep' all the time, but you'll always tell the truth."

Bleep looked at Molly and said, "Bleep. Okay, baby."

- Why would Molly want to take Bleep apart? (Call on a child. Idea: *To fix him.*)

WORKBOOK

EXERCISE 9 Workbook Activity

1. Everybody, open your workbook to Lesson 45. Write your name at the top of the page. ✔
- Look at those vehicles. Do they look ugly? (Children respond.)
- Touch Mrs. Anderson in the picture. ✔
- What do you think she's saying? (Call on a child. Idea: *"Ugh. What happened to my beautiful sports car?"*)

- Touch Molly. ✔
- What do you think she's saying? (Call on a child. Idea: *"Well, I think they look kind of cute."*)
- Look at the workers. Everybody, what are they doing? (Signal.) *Laughing.*
- Why do you think they're laughing? (Call on a child. Idea: *Because the cars look so ugly.*)
- The story doesn't tell us which vehicle Molly drove home and which one Mrs. Anderson drove home. I guess Mrs. Anderson would cry if she had either one of those vehicles.

2. Later you can color the picture. When you color the picture, remember what color those vehicles are.

EXERCISE 10 Classification

1. Everybody, find the next page in your workbook. ✔
- (Hold up workbook. Point to first half.) The boxes show two pictures. **Some** of the clothing in one picture are coats. **All** of the clothing in the other picture are coats.

2. Touch the picture where **some** of the clothing are coats. ✔
- Here's the rule about the picture where **some** of the clothing are coats. The coats should have a red collar and black sleeves. What's the rule? (Signal.) *The coats should have a red collar and black sleeves.*
- Mark the coats in the picture where **some** of the clothing are coats. (Observe children and give feedback.)

3. Here's the rule about the picture where **all** of the clothing are coats. The coats should have a black collar and red sleeves. What's the rule? (Signal.) *The coats should have a black collar and red sleeves.*
- Mark one of the coats. (Observe children and give feedback.)

EXERCISE 11 Location

1. (Hold up workbook. Point to second half.) Everybody, what place do you see in this picture? (Signal.) *A bus station.*
2. Here's a coloring rule for this picture. Listen: Color the containers yellow. What's the rule? (Signal.) *Color the containers yellow.*
3. (Repeat step 2 until firm.)
4. Put a yellow mark on **one** container. ✔
5. Here's another coloring rule for this picture. Listen: Color the vehicles blue. What's the rule? (Signal.) *Color the vehicles blue.*
6. (Repeat step 5 until firm.)
7. Put a blue mark on **one** of the vehicles. ✔
8. There's one more thing to do. One of these containers has a part missing. What container is that? (Call on a child.) *A locker.* Yes, a locker.
- What part of the locker is missing? (Signal.) *The door.* Yes, the door. Before you color the locker, follow the dots and make the door.

Materials: For Lessons 46–130 you will need to make four cards with **north, south, east,** and **west** printed on them. Place these cards on the appropriate walls of the classroom.

Objectives

- Generate statements utilizing past, present and future tenses of the verb "to be." (Exercise 1)
- Given a calendar, identify the day and date for "today" and "tomorrow" and one week from today. (Exercise 2)
- Given a common noun, name three classes containing the noun (smallest, next bigger, really big). (Exercise 3)
- Given a common noun, answer questions involving "can do." (Exercise 4)
- Listen to a short story and answer questions involving "who," "when," "why," "where" and "what". (Exercise 5)
- **Replace a word in a sentence with an opposite.** (Exercise 6)
- **Identify cardinal directions (north, south, east, west).** (Exercise 7)
- Write numbers and draw paths to show a sequence of events and tell a story that involves an interaction of events. (Exercise 8)

EXERCISE 1 Verb Tense

1. Listen: Today the bugs **are** in the garden. Yesterday the bugs **were** in the garden. Tomorrow the bugs **will be** in the garden.
2. Make the statement about the bugs today. (Signal.) *Today the bugs are in the garden.*
3. Make the statement about the bugs yesterday. (Signal.) *Yesterday the bugs were in the garden.*
4. Make the statement about the bugs tomorrow. (Signal.) *Tomorrow the bugs will be in the garden.*
5. (Repeat steps 2 through 4 until firm.)

EXERCISE 2 Calendar

1. (Present calendar.) We're going to talk about today, tomorrow, and one week from today.
2. Tell me the day of the week it is today. Get ready. (Signal.)
- Tell me the day of the week it will be tomorrow. Get ready. (Signal.)
- Tell me the day of the week it will be one week from today. Get ready. (Signal.)
3. (Repeat step 2 until firm.)
4. Now the dates. Tell me today's date. Get ready. (Signal.)
- Look at the calendar. ✔
- Tell me the date it will be one week from today. Get ready. (Signal.)

5. Once more. Listen: Tell me today's date. Get ready. (Signal.)
- Tell me tomorrow's date. Get ready. (Signal.)
- Tell me the date it will be one week from today. Get ready. (Signal.)
6. (Repeat step 5 until firm.)

EXERCISE 3 Classification

1. I'm thinking of a spotted dog. I'm going to name some classes a spotted dog is in.
2. (Make a small circle with your hands.) Here's the smallest class: spotted dogs.
- (Make a wider circle.) Here's the next bigger class: dogs.
- (Make a still wider circle.) Here's the next bigger class: animals.
- (Make an even wider circle.) Here's a really big class: living things.
3. Tell me which class has the most kinds of things in it, spotted dogs, dogs, animals, or living things. Get ready. (Signal.) *Living things.*
4. Now it's your turn to name some classes a spotted dog is in. (Make a small circle with your hands.) What's the smallest class for a spotted dog? (Signal.) *Spotted dogs.*

- (Make a wider circle.) What's the next bigger class? (Signal.) *Dogs.*
- (Make a still wider circle.) What's the next bigger class? (Signal.) *Animals.*
- (Make an even wider circle.) What's a really big class? (Signal.) *Living things.*

5. There is one kind of object you would find in all those classes. Everybody, name the kind of object you would find in all those classes. Get ready. (Signal.) *A spotted dog.*

EXERCISE 4 Can Do

1. Get ready to answer some questions about a fence.
2. What are you going to answer questions about? (Signal.) *A fence.*
3. Can you sit on a fence? (Signal.) *Yes.*
- Can you wear a fence? (Signal.) *No.*
- Can you hide behind a fence? (Signal.) *Yes.*
- Can you use a fence to iron clothes? (Signal.) *No.*
4. (Repeat step 3 until firm.)
5. Here are some more questions about what you can do with a fence.
6. Can you cook hotdogs with a fence? (Signal.) *No.*
- Can you use a fence to keep a dog in the yard? (Signal.) *Yes.*
- Can you draw with a fence? (Signal.) *No.*
- Can you climb over a fence? (Signal.) *Yes.*
- (Repeat step 6 until firm.)
7. Now I'm going to ask you about what a girl can do with a fence.
8. Can a girl climb over a fence? (Signal.) *Yes.*
- Say the whole thing. Get ready. (Signal.) *A girl can climb over a fence.*
- Can a girl wear a fence? (Signal.) *No.*
- Say the whole thing. Get ready. (Signal.) *A girl cannot wear a fence.*
9. (Repeat step 8 until firm.)

EXERCISE 5 Who—What—When—Where—Why

1. Listen to this story.
2. Yesterday the baby was playing with a dog. The dog licked the baby, so the baby began to laugh. The baby laughed so hard that it fell down in front of the dog.
3. Listen again. (Repeat step 2.)

4. Tell who was playing with a dog. Get ready. (Signal.) *The baby.*
- Tell when the baby was playing with a dog. Get ready. (Signal.) *Yesterday.*
- Tell what the dog did to the baby. Get ready. (Signal.) *Licked the baby.*
- Tell why the baby fell down. Get ready. (Signal.) *Because it laughed so hard.*
- Tell where the baby fell down. Get ready. (Signal.) *In front of the dog.*
5. (Repeat step 4 until firm.)

EXERCISE 6 Opposites

1. Let's make up statements with the opposite word.
2. Listen: The boy is **laughing.** Say that statement. (Signal.) *The boy is laughing.*
3. Now say a statement with the opposite of **laughing.** Get ready. (Signal.) *The boy is crying.*
4. (Repeat steps 2 and 3 until firm.)
5. Listen: The door is **narrow.** Say that statement. Get ready. (Signal.) *The door is narrow.*
6. Now say a statement with the opposite of **narrow.** Get ready. (Signal.) *The door is wide.*
7. (Repeat steps 5 and 6 until firm.)

EXERCISE 7 Map Reading

Note: Make sure **north, south, east,** and **west** cards are placed on the appropriate walls.

1. Everybody, we're going to learn about directions. What are we going to learn about? (Signal.) *Directions.*
2. (Point north.) The signs on the walls show the four directions. (Point to each sign and read them in this order:) North, south, east, west.
3. Your turn. I'll point in different directions. You tell me the directions.
- (Point north.) Everybody, which direction is this? (Signal.) *North.*
- (Point south.) Everybody, which direction is this? (Signal.) *South.*
- (Point east.) Everybody, which direction is this? (Signal.) *East.*
- (Point west.) Everybody, which direction is this? (Signal.) *West.*
4. (Repeat step 3 until firm.)

5. (Move to the middle of the room.) Look at me. I'm going to walk. You point to the wall I'm walking to. That's the **direction** I'm walking.

6. Watch. (Walk toward the south wall.) Everybody, which direction? (Signal.) *South.* Yes, I walked south.

• (Return to the middle of the room.)

Error:
The children don't say *south.*
Correction:
1. (Point to the south wall.)
   Which wall am I pointing to? (Signal.)
   The south wall.
2. So which direction am I pointing?
   (Signal.) *South.*
3. (Repeat step 6.)

---

7. Watch. (Walk toward the north wall.) Everybody, which direction? (Signal.) *North.* Yes, I walked north.

• (Return to the middle of the room.)

8. (Repeat steps 6 and 7 until firm.)

WORKBOOK

EXERCISE 8   Sequence Story

Sweetie And Andrea

1. Everybody, open your workbook to Lesson 46. Write your name at the top of the page. ✔

• This is a new kind of story. In this story, Andrea does some things and Sweetie does some things.

• You're going to make a path for Andrea and a path for Sweetie. You'll make Andrea's path **gray** and Sweetie's path **yellow.** So take out a **gray** crayon and a **yellow** crayon.

• Listen:

> Andrea the mouse was hungry. She looked out from her hole in the wall and saw that there were some peanuts on the table. Andrea loved peanuts. But she also saw that there was something else in the room. Something she didn't like very much.

• Everybody, what was that? (Signal.) *Sweetie.*

> As you know, that cat was named Sweetie and he was the meanest cat in town. Sweetie seemed to be sleeping on the rug, so Andrea crept into the room. Sweetie moved, so Andrea hid behind the scratching post.

2. Touch the place where Andrea went to first. ✔
• Where was Andrea first? (Call on a child. Idea: *Behind the scratching post.*)
• Remember, Andrea's on the side of the scratching post where the cat can't see her. That's the **right** side of the scratching post.
• Use your pencil and make a **1** in the circle to show that this is the first place Andrea went to. Make sure your **1** is on the **right** side of the post that is **away** from Sweetie, or your story may not have a very happy ending at all. Raise your hand when you're finished.
(Observe children and give feedback.)
3. That part of the story tells about **Andrea.** So you'll show the path with a **gray** crayon. Draw a path from the picture of Andrea to the circle with a **1** in it. Raise your hand when you're finished.
(Observe children and give feedback.)
• Here's the next thing that happened.

Sweetie woke up and walked over to the scratching post. Sweetie stopped right across from where Andrea was hiding.

4. Touch the circle that shows where Sweetie is now. ✔
- You should be touching the circle on the **left** side of the scratching post. Use your pencil and make a **2** in the circle to show that this is where Sweetie was. Raise your hand when you're finished.
(Observe children and give feedback.)
5. This part of the story tells about **Sweetie.** So you'll show the path with a **yellow** crayon. Draw a yellow path from the picture of Sweetie to the circle with the **2** in it. Raise your hand when you're finished.
(Observe children and give feedback.)

Andrea held her breath and waited. Sweetie scratched on the scratching post. Then Sweetie went in his bed and curled up with his eyes closed.

6. Touch the circle that shows where Sweetie was after he scratched on the scratching post. ✔
- Everybody, where was Sweetie now? (Signal.) *In his bed.*
- Use your pencil and make a **3** in the circle to show that this is the next place Sweetie was. Raise your hand when you're finished. (Observe children and give feedback.)
7. Does this last part of the story tell what **Andrea** did or what **Sweetie** did? (Signal.) *What Sweetie did.*
- So what color will the path be? (Signal.) *Yellow.*
- Draw a yellow path from circle **2** to circle **3**. Raise your hand when you're finished. (Observe children and give feedback.)

While Sweetie was snoozing, Andrea climbed up the scratching post to the very top of it.

8. Touch the circle that shows where Andrea went. ✔
- Where was Andrea now? (Call on a child. Idea: *At the top of the scratching post.*)
- Everybody, use your pencil and make a **4** in the circle to show that this is the next thing that happened. Raise your hand when you're finished.
(Observe children and give feedback.)
9. Does the last part of the story tell what **Andrea** did or what **Sweetie** did? (Signal.) *What Andrea did.*
- So what color will the path be? (Signal.) *Gray.*
- Draw a gray path from circle **1** to circle **4**. Raise your hand when you're finished.
(Observe children and give feedback.)

Then Andrea jumped onto the table. She was pretty close to the peanuts.

10. Touch the circle that shows where Andrea went this time. ✔
- Use your pencil and make a **5** in the circle to show that this is the next thing that happened. Raise your hand when you're finished.
(Observe children and give feedback.)
11. Does this last part of the story tell what **Andrea** did or what **Sweetie** did? (Signal.) *What Andrea did.*
- So what color will the path be? (Signal.) *Gray.*
- Draw a gray path from circle **4** to circle **5**. Raise your hand when you're finished.
(Observe children and give feedback.)

The last thing Andrea did was to eat the peanuts.

12. Uh-oh, there's no circle to show where Andrea was when she ate the peanuts. Draw a path to the peanuts. Make sure the path is the right color. Raise your hand when you're finished.
(Observe children and give feedback.)
- Later you can draw a picture of Andrea eating the peanuts.

13. Now you're going to help me retell the story. You'll do the numbers in order, starting with **1**. That's important. You first tell about **1**. Then you tell about **2**. Then you tell about **3** and so forth. At each number, you have to tell me **who** did something. You can tell by looking at the color of the path that goes **to** the number.

14. Touch number 1. ✔
   - What's the color of the path that goes to that number? (Signal.) *Gray.*
   - So you have to tell about **Andrea.** I'll show you how to do it: Andrea was by her mouse hole. She was hungry. So she snuck over to the scratching post.

15. Touch number 2. ✔
   - What's the color of the path that goes to number 2? (Signal.) *Yellow.*
   - So who do you have to tell about? (Signal.) *Sweetie.*
   - Tell where Sweetie was and what he did. (Call on a child. Idea: *Sweetie was sleeping on a rug. He got up and went to the scratching post, right across from Andrea.*)

16. You just told about number 2. What's the next number you'll touch? (Signal.) *Three.*
   - Look at the path that leads to number 3. Everybody, who do you have to tell about for number 3? (Signal.) *Sweetie.*
   - Tell where Sweetie was and what he did. (Call on a child. Idea: *After Sweetie scratched for a while, he went to his bed and went to sleep.*)

17. You just told about number 3. What's the next number you'll touch? (Signal.) *Four.*
   - Look at the path that leads to number 4. Everybody, who do you have to tell about for number 4? (Signal.) *Andrea.*
   - Tell where Andrea was and what she did. (Call on a child. Idea: *Andrea climbed to the top of the scratching post.*)

18. You just told about number 4. What's the next number you'll touch? (Signal.) *Five.*
   - Look at the path that leads to number 5.
   - Who do you tell about for number 5? (Signal.) *Andrea.*
   - Tell where Andrea was and what she did. (Call on a child. Idea: *Andrea jumped from the scratching post to the table.*)

19. Everybody, is that the end of the story? (Signal.) *No.*
   - How does it end? (Call on a child. Idea: *Andrea goes to the peanuts and eats them.*)

20. Your turn: See if anybody can tell this hard, hard story. Remember, you have to tell about the numbers in order, starting with number 1. For each number, you look at the color of the path. If it's yellow, you tell what Sweetie did. If it's gray, you tell what Andrea did.
   - Who can do it? (Call on a child.) Everybody else, follow along. If you hear a mistake, raise your hand. (Praise children who correctly describe the sequence.)

LESSON 47

Objectives

- Follow directions involving if-then. (Exercise 1)
- Given a calendar, identify the day and date of "today" and "tomorrow" and one week from today. (Exercise 2)
- **Given a common noun, name four classes containing the noun.** (Exercise 3)
- **Generate a list of objects that fit stated criteria.** (Exercise 4)
- Listen to a short story and answer questions involving "who," "when," "why," "where" and "what". (Exercise 5)
- Identify an absurdity of location. (Exercise 6)
- Given a common noun, name things that "can" and "cannot" be done with the noun. (Exercise 7)
- Given a common noun, answer questions involving "can do." (Exercise 8)
- Identify cardinal directions (north, south, east, west). (Exercise 9)
- Answer questions about a familiar story. (Exercises 10 & 11)
- Given a picture, identify an object being moved away "from" and the object being moved "to." (Exercise 12)
- Follow coloring rules involving material. (Exercise 13)

EXERCISE 1 Actions

1. We're going to learn a rule and play a game.
2. Listen to this rule. If I hold up my hand and stamp my foot, say **do it.** Everybody, say the rule with me. Get ready. (Signal.) *If you hold up your hand and stamp your foot, say do it.*
3. What's the rule? (Signal.) *If you hold up your hand and stamp your foot, say do it.*
- What are you going to say if I hold up my hand and stamp my foot? (Signal.) *Do it.*
4. Are you going to say **do it** if I only stamp my foot? (Signal.) *No.*
- Are you going to say **do it** if I hold up my hand and stand up? (Signal.) *No.*
- Are you going to say **do it** if I hold up my hand and stamp my foot? (Signal.) *Yes.*
5. Now we're going to play the game.
6. What's the rule? (Signal.) *If you hold up your hand and stamp your foot, say do it.*
7. Let's see if I can fool you. (Pause.) (Clap and stamp your foot.) (Signal.) (The children should not do anything.)
8. See if I can fool you. (Pause.) (Hold up your hand and stamp your foot.) (Signal.) (Every child should say **do it.**)
9. See if I can fool you this time. (Pause.) (Hold up your hand and stamp your foot.) (Signal.) (Every child should say **do it.**)

EXERCISE 2 Calendar

1. (Present calendar.) We're going to talk about today, tomorrow, and one week from today.
2. Tell me the day of the week it is today. Get ready. (Signal.)
- Tell me the day of the week it will be tomorrow. Get ready. (Signal.)
- Tell me the day of the week it will be one week from today. Get ready. (Signal.)
3. (Repeat step 2 until firm.)
4. Now the dates. Tell me today's date. Get ready. (Signal.)
- Look at the calendar. ✔
- Tell me the date it will be one week from today. Get ready. (Signal.)
5. Once more. Listen: Tell me today's date. Get ready. (Signal.)
- Tell me tomorrow's date. Get ready. (Signal.)
- Tell me the date it will be one week from today. Get ready. (Signal.)
6. (Repeat step 5 until firm.)

EXERCISE 3　Classification

1. We're going to talk about **glasses, containers,** and **things to drink from.** What are we going to talk about? (Signal.) *Glasses, containers, and things to drink from.*

2. You're going to name three classes a glass is in.
   - (Make a small circle with your hands.) What's the smallest class for a glass? (Signal.) *Glasses.*
   - (Make a wider circle.) What's the next bigger class? (Signal.) *Things to drink from.*
   - (Make a still wider circle.) What's a really big class? (Signal.) *Containers.*
3. (Repeat step 2 until firm.)
4. There is one kind of object you would find in all those classes. Everybody, name the kind of object you would find in all those classes. Get ready. (Signal.) *A glass.*
5. Now we're going to talk about **frying pans, containers,** and **things to cook in.** What are we going to talk about? (Signal.) *Frying pans, containers, and things to cook in.*
6. You're going to name three classes a frying pan is in. (Make a small circle with your hands.) What's the smallest class for a frying pan? (Signal.) *Frying pans.*
   - (Make a larger circle.) What's the next bigger class? (Signal.) *Things to cook in.*
   - (Make a still larger circle.) What's a really big class? (Signal.) *Containers.*
7. (Repeat step 6 until firm.)
8. There is one kind of object you would find in all those classes. Everybody, name the kind of object you would find in all those classes. Get ready. (Signal.) *A frying pan.*

EXERCISE 4　Description

1. I'm thinking of an object. See if you can figure out what object I'm thinking of. I'll tell you something about the object.
2. Listen: It's made of metal. Everybody, what do you know about the object? (Signal.) *It's made of metal.*
3. Is a can made of metal? (Signal.) *Yes.* So could I be thinking of a can? (Signal.) *Yes.*
4. Is a fish made of metal? (Signal.) *No.* So could I be thinking of a fish? (Signal.) *No.*

5. Is a baseball made of metal? (Signal.) *No.* So could I be thinking of a baseball? (Signal.) *No.*
6. Is a spoon made of metal? (Signal.) *Yes.* So could I be thinking of a spoon? (Signal.) *Yes.*
7. Listen: The object I'm thinking of is (hold up one finger) made of metal and (hold up two fingers) it's round.
8. Everybody, what is the first thing you know about the object? (Hold up one finger.) *It's made of metal* **and** (hold up two fingers) *it's round.*
9. (Repeat step 8 until firm.)
10. Is a rubber ball made of metal and is it round? (Signal.) *No.*
    - So could I be thinking of a rubber ball? (Signal.) *No.*
    - Why not? (Signal.) *It's not made of metal.*
11. (Repeat step 10 until firm.)
12. Is a coin made of metal and is it round? (Signal.) *Yes.*
    - So could I be thinking of a coin? (Signal.) *Yes.*
13. (Repeat step 12 until firm.)
14. Is a can made of metal and is it round? (Signal.) *Yes.*
    - So could I be thinking of a can? (Signal.) *Yes.*
15. (Repeat step 14 until firm.)
16. Listen: The object I'm thinking of is (hold up one finger) made of metal **and** (hold up two fingers) it's round **and** (hold up three fingers) you can use it to buy things in a store.
17. Everybody, name the object I am thinking of. (Pause two seconds.) Get ready. (Signal.) *A coin.* Yes, a coin.
18. How do you know I'm thinking of a coin? (Hold up one finger.) *It's made of metal* **and** (hold up two fingers) *it's round* **and** (hold up three fingers) *you can use it to buy things in a store.*
19. (Repeat step 18 until firm.)

EXERCISE 5　Who—What—When—Where—Why

1. Listen to this story.
2. The girl was in high school. She told a funny joke. The class laughed because they liked the joke. After the class stopped laughing, they all went back to work.
3. Listen again. (Repeat step 2.)

4. Tell where the girl was. Get ready. (Signal.) *In high school.*
- Tell what the girl did. Get ready. (Signal.) *She told a funny joke.*
- Tell why the class laughed. Get ready. (Signal.) *Because they liked the joke.*
- Tell who went back to work. Get ready. (Signal.) *The class.*
- Tell when the class went back to work. Get ready. (Signal.) *After they stopped laughing.*
5. (Repeat steps 3 and 4 until firm.)

EXERCISE 6 Absurdity

1. Name something you would find in a barbershop. (Call on individual children. Praise and repeat appropriate answers.)
2. We find chairs in a barbershop. Let's all say it. Get ready. (Signal.) *We find chairs in a barbershop.*
- Would you see a horse in a barbershop? (Signal.) *No.*
- That would be absurd.
- Would you find scissors in a barbershop? (Signal.) *Yes.*
  Yes, you find scissors in a barbershop.
- Would you find a train in a barbershop? (Signal.) *No.*
- That would be absurd.

EXERCISE 7 Can Do

Note: In this task, praise children who name things not previously presented in class.

1. Everybody, I'm going to call on individual children to name things we can do with a table.
2. (Call on a child.)
   What's one thing we can do with a table? (After the child gives a correct response, call on the group.) Let's all say the whole thing. Get ready. (Signal.) (The group repeats the child's response.)
3. (Call on another child.)
   What's another thing we can do with a table? (After the child gives a correct response, call on the group.) Let's all name those things we can do with a table.
- What's the first thing? (Hold up one finger.) (The group repeats the first response.)

- What's the second thing? (Hold up two fingers.) (The group repeats the second response.)
4. (Call on another child.)
- What's another thing we can do with a table? (After the child gives a correct response, call on the group.) Let's all name those things we can do with a table.
- What's the first thing? (Hold up one finger.) (The group repeats the first response.)
- What's the second thing? (Hold up two fingers.) (The group repeats the second response.)
- What's the third thing? (Hold up three fingers.) (The group repeats the third response.)
5. Now I'm going to call on individual children to name things we cannot do with a table.
6. (Call on a child.)
   What's one thing we cannot do with a table? (After the child gives a correct response, call on the group.) Let's all say the whole thing. Get ready. (Signal.) (The group repeats the child's response.)
7. (Call on another child.)
   What's another thing we cannot do with a table? (After the child gives a correct response, call on the group.) Let's all name those things we cannot do with a table.
- What's the first thing? (Hold up one finger.) (The group repeats the child's response.)
- What's the second thing? (Hold up two fingers.) (The group repeats the second response.)
8. (Call on another child.)
   What's another thing we cannot do with a table? (After the child gives a correct response, call on the group.) Let's all name those things we cannot do with a table.
- What's the first thing? (Hold up one finger.) (The group repeats the child's response.)
- What's the second thing? (Hold up two fingers.) (The group repeats the second response.)
- What's the third thing? (Hold up three fingers.) (The group repeats the third response.)
9. Now I'm going to call on individual children to name things we cannot do with a rug.

10. (Call on a child.)
What's one thing we cannot do with a rug?
(After the child gives a correct response,
call on the group.) Let's all say the whole
thing. Get ready. (Signal.) (The group
repeats the first response.)

11. (Call on another child.)
What's another thing we cannot do with
a rug? (After the child gives a correct
response, call on the group.) Let's all name
those things we cannot do with a rug.
• What's the first thing? (Hold up one finger.)
(The group repeats the first response.)
• What's the second thing? (Hold up two
fingers.) (The group repeats the second
response.)

12. (Call on another child.)
What's another thing we cannot do with
a rug? (After the child gives a correct
response, call on the group.) Let's all name
those things we cannot do with a rug.
• What's the first thing? (Hold up one finger.)
(The group repeats the first response.)
• What's the second thing? (Hold up two
fingers.) (The group repeats the second
response.)
• What's the third thing? (Hold up three
fingers.) (The group repeats the third
response.)

EXERCISE 8 Can Do

1. Get ready to answer some questions about
a needle.
2. Can you hide a needle? (Signal.) *Yes.*
• Can you brush your teeth with a needle?
(Signal.) *No.*
• Can you step on a needle? (Signal.) *Yes.*
• Can you pave a road with a needle?
(Signal.) *No.*
• Can you sew with a needle? (Signal.) *Yes.*
• Can you take out a splinter with a needle?
(Signal.) *Yes.*

EXERCISE 9 Map Reading

1. Everybody, we're going to learn about
directions. What are we going to learn
about? (Signal.) *Directions.*
2. (Point north.) The signs on the walls show the
four directions. (Point to each sign and read
them in this order:) north, south, east, west.

3. Your turn. I'll point in different directions.
You tell me the directions.
• (Point north.) Everybody, which direction is
this? (Signal.) *North.*
• (Point south.) Everybody, which direction is
this? (Signal.) *South.*
• (Point east.) Everybody, which direction is
this? (Signal.) *East.*
• (Point west.) Everybody, which direction is
this? (Signal.) *West.*
4. (Repeat step 3 until firm.)
5. (Move to the middle of the room.) Look at
me. I'm going to walk. You point to the wall
I'm walking to.
That's the **direction** I'm walking.

6. Watch. (Walk toward the east wall.)
Everybody, which direction? (Signal.) *East.*
Yes, I walked east.
• (Return to the middle of the room.)
7. Watch. (Walk toward the west wall.)
Everybody, which direction? (Signal.) *West.*
Yes, I walked west.
• (Return to the middle of the room.)
8. Watch. (Walk toward the south wall.)
Everybody, which direction? (Signal.)
South.
Yes, I walked south.
• (Return to the middle of the room.)
9. Watch. (Walk toward the north wall.)
Everybody, which direction? (Signal.) *North.*
Yes, I walked north.
• (Return to the middle of the room.)
10. (Repeat steps 6 through 9 until firm.)

EXERCISE 10 Molly Mix-up And Bleep

Review

• I'm going to read the whole story about
Molly Mix-up and Bleep again. We'll see
how well you remember the things that
happened in that story.

There once was an inventor named
Molly Mix-up. Her last name wasn't really
Mix-up, but that's what people called her:
Molly Mix-up.

• Why did people call Molly that? (Call on a
child. Idea: *Something was always wrong
with her inventions.*)

Molly once invented an electric can
opener.

- I'll bet nobody remembers what was wrong with that can opener. Raise your hand if you remember. (Call on a child. Idea: *It ripped cans into little pieces.*)

Molly once invented a toaster that toasted eight slices of bread at the same time.

- I'll bet nobody remembers what was wrong with that toaster. Raise your hand if you remember. (Call on a child. Idea: *It toasted only one side of each slice.*)

Molly Mix-up invented over 50 different things, but they had the same old problem. The invention Molly was most proud of was . . .

- Everybody, which invention? (Signal.) *Bleep.*

It took Molly over seven years to make Bleep and when she was done, that robot could do all kinds of things.

- Like what? (Call on a child. Idea: *Follow directions, fix breakfast, answer the telephone and talk.*)

That robot had the same problem as the other things Molly invented. The problem with Bleep was that he could answer questions and make statements. But . . .

- What was wrong with the answers? (Call on a child. Idea: *They weren't always correct.*)
- Everybody, would Bleep make **false** statements **all** the time? (Signal.) *No.*
- You just never knew when Bleep would say something that wasn't true.

Sometimes that robot got Molly in a lot of trouble, because when Bleep talked, he sounded a lot like Molly when she talked. There was one little difference.

- What was that? (Call on a child. Idea: *Bleep said, "bleep," all the time.*)

Sometimes, people would not listen carefully and would get fooled, particularly a friend of Molly's.

- Everybody, what was her name? (Signal.) *Mrs. Anderson.*
- Why did she get fooled a lot by Bleep? (Call on a child. Idea: *She didn't hear too well.*)

One day, Mrs. Anderson called Molly. The two women were supposed to meet for lunch. When Mrs. Anderson called, Molly was out in the garage working on a new invention.

- Everybody, so who answered the phone? (Signal.) *Bleep.*

Mrs. Anderson said, "Hello, Molly. Today's the day we're supposed to meet for lunch."

Bleep said, "Bleep. That is correct."

Mrs. Anderson then said, "Where do you want to meet?"

- Who remembers what Bleep said? (Call on a child. Idea: *Bleep. The corner of 13th and Elm Street.*)

Mrs. Anderson said, "I don't know what restaurant is on that corner."

Bleep said, "Bleep. You will like it a lot."

Mrs. Anderson said, "Okay, I'll see you there around noon."

Bleep said, "Bleep. Okay, baby."

Just after Bleep hung up the phone, Molly came in and said, "Were there any calls?"

- Everybody, what did Bleep say? (Signal.) *Bleep. Yes.*

"Oh," Molly said, "who called?"

- What did Bleep tell her? (Call on a child. Idea: *Mrs. Anderson suggested meeting at a restaurant on the corner of 13th and Elm.*)

Molly thanked Bleep for giving her the message and Bleep said, "Bleep. Okay, baby."

So Molly went to the address that Bleep had told her. And Mrs. Anderson went to the same address.

Mrs. Anderson and Molly went in their own cars to meet for lunch.

- Everybody, what kind of vehicle did Molly drive? (Signal.) *A van.*
- What kind of vehicle did Mrs. Anderson drive? (Signal.) *A sports car.*
- How were those vehicles the same? (Signal.) *They were red.*

What a surprise the women had when they got to 13th and Elm. The only business on the corner of 13th and Elm was **not** a restaurant or even a market.

- What was on the corner? (Call on a child. Idea: *A wrecking yard.*)
- What do they do with cars at a wrecking yard? (Call on a child. Idea: *They take them apart and scrunch up what's left.*)

Well, Molly arrived at 13th and Elm first. She didn't see a restaurant, so she parked her car in front of the wrecking yard in a parking space that had a sign in front of it.

- Everybody, what did that sign say? (Signal.) *Drop-off zone.*
- Was that a good place to park? (Signal.) *No.*
- Why not? (Call on a child. Idea: *The cars will get taken apart.*)

Molly began to walk around, looking for a restaurant.

When Mrs. Anderson got to the corner of 13th and Elm, she didn't see Molly, so she parked her car in front of the wrecking yard right next to Molly's car—in the drop-off zone. Then she walked around, looking for Molly. She finally found Molly.

- Where did she find Molly? (Call on a child. Idea: *About a block away.*)

Mrs. Anderson said, "Molly, what a terrible place this is. Where's the restaurant you told me about?"

"**I** didn't tell **you** about a restaurant. **You** told **me** about a restaurant."

"No, no," Mrs. Anderson said. "I remember exactly what you said when I asked you where you wanted to meet. You said, 'Bleep. The corner of 13th and Elm Street.'"

Molly said, "Oh, you were talking to Bleep. Let's go back to our cars and find a decent restaurant."

Mrs. Anderson said, "Yes, let's get out of this terrible place."

But it wasn't that easy to get out of that terrible place because when they got back to the wrecking yard, they discovered that their cars were no longer parked in front of the wrecking yard.

- Where were their cars? (Call on a child. Idea: *In the wrecking yard.*)
- Everybody, whose vehicle was just about to be scrunched up by the scrunching machine? (Signal.) *Molly's.*

Their cars were piles of parts and pieces.

The workers at the wrecking yard were just ready to put what was left of Molly's car in the scrunching machine when the two women realized what had happened to their cars. "Stop, stop," they yelled.

And the workers **did** stop.

Mrs. Anderson shouted at them, "How dare you take my beautiful sports car apart?"

One worker said, "Lady, here's the rule about this place."

- What was that rule? (Call on a child. Idea: *If a car is parked in the drop-off zone, the workers take it apart.*)

"Oh, oh. What will we do?" Mrs. Anderson said.

"I don't know," the worker said. "We only know how to take cars **apart.** We can't put them back together."

The women thought and thought. The workers thought and thought. Finally Molly said, "Well, I'm pretty good at making things. I can tell everybody how to put the cars back together, and if we all pitch in, we can put those two cars together before suppertime."

The workers said they would help. And so, everybody pitched in.

- Everybody, were the cars in good shape by suppertime? (Signal.) *No.*
- What was wrong with them? (Call on a child. Idea: *They were all mixed up.*)

Molly and Mrs. Anderson and the workers started gathering up parts and pieces—wheels and engines and rods and doors and seats and steering wheels. Molly was in charge and she told everybody what parts and pieces to put where.

And by suppertime, there were two cars, but those cars had a **very** serious problem. That problem probably wouldn't have happened if one of the cars was yellow and the other one was red, or even if one was red and one was pink or purple. But **both** cars were red. And Molly wasn't always sure which doors went with which car or which fenders went with which car.

So when the cars were finally put together, there was not a red **van** and a red **sports car.** There were two cars, but each of them was part-van and part-sports car.

Mrs. Anderson said, "Ugh. What happened to my beautiful sports car? All I see are two ugly red things."

The workers were laughing pretty hard, but one of them managed to say, "Yeah, those things look pretty ugly."

- Everybody, who didn't think the cars were so ugly? (Signal.) *Molly.*

Molly said, "Well, I think they look kind of cute."

The women didn't know what else to do, so Molly drove one of those red things home and Mrs. Anderson drove the other red thing home.

When Mrs. Anderson got home, she went inside and . . .

- Did what? (Signal.) *Cried and cried.*

And when Molly got home, she looked at the red thing she was driving and finally said to herself, "They are right. This thing **is** ugly."

Then she went inside. Bleep met her at the door and said. "Bleep. Did you enjoy lunch at the corner of 13th and Elm?"

Molly looked at Bleep a long time. Here's what Molly **thought** about doing. She thought about taking Bleep to a place she'd been to before and dropping Bleep off in a zone that she knew about.

- Where was that place? (Call on a child. Idea: *A wrecking yard.*)
- Everybody, what was that zone? (Signal.) *A drop-off zone.*
- Did Molly **actually** do that? (Signal.) *No.*

After Molly thought about it some more, she came up with another plan.

- What was that plan? (Call on a child. Idea: *Fix Bleep up; take Bleep apart.*)
- Let's see if you are right.

Molly got a set of wrenches and a screwdriver and said to Bleep, "I'm going to make some changes in you so you won't say 'bleep' all the time, but you'll always tell the truth."

- And what did Bleep say? (Signal.) *Bleep. Okay, baby.*
- I wonder if Molly will be able to fix Bleep up the right way. Maybe we'll find out later.

EXERCISE 11

1. Everybody, open your workbook to Lesson 47. Write your name at the top of the page. ✔
- Look at the picture. What is Molly doing in this picture? (Call on a child. Idea: *Starting to take Bleep apart.*)
- Everybody, does this picture take place **before** they went to the wrecking yard or **after** they went to the wrecking yard? (Signal.) *After they went to the wrecking yard.*
- What kind of tool is Molly using on Bleep? (Signal.) *A screwdriver.*
- Bleep is saying something in this picture. Can anybody read what Bleep is saying? (Call on a child. Idea: *Bleep.*)
2. Later you can color the picture.

EXERCISE 12   From—To

1. Everybody, find the next page in your workbook. ✔
- (Hold up workbook. Point to first half.)

2. The girl is moving **from** one thing **to** another thing. What is the girl moving **from?** (Signal.) *The tree.*
- What is the girl moving **to?** (Signal.) *The house.*
3. (Repeat step 2 until firm.)
4. Touch the thing the girl is moving **from.** ✔
- Everybody, what are you touching? (Signal.) *The tree.*
- Touch the thing the girl is moving **to.** ✔
- Everybody, what are you touching? (Signal.) *The house.*
5. Here's the rule about the thing the girl is moving **to.** It should be blue. Name the thing you are going to color blue. Get ready. (Signal.) *The house.*
- Make a blue mark on the thing the girl is moving **to.**
  (Observe children and give feedback.)
- Here's a rule about the thing the girl is moving **from.** It should be green. Name the thing you are going to color green. Get ready. (Signal.) *The tree.*
- Make a green mark on the thing the girl is moving **from.**
  (Observe children and give feedback.)

EXERCISE 13   Materials

1. (Hold up workbook. Point to second half.)
2. Here's one coloring rule for this picture. If an object is made of rubber, color it black. What's the rule? (Signal.) *If an object is made of rubber, color it black.*
3. (Repeat step 2 until firm.)
4. Make a black mark on one of the objects made of rubber. ✔
5. Here's another coloring rule for this picture. If an object is made of metal, color it red. What's the rule? (Signal.) *If an object is made of metal, color it red.*
6. (Repeat step 5 until firm.)
7. Make a red mark on one of the objects made of metal. ✔
8. Here's one more thing to do. Part of the raincoat is missing. What part is missing? (Signal.) *The sleeve.* Yes, the sleeve. Before you color the raincoat, follow the dots and make the sleeve.

Objectives

- Follow directions involving if-then. (Exercise 1)
- Given an action, answer questions involving movement "from" and "to" and generate statements about the movement. (Exercise 2)
- Generate statements utilizing past, present and future tenses of the verb "to be." (Exercise 3)
- Given a calendar, identify the day and date for "today" and "tomorrow" and one week from today. (Exercise 4)
- Given a common noun, name things that "can" and "cannot" be done with the noun. (Exercise 5)
- Given a common noun, answer questions involving "can do." (Exercise 6)
- Given a common noun, name four classes containing the noun. (Exercise 7)
- **Apply narrowing criteria to guess a mystery object.** (Exercise 8)
- Listen to a short story and answer questions involving "who," "when," "why," "where" and "what". (Exercise 9)
- Identify cardinal directions (north, south, east, west). (Exercise 10)
- Retell a familiar story. (Exercise 11)
- Follow coloring rules involving classes and subclasses. (Exercise 12)
- Follow coloring rules involving material. (Exercise 13)

EXERCISE 1 Actions

1. (Sit down.) We're going to play some action games.
2. Listen to this rule. If I clap **and** stamp my foot, stand up. Listen again. If I clap and stamp my foot, stand up. Everybody, say the rule with me. Get ready. (Signal.) *If you clap and stamp your foot, stand up.*
- All by yourselves. Say the rule. Get ready. (Signal.) *If you clap and stamp your foot, stand up.*
3. (Repeat step 2 until firm.)
4. What's the rule? (Signal.) *If you clap and stamp your foot, stand up.*
- What are you going to do if I clap and stamp my foot? (Signal.) *Stand up.*
5. Let's see if I can fool you. (Pause.) (Stand up.) (Signal.)
   (The children should not do anything.)
6. (Sit.) See if I can fool you. (Pause.) (Clap and stamp your foot.) (Signal.) (Every child should stand up.)
7. See if I can fool you this time. (Pause.) (Stamp your foot.) (Signal.)
   (The children should not do anything.)
8. (Repeat steps 5 through 7 until firm.)

EXERCISE 2 From—To

1. Look at me.
2. Everybody, I'm going to move my finger from something to something else. See if you can tell me how my finger moves. My turn. (Place your finger on your ear.) Watch. (Move it to your nose.) I did it.
3. Your turn. Where did my finger move from? (Signal.) *Your ear.*
- Where did my finger move to? (Signal.) *Your nose.*
4. Everybody, how did I move my finger? (Signal.) *From your ear to your nose.*
5. Again. How did I move my finger? (Signal.) *From your ear to your nose.*
6. (Repeat step 5 until firm.)
7. Everybody, say the whole thing about how I moved my finger. Get ready. (Signal.) *You moved your finger from your ear to your nose.*
8. (Repeat step 7 until firm.)

EXERCISE 3 Verb Tense

1. Listen: Yesterday the flowers **were** in the yard. Today the flowers **are** in the yard. Tomorrow the flowers **will be** in the yard.
2. Make the statement about the flowers yesterday. Get ready. (Signal.) *Yesterday the flowers were in the yard.*
3. Make the statement about the flowers today. Get ready. (Signal.) *Today the flowers are in the yard.*
4. Make the statement about the flowers tomorrow. Get ready. (Signal.) *Tomorrow the flowers will be in the yard.*
5. (Repeat steps 2 through 4 until firm.)

EXERCISE 4 Calendar

1. (Present calendar.) We're going to talk about today, tomorrow, and one week from today.
2. Tell me the day of the week it is today. Get ready. (Signal.)
   - Tell me the day of the week it will be tomorrow. Get ready. (Signal.)
   - Tell me the day of the week it will be one week from today. Get ready. (Signal.)
3. (Repeat step 2 until firm.)
4. Now the dates. Tell me today's date. Get ready. (Signal.)
   - Look at the calendar. ✔
   - Tell me the date it will be one week from today. Get ready. (Signal.)
5. Once more. Tell me today's date. Get ready. (Signal.)
   - Tell me tomorrow's date. Get ready. (Signal.)
   - Tell me the date it will be one week from today. Get ready. (Signal.)
6. (Repeat step 5 until firm.)

EXERCISE 5 Can Do

> *Note:* In this task, praise children who name things not previously presented in class.

1. Everybody, I'm going to call on individual children to name things we can do with a rug.
2. (Call on a child.)
   What's one thing we can do with a rug? (After the child gives a correct response, call on the group.) Let's all say the whole thing. Get ready. (Signal.) (The group repeats the child's response.)

3. (Call on another child.)
   What's another thing we can do with a rug? (After the child gives a correct response, call on the group.) Let's all name those things we can do with a rug.
   - What's the first thing? (Hold up one finger.) (The group repeats the first response.)
   - What's the second thing? (Hold up two fingers.) (The group repeats the second response.)
4. (Call on another child.)
   What's another thing we can do with a rug? (After the child gives a correct response, call on the group.) Let's all name those things we can do with a rug.
   - What's the first thing? (Hold up one finger.) (The group repeats the first response.)
   - What's the second thing? (Hold up two fingers.) (The group repeats the second response.)
   - What's the third thing? (Hold up three fingers.) (The group repeats the third response.)
5. Now I'm going to call on individual children to name things we can**not** do with a rug.
6. (Call on a child.)
   What's one thing we cannot do with a rug? (After the child gives a correct response, call on the group.) Let's all say the whole thing. (Signal.) (The group repeats the first response.)
7. (Call on another child.)
   What's another thing we cannot do with a rug? (After the child gives a correct response, call on the group.) Let's all name those things we cannot do with a rug.
   - What's the first thing? (Hold up one finger.) (The group repeats the first response.)
   - What's the second thing? (Hold up two fingers.) (The group repeats the second response.)
8. (Call on another child.)
   What's another thing we cannot do with a rug? (After the child gives a correct response, call on the group.) Let's all name those things we cannot do with a rug.
   - What's the first thing? (Hold up one finger.) (The group repeats the first response.)

- What's the second thing? (Hold up two fingers.) (The group repeats the second response.)
- What's the third thing? (Hold up three fingers.) (The group repeats the third response.)

EXERCISE 6 Can Do

1. Get ready to answer some questions about a needle.
2. Can you hide a needle? (Signal.) *Yes.*
- Can you brush your teeth with a needle? (Signal.) *No.*
- Can you step on a needle? (Signal.) *Yes.*
- Can you pave a road with a needle? (Signal.) *No.*
- Can you sew with a needle? (Signal.) *Yes.*
- Can you take out a splinter with a needle? (Signal.) *Yes.*
- Can you put your hand inside a needle? (Signal.) *No.*

EXERCISE 7 Classification

1. We're going to talk about **oak trees, plants, trees,** and **living things.** What are we going to talk about? (Signal.) *Oak trees, plants, trees, and living things.*
- You're going to name four classes an oak tree is in.
2. (Make a small circle with your hands.) What's the smallest class for an oak tree? (Signal.) *Oak trees.*
- (Make a wider circle.) What's the next bigger class? (Signal.) *Trees.*
- (Make a still wider circle.) What's the next bigger class? (Signal.) *Plants.*
- (Make an even wider circle.) What's a really big class? (Signal.) *Living things.*
3. (Repeat step 2 until firm.)
4. There is one kind of object you would find in all of those classes. Everybody, name the kind of object you would find in all of those classes. Get ready. (Signal.) *An oak tree.*
5. Now we're going to talk about **goats, animals, living things,** and **farm animals.** What things? (Signal.) *Goats, animals, living things, and farm animals.*
- You're going to name four classes a goat is in.

6. (Make a small circle with your hands.) What's the smallest class for a goat? (Signal.) *Goats.*
- (Make a wider circle.) What's the next bigger class? (Signal.) *Farm animals.*
- (Make a still wider circle.) What's the next bigger class? (Signal.) *Animals.*
- (Make an even wider circle.) What's a really big class? (Signal.) *Living things.*
7. (Repeat step 6 until firm.)
8. There is one kind of object you would find in all of those classes. Everybody, name the kind of object you would find in all of those classes. Get ready. (Signal.) *A goat.*

EXERCISE 8 Description

1. I'm thinking of an object. See if you can figure out what object I'm thinking of. I'll tell you something about the object.
2. Listen: It's an animal. Everybody, what do you know about the object? (Signal.) *It's an animal.*
- Could I be thinking of a wagon? (Signal.) *No.*
- Could I be thinking of a tree? (Signal.) *No.*
- Could I be thinking of a cow? (Signal.) *Yes.*
- Could I be thinking of a lion? (Signal.) *Yes.*
3. Listen: The object I'm thinking of is (hold up one finger) an animal **and** (hold up two fingers) you find it in the jungle.
4. Everybody, what do you know about the object? (Hold up one finger.) *It's an animal* **and** (hold up two fingers) *you find it in a jungle.*
5. (Repeat step 4 until firm.)
6. Is a monkey an animal and do you find it in a jungle? (Signal.) *Yes.*
- Could I be thinking of a monkey? (Signal.) *Yes.*
7. (Repeat step 6 until firm.)
8. Is an elephant an animal and do you find it in a jungle? (Signal.) *Yes.*
- Could I be thinking of an elephant? (Signal.) *Yes.*
9. (Repeat step 8 until firm.)
10. Is a polar bear an animal and do you find it in the jungle? (Signal.) *No.*
- Could I be thinking of a polar bear? (Signal.) *No.*
- Why not? (Hold up two fingers.) *You do not find it in a jungle.*
11. (Repeat step 10 until firm.)

12. Listen: The object I'm thinking of is (hold up one finger) an animal **and** (hold up two fingers) you find it in a jungle **and** (hold up three fingers) it has a trunk.

13. Everybody, name the object I am thinking of. Get ready. (Signal.) *An elephant.* Yes, an elephant.

EXERCISE 9   Who—What—When—Where—Why

1. Listen to this story.

2. The horse was running next to a fence. The horse was running so fast, it was sweating. Before the horse went back to the barn, it took a swim in the river to cool off.

3. Listen again. (Repeat step 2.)

4. Tell who was running. Get ready. (Signal.) *The horse.*
   - Tell where the horse was running. Get ready. (Signal.) *Next to a fence.*
   - Tell why the horse was sweating. Get ready. (Signal.) *Because it was running fast.*
   - Tell what the horse did to cool off. Get ready. (Signal.) *Took a swim in the river.*
   - Tell when the horse took a swim in the river. Get ready. (Signal.) *Before it went back to the barn.*

5. (Repeat step 4 until firm.)

EXERCISE 10   Map Reading

1. I'll point in different directions. You tell me the directions.

2. (Point north.) Which direction is this? (Signal.) *North.*
   (Point south.) Which direction is this? (Signal.) *South.*
   (Point east.) Which direction is this? (Signal.) *East.*
   (Point west.) Which direction is this? (Signal.) *West.*

3. Watch me. I'm going to walk. You point to the wall I'm walking to. That's the **direction** I'm walking.

4. Watch. (Walk toward the north wall.) Everybody, which direction? (Signal.) *North.* Yes, I walked north.

5. Watch. (Walk toward the east wall.) Everybody, which direction? (Signal.) *East.* Yes, I walked east.
   (Return to the middle of the room.)

6. Watch. (Walk toward the north wall.) Everybody, which direction? (Signal.) *North.* Yes, I walked north.

7. Watch. (Walk toward the west wall.) Everybody, which direction? (Signal.) *West.* Yes, I walked west.

8. Watch. (Walk toward the south wall.) Everybody, which direction? (Signal.) *South.* Yes, I walked south.

9. Watch. (Walk toward the east wall.) Everybody, which direction? (Signal.) *East.* Yes, I walked east.

10. (Repeat steps 6 through 9 until firm.)

WORKBOOK

EXERCISE 11   Sweetie And The Birdbath Sequencing

1. Everybody, open your workbook to Lesson 48. Write your name at the top of the page. ✔
   - These are pictures that show the story about Sweetie and the birdbath. The pictures are in order. That means that the **first** picture shows something that happened at the **beginning** of the story. The **next** picture shows something that happened **next** in the story. The very **last** picture shows something that happened at the **end** of the story.

2. Everybody, touch picture 1. ✔
- What's happening in that picture? (Call on a child. Ideas: *Sweetie is looking at the birds in the birdbath; Sweetie is saying, "Yum, yum;" Little birds are splashing in the birdbath.*)
3. Everybody, touch picture 2. ✔
- What's happening in that picture? (Call on a child. Ideas: *Sweetie is sneaking through the bushes close to the birdbath; An eagle is flying toward the birdbath; Little birds are starting to leave.*)
4. Everybody, touch picture 3. ✔
- What's happening in that picture? (Call on a child. Ideas: *Sweetie is getting grabbed by the eagle; The eagle is slamming Sweetie into the birdbath.*)
5. Everybody, touch picture 4. ✔
- What's happening in that picture? (Call on a child. Ideas: *Sweetie is all wet; Sweetie is looking at the birds through the hole in the fence; Sweetie is wondering how those birds could look so small and helpless but be so strong.*)
6. You can use these pictures to tell the **whole** story about Sweetie and the birdbath. You have to start out by telling **why** Sweetie wanted to sneak through the bushes in the first place. Then tell the things that happened in each picture. Be sure to tell what Sweetie is saying in that last picture. Raise your hand if you think you can tell about each picture.
7. (Call on several children to tell the story. Instruct the other children to follow along and raise their hand if they hear a problem. Praise stories that tell what happens in each picture.)
8. Later you can color the pictures. I know that everybody remembers what color Sweetie is and what colors the eagle is.

EXERCISE 12 Classification

1. Everybody, find the next page in your workbook. ✔
- (Hold up workbook. Point to first half.)
- These pictures show two classes. One class has **one** kind of thing in it, the other class has **more** kinds of things in it.
- Touch the picture that shows only one kind of thing. ✔
- What kind of thing is that in the picture? (Signal.) *Pants.*
2. Touch the picture that shows **more** than one kind of thing. ✔
- That picture shows pants and other things too. Raise your hand if you can figure out the name of the class that has pants and other things in it. ✔
- Everybody, what's the name of that class? (Signal.) *Clothing.*
- Everybody, circle the picture that shows **more** kinds of things. ✔
3. Here's the coloring rule for the picture that shows more kinds of things. The pants in that picture should be blue. What color? (Signal.) *Blue.*
- Make a mark to show the color in that picture. ✔
4. Everybody, touch the picture that shows **one** kind of thing. ✔
- The pants in that picture should be green or black. Mark two pairs of pants in that picture. ✔

EXERCISE 13   **Materials**

1. (Hold up workbook. Point to second half.)
2. Here's a coloring rule for this picture. If an object could be made of plastic, color it blue. What's the rule? (Signal.) *If an object could be made of plastic, color it blue.*
3. (Repeat step 2 until firm.)
4. Make a blue mark on one of the objects that could be made of plastic. ✔

5. Here's another coloring rule for this picture. If an object is made of wood, color it green. What's the rule? (Signal.) *If an object is made of wood, color it green.*
6. (Repeat step 5 until firm.)
7. Make a green mark on one of the objects made of wood. ✔
8. Here's one more thing to do. One part of each chair is missing. What part is missing? (Signal.) *The back.*
• Yes, the back. Before you color the chairs, follow the dots and make the backs.

LESSON 49

Objectives

- **Follow directions involving "from"/"to."** (Exercise 1)
- Given a common noun, name four classes containing the noun. (Exercise 2)
- Given a calendar, identify the day and date for "today" and "tomorrow" and one week from today. (Exercise 3)
- Apply narrowing criteria to guess a mystery object. (Exercise 4)
- Generate statements involving "can do" and "cannot do." (Exercise 5)
- **Name objects that could be made of a given material using true and false statements.** (Exercise 6)
- Discriminate between true and false statements and generate true and false statements. (Exercise 7)
- Identify cardinal directions (north, south, east, west). (Exercise 8)
- Answer questions about a new story. (Exercise 9)
- Make a picture consistent with the details of a story. (Exercise 10)
- **Complete an analogy involving parts of a whole.** (Exercise 11)
- Follow coloring rules involving class. (Exercise 12)

EXERCISE 1 Actions

1. Everybody, you're going to move your finger from your elbow to your ear. How are you going to move your finger? (Signal.) *From my elbow to my ear.*
2. (Repeat step 1 until firm.)
3. Move your finger from your elbow to your ear. Get ready. (Signal.) ✔
   - (Every child is to move a finger from an elbow to an ear.)
4. (Repeat step 3 until firm.)
5. How did you move your finger? (Signal.) *From my elbow to my ear.*
6. (Repeat step 5 until firm.)

EXERCISE 2 Classification

1. Now we're going to talk about **living things, cats, pets,** and **animals.** What are we going to talk about? (Signal.) *Living things, cats, pets, and animals.*
2. You're going to name four classes a cat is in.
   - (Make a small circle with your hands.) What's the smallest class for a cat? (Signal.) *Cats.*
   - (Make a wider circle.) What's the next bigger class? (Signal.) *Pets.*
   - (Make a still wider circle.) What's the next bigger class? (Signal.) *Animals.*
   - (Make an even wider circle.) What's a really big class? (Signal.) *Living things.*
3. (Repeat step 2 until firm.)

4. There is one kind of object you would find in all of those classes. Everybody, name the kind of object you would find in all of those classes. Get ready. (Signal.) *A cat.*

EXERCISE 3 Calendar

1. (Present calendar.) We're going to talk about today, tomorrow, and one week from today.
2. Tell me the day of the week it is today. Get ready. (Signal.)
   - Tell me the day of the week it will be tomorrow. Get ready. (Signal.)
   - Tell me the day of the week it will be one week from today. Get ready. (Signal.)
3. (Repeat step 2 until firm.)
4. Now the dates. Tell me today's date. Get ready. (Signal.)
   - Look at the calendar. ✔
   - Tell me tomorrow's date. Get ready. (Signal.)
   - Tell me the date it will be one week from today. Get ready. (Signal.)
5. Once more. Listen: Tell me today's date. Get ready. (Signal.)
   - Tell me tomorrow's date. Get ready. (Signal.)
   - Tell me the date it will be one week from today. Get ready. (Signal.)
6. (Repeat step 5 until firm.)

EXERCISE 4 Description

1. I'm thinking of an object. See if you can figure out what object I'm thinking of. I'll tell you something about the object.
2. Listen: It's made of wood. Everybody, what do you know about the object? (Signal.) *It's made of wood.*
   - Could I be thinking of a dress? (Signal.) *No.*
   - Could I be thinking of a ruler? (Signal.) *Yes.*
   - Could I be thinking of a suitcase? (Signal.) *No.*
   - Could I be thinking of a table? (Signal.) *Yes.*
3. Listen: The object I'm thinking of is (hold up one finger) made of wood **and** (hold up two fingers) it's found in a classroom.
4. Everybody, what do you know about the object? (Hold up one finger.) *It's made of wood* **and** (hold up two fingers) *it's found in a classroom.*
5. (Repeat step 4 until firm.)
6. Is a boat made of wood and is it found in the classroom? (Signal.) *No.*
   - Could I be thinking of a boat? (Signal.) *No.* Why not? (Signal.) *It's not found in the classroom.*
   - Is a ruler made of wood and is it found in the classroom? (Signal.) *Yes.*
   - Could I be thinking of a ruler? (Signal.) *Yes.*
   - Could I be thinking of a pencil? (Signal.) *Yes.*
7. (Repeat step 6 until firm.)
8. Listen: The object I'm thinking of is (hold up one finger) made of wood **and** (hold up two fingers) it's found in a classroom **and** (hold up three fingers) you use it to write with.
9. Everybody, name the object I am thinking of. (Pause two seconds.) Get ready. (Signal.) *A pencil.* Yes, a pencil.

EXERCISE 5 Can Do

1. I'm going to ask questions about a man and a spoon.
2. Everybody, can a man put a spoon on the table? (Signal.) *Yes.*
   - Say the statement. Get ready. (Signal.) *A man can put a spoon on the table.*
3. Everybody, can a man hide in a spoon? (Signal.) *No.*
   - Say the statement. Get ready. (Signal.) *A man cannot hide in a spoon.*

4. (Call on a child.) Your turn. Make up another statement that tells something a man can do with a spoon. (After the child makes the statement, call on the group.) Everyone, say that statement about what a man can do with a spoon. Get ready. (Signal.) (The group repeats the child's statement.)
5. (Call on another child.) Your turn. Make up a statement that tells something a man can**not** do with a spoon. (After the child makes the statement, call on the group.) Everyone, say that statement about what a man cannot do with a spoon. (Signal.) (The group repeats the child's statement.)
6. (Repeat steps 4 and 5 until firm.)

EXERCISE 6 Materials

1. A woman is going to make some objects.
2. A woman is going to make some objects from plastic. What will the objects be made of? (Signal.) *Plastic.*
3. (Write on the board:)

true	false

   - (Point to each word.) This word says **true.** This word says **false.** See if you can name objects she could make. Every time you name an object that she could make, I'll put a mark by the word **true.** If you name something that is not made of plastic, I'll put a mark by the word **false.**
   - Your turn. Name things the woman could make. (Call on several individual children. Keep a tally. The children should name a number of objects that can be made of plastic. When they have finished, add up the number of marks by the word **true.**)
   - You made _____ statements that are true.

EXERCISE 7 True—False

1. I'm going to say statements. Some of these statements are true and some are false. You tell me about each statement.

2. You use an umbrella to sweep with. True or false? (Signal.) *False.*

- A hammer is a tool. True or false? (Signal.) *True.*

- An umbrella does not have petals. True or false? (Signal.) *True.*

- Ice cream is not food. True or false? (Signal.) *False.*

- Umbrellas have feathers. True or false? (Signal.) *False.*

3. (Repeat step 2 until firm.)

4. Your turn. Make up a statement about an umbrella that is true. (Call on three children. Praise each acceptable statement and have the group repeat it. Then say:) Everybody, that statement is . . . (Signal.) *true.*

5. Your turn. Now make up a statement about an umbrella that is false. (Call on three children. Praise each acceptable statement and have the group repeat it. Then say:) Everybody, that statement is . . . (Signal.) *false.*

EXERCISE 8 Map Reading

1. I'll point in different directions. You tell me the directions.

2. (Point north.) Which direction is this? (Signal.) *North.*
(Point south.) Which direction is this? (Signal.) *South.*
(Point east.) Which direction is this? (Signal.) *East.*
(Point west.) Which direction is this? (Signal.) *West.*

3. Watch me. I'm going to walk. You point to the wall I'm walking to. That's the **direction** I'm walking.

4. Watch. (Walk toward the south wall.) Everybody, which direction? (Signal.) *South.* Yes, I walked south.

5. Watch. (Walk toward the east wall.) Everybody, which direction? (Signal.) *East.* Yes, I walked east.

6. Watch. (Walk toward the north wall.) Everybody, which direction? (Signal.) *North.* Yes, I walked north.

7. Watch. (Walk toward the west wall.) Everybody, which direction? (Signal.) *West.* Yes, I walked west.

8. Watch. (Walk toward the south wall.) Everybody, which direction? (Signal.) *South.* Yes, I walked south.

9. Watch. (Walk toward the east wall.) Everybody, which direction? (Signal.) *East.* Yes, I walked east.

10. (Repeat steps 4 through 9 until firm.)

EXERCISE 9 Molly Fixes Bleep

Storytelling

1. Today I'm going to read you another story about Molly and that robot named Bleep. At the end of the last story about Bleep, was Molly going to leave Bleep in the drop-off zone? (Signal.) *No.*

- What was Molly going to do with Bleep? (Call on a child. Idea: *Fix Bleep so Bleep would not say "bleep" anymore and would not tell lies.*)

2. Here's the new story.

Molly decided to fix up Bleep so that Bleep would not say that word every time he talked.

- Everybody, what word was that? (Signal.) *Bleep.*

Molly also wanted to fix up Bleep so Bleep wouldn't do something else that was bothersome.

- What was the other bothersome thing that Bleep did? (Call on a child. Idea: *Told lies.*)

Molly took the top off Bleep's head. With the top of Bleep's head removed, Molly could see all the wires and the screws that made Bleep work. There were many screws that changed the way Bleep talked and the way he thought. Each screw was a different color. One screw was black. One screw was yellow. Another screw was pink. And there were many other screws.

Molly didn't know which screw to turn or whether she should turn a screw to the right or to the left. So Molly said, "I'll just have to figure out which screw will fix the problem."

She started with the **purple** screw. She turned it to the **right.** When she did that, Bleep didn't say, "Bleep. Okay, baby." Here's what he said: "Bloop. Okay, babe-oo."

- What did Bleep say? (Signal.) *Bloop. Okay, babe-oo.*

Molly said, "Well, that's not the right screw." So she turned the purple screw back to where it was when she started.

Next she tried the **black** screw. She turned it to the **right.** Bleep didn't say, "Bleep. Okay, baby," and he didn't say, "Bloop. Okay, babe-oo." He said, "Blipe. Okay, babe-eye."

- What did he say? (Signal.) *Blipe. Okay, babe-eye.*

So Molly turned the black screw back to where it was when she started.

Next, Molly tried the **green** screw. But when she turned that screw to the **right,** Bleep said, "Blope. Okay, babe-oh."

"No, no,"Molly said and went to the next screw and the next screw and the next screw. Finally, she came to the **blue** screw. When she turned the **blue** screw to the **right,** Bleep said something that was really strange. He didn't say "Bleep," or "bloop," or "blipe" or "blap." He didn't say "blope," or "blup," or even "blurp." Here's what he said when Molly turned the blue screw a **little** bit to the **right:** "Bleep. Bleep. Okay, baby. Okay, baby."

- Listen again: Bleep. Bleep. Okay, baby. Okay, baby.
- What did Bleep say? (Signal.) *Bleep. Bleep. Okay, baby. Okay, baby.*

Molly turned the blue screw even farther to the right and Bleep said, "Bleep, bleep, bleep. Okay, baby. Okay, baby. Okay, baby."

Then Molly turned the blue screw **all** the way to the right and Bleep said . . .

- What do you think he said? (Call on a child. Praise responses with multiple "bleeps" and "Okay, babies.")

Bleep said, "Bleep, bleep, bleep, bleep. Okay, baby. Okay, baby. Okay, baby. Okay, baby."

Molly said, "Well, at least he's not saying, 'blipe' or 'bloop' or 'blup.'"

So she said, "Maybe I'm turning the blue screw the wrong way. Maybe I should be turning it to the **left,** not the **right.** So she turned the screw back to where it was when she started.

Bleep said, "Bleep. Okay, baby."

Then she turned the blue screw to the **left**—just a **little** bit to the left.

Bleep said, "Blee. Okay, baby." He didn't say, "**Bleep.** Okay, baby." He said, "**Blee.** Okay, baby."

- What did Bleep say now? (Signal.) *Blee. Okay, baby.*

Molly turned the blue screw a little **more** to the left.

Bleep said, "Bl. Okay, baby."

Then she turned the blue screw **all** the way to the left, and you'll never guess what Bleep said.

- What do you think Bleep said? (Call on a child.) *Okay, baby.*

Bleep looked at Molly and said, "Okay, baby."

Molly said, "I did it. I fixed up Bleep so he wouldn't say 'bleep' all the time." And Molly was right.

But Bleep still had one problem that wasn't fixed up.

- What was the problem that was not fixed up? (Call on a child. Idea: *Bleep still told lies.*)
- Maybe we'll read about that problem later.
3. I'm going to read the story again. But when I tell about a screw turning to the right or to the left, you have to hold up your finger and show me which way it's turning.

Molly decided to fix up Bleep so that Bleep would not say that word every time he talked.

Molly also wanted to fix up Bleep so Bleep wouldn't do something else that was bothersome.

Molly took the top off Bleep's head. With the top of Bleep's head removed, Molly could see all the wires and the screws that made Bleep work. There were many screws that changed the way Bleep talked and the way he thought. Each screw was a different color. One screw was black. One screw was yellow. Another screw was pink. And there were many other screws.

Molly didn't know which screw to turn or whether she should turn a screw to the right or to the left. So Molly said, "I'll just have to figure out which screw will fix the problem."

She started with the **purple** screw. She turned it to the **right.**

- Everybody, hold your finger and show me which way the purple screw turned. ✔

When she did that, Bleep didn't say, "Bleep. Okay, baby." Here's what he said: "Bloop. Okay, babe-oo."

Molly said, "Well, that's not the right screw." So she turned the purple screw back to where it was when she started.

Next she tried the **black** screw. She turned it to the **right.**

- Everybody, hold up your finger and show me which way the black screw turned. ✔

Bleep didn't say, "Bleep. Okay, baby," and he didn't say, "Bloop. Okay, babe-oo." He said, "Blipe. Okay, babe-eye."

So Molly turned the black screw back to where it was when she started.

Next, Molly tried the **green** screw. But when she turned that screw to the **right,** Bleep said, "Blope. Okay, babe-oh."

"No, no," Molly said and went to the next screw and the next screw and the next screw. Finally, she came to the **blue** screw. When she turned the **blue** screw to the **right,** Bleep said something that was really strange. He didn't say "bleep," or "bloop," or "blipe" or "blap." He didn't say "blope," or "blup," or even "blurp." Molly turned the blue screw a **little** bit to the **right.**

- Everybody, hold up your finger and show me a **little** bit to the **right.** ✔
- Here's what Bleep said:

"Bleep. Bleep. Okay, baby. Okay, baby."

Molly turned the blue screw even farther to the right.

- Everybody, hold up your finger and show me even farther to the right. ✔

Bleep said, "Bleep, bleep, bleep. Okay, baby. Okay, baby. Okay, baby."

Then Molly turned the blue screw **all** the way to the right and Bleep said, "Bleep, bleep, bleep, bleep. Okay, baby. Okay, baby. Okay, baby. Okay, baby."

Molly said, "Well, at least he's not saying, 'blipe' or 'bloop' or 'blup.'"

So she said, "Maybe I'm turning the blue screw the wrong way. Maybe I should be turning it to the **left,** not the **right.** So she turned the screw back to where it was when she started.

- Everybody, hold up your finger and show me where the blue screw was when she started. ✔

Bleep said, "Bleep. Okay, baby."

Then she turned the blue screw to the **left**—just a **little** bit to the left.

- Everybody, show me a **little** bit to the **left** with your finger. ✔

Bleep said, "Blee. Okay, baby." He didn't say, "**Bleep.** Okay, baby." He said, "**Blee.** Okay, baby."

Molly turned the blue screw a little **more** to the left.

- Everybody, show me a **little** more to the **left** with your finger. ✔

Bleep said, "Bl. Okay, baby."

Then she turned the blue screw **all** the way to the left, and you'll never guess what Bleep said.

Bleep looked at Molly and said, "Okay, baby."

Molly said, "I did it. I fixed up Bleep so he wouldn't say 'bleep' all the time." And Molly was right.

But Bleep still had one problem that wasn't fixed up.

EXERCISE 10

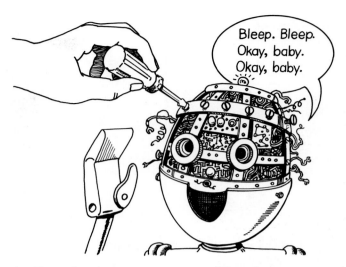

1. Everybody, open your workbook to Lesson 49. Write your name at the top of the page. ✔
- There's poor Bleep with the top of his head off. What is Molly doing? (Call on a child. Idea: *Turning one of the screws.*)
2. You can see that Molly is turning one of the screws. But we don't know which screw she is turning. Maybe we can figure out which screw she is turning.
- Bleep is saying something. I'll read what Bleep is saying and maybe that will give you a clue about the color of the screw. Don't say the answer. Just raise your hand if you know which screw Molly is turning.
- Here's what Bleep is saying: "Bleep, bleep. Okay, baby. Okay, baby."
- Everybody with your hand raised, which screw is Molly turning? (Signal.) *The blue screw.*
- Put a blue mark on the screw to show that it should be blue. Later you can color the rest of the picture.

EXERCISE 11 Analogies

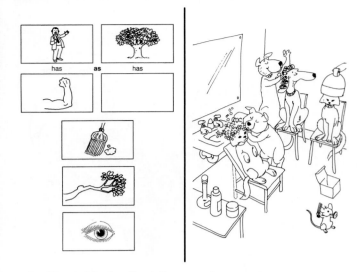

1. Everybody, find the next page in your workbook. ✔
• (Hold up workbook. Point to first half.)
• The pictures show something and part of the thing.
2. Touch the man. ✔
3. Now touch the picture that's right below the man. It shows part of the man. Everybody, what part? (Signal.) *An arm.* Yes, those pictures show that a man has an arm.
4. Touch the tree. ✔
• One of the pictures below the tree shows the part it has. Touch the picture that shows the part a tree has. ✔
• Everybody, what part does a tree have? (Signal.) *A branch.*

5. Listen: A man has an arm **as** a tree has a branch.
• Tell me about a man. Get ready. (Signal.) *A man has an arm.*
• Tell me about a tree. Get ready. (Signal.) *A tree has a branch.*
6. Draw a line from the tree to the part it has. (Observe children and give feedback.)

EXERCISE 12 Location

1. (Hold up workbook. Point to second half.)
2. What place do you see in this picture? (Call on a child. Idea: *a beauty parlor or barbershop.*)
3. Here's a coloring rule for this picture. Listen: Color the furniture brown. What's the rule? (Signal.) *Color the furniture brown.*
4. (Repeat step 3 until firm.)
5. Put a brown mark on **one** piece of furniture. ✔
6. Here's another coloring rule for this picture. Listen: Color the containers red. What's the rule? (Signal.) *Color the containers red.*
7. (Repeat step 6 until firm.)
8. Put a red mark on **one** container. ✔
9. There's one more thing to do.
10. One piece of furniture has a missing part. What piece of furniture is that? (Signal.) *A chair.* Yes, a chair.
11. What part of the chair is missing? (Signal.) *The leg.* Yes, the leg.
• Before you color the chair, follow the dots and make the leg.

Objectives

- Generate statements to describe actions using past, present and future tense and describe actions involving "to" and "from." (Exercise 1)
- Given a common noun, name four classes containing the noun. (Exercise 2)
- Given a common noun, name things that "can" and "cannot" be done with the noun. (Exercise 3)
- Apply narrowing criteria to guess a mystery object. (Exercise 4)
- Name objects that could be made of a given material. (Exercise 5)
- Replace a word in a sentence with an opposite. (Exercise 6)
- Given a calendar, identify the day and date for "today" and "tomorrow" and one week from today. (Exercise 7)
- Identify cardinal directions (north, south, east, west). (Exercise 8)
- Collect data on groups and tell whether statements about groups are true or false. (Exercise 9)
- **Complete an analogy involving location.** (Exercise 10)
- Follow coloring rules involving material. (Exercise 11)

EXERCISE 1 Actions

1. (Sit down.) It's time for some actions.
2. Everybody, I will stand up. Say the whole thing about what I will do. Get ready. (Signal.) *You will stand up.*
3. Am I standing up now? (Signal.) *No.*
4. What am I doing now? (Signal.) *Sitting down.*
   - What will I do? (Signal.) *Stand up.*
5. (Stand up.) What am I doing now? (Signal.) *Standing up.*
6. What was I doing before I stood up? (Signal.) *Sitting down.*
7. (Sit down.)
8. (Repeat steps 2 through 7 until firm.)
9. Look at me.
10. Everybody, I'm going to move my finger from something to something else. See if you can tell me how my finger moves. My turn. (Place your finger on your head. Move it to your elbow.) I did it.
11. Your turn. Where did my finger move from? (Signal.) *Your head.*
12. Everybody, how did I move my finger? (Signal.) *From your head to your elbow.*
13. Again. How did I move my finger? (Signal.) *From your head to your elbow.*
14. (Repeat step 13 until firm.)
15. Everybody, say the whole thing about how I moved my finger. Get ready. (Signal.) *You moved your finger from your head to your elbow.*
16. (Repeat step 15 until firm.)

17. Your turn. Move your finger from your head to your elbow. Get ready. (Signal.) ✔
    - How did you move your finger? (Signal.) *From my head to my elbow.*
    - Everybody, say the whole thing about how you moved your finger. Get ready. (Signal.) *I moved my finger from my head to my elbow.*

EXERCISE 2 Classification

1. We're going to talk about **spotted dogs, dogs, animals,** and **pets.** What are we going to talk about? (Signal.) *Spotted dogs, dogs, animals, and pets.*
   - You're going to name four classes a spotted dog is in.
2. (Make a small circle with your hands.) What's the smallest class for a spotted dog? (Signal.) *Spotted dogs.*
   - (Make a wider circle.) What's the next bigger class? (Signal.) *Dogs.*
   - (Make a still wider circle.) What's the next bigger class? (Signal.) *Pets.*
   - (Make an even wider circle.) What's a really big class? (Signal.) *Animals.*
3. (Repeat step 2 until firm.)
4. There is one kind of object you would find in all of those classes. Everybody, name the kind of object you would find in all those classes. Get ready. (Signal.) *A spotted dog.*

5. Now we're going to talk about **things made of cloth, shirts, clothing,** and **striped shirts.** What are we going to talk about? (Signal.) *Things made of cloth, shirts, clothing, and striped shirts.*

• You're going to name four classes a striped shirt is in.

6. (Make a small circle with your hands.) What's the smallest class for a striped shirt? (Signal.) *Striped shirts.*

• (Make a wider circle.) What's the next bigger class? (Signal.) *Shirts.*

• (Make a still wider circle.) What's the next bigger class? (Signal.) *Clothing.*

• (Make an even wider circle.) What's a really big class? (Signal.) *Things made of cloth.*

7. (Repeat step 6 until firm.)

8. There is one kind of object you would find in all of those classes. Everybody, name the kind of object you would find in all those classes. Get ready. (Signal.) *A striped shirt.*

EXERCISE 3   Can Do

1. Get ready to answer some questions about a jump rope.

2. What are you going to answer questions about? (Signal.) *A jump rope.*

3. Can you carry a jump rope? (Signal.) *Yes.*

• Can you paint a picture with a jump rope? (Signal.) *No.*

• Can you make a jump rope walk? (Signal.) *No.*

• Can you step on a jump rope? (Signal.) *Yes.*

• Can you leave a jump rope out in the rain? (Signal.) *Yes.*

• Can you play with a jump rope? (Signal.) *Yes.*

4. (Repeat step 3 until firm.)

5. Can a boy play with a jump rope? (Signal.) *Yes.* Say the whole thing. Get ready. (Signal.) *A boy can play with a jump rope.*

• Can a boy make a jump rope walk? (Signal.) *No.* Say the whole thing. Get ready. (Signal.) *A boy cannot make a jump rope walk.*

6. (Repeat step 5 until firm.)

EXERCISE 4   Description

1. I'm thinking of an object. See if you can figure out what object I'm thinking of. I'll tell you something about the object.

2. Listen: It's a vehicle. Everybody, what do you know about the object? (Signal.) *It's a vehicle.*

• Could I be thinking of a car? (Signal.) *Yes.*

• Could I be thinking of a bucket? (Signal.) *No.*

• Could I be thinking of a boat? (Signal.) *Yes.*

• Could I be thinking of a chair? (Signal.) *No.*

3. Listen: The object I'm thinking of is (hold up one finger) a vehicle **and** (hold up two fingers) it has four wheels.

4. Everybody, what do you know about the object?
(Hold up one finger.) *It's a vehicle* **and** (hold up two fingers) *it has four wheels.*

5. (Repeat step 4 until firm.)

6. Could I be thinking of a bicycle? (Signal.) *No.*

• Why not? (Signal.) *It does not have four wheels.*

• Could I be thinking of a car? (Signal.) *Yes.*

• Could I be thinking of a wagon? (Signal.) *Yes.*

7. (Repeat step 6 until firm.)

8. Listen: The object I'm thinking of is (hold up one finger) a vehicle **and** (hold up two fingers) it has four wheels **and** (hold up three fingers) you pull it.

9. Everybody, name the object I'm thinking of. (Pause two seconds.) Get ready. (Signal.) *A wagon.* Yes, a wagon.

10. How do you know I'm thinking of a wagon? (Hold up one finger.) *It's a vehicle* **and** (hold up two fingers) *it has four wheels* **and** (hold up three fingers) *you pull it.*

11. (Repeat step 10 until firm.)

EXERCISE 5   Materials

1. Think of things that are made of concrete.

2. Let's see who can name at least three things made of concrete.
(Call on individual children to name objects made of concrete. Each child should name at least three things.)

3. Everybody, think of things that are made of rubber.

4. Let's see who can name at least three things made of rubber. (Call on individual children to name objects made of rubber. Each child should name at least three things.)

5. Everybody, think of things that are made of glass.

6. Let's see who can name at least three things made of glass. (Call on individual children to name objects made of glass. Each child should name at least three things.)

EXERCISE 6 Opposites

1. Let's make up statements with the opposite word.
2. Listen: The ocean is **noisy.** Say that statement. Get ready. (Signal.) *The ocean is noisy.*
3. Now say a statement with the opposite of **noisy.** Get ready. (Signal.) *The ocean is quiet.*
4. (Repeat steps 2 and 3 until firm.)
5. Listen: The frog is **slow.** Say that statement. Get ready. (Signal.) *The frog is slow.*
6. Now say a statement with the opposite of **slow.** Get ready. (Signal.) *The frog is fast.*
7. (Repeat steps 5 and 6 until firm.)

EXERCISE 7 Calendar

1. (Present calendar.) We're going to talk about today, tomorrow, and one week from today.
2. Tell me the day of the week it is today. Get ready. (Signal.)
• Tell me the day of the week it will be tomorrow. Get ready. (Signal.)
• Tell me the day of the week it will be one week from today. Get ready. (Signal.)
3. (Repeat step 2 until firm.)
4. Now the dates. Tell me today's date. Get ready. (Signal.)
• Look at the calendar. ✔
• Tell me the date it will be one week from today. Get ready. (Signal.)
5. Once more. Listen: Tell me today's date. Get ready. (Signal.)
• Tell me tomorrow's date. Get ready. (Signal.)
• Tell me the date it will be one week from today. Get ready. (Signal.)
6. (Repeat step 5 until firm.)

EXERCISE 8 Map Reading

1. Let's all stand up. (Signal.) (All stand.)
2. I'm going to face east. Watch. (Face the east wall.)
• What am I doing? (Signal.) *Facing east.*
• Say the statement. (Signal.) *You are facing east.*
3. Everybody, now you're going to face east. (Pause.) Get ready. (Signal.) (The children face east.)
• What are you doing? (Signal.) *Facing east.*
• Say the statement. (Signal.) *I am facing east.*
4. Everybody, you're going to face north. (Pause.) Get ready. (Signal.) (The children face north.)
• What are you doing? (Signal.) *Facing north.*
• Say the statement. (Signal.) *I am facing north.*
5. Everybody, you're going to face south. (Pause.) Get ready. (Signal.) (The children face south.)
• What are you doing? (Signal.) *Facing south.*
• Say the statement. (Signal.) *I am facing south.*
6. (Repeat steps 2 through 5 until firm.)
7. Let's sit. (Signal.) (All sit.)
8. (Point east.) Tell me the direction I'm pointing. Get ready. (Signal.) *East.*
• Say the statement. Get ready. (Signal.) *You are pointing east.* Yes, if I walked all day in this direction, I would be going east.
9. (Point north.) Tell me the direction I'm pointing. Get ready. (Signal.) *North.*
• Say the statement. Get ready. (Signal.) *You are pointing north.* Yes, if I walked for an hour in this direction, I would be going north.
10. (Repeat steps 8 and 9 until firm.)

WORKBOOK

EXERCISE 9   Data Collection

1. Everybody, open your workbook to Lesson 50. Write your name at the top of the page. ✔
2. The picture shows a lot of nuts under a tree. In the background, you can see the bragging rats, the little black rat and the wise old rat. The bragging rats had a contest to see who could pick up the most nuts from under that tree in the picture.
   - Some of the nuts have the letter **Y** on them. Touch one of those nuts. ✔
   - The nuts with a **Y** were picked up by the rat with the yellow teeth.
   - Put a **yellow** mark on all the nuts the yellow-toothed rat collected. Remember, those nuts have a **Y** on them. Raise your hand when you're finished.
     (Observe children.)
3. Some of the nuts have the letter **B** on them. Touch one of those nuts. ✔
   - The nuts with a **B** were picked up by the little black rat.
   - Make a **black** mark on each nut the black rat collected. Raise your hand when you're finished.
     (Observe children.)
4. Some of the nuts have the letter **G** on them. Touch one of those nuts. ✔
   - Those nuts were collected by the long-tailed gray rat.
   - Make a **gray** mark on each nut the long-tailed gray rat collected. Raise your hand when you're finished.
     (Observe children.)

5. Your turn to count the nuts collected by each rat and write the numbers in the big box at the bottom of the page. Listen: Count the nuts collected by the **yellow-toothed** rat and write that number in the top box. Write the number for the nuts with a **Y** on them. Use your pencil. Raise your hand when you're finished. (Observe children.)
6. Now count the nuts collected by the **gray** rat and write that number in the middle box. Write the number for the nuts with a **G** on them. Use your pencil. Raise your hand when you're finished.
   (Observe children.)
7. Now count the nuts collected by the little **black** rat and write that number in the bottom box. Write the number for the nuts with a **B** on them. Use your pencil. Raise your hand when you're finished.
   (Observe children.)
8. Listen: Put your pencil down and pick up your **red** crayon. ✔
   - Touch the **top** number box. ✔
   - Everybody, what number did you write for the yellow-toothed rat? (Signal.) *Six.*
   - Listen: If you did **not** write **six,** use your red crayon and write **six** on the line right after the box for the yellow-toothed rat. If you wrote **six,** don't do anything with your red crayon. (Observe children.)
9. Touch the **middle** number box. ✔
   - Everybody, what did you write for the long-tailed gray rat? (Signal.) *Eight.*
   - Listen: If you did **not** write **eight,** use your red crayon and write **eight** on the line right after the box for the long-tailed gray rat. If you wrote **eight,** don't do anything with your red crayon. (Observe children.)
10. Touch the **bottom** number box. ✔
    - Everybody, what did you write for the little black rat? (Signal.) *Ten.*
    - Listen: If you did **not** write **ten,** use your red crayon and write **ten** on the line right after the box for the little black rat. If you wrote **ten,** don't do anything with your red crayon. (Observe children.)
11. Everybody, who won the nut collecting contest? (Signal.) *The little black rat.*
    - I wonder if one of those bragging rats will ever win a contest.

EXERCISE 10 Analogies

1. Everybody, find the next page in your workbook. ✔
- (Hold up workbook. Point to first half.)
- The pictures show something and where that thing goes.
2. Touch the boat. ✔
3. Now touch the picture that's right below the boat. It shows where the boat goes.
- Everybody, where does it go? (Signal.) *In the water.* Yes, that picture shows that a boat goes in the water.
4. Touch the picture of the plane. ✔
- One of the pictures below shows where the plane goes. Touch the picture that shows where the plane goes. ✔
- Everybody, where does the plane go? (Signal.) *In the sky.*

5. Listen: A boat goes in the water **as** a plane goes in the sky.
- Tell me about a boat. Get ready. (Signal.) *A boat goes in the water.*
- Tell me about a plane. Get ready. (Signal.) *A plane goes in the sky.*
- Draw a line from the plane to where it goes. (Observe children and give feedback.)

EXERCISE 11 Materials

1. (Hold up workbook. Point to second half.)
2. Here's a coloring rule for this picture. If an object is made of cloth, color it red. What's the rule? (Signal.) *If an object is made of cloth, color it red.*
3. (Repeat step 2 until firm.)
4. Make a red mark on one of the objects made of cloth. ✔
5. Here's another coloring rule for this picture. If an object is made of metal, color it brown. What's the rule? (Signal.) *If an object is made of metal, color it brown.*
6. (Repeat step 5 until firm.)
7. Make a brown mark on one of the objects made of metal. ✔
8. Here's one more thing to do. Part of the garbage can is missing. What part is missing? (Signal.) *The lid.* Yes, the lid. Before you color the can, follow the dots with your pencil and make the lid.

Objectives

- Generate statements to describe actions using past, present and future tenses. (Exercise 1)
- Identify an object that fits stated criteria. (Exercise 2)
- Name objects that could be made of a given material. (Exercises 3 & 4)
- Given a calendar, identify the day and date for "today" and "tomorrow" and one week from today. (Exercise 5)
- Generate sentences using forms of the verb "to be." (Exercise 6)
- Identify cardinal directions (north, south, east, west). (Exercise 7)
- **Construct word-picture sentences for story illustrations.** (Exercise 8)

EXERCISE 1 Actions

1. It's time for some actions.
2. Listen, you will stand up. Everybody, say the whole thing about what you will do. Get ready. (Signal.) *I will stand up.*
3. What are you going to do? (Signal.) *Stand up.*
4. Are you standing up now? (Signal.) *No.* Will you stand up? (Signal.) *Yes.*
5. Everybody, do it. (Signal.) (Every child should stand up.)
6. What were you doing before you stood up? (Signal.) *Sitting down.*
- Sit down. ✔
7. (Repeat steps 2 through 6 until firm.)
8. It's time for a different action game. You are going to do two things at the same time.
9. Everybody, you're going to point to the wall and point to the ceiling. What are you going to do? (Signal.) *Point to the wall and point to the ceiling.*
- Everybody, do it and keep pointing. (Signal.) ✔
- What are you doing? (Signal.) *Pointing to the wall and pointing to the ceiling.*
10. Say the whole thing. Get ready. (Signal.) *I am pointing to the wall and pointing to the ceiling.*
- (Repeat step 10 until firm.)
11. Hands down. Everybody, you're going to hold up your hand and hold up your foot. What are you going to do? (Signal.) *Hold up my hand and hold up my foot.*
- Do it. (Signal.) ✔
- What are you doing? (Signal.) *Holding up my hand and holding up my foot.*
12. Say the whole thing. Get ready. (Signal.) *I am holding up my hand and holding up my foot.*
- (Repeat step 12 until firm.)
13. Hands and feet down. ✔

EXERCISE 2 Description

1. I'm thinking of an object. See if you can figure out what object I'm thinking of. I'll tell you something about the object.
2. Listen: It's made of paper. Everybody, what do you know about the object? (Signal.) *It's made of paper.*
- Could I be thinking of a paper napkin? (Signal.) *Yes.*
- Could I be thinking of a chair? (Signal.) *No.*
- Could I be thinking of a pillow? (Signal.) *No.*
3. Listen: The object I'm thinking of is (hold up one finger) made of paper **and** (hold up two fingers) you put things in it.
4. Everybody, what do you know about the object? (Hold up one finger.) *It's made of paper* **and** (hold up two fingers) *you put things in it.*
5. (Repeat step 4 until firm.)
6. Could I be thinking of a garbage can? (Signal.) *No.*
- Why not? (Signal.) *It's not made of paper.*
- Could I be thinking of an envelope? (Signal.) *Yes.*
- Could I be thinking of a paper bag? (Signal.) *Yes.*
7. (Repeat step 6 until firm.)
8. Listen: The object I'm thinking of is (hold up one finger) made of paper **and** (hold up two fingers) you put things in it **and** (hold up three fingers) you put it in a mailbox.
9. Everybody, name the object I am thinking of. (Pause two seconds.) Get ready. (Signal.) *An envelope.* Yes, an envelope.

10. How do you know I'm thinking of an envelope?
(Hold up one finger.) *It's made of paper and* (hold up two fingers) *you put things in it and* (hold up three fingers) *you put it in a mailbox.*
11. (Repeat step 10 until firm.)

EXERCISE 3   Materials

1. A man is going to make some objects from wood. What will the objects be made of? (Signal.) *Wood.*
2. (Write on the board:)

true	false

(Point to each word.) This word says **true.** This word says **false.** See if you can name all the objects he could make. Every time you name an object that could be made of wood, I'll put a mark by the word **true.** If you name something that is not made of wood, I'll put a mark by the word **false.**
- Your turn. Name things the man could make. (Call on several individual children. Keep a tally. The children should name a number of objects that can be made of wood. When they have finished, add up the number of marks by the word **true.**)
- You made _____ statements that are true.

EXERCISE 4   Materials

1. Think of things that are made of rubber.
2. Let's see who can name at least three things made of rubber. (Call on individual children to name objects made of rubber. Each child should name at least three things.)
3. Everybody, think of things that are made of glass.
4. Let's see who can name at least three things made of glass. (Call on individual children to name objects made of glass. Each child should name at least three things.)
5. Everybody, think of things that are made of wood.
6. Let's see who can name at least three things made of wood. (Call on individual children to name objects made of wood. Each child should name at least three things.)

EXERCISE 5   Calendar

1. (Present calendar.)
- We're going to talk about today, tomorrow, and one week from today.
2. Tell me the day of the week it is today. Get ready. (Signal.)
- Tell me the day of the week it will be tomorrow. Get ready. (Signal.)
- Tell me the day of the week it will be one week from today. Get ready. (Signal.)
3. (Repeat step 2 until firm.)
4. Now the dates. Tell me today's date. Get ready. (Signal.)
- Look at the calendar. ✔
- Tell me the date it will be one week from today. Get ready. (Signal.)
5. Once more.
- Listen: Tell me today's date. Get ready. (Signal.)
- Tell me tomorrow's date. Get ready. (Signal.)
- Tell me the date it will be one week from today. Get ready. (Signal.)
6. (Repeat step 5 until firm.)

EXERCISE 6   Verb Tense

1. Listen: Tomorrow the water **will be** in the ocean. Yesterday the water **was** in the ocean. Today the water **is** in the ocean.
2. Make the statement about the water tomorrow. Get ready. (Signal.) *Tomorrow the water will be in the ocean.*
3. Make the statement about the water yesterday. Get ready. (Signal.) *Yesterday the water was in the ocean.*
4. Make the statement about the water today. Get ready. (Signal.) *Today the water is in the ocean.*
5. (Repeat steps 2 through 4 until firm.)

EXERCISE 7 Map Reading

1. Everybody, stand up. (Signal.) (Children stand.)
2. Everybody, you're going to face south. (Pause.) Get ready. (Signal.) (The children face south.)
   - What are you doing? (Signal.) *Facing south.*
   - Say the statement. (Signal.) *I am facing south.*
3. Everybody, you're going to face east. (Pause.) Get ready. (Signal.) (The children face east.)
   - What are you doing? (Signal.) *Facing east.*
   - Say the statement. (Signal.) *I am facing east.*
4. (Repeat steps 2 and 3 until firm.)
5. Everybody, you're going to face north. (Pause.) Get ready. (Signal.) (The children face north.)
   - What are you doing? (Signal.) *Facing north.*
   - Say the statement. (Signal.) *I am facing north.*
6. (Repeat step 5 until firm.)
7. Sit down. ✔
8. (Point west.) Tell me the direction I'm pointing. Get ready. (Signal.) *West.*
   - Say the statement. (Signal.) *You are pointing west.*
   - Yes, if I flew in an airplane for two hours in this direction, I would be going west.
9. (Point south.) Tell me the direction I'm pointing. Get ready. (Signal.) *South.*
   - Say the statement. (Signal.) *You are pointing south.*
   - Yes, if I flew in an airplane for ten hours in this direction, I would be going south.
10. (Repeat steps 8 and 9 until firm.)

EXERCISE 8 Sentence Construction

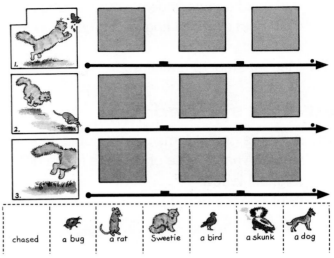

1. Everybody, open your workbook to Lesson 51. Write your name at the top of the page. ✔
2. The pictures show what Sweetie did. You're going to use cutouts to make up sentences that show what Sweetie did in the pictures.
3. Look at the cutouts at the bottom of the page. There are words at the bottom of each cutout.
   I'll read the words.
   - Touch the first cutout. ✔
     The word says: **chased.**
   - Touch the next cutout. ✔
     The words say: **a bug.**
   - Touch the next cutout. ✔
     The words say: **a rat.**
   - Touch the next cutout. ✔
     The word says: **Sweetie.**
   - Touch the next cutout. ✔
     The words say: **a bird.**
   - Touch the next cutout. ✔
     The words say: **a skunk.**
   - Touch the last cutout. ✔
     The words say: **a dog.**
4. Your turn: Cut out your cutouts. Raise your hand when you're finished.
   (Observe children and give feedback.)

5. One of your cutouts does not have a picture, just a word. Hold up that cutout. ✔
- Remember: The word on that cutout is **chased.** What word? (Signal.) *Chased.*
- That's what Sweetie did in all these pictures.
6. Everybody, touch picture 1. ✔
- What did Sweetie do in this picture? (Signal.) *Chased a bird.*
- Here's the sentence that tells what Sweetie did: **Sweetie chased a bird.**
7. Everybody, say that sentence. (Signal.) *Sweetie chased a bird.*
- (Repeat step 7 until firm.)
8. Listen to the sentence again: **Sweetie** (pause) **chased** (pause) **a bird.**
- What's the first word in that sentence? (Signal.) *Sweetie.*
- What's the next word in that sentence? (Signal.) *Chased.*
- What are the last words in that sentence? (Signal.) *A bird.*
- (Repeat step 8 until firm.)
9. Your turn: Put the cutouts in place in the three boxes next to picture 1. Put the cutouts that show: **Sweetie chased a bird.** Raise your hand when you're finished. (Observe children and give feedback.)
- (Write on the board:)

Sweetie chased a bird

- Here's what the words in your boxes should say. Raise your hand if you got it right. ✔
10. Your turn: Write the sentence on the arrow for picture 1. Write the words **Sweetie, chased, a bird.** Write the whole sentence. Copy the words carefully. Raise your hand when you're finished. (Observe children and give feedback.)
- Take your cutouts off the first arrow. ✔
11. Now you're going to make up a sentence for picture 2.
- Touch picture 2. ✔
- That picture shows something else that Sweetie did. Raise your hand when you can say the whole sentence about what Sweetie did in picture 2. ✔

12. Everybody, say the sentence. (Signal.) *Sweetie chased a rat.*
13. (Repeat step 12 until firm.)
14. Put the cutouts in place in the three boxes next to picture 2. Put the cutouts that show: **Sweetie chased a rat.** Raise your hand when you're finished. (Observe children and give feedback.)
- (Write on the board:)

Sweetie chased a rat

- Here's what the words should say for picture 2. Raise your hand if you got it right. ✔
15. Your turn: Write the sentence on the arrow for picture 2. Write the words **Sweetie, chased, a rat.** Write the whole sentence. Copy the words carefully. Raise your hand when you're finished. (Observe children and give feedback.)
- Take your cutouts off the second arrow. ✔
16. Oh, dear. There's another picture of Sweetie on the page, but the picture doesn't show what Sweetie chased. In fact, it looks like something might be chasing Sweetie. If you think Sweetie is chasing something, make up your sentence about what Sweetie chased. If you think something chased Sweetie, make up that sentence.
- Put your cutouts in the boxes for picture 3 so you make up a sentence. Don't make up one of the sentences you've already written. Raise your hand when you're finished. (Observe children and give feedback.)
17. (Call on several children:) Read the sentence you made up. (Praise appropriate sentences.)
- Everybody, copy the last sentence you made up. Raise your hand when you're finished. (Observe children and give feedback.)
18. Everybody, turn your cutouts over and put them in a pile. Let's see who can read all three of their sentences. (Call on several children. Praise correct responses.)

LESSON 52

Objectives

- Describe actions involving same/different/and from/to. (Exercise 1)
- Name three classes containing a common noun and answer questions about members of those classes. (Exercise 2)
- Apply narrowing criteria to guess a mystery object. (Exercise 3)
- Given a common noun, answer questions involving "can do." (Exercise 4)
- Given a calendar, identify the day and date for "today" and "tomorrow" and one week from today. (Exercise 5)
- **Identify cardinal directions on a map.** (Exercise 6)
- Listen to a familiar story. (Exercise 7)
- Answer questions about a familiar story and make a picture consistent with the details of the story. (Exercise 8)
- Follow coloring rules involving classes and subclasses. (Exercise 9)
- **Complete an analogy involving class.** (Exercise 10)

EXERCISE 1 Actions

1. (Sit down.) It's time for an action game.
2. Everybody, stand up. (Signal.) (Every child should stand up and remain standing while you sit.) Good.
3. Now tell me if I do the same thing you did or something different. Watch me. (Stand up.) Did I do the same thing or something different? (Signal.) *The same thing.*
4. Watch me. (Sit down.) Did I do the same thing or something different? (Signal.) *Something different.*
5. Watch me. (Stand up.) Did I do the same thing or something different? (Signal.) *The same thing.*
- Everybody, sit down. ✔
6. (Move to your desk.) Look at me. I'm going to move my finger from something to something else. See if you can tell me how many finger moves. My turn. (Place your finger on your desk.) Watch. (Move it to your chair.) I did it.
7. Your turn. Where did my finger move from? (Signal.) *Your desk.*
- Where did my finger move to? (Signal.) *Your chair.*
8. Everybody, how did I move my finger? (Signal.) *From your desk to your chair.*
9. Again. How did I move my finger? (Signal.) *From your desk to your chair.*
10. (Repeat step 9 until firm.)

11. Everybody, say the whole thing about how I moved my finger. Get ready. (Signal.) *You moved your finger from your desk to your chair.*
12. (Repeat step 11 until firm.)

EXERCISE 2 Classification

1. Today we're going to talk about a brick house. We can put a brick house into three different classes. See how many classes you can name, starting with the smallest class.
2. Everybody, tell me the smallest class for brick houses. Get ready. (Signal.) *Brick houses.*
- What's the next bigger class? (Signal.) *Houses.*
- What's the biggest class? (Signal.) *Buildings.*
3. (Repeat step 2 until firm.)
4. What is one kind of object you would find in all those classes? (Signal.) *A brick house.*
5. Think of these classes: brick houses, houses, buildings.
- Would you find a factory in all those classes? (Signal.) *No.*
- Would you find a wooden house in all those classes? (Signal.) *No.*
- Name two of those classes you would find a wooden house in. (Pause.) Get ready. (Tap 2 times.) *Houses. Buildings.*
6. (Repeat step 5 until firm.)

EXERCISE 3　Description

1. I'm thinking of an object. See if you can figure out what object I'm thinking of. I'll tell you something about the object.
2. Listen: It's a building. Everybody, what do you know about the object? (Signal.) *It's a building.*
- Could I be thinking of a restaurant? (Signal.) *Yes.*
- Could I be thinking of a tree? (Signal.) *No.*
3. Is a swing a building? (Signal.) *No.*
- So could I be thinking of a swing? (Signal.) *No.*
4. Is a school a building? (Signal.) *Yes.*
- Could I be thinking of a school? (Signal.) *Yes.*
5. Listen: The object I'm thinking of is (hold up one finger) a building **and** (hold up two fingers) it has a lot of chairs in it.
6. Everybody, what do you know about the object? (Hold up one finger.) *It's a building* **and** (hold up two fingers) *it has a lot of chairs.*
7. (Repeat step 6 until firm.)
8. Is a theater a building and does it have a lot of chairs in it? (Signal.) *Yes.*
- What do you know about the object I'm thinking of? (Hold up one finger.) *It's a building* **and** (hold up two fingers) *it has a lot of chairs.*
- Could I be thinking of a theater? (Signal.) *Yes.*
9. (Repeat step 8 until firm.)
10. Is a grocery store a building and does it have a lot of chairs in it? (Signal.) *No.*
- What do you know about the object I'm thinking of? (Hold up one finger.) *It's a building* **and** (hold up two fingers) *it has a lot of chairs.*
- Could I be thinking of a grocery store? (Signal.) *No.*
- Why not? (Signal.) *It does not have a lot of chairs in it.*
11. (Repeat step 10 until firm.)
12. Is a school a building and does it have a lot of chairs in it? (Signal.) *Yes.*
- What do you know about the object I'm thinking of? (Hold up one finger.) *It's a building* **and** (hold up two fingers) *it has a lot of chairs.*
- Could I be thinking of a school? (Signal.) *Yes.*
13. (Repeat step 12 until firm.)
14. Listen: The object I'm thinking of is (hold up one finger) a building **and** (hold up two fingers) it has a lot of chairs in it **and** (hold up three fingers) you watch movies in it.
15. Everybody, name the object I am thinking of. (Pause two seconds.) Get ready. (Signal.) *A theater.* Yes, a theater.
16. How do you know I'm thinking of a theater? (Hold up one finger.) *It's a building* **and** (hold up two fingers) *it has a lot of chairs* **and** (hold up three fingers) *you watch movies in it.*
17. (Repeat step 16 until firm.)

EXERCISE 4　Can Do

1. Get ready to answer some questions about a suitcase.
2. What are you going to answer questions about? (Signal.) *A suitcase.*
3. Can you go swimming in a suitcase? (Signal.) *No.*
- Can you wear a suitcase? (Signal.) *No.*
- Can you put clothes in a suitcase? (Signal.) *Yes.*
- Can you drop a suitcase? (Signal.) *Yes.*
- Can you carry a suitcase? (Signal.) *Yes.*
- Can you put a suitcase in a car? (Signal.) *Yes.*
- Can you cut paper with a suitcase? (Signal.) *No.*
4. (Repeat step 3 until firm.)
5. Can a woman put clothes in a suitcase? (Signal.) *Yes.*
- Say the whole thing. Get ready. (Signal.) *A woman can put clothes in a suitcase.*
- Can a woman go swimming in a suitcase? (Signal.) *No.*
- Say the whole thing. Get ready. (Signal.) *A woman cannot go swimming in a suitcase.*
6. (Repeat step 5 until firm.)

EXERCISE 5 Calendar

1. (Present calendar.)
- We're going to talk about today, tomorrow, and one week from today.

2. Tell me the day of the week it is today. Get ready. (Signal.)
- Tell me the day of the week it will be tomorrow. Get ready. (Signal.)
- Tell me the day of the week it will be one week from today. Get ready. (Signal.)

3. (Repeat step 2 until firm.)

4. Now the dates.
- Tell me today's date. Get ready. (Signal.)
- Look at the calendar. ✔
- Tell me the date it will be one week from today. Get ready. (Signal.)

5. Once more.
- Listen: Tell me today's date. Get ready. (Signal.)
- Tell me tomorrow's date. Get ready. (Signal.)
- Tell me the date it will be one week from today. Get ready. (Signal.)

6. (Repeat step 5 until firm.)

EXERCISE 6 Map Reading

1. (Draw a large rectangle on the board. Label as indicated:)

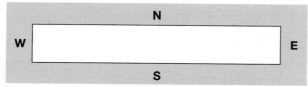

2. We're going to learn a rule about reading maps.

3. Here's the rule about maps. (Touch each letter as you say:) **North** is on the top; **south** is on the bottom; **east** is on this side; **west** is on this side.

4. (Repeat step 3.)

5. See if you can say the rule with me. Get ready. (Touch each letter as you and the children say the rule.)
North is on the top; south is on the bottom; east is on this side; west is on this side.

6. Listen: North is on the top; south is on the bottom. Say that. (Touch each letter as the children respond. Do **not** respond with the children.) *North is on the top; south is on the bottom.*

7. (Repeat step 6 until firm.)

8. Listen: East is on this side; west is on this side. Say that. (Touch each letter as the children respond without you.) *East is on this side; west is on this side.*

9. (Repeat step 8 until firm.)

10. Now say the whole rule. (Touch each letter as the children respond. Do **not** respond with the children.) *North is on the top; south is on the bottom; east is on this side; west is on this side.*

11. (Repeat steps 6 through 10 until firm.)

12. I'm going to move my finger. Tell me the direction I go.

13. (Touch the middle of the rectangle.) Watch. (Move toward the north.) Everybody, which direction did I go? (Touch.) *North.* Yes, north. I went north.

14. (Touch the middle of the rectangle.) Watch. (Move toward the south.) Everybody, which direction did I go? (Touch.) *South.* Yes, south. I went south.

15. (Touch the middle of the rectangle.) Watch. (Move toward the west.) Everybody, which direction did I go? (Touch.) *West.* Yes, west. I went west.

16. (Repeat steps 13 through 15 until firm.)

17. Let's say the rule about the map one more time. (Touch each letter as you and the children say the rule.) *North is on the top; south is on the bottom; east is on this side; west is on this side.*

EXERCISE 7 Molly Fixes Bleep

Review

- Everybody, open your workbook to Lesson 52. Write your name at the top of the page. ✔
- These pictures show Bleep saying different things. Next to each picture of Bleep is the blue screw.

Molly decided to fix up Bleep so that Bleep would not say that word every time he talked.

Molly also wanted to fix up Bleep so Bleep wouldn't do something else that was bothersome.

Molly took the top off Bleep's head. With the top of Bleep's head removed, Molly could see all the wires and the screws that made Bleep work. There were many screws that changed the way Bleep talked and the way he thought. Each screw was a different color. One screw was black. One screw was yellow. Another screw was pink. And there were many other screws.

Molly didn't know which screw to turn or whether she should turn a screw to the right or to the left. So Molly said, "I'll just have to figure out which screw will fix the problem."

She started with the **purple** screw. She turned it to the **right.** When she did that, Bleep didn't say, "Bleep. Okay, baby." Here's what he said: "Bloop. Okay, babe-oo."

Molly said, "Well, that's not the right screw." So she turned the purple screw back to where it was when she started.

Next she tried the **black** screw. She turned it to the **right.** Bleep didn't say, "Bleep. Okay, baby," and he didn't say, "Bloop. Okay, babe-oo." He said, "Blipe. Okay, babe-eye."

So Molly turned the black screw back to where it was when she started.

Next, Molly tried the **green** screw. But when she turned that screw to the **right,** Bleep said, "Blope. Okay, babe-oh."

"No, no," Molly said and went to the next screw and the next screw and the next screw. Finally, she came to the **blue** screw. When she turned the **blue** screw to the **right,** Bleep said something that was really strange. He didn't say "bleep," or "bloop," or "blipe" or "blap." He didn't say "blope," or "blup," or even "blurp." Here's what he said when Molly turned the blue screw a **little** bit to the **right:** "Bleep. Bleep. Okay, baby. Okay, baby."

Molly turned the blue screw even farther to the right and Bleep said, "Bleep, bleep, bleep. Okay, baby. Okay, baby. Okay, baby."

Then Molly turned the blue screw **all** the way to the right and Bleep said, "Bleep, bleep, bleep, bleep. Okay, baby. Okay, baby. Okay, baby. Okay, baby."

Molly said, "Well, at least he's not saying, 'blipe' or 'bloop' or 'blup.'"

So she said, "Maybe I'm turning the blue screw the wrong way. Maybe I should be turning it to the **left,** not the **right.**" So she turned the screw back to where it was when she started.

Bleep said, "Bleep. Okay, baby."

Then she turned the blue screw to the **left**—just a **little** bit to the left.

Bleep said, "Blee. Okay, baby." He didn't say, "**Bleep.** Okay, baby." He said, "**Blee.** Okay, baby."

Molly turned the blue screw a little **more** to the left.

Bleep said, "Bl. Okay, baby."

Then she turned the blue screw **all** the way to the left, and you'll never guess what Bleep said.

Bleep looked at Molly and said, "Okay, baby."

Molly said, "I did it. I fixed up Bleep so he wouldn't say 'bleep' all the time." And Molly was right.

But Bleep still had one problem that wasn't fixed up.

EXERCISE 8 Workbook Activity

1. Everybody, look at page 91 again. ✔
- In each picture, Bleep is saying different things.
2. Touch picture 1. ✔
- I'll read what Bleep said. Listen: "Blee. Okay, baby." That's what Bleep would say if Molly turned the blue screw to the left.
3. Touch the screw in picture 2. ✔
- Listen: Here's what Bleep said: "Bl. Okay, baby." That's what Bleep said when Molly turned the blue screw a little more to the left.
4. Touch the screw in picture 3. ✔
- Listen: Here's what Bleep said: "Bleep, bleep. Okay, baby. Okay, baby." That's what Bleep said when Molly turned the blue screw to the right.

5. There isn't a picture that shows what Bleep said when Molly turned the blue screw **all** the way to the left. Everybody, what would Bleep be saying in that picture? (Signal.) *"Okay, baby."*
6. Later you can color the pictures of Bleep and show some of the different-colored screws.

EXERCISE 9 Classification

1. Everybody, find the next page in your workbook. ✔
- (Hold up workbook. Point to first half.) These pictures show two classes. One class has **one** kind of thing in it, the other class has **more** kinds of things in it.
- Touch the picture that shows only **one** kind of thing. ✔
- What kind of thing is that in the picture? (Signal.) *Tables.*
2. Touch the picture that shows **more** than one kind of thing. ✔
- That picture shows tables and other things, too. Raise your hand if you can figure out the name of the class that has tables and other things in it. ✔
- Everybody, what's the name of that class? (Signal.) *Furniture.*
- Everybody, circle the picture that shows **more** kinds of things. ✔
3. Here's the coloring rule for the picture that shows **more** kinds of things. The tables in that picture should be orange. What color? (Signal.) *Orange.*
- Make marks to show the color in that picture. ✔
4. Everybody, touch the picture that shows **one** kind of thing. ✔
- The tables in that picture should be green or purple. Mark two tables in that picture. ✔

EXERCISE 10 Analogies

1. (Hold up workbook. Point to second half.)
   The pictures show something and the class
   it is in.
2. Touch the hammer. ✔
3. Now touch the picture that's right below
   the hammer. ✔
   • That picture shows what class the hammer
     is in. Everybody, what class? (Signal.)
     Tools.
   • Yes, that picture shows that a hammer is a
     tool.
4. Touch the picture of the boat. ✔

   • One of the pictures below shows what
     class the boat is in. Touch the picture that
     shows what class a boat is in. ✔
   • Everybody, what class is it in? (Signal.)
     Vehicles.
5. Listen: A hammer is a tool **as** a boat is a
   vehicle.
   • Tell me about a hammer. Get ready.
     (Signal.) *A hammer is a tool.*
   • Tell me about a boat. Get ready. (Signal.)
     A boat is a vehicle.
   • Draw a line from the boat to the class it is in.
     (Observe children and give feedback.)

Objectives

- Generate statements to describe actions using present, past and future tense and answer questions involving "or" and "same/different." (Exercise 1)
- Given a common noun, answer questions involving "can do." (Exercise 2)
- Name objects that could be made of a given material. (Exercise 3)
- Discriminate between true and false statements and generate true and false statements. (Exercise 4)
- Name three classes containing a common noun and answer questions about members of those classes. (Exercise 5)
- Given a calendar, identify the day and date for "today" and "tomorrow" and one week from today. (Exercise 6)
- Identify cardinal directions on a map. (Exercise 7)
- Construct word-picture sentences for story illustrations. (Exercise 8)

EXERCISE 1 Actions

1. Here's the first action game.
2. (Stand up.) Listen: I'm going to walk or hop or stamp my foot. What am I going to do? (Signal.) *Walk or hop or stamp your foot.*
3. Yes, I'm going to walk or hop or stamp my foot.
- Am I going to walk? (Signal.) *Maybe.*
- Am I going to hold a pencil? (Signal.) *No.*
- Am I going to hop? (Signal.) *Maybe.*
- Am I going to stamp my foot? (Signal.) *Maybe.*
4. I'm going to walk or hop or stamp my foot. What am I going to do? (Signal.) *Walk or hop or stamp your foot.*
5. Here I go. (Stamp your foot.)
- What did I do? (Signal.) *Stamped your foot.*
6. Everybody, touch the back of your chair. Get ready. (Signal.) ✔
- Good. Stop touching the back of your chair.
7. Now tell me if I do the same thing you did or something different.
- Watch me. (Touch your knee.) Did I do the same thing or something different? (Signal.) *Something different.*
8. Watch me. (Touch the back of your chair.) Did I do the same thing or something different? (Signal.) *The same thing.*
9. Watch me. (Touch your nose.) Did I do the same thing or something different? (Signal.) *Something different.*

EXERCISE 2 Can Do

1. Get ready to answer some questions about a pencil.
2. What are you going to answer questions about? (Signal.) *A pencil.*
3. Can you break a pencil? (Signal.) *Yes.*
- Can you wash windows with a pencil? (Signal.) *No.*
- Can you chew on a pencil? (Signal.) *Yes.*
- Can you park a car in a pencil? (Signal.) *No.*
- Can you cut your hair with a pencil? (Signal.) *No.*
- Can you put a pencil in your pocket? (Signal.) *Yes.*
- Can you draw with a pencil? (Signal.) *Yes.*
4. (Repeat step 3 until firm.)
5. Can a girl write with a pencil? (Signal.) *Yes.*
- Say the whole thing. Get ready. (Signal.) *A girl can write with a pencil.*
- Can a girl cut her hair with a pencil? (Signal.) *No.*
- Say the whole thing. Get ready. (Signal.) *A girl cannot cut her hair with a pencil.*
6. (Repeat step 5 until firm.)

EXERCISE 3 Materials

1. Everybody, think of things that are made of wood. Let's see who can name at least three things made of wood. (Call on individual children to name objects made of wood. Each child should name at least three things.)

2. Everybody, think of things that are made of cloth. Let's see who can name at least three things made of cloth. (Call on individual children to name objects made of cloth. Each child should name at least three things.)

3. Everybody, think of things that are made of rubber. Let's see who can name at least three things made of rubber. (Call on individual children to name objects made of rubber. Each child should name at least three things.)

EXERCISE 4 True—False

1. I'm going to say statements. Some of these statements are **true** and some are **false.** You tell me about each statement.

2. A toothbrush is used to carry things in. True or false? (Signal.) *False.*
• A toothbrush is not furniture. True or false? (Signal.) *True.*
3. (Repeat step 2 until firm.)
4. Your turn. Make up a statement about a toothbrush that is true. (Call on three children. Praise each acceptable statement and have the group repeat it. Then say:) Everybody, that statement is . . . (Signal.) *true.*

5. Your turn. Now make up a statement about a toothbrush that is false. (Call on three children. Praise each acceptable statement and have the group repeat it. Then say:) Everybody, that statement is . . . (Signal.) *false.*

EXERCISE 5 Classification

1. Today we're going to talk about a tire factory. We can put a tire factory into three different classes. See how many classes you can name, starting with the smallest class.

2. Everybody, what's the smallest class for a tire factory? (Signal.) *Tire factories.*
• What's the next bigger class? (Signal.) *Factories.*
• What's the biggest class? (Signal.) *Buildings.*
3. (Repeat step 2 until firm.)
4. What is the one kind of object you would find in all those classes? (Signal.) *A tire factory.*

5. Think of these classes: tire factories, factories, buildings.
• Would you find a car factory in all those classes? (Signal.) *No.*
• Name the two classes you would find a car factory in. (Pause.) Get ready. (Tap 2 times.) *Factories. Buildings.*
• Would you find a house in all those classes? (Signal.) *No.*
• Name the class you would find a house in. (Pause.) Get ready. (Signal.) *Buildings.*
6. (Repeat step 5 until firm.)

EXERCISE 6 Calendar

1. (Present calendar.)
• We're going to talk about today, tomorrow, and one week from today.
2. Tell me the day of the week it is today. Get ready. (Signal.)
• Tell me the day of the week it will be tomorrow. Get ready. (Signal.)
• Tell me the day of the week it will be one week from today. Get ready. (Signal.)
3. (Repeat step 2 until firm.)
4. Now the dates.
• Tell me today's date. Get ready. (Signal.)
• Look at the calendar. ✔
• Tell me the date it will be one week from today. Get ready. (Signal.)
5. Once more.
• Listen: Tell me today's date. Get ready. (Signal.)
• Tell me tomorrow's date. Get ready. (Signal.)
• Tell me the date it will be one week from today. Get ready. (Signal.)
6. (Repeat step 5 until firm.)

EXERCISE 7 Map Reading

1. (Draw a large rectangle on the board. Label as indicated:)

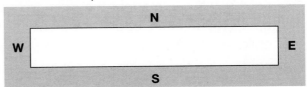

2. We're going to learn a rule about reading maps.

3. Here's the rule about maps. (Touch each letter as you say:) **North** is on the top; **south** is on the bottom; **east** is on this side; **west** is on this side.

4. (Repeat step 3.)

5. See if you can say the rule with me. Get ready. (Touch each letter as you and the children say the rule.) *North is on the top: south is on the bottom; east is on this side; west is on this side.*

6. Listen: North is on the top: south is on the bottom. Say that. (Touch each letter as the children respond. Do **not** respond with the children.) *North is on the top; south is on the bottom.*

7. (Repeat step 6 until firm.)

8. Listen: East is on this side (touch); west is on this side (touch). Say that. (Touch each letter as the children respond without you.) *East is on this side; west is on this side.*

9. (Repeat step 8 until firm.)

10. Now say the whole rule. (Touch each letter as the children respond. Do **not** respond with the children.) *North is on the top; south is on the bottom; east is on this side; west is on this side.*

11. (Repeat steps 5 through 10 until firm.)

12. Watch. I'm going to move my finger. Tell me the direction I go.

13. (Touch the middle of the rectangle.) Watch. (Move toward the east.) Everybody, which direction did I go? (Touch.) *East.*
   • Yes, east. I went east.

14. (Touch the middle of the rectangle.) Watch. (Move toward the west.) Everybody, which direction did I go? (Touch.) *West.*
   • Yes, west. I went west.

15. (Touch the middle of the rectangle.) Watch. (Move toward the south.) Everybody, which direction did I go? (Touch.) *South.*
   • Yes, south. I went south.

16. (Repeat steps 12 through 16 until firm.)

17. Let's say the rule about the map one more time. (Touch each letter as you and the children say the rule.) *North is on the top; south is on the bottom; east is on this side; west is on this side.*

EXERCISE 8 Sentence Construction

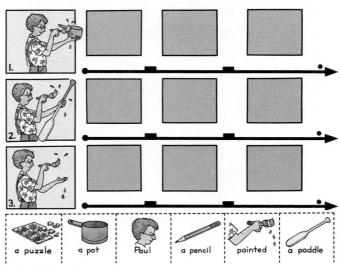

a puzzle   a pot   Paul   a pencil   painted   a paddle

1. Everybody, open your workbook to Lesson 53. Write your name at the top of the page. ✔

2. The pictures show what Paul did. You're going to make up sentences that tell what he did.

3. Look at the cutouts at the bottom of the page. There are words at the bottom of each cutout. I'll read the words.
   • Touch the first cutout. ✔
     The words say: **a puzzle.**
   • Touch the next cutout. ✔
     The words say: **a pot.**
   • Touch the next cutout. ✔
     The word says: **Paul.**
   • Touch the next cutout. ✔
     The words say: **a pencil.**
   • Touch the next cutout. ✔
     The word says: **painted.**
   • Touch the last cutout. ✔
     The words say: **a paddle.**

4. Your turn: Cut out the pictures at the bottom of the page along the dotted lines. Raise your hand when you have all your cutouts ready.
   (Observe children and give feedback.)

5. Everybody, touch picture 1. ✔
   • That picture shows something Paul did. What did he do in that picture? (Signal.) *Painted a pot.*
   • Here's the sentence that tells what Paul did: **Paul painted a pot.**

6. Everybody, say that sentence. (Signal.) *Paul painted a pot.*
    (Repeat step 6 until firm.)
7. (Write on the board:)

*   You're going to use your cutout pictures to show that sentence. Here's how you'll do it: You'll put the cutouts for picture 1 in the three boxes next to picture 1.
*   (Write **Paul painted** in the first and second boxes on the board:)

Paul	painted	

    Listen: **Paul painted** a pot.
*   (Touch the first box.) So you put the cutout for **Paul** here.
*   (Touch the second box.) Then you put the cutout for **painted** here.
*   Do that much. Put the cutouts for **Paul** and **painted** in the first two boxes. The words are on the cutouts. Raise your hand when you're finished.
    (Observe children and give feedback.)
8. Everybody, touch picture 1 again. ✔
*   Say the whole sentence for that picture. (Signal.) *Paul painted a pot.*
*   Fix up the cutouts by putting the right cutout in the last box. Remember, you want your cutouts to say: **Paul painted a pot.** Raise your hand when you're finished.
    (Observe children and give feedback.)
*   Everybody, what picture did you put in the last box? (Signal.) *A pot.*
*   (Write to show:)

Paul	painted	a pot

*   Here's what the words in your boxes should say. Raise your hand if you got it right. ✔
9. Your turn: Everybody, touch the **arrow** for picture 1. ✔
*   Listen: Write the sentence on the arrow for picture 1. Write the words **Paul, painted, a pot.** Those words are written on the bottom of your cutouts. **Paul painted a pot.** Write the whole sentence. Copy the words carefully. Raise your hand when you're finished.
    (Observe children and give feedback.)
*   Take your cutouts off the first arrow. ✔
10. Now you're going to make up a sentence for picture 2.

*   Everybody, touch picture 2. ✔
    That picture shows something else Paul did. Raise your hand when you can say the whole sentence about what Paul did in picture 2. ✔
11. Everybody, say the sentence. (Signal.) *Paul painted a paddle.*
*   (Repeat step 11 until firm.)
12. Put the cutouts in place in the three boxes next to picture 2.
*   Make up the sentence: **Paul painted a paddle.** Raise your hand when you're finished.
    (Observe children and give feedback.)
*   (Write on the board:)

Paul	painted	a paddle

*   Here's what the words should say for picture 2. Raise your hand if you got it right. ✔
*   Your turn: Everybody, touch the **arrow** for picture 2. ✔
*   Listen: Write the sentence on the arrow for picture 2. Write the words **Paul, painted, a paddle.** Those words are written on the bottom of your cutouts. **Paul painted a paddle.** Write the whole sentence. Copy the words carefully. Raise your hand when you're finished.
    (Observe children and give feedback.)
*   Take your cutouts off the second arrow. ✔
13. Oh, dear. There's another picture of Paul on the page, but the picture doesn't show what Paul painted. Maybe you could make up a sentence about what Paul did by using your cutouts.
*   Put your cutouts in the boxes for picture 3 so you make up a sentence that tells about something else Paul did. Don't make up one of the sentences you've already written. Raise your hand when you're finished.
    (Observe children and give feedback.)
*   (Call on several children:) Read the sentence you made up about Paul.
    (Praise appropriate sentences.)
14. Everybody, touch the **arrow** for picture 3. ✔
*   Listen: Copy the sentence you made up for picture 3. Raise your hand when you're finished.
    (Observe children and give feedback.)
15. Everybody, turn your cutouts over and put them in a pile. Let's see who can read all three of their sentences. (Call on several children. Praise correct responses.)

Lesson 53   **285**

LESSON 54

Objectives

- Generate statements to describe actions using present, past and future tense. (Exercise 1)
- Name objects that could be made of a given material. (Exercise 2)
- Given a common noun, answer questions involving "can do." (Exercise 3)
- Given a calendar, identify the day and date for "today" and "tomorrow" and one week from today. (Exercise 4)
- Answer questions about a new story. (Exercise 5)
- Make a picture consistent with the details of the story. (Exercise 6)
- **Follow coloring rules involving cardinal directions.** (Exercise 7)
- Follow coloring rules involving materials. (Exercise 8)

EXERCISE 1 Actions

1. (Sit down.) Everybody, we will stand up. Say the whole thing about what we will do. Get ready. (Signal.) *We will stand up.*
2. Are we standing up now? (Signal.) *No.*
- What are we doing now? (Signal.) *Sitting down.*
3. What will we do? (Signal.) *Stand up.*
4. Let's do it. (Signal.) (Stand up with the children.)
5. What were we doing? (Signal.) *Sitting down.*
- Sit down. ✔
6. (Repeat steps 1 through 5 until firm.)

EXERCISE 2 Materials

1. A woman is going to make some objects from cloth. What will the objects be made of? (Signal.) *Cloth.*
2. (Write on the board:)

true	false

(Point to each word.) This word says **true.** This word says **false.**
- See if you can guess all the objects she's going to make. Every time you name an object that could be made of cloth, I'll put a mark by the word **true.** If you name something that is not made of cloth, I'll put a mark by the word **false.**
- Your turn. Guess what the woman is going to make. (Call on several individual children. Keep a tally. The children should name a number of objects that can be made of cloth. When they have finished, add up the number of marks by the word **true.**)

- You made _____ statements that are true.
3. You have named lots of objects she could make from cloth. I'll tell you the objects she made: Curtains, skirts, and jackets. Name the objects. Get ready. (Signal.) *Curtains, skirts, and jackets.*

EXERCISE 3 Can Do

1. Get ready to answer some questions about an umbrella.
2. Can you stand under an umbrella? (Signal.) *Yes.*
- Can you write with an umbrella? (Signal.) *No.*
- Can you fly in an umbrella? (Signal.) *No.*
- Can you hide under an umbrella? (Signal.) *Yes.*
- Can you cook dinner in an umbrella? (Signal.) *No.*
- Can you jump over an umbrella? (Signal.) *Yes.*
3. (Repeat step 2 until firm.)
4. Can a man use an umbrella to keep dry in the rain? (Signal.) *Yes.*
- Say the whole thing. Get ready. (Signal.) *A man can use an umbrella to keep dry in the rain.*
- Can a man fly in an umbrella? (Signal.) *No.*
- Say the whole thing. Get ready. (Signal.) *A man cannot fly in an umbrella.*
5. (Repeat step 4 until firm.)

EXERCISE 4 Calendar

1. (Present calendar.)
- We're going to talk about today, tomorrow, and one week from today.
2. Tell me the day of the week it is today. Get ready. (Signal.)
- Tell me the day of the week it will be tomorrow. Get ready. (Signal.)
- Tell me the day of the week it will be one week from today. Get ready. (Signal.)
3. (Repeat step 2 until firm.)
4. Now the dates.
- Tell me today's date. Get ready. (Signal.)
- Look at the calendar. ✔
- Tell me the date it will be one week from today. Get ready. (Signal.)
5. Once more.
- Listen: Tell me today's date. Get ready. (Signal.)
- Tell me tomorrow's date. Get ready. (Signal.)
- Tell me the date it will be one week from today. Get ready. (Signal.)
6. (Repeat step 5 until firm.)

EXERCISE 5 Sweetie And The Snapping Turtle

Storytelling

- I'm going to tell you another story about Sweetie.

One evening, the woman who owned Sweetie went to visit her uncle. She took Sweetie with her. Sweetie didn't want to go. He growled and refused to purr. But when he got there, he saw something that was very interesting.

Sweetie was in the kitchen. He looked through the doorway into the next room. And in the middle of that room were two tables.

- Get a picture of that place. Which room was Sweetie in? (Signal.) *The kitchen.*
- Which room were the tables in? (Signal.) *The other room.*

There seemed to be something good to eat on one of the tables. So Sweetie walked into the room to get a closer look.

One table was to Sweetie's **right.** And the other table was to Sweetie's **left.** Sweetie looked at the table to his **right** and said to himself, "Yummitie, yummers. Look at what is on that table—tasty little goldfish swimming around inside a bowl."

- Listen: One table had tasty goldfish on it. Was that table to Sweetie's **right** or his **left?** (Signal.) *His right.*
- Remember that.

Then Sweetie looked at the table to his **left** and said to himself, "Ugh." On that table was another bowl, but it didn't have tasty little goldfish swimming around inside it. It had one huge snapping turtle. And that turtle looked mighty mean.

- Get a picture of both tables: One to Sweetie's **right** and one to his **left.** Something was in the bowl to his **left.** What was in that bowl? (Signal.) *A turtle.*
- What was in the bowl to his **right?** (Signal.) *Goldfish.*

Sweetie said to himself, "When nobody is looking, I'll sneak back in this room, jump up on that table to my right, and grab myself a pawful of yummy little goldfish."

Well, that was Sweetie's plan, but things didn't work out quite the way Sweetie thought they would. The reason is that the room with the tables had **two** doors, one door at each end.

The door on one side led to the kitchen. The door on the other end led to the living room.

- Let's see if we have a good picture of that room. How many doors does the room have? (Signal.) *Two.*
- One door leads to the kitchen. The other door leads to the living room. Which door did Sweetie go through when he went into the room with the tables? (Signal.) *The kitchen door.*

Sweetie had come in from the **kitchen.** Sweetie didn't know it, but if he came in from the **living room,** he would be facing the other way. So the tasty little goldfish would not be on his **right** anymore. They would be on his **left.** And the mean snapping turtle wouldn't be on his **left** anymore. That turtle would be on his **right.**

- Oh, dear. Sweetie thought that the goldfish would **always** be on his **right,** but if he came in from the living room, they'd be on his **left.**

Well, Sweetie went into the living room and pretended to take a nap. All the time he was pretending, he was thinking about what he would do. He pictured himself going back into the room with the tables, jumping up on the table to his right and grabbing a pawful of yummy goldfish.

- Where was Sweetie when he was thinking about what he'd do? (Signal.) *In the living room.*
- Uh-oh.

Things might have worked out for Sweetie if something else hadn't happened. Somebody shut off the lights in the room with the tables. That room was dark, dark, dark.

Pretty soon, everybody left the living room and there was Sweetie, all alone. That picture in his mind of what he would do was so strong, he could almost taste those yummy little fish.

- What was he going to do? (Call on a child. Idea: *Go into the room with the tables, jump up on the table to his right and grab a pawful of goldfish.*)

Sweetie crept out of the living room and into the dark room with the tables. Then he did just what he planned. He sniffed around until he found the two tables. Then he jumped on one of them.

- Was that the table to his **left** or his **right?** (Signal.) *To his right.*
- What was in the bowl on that table? (Signal.) *The turtle.*

Then Sweetie shot his paw into the bowl to his right and . . . Sweetie let out such a yowl that you could hear it two blocks away. Everybody in the house jumped about two feet when Sweetie started yowling. The woman who owned Sweetie ran around trying to find him. "Sweetie, Sweetie," she called, "What's wrong?" She ran into the room with the tables and turned on the lights.

Sweetie's owner ran after Sweetie, but she didn't catch up with him because he moved like a yellow blur. And he did that while running on three legs and holding his right paw out in front of him.

- Why wasn't Sweetie running on all four legs? (Call on a child. Idea: *One paw was sore.*)
- Poor Sweetie had a sore right paw.

At last, Sweetie settled down and went into the **kitchen.** Sweetie's owner said, "I wonder if poor Sweetie stepped on something. He seems to have a very sore front paw."

Sweetie looked into the room with the tables. The lights were back on in that room and he could see the goldfish clearly. They were on the table to his **right.** Then he said to himself, "From here, those goldfish look pretty helpless, but . . . "

- Who can finish what Sweetie said? (Call on a child. Idea: *Let me tell you, they can really bite.*)
- Yes.

Sweetie said, "From here those goldfish look pretty helpless, but let me tell you, they can **really** bite."

WORKBOOK 54

EXERCISE 6   Story Details

1. Everybody, open your workbook to Lesson 54. Write your name at the top of the page. ✔
* This is a picture of that room with two tables.
2. Touch number 1. ✔
* That's where Sweetie was when he went into the room the **first** time.
* Which room did he come from? (Signal.) *The kitchen.*
* So that door behind him in picture 1 is the door that leads to the kitchen. You can see the two tables. But there are no bowls on them.
* Were the goldfish on the table to Sweetie's right or his left? (Signal.) *To his right.*
* Listen: Make an **R** on Sweetie's **right** front paw at number 1. Then make a little **X** on the table that should have the goldfish bowl on it. Make the **R** on Sweetie's right paw. Then make an **X** on the table to his **right.** Raise your hand when you're finished.
(Observe children and give feedback.)
3. Now later on, Sweetie came in from the **living room.**
* Touch number 2. ✔
* That's where Sweetie was when the room was dark.
* Make an **R** on his **right** paw at number 2. Raise your hand when you're finished.
(Observe children and give feedback.)

* When Sweetie jumped on the table that was to his right, he got one big surprise, didn't he?
4. You're going to fix up the picture. You're going to cut out the pictures and put them where they belong. The cutout with the stove on it goes over the door to the kitchen. Remember where that room is. The cutout with the couch on it goes over the doorway to the living room. And the bowls go on the tables. Remember, the goldfish go on the table with the **X.** The turtle goes on the other table. Don't get mixed up or your picture won't match the story. Raise your hand when you're finished.
(Observe children and give feedback.)

> *Optional:* Children paste pictures in place and color picture.

EXERCISE 7   Map Reading

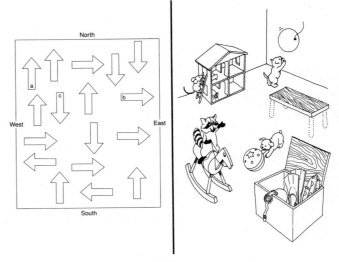

1. Everybody, find the next page in your workbook. ✔
* (Hold up workbook. Point to first half.)
* Some of the arrows have letters on them. Find the arrow with the letter **A.** ✔
* That arrow is pointing **north.** Which direction? (Signal.) *North.*
2. Find the arrow with the letter **B.** ✔
* That arrow is pointing **east.** Which direction? (Signal.) *East.*
3. Find the arrow with the letter **C.** ✔
* That arrow is pointing **south.** Which direction? (Signal.) *South.*
4. Touch **A.** ✔
* Everybody, which direction is that arrow pointing? (Signal.) *North.*

- Touch **B.** ✔
- Everybody, which direction is that arrow pointing? (Signal.) *East.*
- Touch **C.** ✔
- Everybody, which direction is that arrow pointing? (Signal.) *South.*

5. Listen: Here's a rule about the arrows that are pointing **north.** All arrows that are pointing **north** should be blue. What color? (Signal.) *Blue.*

- There are six arrows that are pointing **north.** Put a blue mark on each arrow that is pointing **north.**
  (Observe children and give feedback.)

6. Here's a rule about the arrows that are pointing **east.** All the arrows that are pointing **east** should be red. What color? (Signal.) *Red.*

- There are five arrows pointing **east.** Put a red mark on each of them.
  (Observe children and give feedback.)

7. Later you can color the arrows that are pointing **north** and the arrows that are pointing **east.**

EXERCISE 8 Materials

1. (Hold up workbook. Point to second half.)
2. Here's a coloring rule for this picture. If an object is made of rubber, color it green. What's the rule? (Signal.) *If an object is made of rubber, color it green.*
3. (Repeat step 2 until firm.)
4. Make a green mark on one of the objects made of rubber. ✔
5. Here's another coloring rule for this picture. If an object is made of wood, color it black. What's the rule? (Signal.) *If an object is made of wood, color it black.*
6. (Repeat step 5 until firm.)
7. Make a black mark on one of the objects made of wood. ✔
8. Here's one more thing to do. Part of the bench is missing. What part is missing? (Signal.) *The legs.*

- Yes, the legs. Before you color the bench, follow the dots with your pencil to make the legs.

Objectives

- Given a common noun, answer questions involving "can do." (Exercise 1)
- Name three classes containing a common noun and answer questions about members of those classes. (Exercise 2)
- Name objects that could be made of a given material. (Exercise 3)
- Replace a word in a sentence with an opposite. (Exercise 4)
- Given a calendar, identify the day and date for "today" and "tomorrow" and one week from today. (Exercise 5)
- Construct word-picture sentences for story illustrations. (Exercise 6)

EXERCISE 1 Can Do

1. Get ready to answer some questions about a chair.
2. Can you put your clothes on a chair? (Signal.) *Yes.*
- Can you mow the lawn with a chair? (Signal.) *No.*
- Can you carry a chair? (Signal.) *Yes.*
- Can you stand on a chair? (Signal.) *Yes.*
- Can you skate on a chair? (Signal.) *No.*
- Can you ride a chair to school? (Signal.) *No.*
- Can you sit in a chair? (Signal.) *Yes.*
- Can you sharpen a pencil with a chair? (Signal.) *No.*
3. Can a boy sit in a chair? (Signal.) *Yes.* Say the whole thing. Get ready. (Signal.) *A boy can sit in a chair.*
- Can a boy mow the lawn with a chair? (Signal.) *No.*
- Say the whole thing. Get ready. (Signal.) *A boy cannot mow the lawn with a chair.*

EXERCISE 2 Classification

1. Today we're going to talk about a rocking chair. We can put a rocking chair into three different classes. See how many classes you can name, starting with the smallest class.
2. Everybody, what's the smallest class for a rocking chair? (Signal.) *Rocking chairs.*
- What's the next bigger class? (Signal.) *Chairs.*
- What's the next bigger class? (Signal.) *Furniture.*
3. (Repeat step 2 until firm.)
4. What is one kind of object you would find in all those classes? (Signal.) *A rocking chair.*

5. Think of these classes: rocking chairs, chairs, furniture.
- Would you find a table in all those classes? (Signal.) *No.*
- Name the class you would find a table in. (Pause.) Get ready. (Signal.) *Furniture.*
6. (Repeat step 5 until firm.)

EXERCISE 3 Materials

1. Think of things that are made of metal. Let's see who can name at least three things made of metal. (Call on individual children to name objects made of metal. Each child should name at least three things.)
2. Everybody, think of things that are made of glass. Let's see who can name at least three things made of glass. (Call on individual children to name objects made of glass. Each child should name at least three things.)
3. Everybody, think of things that are made of leather. Let's see who can name at least three things made of leather. (Call on individual children to name objects made of leather. Each child should name at least three things.)

EXERCISE 4 Opposites

1. Here are some new opposites.
2. Listen: The opposite of pushing is pulling.
- What's the opposite of pushing? (Signal.) *Pulling.*
- What's the opposite of pulling? (Signal.) *Pushing.*

3. Listen: The opposite of shiny is dull.
- What's the opposite of shiny? (Signal.) *Dull.*
- What's the opposite of dull? (Signal.) *Shiny.*
4. Listen: The opposite of dangerous is safe.
- What's the opposite of dangerous? (Signal.) *Safe.*
- What's the opposite of safe? (Signal.) *Dangerous.*
5. Listen: The opposite of raw is cooked.
- What's the opposite of raw? (Signal.) *Cooked.*
- What's the opposite of cooked? (Signal.) *Raw.*
6. Let's review.
- What's the opposite of pushing? (Signal.) *Pulling.*
- What's the opposite of shiny? (Signal.) *Dull.*
- What's the opposite of safe? (Signal.) *Dangerous.*
- What's the opposite of raw? (Signal.) *Cooked.*

EXERCISE 5 Calendar

1. (Present calendar.)
- We're going to talk about today, tomorrow, and one week from today.
2. Tell me the day of the week it is today. Get ready. (Signal.)
- Tell me the day of the week it will be tomorrow. Get ready. (Signal.)
- Tell me the day of the week it will be one week from today. Get ready. (Signal.)
3. (Repeat step 2 until firm.)
4. Now the dates.
- Tell me today's date. Get ready. (Signal.)
- Look at the calendar. ✔
- Tell me the date it will be one week from today. Get ready. (Signal.)
5. Once more.
- Listen: Tell me today's date. Get ready. (Signal.)
- Tell me tomorrow's date. Get ready. (Signal.)
- Tell me the date it will be one week from today. Get ready. (Signal.)
6. (Repeat step 5 until firm.)

EXERCISE 6 Sentence Construction

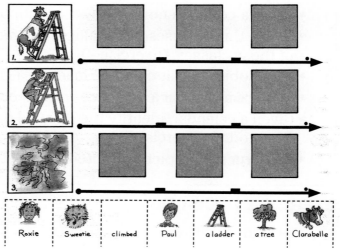

1. Everybody, open your workbook to Lesson 55. Write your name at the top of the page. ✔
- The pictures show what different characters did. You're going to use the cutouts to make up sentences that show what the characters did in the pictures.
2. Look at the cutouts at the bottom of the page. There are words at the bottom of each cutout. I'll read the words.
- Touch the first cutout. ✔ The word says: **Roxie.**
- Touch the next cutout. ✔ The word says: **Sweetie.**
- Touch the next cutout. ✔ The word says: **climbed.**
- Touch the next cutout. ✔ The word says: **Paul.**
- Touch the next cutout. ✔ The words say: **a ladder.**
- Touch the next cutout. ✔ The words say: **a tree.**
- Touch the last cutout. ✔ The word says: **Clarabelle.**
3. Your turn: Cut out your cutouts. Raise your hand when you're finished.
(Observe children and give feedback.)

4. One of your cutouts doesn't have a picture, just a word. Hold up that cutout. ✔
- Remember: The word on that cutout is **climbed.** What word? (Signal.) *Climbed.* That's what the characters did in all these pictures.
5. Everybody, touch picture 1. ✔
- Who's in that picture? (Signal.) *Clarabelle.*
- Everybody, what did Clarabelle do in this picture? (Signal.) *Climbed a ladder.*
- Here's the sentence that tells what Clarabelle did: **Clarabelle climbed a ladder.**
6. Everybody, say that sentence. (Signal.) *Clarabelle climbed a ladder.* (Repeat step 6 until firm.)
7. Listen to the sentence again: **Clarabelle** (pause) **climbed** (pause) **a ladder.**
- What's the first word in that sentence? (Signal.) *Clarabelle.*
- What's the next word in that sentence? (Signal.) *Climbed.*
- What are the last words in that sentence? (Signal.) *A ladder.*
(Repeat step 7 until firm.)
8. Your turn: Put the cutouts in the three boxes next to picture 1. Put the cutouts that show: **Clarabelle climbed a ladder.** Raise your hand when you're finished. (Observe children and give feedback.)
- (Write on the board:)

Clarabelle climbed a ladder

- Here's what the words in your boxes should say. Raise your hand if you got it right. ✔
9. Your turn: Write the sentence on the arrow for picture 1. Write the words **Clarabelle, climbed, a ladder.** Copy the words carefully. Raise your hand when you're finished.
(Observe children and give feedback.)
- Take your cutouts off the first arrow. ✔
10. Now you're going to make up a sentence for picture 2.
- Touch picture 2. ✔
- That picture shows something another character did.

- Who's in that picture? (Signal.) *Roxie.* Raise your hand when you can say the whole sentence about what Roxie did in picture 2. ✔
11. Everybody, say the sentence. (Signal.) *Roxie climbed a ladder.* (Repeat step 11 until firm.)
12. Put the cutouts in the three boxes next to picture 2. Put the cutouts that show: **Roxie climbed a ladder.** Raise your hand when you're finished.
(Observe children and give feedback.)
- (Write on the board:)

Roxie climbed a ladder

- Here's what the words should say for picture 2. Raise your hand if you got it right. ✔
13. Your turn: Write the sentence on the arrow for picture 2. Write the words **Roxie, climbed, a ladder.** Copy the words carefully. Raise your hand when you're finished.
(Observe children and give feedback.)
- Take your cutouts off the second arrow. ✔
14. Now you're going to make up a sentence for picture 3. Oh, dear, you can't see who is climbing the ladder in that picture. In fact, maybe there's not even a ladder in that picture. Maybe there's a tree and maybe somebody is climbing that tree.
- Put your cutouts in the boxes for picture 3 so you make up a sentence. Don't make up one of the sentences you've already written. Raise your hand when you're finished.
(Observe children and give feedback.)
15. (Call on several children.) Read the sentence you made up. (Praise appropriate sentences.)
- Everybody, copy the last sentence you made up. Raise your hand when you're finished.
(Observe children and give feedback.)
16. Everybody, turn your cutouts over and put them in a pile. Let's see who can read all three of their sentences. (Call on several children. Praise correct responses.)

LESSON 56

EXERCISE 1 Can Do

1. Get ready to answer some questions about a hairbrush.
2. Can you brush your hair with a hairbrush? (Signal.) *Yes.*
- Can you drink a hairbrush? (Signal.) *No.*
- Can you sleep on a hairbrush? (Signal.) *No.*
- Can you hide in a hairbrush? (Signal.) *No.*
- Can you fix a broken chair with a hairbrush? (Signal.) *No.*
- Can you brush a dog with a hairbrush? (Signal.) *Yes.*
- Can you ride on a hairbrush? (Signal.) *No.*
- Can a girl hide in a hairbrush? (Signal.) *No.*
- Say the whole thing. Get ready. (Signal.) *A girl cannot hide in a hairbrush.*
3. (Repeat step 2 until firm.)

EXERCISE 2 Opposites

1. Here are some new opposites.
2. Listen: The opposite of smooth is rough.
- What's the opposite of smooth? (Signal.) *Rough.*
- What's the opposite of rough? (Signal.) *Smooth.*
3. Listen: The opposite of shallow is deep.
- What's the opposite of shallow? (Signal.) *Deep.*

4. Let's review.
- What's the opposite of deep? (Signal.) *Shallow.*
- What's the opposite of dangerous? (Signal.) *Safe.*
- What's the opposite of pushing? (Signal.) *Pulling.*
- What's the opposite of shallow? (Signal.) *Deep.*
- What's the opposite of rough? (Signal.) *Smooth.*
- What's the opposite of cooked? (Signal.) *Raw.*
- What's the opposite of raw? (Signal.) *Cooked.*
5. (Repeat step 4 until firm.)

EXERCISE 3 Calendar Facts

1. We're going to talk about days, months, and seasons.
2. Everybody, how many days are in a week? (Signal.) *Seven.*
- Say the whole thing. Get ready. (Signal.) *There are seven days in a week.*
3. Everybody, name the seven days of the week. Get ready. (Signal.) *Sunday, Monday, Tuesday, Wednesday, Thursday, Friday, Saturday.*
4. (Repeat step 3 until firm.)
5. How many months are in a year? (Signal.) *Twelve.*
- Say the whole thing. Get ready. (Signal.) *There are twelve months in a year.*

6. Name the months of the year through December. Get ready. (Signal.) *January, February, March, April, May, June, July, August, September, October, November, December.*

7. (Repeat step 6 until firm.)

8. Everybody, how many seasons are there in a year? (Signal.) *Four.*
   - Say the seasons of the year. Get ready. (Signal.) *Winter, spring, summer, fall.*

9. (Repeat step 8 until firm.)

EXERCISE 4   True—False

1. I'm going to say statements. Some of these statements are true and some are false. You tell me about each statement.

2. Fish are vehicles. True or false? (Signal.) *False.*
   - You find the moon in the sky. True or false? (Signal.) *True.*
   - A firefighter puts out fires. True or false? (Signal.) *True.*
   - Fish cannot climb trees. True or false? (Signal.) *True.*

3. (Repeat step 2 until firm.)

4. Your turn. Make up a statement about fish that is true. (Call on three children. Praise each acceptable statement and have the group repeat it. Then say:) Everybody, that statement is . . . (Signal.) *true.*

5. Your turn. Now make up a statement about fish that is false. (Call on three children. Praise each acceptable statement and have the group repeat it. Then say:) Everybody, that statement is . . . (Signal.) *false.*

EXERCISE 5   Materials

1. Think of things that are made of paper. Let's see who can name at least three things made of paper. (Call on individual children to name objects made of paper. Each child should name at least three things.)

2. Everybody, think of things that are made of leather.
   Let's see who can name at least three things made of leather. (Call on individual children to name objects made of leather. Each child should name at least three things.)

EXERCISE 6   Calendar

1. (Present calendar.)
   - We're going to talk about today, tomorrow, and one week from today.

2. Tell me the day of the week it is today. Get ready. (Signal.)
   - Tell me the day of the week it will be tomorrow. Get ready. (Signal.)
   - Tell me the day of the week it will be one week from today. Get ready. (Signal.)

3. (Repeat step 2 until firm.)

4. Now the dates.
   - Tell me today's date. Get ready. (Signal.)
   - Look at the calendar. ✔
   - Tell me the date it will be one week from today. Get ready. (Signal.)

5. Once more.
   - Listen: Tell me today's date. Get ready. (Signal.)
   - Tell me tomorrow's date. Get ready. (Signal.)
   - Tell me the date it will be one week from today. Get ready. (Signal.)

6. (Repeat step 5 until firm.)

WORKBOOK

EXERCISE 7   Molly Fixes Bleep

Review

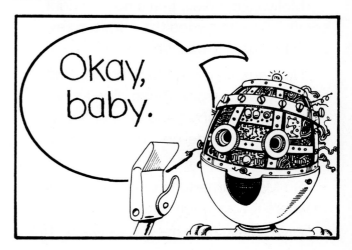

1. Everybody, find Lesson 56 in your workbook. Write your name at the top of the page. ✔
   - This picture shows Bleep after Molly turned the blue screw all the way to the left.

Molly decided to fix up Bleep so that Bleep would not say that word every time he talked. Molly also wanted to fix up Bleep so Bleep wouldn't do something else that was bothersome.

Molly took the top off Bleep's head. With the top of Bleep's head removed, Molly could see all the wires and the screws that made Bleep work. There were many screws that changed the way Bleep talked and the way he thought. Each screw was a different color. One screw was black. One screw was yellow. Another screw was pink. And there were many other screws.

Molly didn't know which screw to turn or whether she should turn a screw to the right or to the left. So Molly said, "I'll just have to figure out which screw will fix the problem."

She started with the **purple** screw. She turned it to the **right.** When she did that, Bleep didn't say, "Bleep. Okay, baby." Here's what he said: "Bloop. Okay, babe-oo."

Molly said, "Well, that's not the right screw." So she turned the purple screw back to where it was when she started.

Next she tried the **black** screw. She turned it to the **right.** Bleep didn't say, "Bleep. Okay, baby," and he didn't say, "Bloop. Okay, babe-oo." He said, "Blipe. Okay, babe-eye."

So Molly turned the black screw back to where it was when she started.

Next, Molly tried the **green** screw. But when she turned that screw to the **right,** Bleep said, "Blope. Okay, babe-oh."

"No, no," Molly said and went to the next screw and the next screw and the next screw. Finally, she came to the **blue** screw. When she turned the **blue** screw to the **right,** Bleep said something that was really strange. He didn't say "bleep," or "bloop," or "blipe" or "blap." He didn't say "blope," or "blup," or even "blurp." Here's what he said when Molly turned the blue screw a **little** bit to the **right:** "Bleep. Bleep. Okay, baby. Okay, baby."

Molly turned the blue screw even farther to the right and Bleep said, "Bleep, bleep, bleep. Okay, baby. Okay, baby. Okay, baby."

Then Molly turned the blue screw **all** the way to the right and Bleep said, "Bleep, bleep, bleep, bleep. Okay, baby. Okay, baby. Okay, baby. Okay, baby."

Molly said, "Well, at least he's not saying, 'blipe' or 'bloop' or 'blup.'"

So she said, "Maybe I'm turning the blue screw the wrong way. Maybe I should be turning it to the **left,** not the **right."** So she turned the screw back to where it was when she started.

Bleep said, "Bleep. Okay, baby."

Then she turned the blue screw to the **left**—just a **little** bit to the left.

Bleep said, "Blee. Okay, baby." He didn't say, **"Bleep.** Okay, baby." He said, **"Blee.** Okay, baby."

Molly turned the blue screw a little **more** to the left.

Bleep said, "Bl. Okay, baby."

Then she turned the blue screw **all** the way to the left, and you'll never guess what Bleep said.

Bleep looked at Molly and said, "Okay, baby."

Molly said, "I did it. I fixed Bleep so he wouldn't say 'bleep' all the time." And Molly was right.

But Bleep still had one problem that wasn't fixed up.

2. Later you can color the picture.

EXERCISE 8 Map Reading

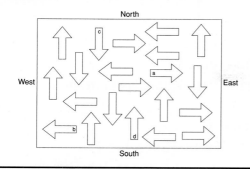

1. Everybody, find the next page in your workbook. ✔
- (Hold up workbook. Point to first half.) Find the arrows. ✔
2. Some of the arrows have letters on them. Find the arrow with the letter **A**. ✔
- Raise your hand when you know which direction that arrow is pointing. ✔
- Everybody, which direction? (Signal.) *East.*
3. Find the arrow with the letter **B**. ✔
- Raise your hand when you know which direction that arrow is pointing. ✔
- Everybody, which direction? (Signal.) *West.*
4. Find the arrow with the letter **C**. ✔
- Everybody, which direction is that arrow pointing? (Signal.) *South.*
5. Find the arrow with the letter **D**. ✔
- Everybody, which direction is that arrow pointing? (Signal.) *North.*
6. Once more.
- Touch **A**. ✔
Everybody, which direction is that arrow pointing? (Signal.) *East.*
- Touch **B**. ✔
Everybody, which direction is that arrow pointing? (Signal.) *West.*
- Touch **C**. ✔
Everybody, which direction is that arrow pointing? (Signal.) *South.*
- Touch **D**. ✔
Everybody, which direction is that arrow pointing? (Signal.) *North.*
7. (Repeat step 6 until firm.)

8. Listen: Here's a rule about the arrows that are pointing **west**. All arrows that are pointing **west** should be black. What color? (Signal.) *Black.*
- There are six arrows that are pointing **west**. Put a black mark on each arrow that is pointing **west**.
(Observe children and give feedback.)
9. Here's a rule about the arrows that are pointing **north**. All arrows that are pointing **north** should be green. What color? (Signal.) *Green.*
- There are six arrows pointing **north**. Put a green mark on each of them.
(Observe children and give feedback.)
10. Later you can color the arrows that are pointing **west** and the arrows that are pointing **north**.

EXERCISE 9 Location

1. (Hold up workbook. Point to second half.) Look at the picture. ✔
- Everybody, what place do you see in this picture? (Signal.) *A pet store.*
2. Here's a coloring rule for this picture. Listen: Color some of the animals brown and some of the animals blue. What's the rule? (Signal.) *Color some of the animals brown and some of the animals blue.*
3. (Repeat step 2 until firm.)
4. Mark the animals. ✔
5. Here's another coloring rule for this picture. Listen: Color the containers yellow. What's the rule? (Signal.) *Color the containers yellow.*
6. (Repeat step 5 until firm.)
7. Put a yellow mark on **one** of the containers. ✔

LESSON 57

Objectives

- Apply narrowing criteria to guess a mystery object. (Exercise 1)
- Discriminate between true and false statements and generate true and false statements. (Exercise 2)
- Replace a word in a sentence with an opposite. (Exercise 3)
- Answer questions involving previously learned calendar facts. (Exercise 4)
- Given a common object, students generate activities that "can" and "cannot do" with the object. (Exercise 5)
- Name objects that could be made of a given material. (Exercise 6)
- **Match unique utterances to the familiar story character who would speak them.** (Exercise 7)
- Follow coloring rules involving classes and subclasses. (Exercise 8)
- Complete an analogy involving class. (Exercise 9)

EXERCISE 1   Description

1. I'm thinking of an object. See if you can figure out what object I'm thinking of. I'll tell you something about the object.
2. Listen: It's made of cloth. Everybody, what do you know about the object? (Signal.) *It's made of cloth.*
   - Could I be thinking of a shirt? (Signal.) *Yes.*
   - Could I be thinking of a pot? (Signal.) *No.*
   - Could I be thinking of a tablecloth? (Signal.) *Yes.*
   - Could I be thinking of a knife? (Signal.) *No.*
3. Listen: The object I'm thinking of is (hold up one finger) made of cloth **and** (hold up two fingers) it's flat.
4. Everybody, what do you know about the object? (Hold up one finger.) *It's made of cloth* **and** (hold up two fingers) *it's flat.*
5. (Repeat step 4 until firm.)
6. Could I be thinking of a rug? (Signal.) *Yes.*
   - Could I be thinking of a plate? (Signal.) *No.*
   - Why not? (Signal.) *It's not made of cloth.*
7. (Repeat step 6 until firm.)
8. Is a tablecloth made of cloth and is it flat? (Signal.) *Yes.*
   - Could I be thinking of a tablecloth? (Signal.) *Yes.*
9. (Repeat step 8 until firm.)
10. Listen: The object I'm thinking of is (hold up one finger) made of cloth
    and (hold up two fingers) it's flat
    and (hold up three fingers) you put it on the floor.
11. Everybody, name the object I am thinking of. (Pause two seconds.) Get ready. (Signal.) *A rug.* Yes, a rug.
12. How do you know I'm thinking of a rug? (Hold up one finger.) (Signal.) *It's made of cloth.*
    and (hold up two fingers) *it's flat*
    and (hold up three fingers) *you put it on the floor.*
13. (Repeat step 12 until firm.)

EXERCISE 2   True—False

1. I'm going to say statements. Some of these statements are true and some are false. You tell me about each statement.
2. You wear shoes on your hands. True or false? (Signal.) *False.*
   - A bottle is a plant. True or false? (Signal.) *False.*
   - Cats have claws. True or false? (Signal.) *True.*
   - A boat has wheels. True or false? (Signal.) *False.*
   - A suitcase is a container. True or false? (Signal.) *True.*
3. (Repeat step 2 until firm.)
4. Your turn. Make up a statement about a boat that is true. (Call on three children. Praise each acceptable statement and have the group repeat it. Then say:) Everybody, that statement is . . . (Signal.) *true.*
5. Your turn. Now make up a statement about boat that is false. (Call on three children. Praise each acceptable statement and have the group repeat it. Then say:) Everybody, that statement is . . . (Signal.) *false.*

EXERCISE 3   Opposites

1. You're going to make up statements that have the opposite word.
2. Listen: The street was dangerous. Say that statement. Get ready. (Signal.) *The street was dangerous.*
   - Now say a statement that tells the opposite about the street. Get ready. (Signal.) *The street was safe.*
3. Listen: The table top was smooth. Say that statement. Get ready. (Signal.) *The table top was smooth.*
   - Now say a statement that tells the opposite about the table top. Get ready. (Signal.) *The table top was rough.*
4. Listen: The car was shiny. Say that statement. Get ready. (Signal.) *The car was shiny.*
   - Now say a statement that tells the opposite about the car. Get ready. (Signal.) *The car was dull.*
5. Listen: The man was pushing the sled. Say that statement. Get ready. (Signal.) *The man was pushing the sled.*
   - Now say a statement that tells the opposite about what the man was doing. Get ready. (Signal.) *The man was pulling the sled.*
6. Listen: The water was shallow. Say that statement. Get ready. (Signal.) *The water was shallow.*
   - Now say a statement that tells the opposite about the water. Get ready. (Signal.) *The water was deep.*
7. Listen: The meat was raw. Say that statement. Get ready. (Signal.) *The meat was raw.*
   - Now say a statement that tells the opposite about the meat. Get ready. (Signal.) *The meat was cooked.*
8. (Repeat step 7 until firm.)

EXERCISE 4   Calendar Facts

1. You learned calendar facts.
   - Everybody, how many days are in a week? (Signal.) *Seven.*
   - Everybody, say the days of the week. Get ready. (Signal.) *Sunday, Monday, Tuesday, Wednesday, Thursday, Friday, Saturday.*
2. How many weeks are in a year? (Signal.) *52.*
   - Say the fact. Get ready. (Signal.) *There are 52 weeks in a year.*
3. How many days are in a year? (Signal.) *365.*
   - Say the fact. Get ready. (Signal.) *There are 365 days in a year.*

4. How many seasons are in a year? (Signal.) *Four.*
   - Name the four seasons. Get ready. (Signal.) *Winter, spring, summer, fall.*
5. (Repeat step 4 until firm.)
6. How many months are in a year? (Signal.) *12.*
   - Everybody, say the months. Get ready. (Signal.) *January, February, March, April, May, June, July, August, September, October, November, December.*
7. (Repeat step 6 until firm.)
   - Listen: What day of the week is it today? (Signal.)
   - Listen: What day of the week will it be tomorrow? (Signal.)
   - Listen: What's today's date? (Signal.)

EXERCISE 5   Can Do

1. Everybody, I'm going to call on individual children to name things we can do with a bag.
2. (Call on one child.)
   - What's one thing we can do with a bag? (After the child gives a correct response, call on the group.) Let's all say the whole thing. Get ready. (Signal.) (The group repeats the child's response.)
3. (Call on another child.)
   - What's another thing we can do with a bag? (After the child gives a correct response, call on the group.) Let's all name those things we can do with a bag.
   - What's the first thing? (Hold up one finger.) (The group repeats the first response.)
   - What's the second thing? (Hold up two fingers.) (The group repeats the second response.)
4. (Call on another child.)
   - What's another thing we can do with a bag? (After the child gives a correct response, call on the group.) Let's all name those things we can do with a bag.
   - What's the first thing? (Hold up one finger.) (The group repeats the first response.)
   - What's the second thing? (Hold up two fingers.) (The group repeats the second response.)
   - What's the third thing? (Hold up three fingers.) (The group repeats the third response.)

5. Now I'm going to call on individual children to name things we can**not** do with a bag.

6. (Call on one child.)

• What's one thing we cannot do with a bag? (After the child gives a correct response, call on the group.) Let's all say the whole thing. Get ready. (Signal.) (The group repeats the first response.)

7. (Call on another child.)

• What's another thing we cannot do with a bag? (After the child gives a correct response, call on the group.) Let's all name those things we cannot do with a bag.

• What's the first thing? (Hold up one finger.) (The group repeats the first response.)

• What's the second thing? (Hold up two fingers.) (The group repeats the second response.)

8. (Call on another child.)

• What's another thing we cannot do with a bag? (After the child gives a correct response, call on the group.) Let's all name those things we cannot do with a bag.

• What's the first thing? (Hold up one finger.) (The group repeats the first response.)

• What's the second thing? (Hold up two fingers.) (The group repeats the second response.)

• What's the third thing? (Hold up three fingers.) (The group repeats the third response.)

EXERCISE 6   Materials

1. Think of things that are made of leather. Let's see who can name at least three things made of leather. (Call on individual children to name objects made of leather. Each child should name at least three things.)

2. Everybody, think of things that are made of glass. Let's see who can name at least three things made of glass. (Call on individual children to name objects made of glass. Each child should name at least three things.)

3. Everybody, think of things that are made of rubber. Let's see who can name at least three things made of rubber. (Call on individual children to name objects made of rubber. Each child should name at least three things.)

EXERCISE 7   Extrapolation

What Characters Say

1._____
2._____
3._____
4._____
5._____
6._____

1. Everybody, open your workbook to Lesson 57. Write your name at the top of the page. ✔

2. These are some more pictures of characters you know. Each picture has a letter under it. The letter is the initial of the character in the picture.

3. Touch the first picture. ✔

• Who is in that picture? (Signal.) *Rolla.*

• What letter is under that picture? (Signal.) *R.*
  R is the first letter in **Rolla's** name.

• Who is in the next picture? (Signal.) *Paul.*

• What letter is under Paul? (Signal.) *P.*
  P is the first letter in **Paul's** name.

• Who is in the next picture? (Signal.) *A bragging rat.*

• What letter is under the bragging rat? (Signal.) *B.*
  B is the first letter in the words **Bragging Rat.**

• Who is in the next picture? (Signal.) *Clarabelle.*

• What letter is under Clarabelle? (Signal.) *C.*
  C is the first letter in **Clarabelle's** name.

• Who is in the last picture? (Signal.) *Sweetie.*

• What letter is under Sweetie? (Signal.) *S.*
  S is the first letter in **Sweetie's** name.

4. Here's the game we'll play: I'll say six different things. For each thing I'll say, you're going to write the letter for the character who would say that. You're not going to say anything out loud. You'll just find the right picture and write the letter for that character.

5. Everybody, touch number 1. ✔
- Listen and don't say anything. Here's the statement for number 1: "Oh, I'd love to go skiing just like those children are doing."
- Find the character who would say that. Write the letter for that character on line 1. Raise your hand when you're finished. (Observe children and give feedback.)
- Everybody, which character would love to go skiing just like the children? (Signal.) *Clarabelle.*
- So what letter did you write for number 1? (Signal.) *C.*
- (Write on the board:)

1.	C

- Here's what you should have for number 1. Raise your hand if you got it right. ✔
6. Everybody, touch number 2. ✔
- Listen and don't say anything. Here's the statement for number 2: "If I could just go fast enough, I could pass somebody up."
- Find the character who would say that. Write the letter for that character on line 2. Raise your hand when you're finished. (Observe children and give feedback.)
- Everybody, which character would say, "If I could go fast enough, I could pass somebody up"? (Signal.) *Rolla.*
- So what letter did you write for number 2? (Signal.) *R.*
- (Write to show:)

1.	C
2.	R

- Here's what you should have for number 2. Raise your hand if you got it right. ✔
7. Everybody, touch number 3. ✔
- Listen and don't say anything. Here's the statement for number 3: "Purple pictures of pansies and plums are pleasing."
- Find the character who would say that. Write the letter for that character on line 3. Raise your hand when you're finished. (Observe children and give feedback.)
- Everybody, which character would say, "Purple pictures of pansies and plums are pleasing"? (Signal.) *Paul.*
- So what letter did you write for number 3? (Signal.) *P.*

- (Write to show:)

1.	C
2.	R
3.	P

- Here's what you should have for number 3. Raise your hand if you got it right. ✔
8. Everybody, touch number 4. ✔
- Listen and don't say anything. Here's the statement for number 4: "Oh, a helpless little mouse. Yum, yum."
- Find the character who would say that. Write the letter for that character on line 4. Raise your hand when you're finished. (Observe children and give feedback.)
- Everybody, which character would say, "Oh, a helpless little mouse. Yum, yum"? (Signal.) *Sweetie.*
- So what letter did you write for number 4? (Signal.) *S.*
- (Write to show:)

1.	C
2.	R
3.	P
4.	S

- Here's what you should have for number 4. Raise your hand if you got it right. ✔
9. Everybody, touch number 5. ✔
- Listen and don't say anything. Here's the statement for number 5: "But it's true. I got out of there by doing nothing but turning right."
- Find the character who would say that. Write the letter for that character on line 5. Raise your hand when you're finished. (Observe children and give feedback.)
- Everybody, which character would say, "But it's true. I got out of there by doing nothing but turning right"? (Signal.) *The bragging rat.*
- So what letter did you write for number 5? (Signal.) *B.*
- (Write to show:)

1.	C
2.	R
3.	P
4.	S
5.	B

- Here's what you should have for number 5. Raise your hand if you got it right. ✔

10. Everybody, touch number 6. ✔
   • Listen and don't say anything. Here's the statement for number 6: "That looks pretty poor, but I know how to fix it."
   • Find the character who would say that. Write the letter for that character on line 6. Raise your hand when you're finished. **(Observe children and give feedback.)**
   • Everybody, which character would say, "That looks pretty poor, but I know how to fix it"? (Signal.) *Paul.*
   • So what letter did you write for number 6? (Signal.) *P.*
   • (Write to show:)

1.	C
2.	R
3.	P
4.	S
5.	B
6.	P

   • Here's what you should have for number 6. Raise your hand if you got it right. ✔
11. Raise your hand if you got everything right. ✔
   • You know a lot about these characters.

EXERCISE 8 Classification

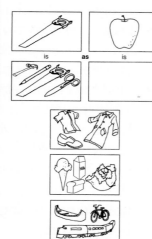

1. Everybody, find the next page in your workbook. ✔
   • (Hold up workbook. Point to first half.) These pictures show two classes. One class has **one** kind of thing in it, the other class has **more** kinds of things in it.
   • Touch the picture that shows only **one** kind of thing. ✔
   • What kind of thing is that in the picture? (Signal.) *Chairs.*
2. Touch the picture that shows **more** than one kind of thing. ✔
   • That picture shows chairs and other things too. Raise your hand if you can figure out the name of the class that has chairs and other things in it. ✔
   • Everybody, what's the name of that class? (Signal.) *Things made of wood.*
   • Everybody, circle the picture that shows **more** kinds of things. ✔
3. Everybody, touch the picture that shows **one** kind of thing. ✔
   • The chairs in that picture should be orange. What color? (Signal.) *Orange.*
   • Mark a chair in that picture. ✔
4. Touch the picture that shows **more** kinds of things. Each chair in that picture should be yellow and white. What colors? (Signal.) *Yellow and white.*
   • Make marks to show the colors in that picture. ✔

EXERCISE 9 Analogies

1. (Hold up workbook. Point to second half.)
   • The pictures show something and the class it is in.
2. Touch the saw. ✔
3. The picture that's right below the saw shows what class the saw is in. Everybody, what class? (Signal.) *Tools.*
   • Yes, that picture shows that a saw is a tool.
4. Touch the picture of the apple. ✔
   • One of the pictures below shows what class the apple is in. Touch the picture that shows what class an apple is in. ✔
   • Everybody, what class is it in? (Signal.) *Food.*
5. Listen: A saw is a tool **as** an apple is food.
   • Tell me about a saw. Get ready. (Signal.) *A saw is a tool.*
   • Tell me about an apple. Get ready. (Signal.) *An apple is food.*
   • Draw a line from the apple to the class it is in. (Observe children and give feedback.)

Objectives

- Generate statements involving "can do" and "cannot do." (Exercise 1)
- **Generate a list of objects that fit stated criteria.** (Exercise 2)
- Generate a statement with the opposite of a given word. (Exercise 3)
- Answer questions involving previously learned calendar facts. (Exercise 4)
- Apply narrowing criteria to guess a mystery object. (Exercise 5)
- Answer questions about a new story. (Exercise 6)
- **Complete a picture by copying the words, to show a familiar character saying the days of the week.** (Exercise 7)
- Follow coloring rules involving cardinal directions. (Exercise 8)
- Follow coloring rules involving "some" and class. (Exercise 9)

EXERCISE 1 Can Do

1. I'm going to ask questions about a girl and a rug.
2. Everybody, can a girl vacuum a rug? (Signal.) *Yes.*
   Say the statement. Get ready. (Signal.)
   A girl can vacuum a rug.
3. Everybody, can a girl read a rug? (Signal.) *No.*
   Say the statement. Get ready. (Signal.)
   A girl cannot read a rug.
4. (Call on one child.)
   Your turn. Make up another statement that tells something a girl can do with a rug.
   (After the child makes the statement, call on the group.)
   - Everybody, say that statement about what a girl can do with a rug. Get ready. (Signal.)
     (The group repeats the statement.)
   - (Repeat until firm.)
5. (Call on another child.)
   Your turn. Now make up a statement that tells something a girl cannot do with a rug.
   (After the child makes the statement, call on the group.)
   - Everybody, say that statement about what a girl cannot do with a rug. Get ready.
     (Signal.) (The group repeats the statement.)
   - (Repeat until firm.)
6. (Repeat steps 4 and 5, calling on individual children.)

EXERCISE 2 Description

1. Get ready to play detective and find out what object I'm thinking of. I'll give you two clues.
2. (Hold up one finger.) It's a building.
   (Hold up two fingers.) It has a lot of seats.
3. Say the two things we know about the object. Get ready.
   (Hold up one finger.) *It's a building.*
   - (Hold up two fingers.) *It has a lot of seats.*
4. (Repeat step 3 until firm.)
5. Those clues don't tell you enough to find the right building. They could tell you about a lot of buildings. See how many buildings you can name that have a lot of seats.
   (Call on individual children. The group is to name at least three buildings that have a lot of seats, such as *a school, a theater,* and *a temple.*)
6. Here's another clue for finding the right object. Listen: Children go there to learn. Everybody, say that. Get ready. (Signal.)
   Children go there to learn.
7. Now here are the three things we know about the object. (Hold up one finger.) It's a building. (Hold up two fingers.) It has a lot of seats. (Hold up three fingers.) Children go there to learn.
8. Everybody, say all the things we know.
   (Hold up one finger.) *It's a building.*
   - (Hold up two fingers.) *It has a lot of seats.*
   - (Hold up three fingers.) *Children go there to learn.*
9. Everybody, tell me what I'm thinking of. (Pause.) Get ready. (Signal.) *A school.*
   Yes, a school.

EXERCISE 3 Opposites

1. You're going to make up statements that have the opposite word.
2. Listen: The paper was smooth. Say that statement. Get ready. (Signal.) *The paper was smooth.*
• Now say a statement that tells the opposite about the paper. Get ready. (Signal.) *The paper was rough.*
3. Listen: Six boys were pushing a cart. Say that statement. Get ready. (Signal.) *Six boys were pushing a cart.*
• Now say a statement that tells the opposite about what the six boys were doing. Get ready. (Signal.) *Six boys were pulling a cart.*
4. Listen: The pot was dull. Say the statement. Get ready. (Signal.) *The pot was dull.*
• Now say a statement that tells the opposite about the pot. Get ready. (Signal.) *The pot was shiny.*
5. Listen: The roof was dangerous. Say the statement. Get ready. (Signal.) *The roof was dangerous.*
• Now say a statement that tells the opposite about the roof. Get ready. (Signal.) *The roof was safe.*
6. Listen: The pot was shallow. Say the statement. Get ready. (Signal.) *The pot was shallow.*
• Now say a statement that tells the opposite about the pot. Get ready. (Signal.) *The pot was deep.*
7. Listen: The egg was raw. Say the statement. Get ready. (Signal.) *The egg was raw.*
• Now say a statement that tells the opposite about the egg. Get ready. (Signal.) *The egg was cooked.*
8. (Repeat step 7 until firm.)

EXERCISE 4 Calendar Facts

1. You learned calendar facts.
• Everybody, how many days are in a week? (Signal.) *Seven.*
• Everybody, say the days of the week. Get ready. (Signal.) *Sunday, Monday, Tuesday, Wednesday, Thursday, Friday, Saturday.*
2. How many weeks are in a year? (Signal.) *52.*
• Say the fact. Get ready. (Signal.) *There are 52 weeks in a year.*
3. How many days are in a year? (Signal.) *365.*
• Say the fact. Get ready. (Signal.) *There are 365 days in a year.*

4. How many seasons are in a year? (Signal.) *Four.*
• Name the four seasons. Get ready. (Signal.) *Winter, spring, summer, fall.*
5. How many months are in a year? (Signal.) *12.*
• Everybody, say the months. Get ready. (Signal.) *January, February, March, April, May, June, July, August, September, October, November, December.*
6. Listen: What day of the week is it today? (Signal.)
• Listen: What day of the week will it be tomorrow? (Signal.)
• Listen: What's today's date? (Signal.)

EXERCISE 5 Description

1. You're going to figure out what object I'm thinking of.
2. Listen: I'm thinking of a vehicle that has wheels. Name some vehicles I could be thinking of. (Call on individual children. Praise examples such as *trains* and *airplanes* as well as *cars, bikes,* and so on.)
3. Listen: I'm thinking of a vehicle with wheels that carries a lot of people. Could I be thinking of a boat? (Signal.) *No.*
• How do you know? (Call on a child. Idea: *It's not a vehicle with wheels.*)
4. (Repeat step 3 until firm.)
5. Everybody, could I be thinking of a motorcycle? (Signal.) *No.*
• How do you know? (Call on a child. Idea: *It doesn't carry a lot of people.*)
• Everybody, could I be thinking of a bus? (Signal.) *Yes.*
• How do you know? (Call on a child. Idea: *It's a vehicle with wheels that carries a lot of people.*)
• Everybody, could I be thinking of a train? (Signal.) *Yes.*
• How do you know? (Call on a child. Idea: *It's a vehicle with wheels that carries a lot of people.*)
6. (Repeat step 5 until firm.)
7. Listen: The object I'm thinking of runs on tracks.
• Could I be thinking of a bus? (Signal.) *No.*
• How do you know? (Call on a child. Idea: *It doesn't run on tracks.*)
8. (Repeat step 7 until firm.)
9. Everybody, could I be thinking of a train? (Signal.) *Yes.*

- How do you know? (Call on a child. Idea: *It's a vehicle with wheels that carries a lot of people and it runs on tracks.*)

10. I couldn't fool you. I was thinking of a train.

EXERCISE 6 Bleep Learns The Days Of The Week *Part 1*

Storytelling

1. Here's another story about Molly and Bleep.

In our last story, Molly adjusted the blue screw so that Bleep did not bleep every time he talked.

At first, Bleep sometimes said things that were not true. One time, Bleep told all the neighbors to go over to somebody's place and pick purple plums.

- Everybody, whose place was that? (Signal.) *Paul's.*

Molly fixed up that problem by taking the top off Bleep's head and adjusting a little yellow screw.

After Molly did that, Bleep did not seem to lie anymore. But there was something different about Bleep.

Molly found out about this problem the day after she adjusted the yellow screw.

Here's what happened: It was Saturday. Molly was getting ready to get in her strange red vehicle and buy some parts for a new invention.

- Listen to that part again.

It was Saturday. Molly was getting ready to get in her strange red vehicle and buy some parts for a new invention.

- Everybody, what day of the week was it? (Signal.) *Saturday.*
- What was Molly getting ready to do? (Call on a child. Idea: *Get in her strange red vehicle and buy some parts for a new invention.*)
- What was strange about her red vehicle? (Call on a child. Idea: *It was part-van and part-sports car.*)

- Everybody, who else had a strange red vehicle? (Signal.) *Mrs. Anderson.*

Molly said to Bleep, "I'm not sure if the hardware store is open on Saturdays. Do you remember?"

Bleep looked at her and said, "Blurp."

He didn't say, "Bleep." He said, "Blurp."

Molly said, "Why did you say, 'blurp'?"

Bleep said, "I do not remember."

- That's important. Molly said, "Why did you say, 'blurp'?" and Bleep said, "I do not remember."

Molly scratched her head and didn't think much about it. She said to herself, "Maybe that was just a strange sound that came out of Bleep's mouth by accident."

On Tuesday, something else happened. Molly was fixing dinner. Bleep was setting the table for her.

- Listen to that part again.

On Tuesday, something else happened. Molly was fixing dinner. Bleep was setting the table for her.

- Everybody, what day was it now? (Signal.) *Tuesday.*
- What was Molly doing? (Signal.) *Fixing dinner.*
- What was Bleep doing? (Signal.) *Setting the table.*

Molly said, "Oh dear. I just remembered that I was supposed to have dinner with Mrs. Anderson sometime this week. But I don't remember whether we were supposed to get together today or on Wednesday. Do you remember which day it was?"

Bleep said, "Blurp."

Molly said, "Why did you say that?"

Bleep said, "I do not remember."

- That's important: Molly said, "Why did you say that?" and Bleep said, "I do not remember."

Well, Molly thought that Bleep was trying to tell her that he didn't remember the day Molly and Mrs. Anderson were supposed to meet. But Bleep was really trying to tell her that he didn't remember anything about Tuesday or anything about Wednesday or anything about the other days of the week.

- Listen:

   Bleep didn't know about the days of the week. He didn't know about Tuesday, Wednesday or any of the other days.

- What are the names of some of the other days? (Call on a child. Idea: *Sunday, Monday, Thursday, Friday, Saturday.*)
- Everybody, so when Molly asked Bleep, "Why did you say, 'blurp'?" what would Bleep always say? (Signal.) *"I do not remember."*
- And Bleep was trying to tell Molly that he didn't remember anything about the days of the week. He must have forgotten all about them when Molly adjusted that yellow screw.

   Molly got another clue about Bleep's new problem on Friday. She said to Bleep, "Where did you put Thursday's newspaper?"

- You know what Bleep said. Everybody, what did Bleep say? (Signal.) *Blurp.*

   Then Molly said, "Why did you say that?" Then Bleep explained.

- What did Bleep say? (Signal.) *"I do not remember."*

   That kind of problem went on for one more week before they finally figured out Bleep's problem. She figured it out when Paul came over one day and asked Molly if he could borrow her big pliers on Saturday.

   Bleep was standing near Molly. He said that word again.

- Everybody, what word? (Signal.) *Blurp.*

   Molly said, "Why did you say 'blurp,' Bleep?" And Bleep explained.

- Everybody, what did Bleep say? (Signal.) *"I do not remember."*

   But just after Paul left, Molly figured out what Bleep's problem was. She looked at Bleep and said, "What day of the week is today?"

   Bleep said that word again.

   Molly said, "Ah, ha. You don't remember the days of the week, do you?"

   Bleep looked at her with a very sad expression and said, "Blurp."

   Poor Bleep.

   Molly said, "Well, let's see if you can **learn** the days of the week if I tell you about them."

   Bleep said, "Okay, baby."

   Molly said, "Here are the days of the week: Sunday, Monday, Tuesday, Wednesday, Thursday, Friday, Saturday."

   Bleep said, "Sunday, Monday, Blurpday, Blurpday . . . "

   "Stop, stop," Molly said. "Let's just try the first four days of the week. Listen and think hard: Sunday, Monday, Tuesday, **Wednesday.** Can you say that much?"

   Bleep said, "Sunday, Monday, Tuesday, Blurpday."

- Everybody, what should Bleep have said instead of **Blurpday?** (Signal.) *Wednesday.*
- Who can say the first four days of the week the way Bleep **should** say them? (Call on a child. Praise children who say all four days.)
- Let's do it together. We'll say the first four days of the week the right way. Get ready. (Signal.) (Respond with the children.) *Sunday, Monday, Tuesday, Wednesday.*
2. Your turn: Say the first four days of the week. Get ready. (Signal.) *Sunday, Monday, Tuesday, Wednesday.*
- (Repeat step 2 until firm.)

After Molly practiced the names with Bleep, he could say the first four days of the week the right way. Molly would say this: "Sunday, Monday, Tuesday, Wednesday."

And Bleep would say this: "Sunday, Monday, Tuesday, Wednesday."

Bleep could do that much perfectly, but you know what he said when he tried to say Thursday, Friday and Saturday.

3. Everybody, what did he say? (Signal.) *Blurpday, Blurpday, Blurpday.*
- Molly still had some work to do with Bleep.

WORKBOOK 58

EXERCISE 7   Writing The Days Of The Week

Sunday	Monday	Tuesday	Wednesday

1. Everybody, find Lesson 58 in your workbook. Write your name at the top of the page. ✔
- Molly is saying something in that picture and Bleep is saying something too.
2. Touch the words that Molly is saying. ✔
- I'll read those words: **Say the days of the week.** That's what Molly is telling Bleep.
- And Bleep is saying something, but some of the words are missing. He is saying: **Blank, blank, blank, Blurpday.** He didn't really say that.
- Everybody, what did he **really** say? (Signal.) *Sunday, Monday, Tuesday, Blurpday.*

3. Touch the words at the top of the page. They are the names of the first four days of the week.
- Touch the first word. ✔ That's **Sunday.**
- Touch the next word. ✔ That's **Monday.**
- Touch the next word. ✔ That's **Tuesday.**
- Touch the last word. ✔ That's **Wednesday.**
4. You're going to write the names so that Bleep says: **Sunday, Monday, Tuesday** and **Wednesday.** So you'll have to fix up that last word Bleep said so it says **Wednesday,** not **Blurpday.** You'll have to cross out the part that says **Blurp** and write the correct letters. Remember to spell the words correctly and start each word with a capital letter. Raise your hand when you're finished. (Observe children and give feedback.)
5. Later you can color the picture.

EXERCISE 8   Map Reading

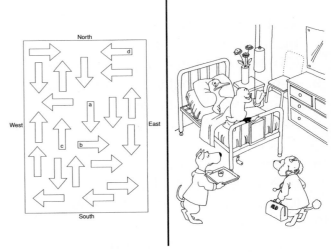

1. Everybody, find the next page in your workbook. ✔
- (Hold up workbook. Point to first half.) Find the arrows. ✔
2. Some of the arrows have letters on them. Find the arrow with the letter **A.** ✔
- Raise your hand when you know which direction that arrow is pointing. ✔
- Everybody, which direction? (Signal.) *South.*
3. Find the arrow with the letter **B.** ✔
- Raise your hand when you know which direction that arrow is pointing. ✔

- Everybody, which direction? (Signal.) *East.*
4. Find the arrow with letter **C. ✔**
- Everybody, which direction is that arrow pointing? (Signal.) *North.*
5. Find the arrow with the letter **D. ✔**
- Everybody, which direction is that arrow pointing? (Signal.) *West.*
6. Once more.
- Touch **A. ✔**
Everybody, which direction is that arrow pointing? (Signal.) *South.*
- Touch **B. ✔**
Everybody, which direction is that arrow pointing? (Signal.) *East.*
- Touch **C. ✔**
Everybody, which direction is that arrow pointing? (Signal.) *North.*
- Touch **D. ✔**
Everybody, which direction is that arrow pointing? (Signal.) *West.*
7. (Repeat step 6 until firm.)
8. Listen: Here's a rule about the arrows that are pointing **south.** All arrows that are pointing **south** should be yellow. What color? (Signal.) *Yellow.*
- There are six arrows that are pointing **south.** Put a yellow mark on each arrow that is pointing **south.**
(Observe children and give feedback.)
9. Here's a rule about the arrows that are pointing **west.** All the arrows that are pointing **west** should be blue. What color? (Signal.) *Blue.*
- There are five arrows pointing **west.** Put a blue mark on each of them.
(Observe children and give feedback.)
10. Later you can color the arrows that are pointing **south** and the arrows that are pointing **west.**

EXERCISE 9   Location

1. (Hold up workbook. Point to second half.) Look at the picture. **✔**
- Everybody, what place do you see in this picture? (Signal.) *A hospital.*
2. Here's a coloring rule for this picture. Listen: Color some of the furniture yellow and some of the furniture green.
- What is the rule? (Signal.) *Color some of the furniture yellow and some of the furniture green.*
3. (Repeat step 2 until firm.)
4. Put marks on the furniture. **✔**
5. Here's another coloring rule for this picture. Listen: Color the clothing blue. What's the rule? (Signal.) *Color the clothing blue.*
6. (Repeat step 5 until firm.)
7. Put a blue mark on **one** piece of clothing. **✔**
8. There's one more thing to do. One piece of furniture has a missing part. What piece of furniture is that? (Signal.) *A chair.* Yes, a chair.
9. What part of the chair is missing? (Signal.) *The back.*
- Yes, the back. Before you color the chair, follow the dots and make the back.

Objectives

- Given a common object, students generate activities that "can" and "cannot do" with the object. (Exercise 1)
- Generate sentences using forms of the verb "to be." (Exercise 2)
- Follow directions involving if-then. (Exercise 3)
- **Name things that a statement does NOT tell.** (Exercise 4)
- Generate a list of objects that fit stated criteria. (Exercise 5)
- Answer questions involving previously learned calendar facts. (Exercise 6)
- Replace a word in a sentence with an opposite. (Exercise 7)
- Answer questions about a familiar story. (Exercise 8)
- Complete a picture by copying the words, to show a familiar character saying the days of the week. (Exercise 9)

EXERCISE 1 Can Do

1. Everybody, I'm going to call on individual children to name things we can do with an envelope.
2. (Call on a child.)
- What's one thing we can do with an envelope? (After the child gives a correct response, call on the group.) Let's all say the whole thing. Get ready. (Signal.) (The group repeats the child's response.)
3. (Call on another child.)
- What's another thing we can do with an envelope? (After the child gives a correct response, call on the group.) Let's all name those things we can do with an envelope.
- What's the first thing? (Hold up one finger.) (The group repeats the first response.)
- What's the second thing? (Hold up two fingers.) (The group repeats the second response.)
4. (Call on another child.)
- What's another thing we can do with an envelope? (After the child gives a correct response, call on the group.) Let's all name those things we can do with an envelope.
- What's the first thing? (Hold up one finger.) (The group repeats the first response.)
- What's the second thing? (Hold up two fingers.) (The group repeats the second response.)
- What's the third thing? (Hold up three fingers.) (The group repeats the third response.)

5. Now I'm going to call on individual children to name things we cannot do with an envelope.
6. (Call on one child.)
- What's one thing we cannot do with an envelope? (After the child gives a correct response, call on the group.) Let's all say the whole thing. Get ready. (Signal. The group repeats the first response.)
7. (Call on another child.)
- What's another thing we cannot do with an envelope? (After the child gives a correct response, call on the group.) Let's all name those things we cannot do with an envelope.
- What's the first thing? (Hold up one finger.) (The group repeats the first response.)
- What's the second thing? (Hold up two fingers.) (The group repeats the second response.)
8. (Call on another child.)
- What's another thing we cannot do with an envelope? (After the child gives a correct response, call on the group.) Let's all name those things we cannot do with an envelope.
- What's the first thing? (Hold up one finger.) (The group repeats the first response.)
- What's the second thing? (Hold up two fingers.) (The group repeats the second response.)
- What's the third thing? (Hold up three fingers.) (The group repeats the third response.)

EXERCISE 2 Verb Tense

1. I'll make a statement about a chair.
2. Listen: Tomorrow the chair will be here. Everybody, say that statement. (Signal.) *Tomorrow the chair will be here.*
  - (Repeat step 2 until firm.)
3. You told me about tomorrow. Now make a statement about the chair yesterday. Get ready. (Signal.) *Yesterday the chair was here.*
  - (Repeat step 3 until firm.)
4. Now make a statement about the chair today. Get ready. (Signal.) *Today the chair is here.*
  - (Repeat step 4 until firm.)

EXERCISE 3 Actions

1. We're going to learn a rule and play a game.
2. Listen to this rule. If the teacher says **go** or **stop,** touch your head.
  - Listen again: If the teacher says **go** or **stop,** touch your head.
3. Everybody, say the rule with me. Get ready. (Signal.) (Respond with the children.) *If the teacher says **go** or **stop,** touch your head.*
  - All by yourselves. Say the rule. Get ready. (Signal.) *If the teacher says **go** or **stop,** touch your head.*
4. (Repeat step 3 until firm.)
5. What's the rule? (Signal.) *If the teacher says **go** or **stop,** touch your head.*
  - What are you going to do if I say **go** or say **stop?** (Signal.) *Touch my head.*
6. Now we're going to play the game.
7. What's the rule? (Signal.) *If the teacher says **go** or **stop,** touch your head.*
8. Let's see if I can fool you. Get ready. (Pause.) (Touch your head.) (Signal.) (The children should not do anything.)
9. See if I can fool you. Get ready. (Pause.) **Go.** (Signal.) (The children should touch their heads.)
10. See if I can fool you this time. Get ready. (Pause.) **Stop.** (Signal.) (The children should touch their heads.)
11. (Repeat steps 7 through 10 until firm.)

EXERCISE 4 Statements

1. Listen to this statement. The girls are jumping rope.
  - Everybody, say that statement. Get ready. (Signal.) *The girls are jumping rope.*
2. Does that statement tell what the girls are doing now? (Signal.) *Yes.*
  - Does that statement tell what the girls did yesterday? (Signal.) *No.*
  - Does that statement tell if the girls are happy? (Signal.) *No.*
  - Does that statement tell if the girls are wearing shoes? (Signal.) *No.*
  - Does that statement tell how many girls are jumping rope? (Signal.) *No.*
3. The girls are jumping rope.
  - Everybody, say that statement again. Get ready. (Signal.) *The girls are jumping rope.*
4. Here's one thing that statement does not tell us. It doesn't tell how long the rope is. Your turn to name two more things the statement does not tell us. (Call on individual children. Repeat both correct responses.)
5. You named two things the statement does not tell us.
  - Everybody, name the first thing. Get ready. (Hold up one finger.) (The group repeats the first response.)
  - Everybody, name the second thing. Get ready. (Hold up two fingers.) (The group repeats the second response.)
6. (Repeat step 5 until firm.)

EXERCISE 5 Description

1. Get ready to play detective and find out what object I'm thinking of. I'll give you two clues.
2. (Hold up one finger.) It's a container.
  - (Hold up two fingers.) It's made of plastic.
3. Say the two things we know about the object. Get ready.
  - (Hold up one finger.) *It's a container.*
  - (Hold up two fingers.) *It's made of plastic.*
4. (Repeat step 3 until firm.)
5. Those clues don't tell you enough to find the right container. They could tell you about a lot of containers. See how many containers you can name that are made of plastic. (Call on individual children. The group is to name at least three containers that are made of plastic, such as *a bottle, a pail,* and *a bowl.*)
6. Here's another clue for finding the right object. Listen: You buy soda pop in it. Everybody, say that. Get ready. (Signal.) *You buy soda pop in it.*

7. Now here are the three things we know about the object.
- (Hold up one finger.) It's a container.
- (Hold up two fingers.) It's made of plastic.
- (Hold up three fingers.) You buy soda pop in it.
8. Everybody, say all the things we know. Get ready.
- (Hold up one finger.) *It's a container.*
- (Hold up two fingers.) *It's made of plastic.*
- (Hold up three fingers.) *You buy soda pop in it.*
9. Everybody, tell me what object I am thinking of. (Pause.) Get ready. (Signal.) *A bottle.* Yes, a bottle.
10. How do you know I was thinking of a bottle? (Hold up one finger.) *It's a container.*
- (Hold up two fingers.) *It's made of plastic.*
- (Hold up three fingers.) *You buy soda pop in it.*

EXERCISE 6 Calendar Facts

1. You learned calendar facts.
- Everybody, how many days are in a week? (Signal.) *Seven.*
- Everybody, say the days of the week. Get ready. (Signal.) *Sunday, Monday, Tuesday, Wednesday, Thursday, Friday, Saturday.*
2. How many weeks are in a year? (Signal.) *52.*
- Say the fact. Get ready. (Signal.) *There are 52 weeks in a year.*
3. How many days are in a year? (Signal.) *365.*
- Say the fact. Get ready. (Signal.) *There are 365 days in a year.*
4. How many seasons are in a year? (Signal.) *Four.*
- Name the four seasons. Get ready. (Signal.) *Winter, spring, summer, fall.*
5. How many months are in a year? (Signal.) *12.*
- Everybody, say the months. Get ready. (Signal.) *January, February, March, April, May, June, July, August, September, October, November, December.*
6. (Repeat step 5 until firm.)
7. What day of the week is it today? (Signal.)
- What day of the week will it be tomorrow? (Signal.)
- What's today's date? (Signal.)

EXERCISE 7 Opposites

1. Here are some new opposites.
2. Listen: The opposite of before is after.
- What's the opposite of before something happened? (Signal.) *After something happened.*
- What's the opposite of after something happened? (Signal.) *Before something happened.*
3. Listen: The opposite of early is late.
- What's the opposite of early? (Signal.) *Late.*
- What's the opposite of late? (Signal.) *Early.*
4. Listen: The opposite of start is finish.
- What's the opposite of start? (Signal.) *Finish.*
- What's the opposite of finish? (Signal.) *Start.*
5. You're going to make up statements that have the opposite word.
6. Listen: The workers were starting a job. Say that statement. Get ready. (Signal.) *The workers were starting a job.*
- Now say a statement that tells the opposite about what the workers were doing. Get ready. (Signal.) *The workers were finishing a job.*
7. Listen: The vegetables were cooked. Say that statement. Get ready. (Signal.) *The vegetables were cooked.*
- Now say a statement that tells the opposite about the vegetables. Get ready. (Signal.) *The vegetables were raw.*
8. Listen: The girls woke up early. Say that statement. Get ready. (Signal.) *The girls woke up early.*
- Now say a statement that tells the opposite about the girls. Get ready. (Signal.) *The girls woke up late.*
9. Listen: The person was old. Say that statement. Get ready. (Signal.) *The person was old.*
- Now say a statement that tells the opposite about the person. Get ready. (Signal.) *The person was young.*
10. (Repeat steps 6 through 9 until firm.)

EXERCISE 8 Bleep Learns The Days Of The Week *Part 2*

Storytelling

1. Listen to the story about Bleep again.

> After Molly adjusted the blue screw, Bleep did not bleep every time he talked. But Bleep sometimes said things that were not true.

- Who remembers one thing that Bleep told everybody that wasn't true? (Call on a child. Idea: *To pick purple plums at Paul's place.*)

> Molly fixed up that problem by adjusting a different screw.

- Everybody, which screw was that? (Signal.) *The yellow screw.*

> After Molly adjusted the yellow screw, Bleep did not seem to lie anymore. But there was something different about Bleep.
>
> Molly found out about this problem the day after she adjusted the yellow screw.
>
> Here's what happened: It was Saturday. Molly was getting ready to get in her strange red vehicle and buy some parts for a new invention.
>
> Molly said to Bleep, "I'm not sure if the hardware store is open on Saturdays. Do you remember?"
>
> Bleep looked at her and said . . .

- Everybody, what did he say? (Signal.) *Blurp.*
- Yes, first Bleep said, "Blurp."
- When Bleep said "Blurp," what was he trying to tell Molly? (Call on a child. Idea: *That he didn't know anything about the days of the week.*)
- But Molly didn't know that.

> Molly asked Bleep, "Why did you say 'blurp?'"

- And what did Bleep say? (Signal.) *"I do not remember."*

> Molly scratched her head and didn't think much about it. She said to herself, "Maybe that was just a strange sound that came out of Bleep's mouth by accident."
>
> On Tuesday, something else happened. Molly was fixing dinner. Bleep was setting the table for her.
>
> Molly said, "Oh dear. I just remembered that I was supposed to have dinner with Mrs. Anderson sometime this week. But I don't remember whether we were supposed to get together today or on Wednesday. Do you remember which day it was?"

- And what did Bleep say? (Signal.) *Blurp.*

> Molly said, "Why did you say that?"

- And, what did Bleep say? (Signal.) *"I do not remember."*
- Right.

> Bleep said, "I do not remember."

- What didn't he remember? (Call on a child. Idea: *Anything about the days of the week.*)

> Well, Molly thought that Bleep was trying to tell her that he didn't remember the day Molly and Mrs. Anderson were supposed to meet. But Bleep was really trying to tell her that he didn't remember anything about Tuesday or anything about Wednesday or anything about the other days of the week.
>
> Molly got another clue about Bleep's new problem on Friday. She said to Bleep, "Where did you put Thursday's newspaper?"

- You know what Bleep said.

> That kind of problem went on for one more week before Molly finally figured out Bleep's problem. She figured it out when Paul came over one day and asked Molly if he could borrow her big pliers on Saturday.

Bleep was standing near Molly. He said that word again.

Molly said, "Why did you say 'blurp,' Bleep?"

And Bleep explained.

- What did he say when he explained? (Signal.) *"I do not remember."*

But just after Paul left, Molly figured out what Bleep's problem was. She looked at Bleep and said, "What day of the week is today?"

Bleep said that word again.

Molly said, "Ah, ha. You don't remember the days of the week, do you?"

Bleep looked at her with a very sad expression and said, "Blurp."

Poor Bleep.

Molly said, "Well, let's see if you can **learn** the days of the week if I tell you about them."

Bleep said, "Okay, baby."

Molly said the days of the week.

- Who can say them? (Call on a child. Praise appropriate response.)

Then it was Bleep's turn to say the days of the week.

Here's what Bleep said: "Sunday, Monday, Blurpday, Blurpday . . . "

"Stop, stop," Molly said. "Let's just try the first four days of the week. Listen and think hard: Sunday, Monday, Tuesday, **Wednesday.** Can you say that much?"

- And what did Bleep say? (Call on a child. Idea: *Sunday, Monday, Tuesday, Blurpday.*)

Bleep said, "Sunday, Monday, Tuesday, Blurpday."

After Molly practiced the names with Bleep, he could say the first four days of the week the right way. Then Molly worked on the rest of the days of the week until Bleep could do all seven days without one blurp.

First Molly told Bleep the days that come after Wednesday.

- Here they are: Thursday, Friday, Saturday. Once more: Thursday, Friday, Saturday.
2. Everybody, say those days without one blurp. (Signal.) *Thursday, Friday, Saturday.*
- (Repeat step 2 until firm.)

At last Bleep could say all the days just like this: Sunday, Monday, Tuesday, Wednesday, Thursday, Friday, Saturday.

- Let's see if you can say all the days as well as Bleep did.
3. Everybody, say all seven days of the week. Get ready. (Signal.) *Sunday, Monday, Tuesday, Wednesday, Thursday, Friday, Saturday.*
- (Repeat step 3 until firm.)
4. If you remember those days really well, we'll put on a play and have somebody play the part of Molly, somebody else play the part of Bleep and somebody else play the part of Paul. Raise your hand if you can say all the days of the week without any mistakes or any blurps. (Call on several children. Praise correct responses.)

EXERCISE 9 Writing The Days Of The Week

1. Everybody, find Lesson 59 in your workbook. Write your name at the top of the page. ✔

- In this picture, Bleep looks very proud and he's saying something. Bleep is supposed to be saying the days of the week, but some of the days are missing. He is saying Sunday, Monday, Tuesday, and then the rest of the lines are blank. You'll have to fill in all the missing days. They're written at the top of the page.

2. Everybody, touch the first word. ✔
That's **Wednesday.**

- Touch the next word. ✔
That's **Thursday.**

- Touch the next word. ✔
That's **Friday.**

- Touch the last word. ✔
What's that word? (Signal.) *Saturday.*

3. So Bleep is supposed to be saying, "Sunday, Monday, Tuesday, Wednesday, Thursday, Friday, Saturday."

- And Molly is saying, "Wow, you can say **all** the days of the week."

4. Fill in the missing days of the week. Remember to spell the words correctly and start each word with a capital letter. Raise your hand when you're finished.
(Observe children and give feedback.)

5. Later you can color the picture.

Objectives

- Identify an object by stated criteria. (Exercise 1)
- Name four classes containing a common noun and answer questions about members of those classes. (Exercise 2)
- Identify an object by stated criteria. (Exercise 3)
- Replace a word in a sentence with an opposite. (Exercise 4)
- Answer questions involving previously learned calendar facts. (Exercise 5)
- Listen to a familiar story. (Exercise 6)
- Put on a play to show a familiar story. (Exercise 7)
- Complete a picture by copying the words, to show a familiar character saying the days of the week. (Exercise 8)

EXERCISE 1 Descriptions

1. You're going to figure out what object I'm thinking of.
- Listen: I'm thinking of an appliance you find in the kitchen. Name some appliances I could be thinking of. (Call on individual children.)
2. Listen: I'm thinking of a kitchen appliance that is big.
- Could I be thinking of a refrigerator? (Signal.) *Yes.*
- Everybody, how do you know? (Signal.) *It's a kitchen appliance that is big.*
3. (Repeat step 2 until firm.)
4. Listen: Could I be thinking of a stove? (Signal.) *Yes.*
- Everybody, how do you know? (Signal.) *It's a kitchen appliance that is big.*
- Could I be thinking of a lawn mower? (Signal.) *No.*
- How do you know? (Call on a child. Idea: *It's not a kitchen appliance that is big.*)
- Everybody, could I be thinking of a toaster? (Signal.) *No.*
- How do you know? (Call on a child. Idea: *It's not a kitchen appliance that is big.*)
5. (Repeat step 4 until firm.)

6. Listen: The object I'm thinking of is used to keep food cold.
- Could I be thinking of a stove? (Signal.) *No.*
- How do you know? (Call on a child. Idea: *It's not used to keep food cold.*)
- Everybody, could I be thinking of a refrigerator? (Signal.) *Yes.*
- How do you know? (Call on a child. Idea: *It's a kitchen appliance that is big and used to keep food cold.*)
7. (Repeat step 6 until firm.)
- Yes, I was thinking of a refrigerator.

EXERCISE 2 Classification

1. Today we're going to talk about a poodle. We can put a poodle into four different classes.
- You'll start with the smallest class for poodles and name all four classes.
2. One of the classes is pets. Everybody, is that class bigger than the class of animals or smaller than the class of animals? (Signal.) *Smaller than the class of animals.*
3. Everybody, what's the smallest class for a poodle? (Signal.) *Poodles.*
- What's the next bigger class? (Signal.) *Dogs.*
- What's the next bigger class? (Signal.) *Pets.*
- What's the biggest class? (Signal.) *Animals.*
4. (Repeat step 3 until firm.)
5. What is one kind of object you would find in all those classes? (Signal.) *A poodle.*

6. Think of these classes: poodles, dogs, pets, animals. What classes? (Signal.) *Poodles, dogs, pets, animals.*
• Would you find a collie in all those classes? (Signal.) *No.*
• Name three of those classes you would find a collie in. (Pause.) Get ready. (Tap 3 times.) *Dogs. Pets. Animals.*
• Would you find a giraffe in all those classes? (Signal.) *No.*
• Name one class you would find a giraffe in. (Pause.) Get ready. (Tap.) *Animals.*
7. (Repeat step 6 until firm.)

EXERCISE 3   Description

1. I'm thinking of an object. See if you can figure out what object I'm thinking of. I'll tell you something about the object.
• Listen: It's furniture. Everybody, what do you know about the object? (Signal.) *It's furniture.*
• Could I be thinking of a cabinet? (Signal.) *Yes.*
• Could I be thinking of a knife? (Signal.) *No.*
• Could I be thinking of a truck? (Signal.) *No.*
• Could I be thinking of a couch? (Signal.) *Yes.*
2. Listen: The object I'm thinking of is (hold up one finger) furniture **and** (hold up two fingers) you find it in a bedroom.
3. Everybody, what do you know about the object? (Hold up one finger.) *It's furniture* **and** (hold up two fingers) *you find it in a bedroom.*
• (Repeat step 3 until firm.)
4. Could I be thinking of couch? (Signal.) *No.*
• Why not? (Signal.) *You don't find it in a bedroom.*
• (Repeat step 4 until firm.)
5. Could I be thinking of a bed? (Signal.) *Yes.*
• How do you know? (Call on a child. Idea: *It's furniture and you find it in a bedroom.*)
6. Listen: The object I'm thinking of is (hold up one finger) furniture **and** (hold up two fingers) you find it in a bedroom **and** (hold up three fingers) you sleep on it.
7. Everybody, name the object I am thinking of. Get ready. (Signal.) *A bed.*

8. How do you know I'm thinking of a bed? (Hold up one finger.) *It is furniture* **and** (hold up two fingers) *you find it in a bedroom* **and** (hold up three fingers) *you sleep on it.*
9. (Repeat step 8 until firm.)

EXERCISE 4   Opposites

1. You're going to make up statements that have the opposite word.
2. Listen: The food was raw. Say that statement. Get ready. (Signal.) *The food was raw.*
• Now say a statement that tells the opposite about the food. Get ready. (Signal.) *The food was cooked.*
3. Listen: The table was rough. Say that statement. Get ready. (Signal.) *The table was rough.*
• Now say a statement that tells the opposite about the table. Get ready. (Signal.) *The table was smooth.*
4. Listen: The car was shiny. Say that statement. Get ready. (Signal.) *The car was shiny.*
• Now say a statement that tells the opposite about the car. Get ready. (Signal.) *The car was dull.*
5. Listen: The man was pushing the sled. Say that statement. Get ready. (Signal.) *The man was pushing the sled.*
• Now say a statement that tells the opposite about the sled. Get ready. (Signal.) *The man was pulling the sled.*
6. Listen: The road was safe. Say that statement. Get ready. (Signal.) *The road was safe.*
• Now say a statement that tells the opposite about the road. Get ready. (Signal.) *The road was dangerous.*

EXERCISE 5   Calendar Facts

1. You learned calendar facts.
• Everybody, how many days are in a week? (Signal.) *Seven.*
• Everybody, say the days of the week. Get ready. (Signal.) *Sunday, Monday, Tuesday, Wednesday, Thursday, Friday, Saturday.*
2. How many weeks are in a year? (Signal.) *52.*
• Say the fact. Get ready. (Signal.) *There are 52 weeks in a year.*
3. How many days are in a year? (Signal.) *365.*

- Say the fact. Get ready. (Signal.) *There are 365 days in a year.*
4. How many seasons are in a year? (Signal.) *Four.*
- Name the four seasons. Get ready. (Signal.) *Winter, spring, summer, fall.*
5. How many months are in a year? (Signal.) *12.*
- Everybody, say the months. Get ready. (Signal.) *January, February, March, April, May, June, July, August, September, October, November, December.*
- (Repeat until firm.)
6. What day of the week is it today? (Signal.)
- What day of the week will it be tomorrow? (Signal.)
- What's today's date? (Signal.)

EXERCISE 6 Bleep Learns The Days Of The Week

Review

1. You did such a good job of remembering the days of the week that we're going to put on a play. Remember, you have to say all the days of the week without one Blurpday.
- Everybody, what's the first day of the week? (Signal.) *Sunday.*
- Say the days of the week, starting with Sunday. Get ready. (Signal.) *Sunday, Monday, Tuesday, Wednesday, Thursday, Friday, Saturday.*
2. Listen to the last story about Bleep very carefully, because after I read it, we're going to act out part of the story. I'll tell you a clue about the part we'll act out: It takes place when someone comes over to borrow something.

After Molly adjusted the blue screw, Bleep did not bleep every time he talked. But Bleep sometimes said things that were not true.

Molly fixed up that problem by adjusting a different screw.

After Molly adjusted the yellow screw, Bleep did not seem to lie anymore. But there was something different about Bleep.

Molly found out about this problem the day after she adjusted the yellow screw.

Here's what happened: It was Saturday. Molly was getting ready to get in her strange red vehicle and buy some parts for a new invention.

Molly said to Bleep, "I'm not sure if the hardware store is open on Saturdays. Do you remember?"

Bleep looked at her and said, "Blurp."

Molly asked Bleep, "Why did you say 'blurp'?"

Bleep said, "I do not remember."

Molly scratched her head and didn't think much about it. She said to herself, "Maybe that was just a strange sound that came out of Bleep's mouth by accident."

On Tuesday, something else happened. Molly was fixing dinner. Bleep was setting the table for her.

Molly said, "Oh dear. I just remembered that I was supposed to have dinner with Mrs. Anderson some time this week. But I don't remember whether we were supposed to get together today or on Wednesday. Do you remember which day it was?"

Bleep said, "Blurp."

Molly said, "Why did you say that?"

Bleep said, "I do not remember."

Well, Molly thought that Bleep was trying to tell her that he didn't remember the day Molly and Mrs. Anderson were supposed to meet. But Bleep was really trying to tell her that he didn't remember anything about Tuesday or anything about Wednesday or anything about the other days of the week.

Molly got another clue about Bleep's new problem on Friday. She said to Bleep, "Where did you put Thursday's newspaper?"

Bleep said, "Blurp."

That kind of problem went on for one more week before Molly finally figured out Bleep's problem. She figured it out when Paul came over one day and asked

Molly if he could borrow her big pliers on Saturday.

Bleep was standing near Molly. He said that word again.

Molly said, "Why did you say 'blurp,' Bleep?"

And Bleep explained.

But just after Paul left, Molly figured out what Bleep's problem was. She looked at Bleep and said, "What day of the week is today?"

Bleep said that word again.

Molly said, "Ah, ha. You don't remember the days of the week, do you?"

Bleep looked at her with a very sad expression and said, "Blurp."

Poor Bleep.

Molly said, "Well, let's see if you can **learn** the days of the week if I tell you about them."

Bleep said, "Okay, baby."

Molly said the days of the week.

Then it was Bleep's turn to say the days of the week. Here's what Bleep said: "Sunday, Monday, Blurpday, Blurpday . . ."

"Stop, stop," Molly said. "Let's just try the first four days of the week. Listen and think hard: Sunday, Monday, Tuesday, **Wednesday.** Can you say that much?"

Bleep said, "Sunday, Monday, Tuesday, Blurpday."

After Molly practiced the names with Bleep, he could say the first four days of the week the right way. Then Molly worked on the rest of the days of the week until Bleep could do all seven days without one blurp.

3. Everybody, say the days of the week the way Bleep could do it after Molly worked with him. Get ready. (Signal.) *Sunday, Monday, Tuesday, Wednesday, Thursday, Friday, Saturday.*

EXERCISE 7 Bleep Learns The Days Of The Week

Putting On A Play

1. Now we're going to act out the part when somebody comes over to borrow something.
- Everybody, who comes over to borrow something? (Signal.) *Paul.*
- What does Paul want to borrow? (Signal.) *Some big pliers.*
- Paul wants to borrow the big pliers on a certain day. What day is that? (Signal.) *Saturday.*
2. We'll need somebody to play the part of Molly, somebody to play the part of Paul and somebody to play the part of Bleep. (Identify children for the parts.)
3. I'll read part of the story. Then our actors will do that part. Listen:

Paul came over and asked Molly, "Can I borrow your big pliers on Saturday?"

Bleep was standing near Molly and he said that word again.

Then Molly said, "Why did you say 'blurp,' Bleep?"

And Bleep explained.

- Everybody, what did Bleep say when he explained? (Signal.) *"I do not remember."*
4. Let's try that part. Bleep, you stand next to Molly. Paul, you come in and ask your question about borrowing the big pliers. Bleep, as soon as Paul asks the question and you hear the word **Saturday,** you say, "blurp." Then, Molly, you ask Bleep why he said "blurp." Then, Bleep, you explain.
- Here we go. Paul, come in and ask your question. Then see how far you can go. Everybody else, watch carefully.
- (Prompt if necessary as children act out the part of the story.)
- Let's do that one more time. Then we'll try it with a different set of characters. (Praise children for saying their lines.)
5. (Identify three individual children for the roles and repeat the scene.)
6. We have some really good actors in this class.

EXERCISE 8 Writing The Days Of The Week

Why did you say _____, Bleep?

Sunday
_____

Monday
_____

Tuesday
_____

Wednesday
_____

Thursday
_____

Blurpday
_____

Saturday
_____

1. Everybody, open your workbook to Lesson 60. Write your name at the top of the page. ✔
- Look at the picture. It shows Paul and Molly and Bleep.
- Molly is saying, "Why did you say **blank,** Bleep?" There should be a word in the blank. What word? **(Signal.)** *Blurp.*

- So this part of the story must have taken place just **after** Bleep said, "blurp."
- What made Bleep say "blurp" in the first place? **(Call on a child. Idea:** *Paul said the word Saturday.***)**
2. You're going to write the missing word in the blank.
- (Write on the board:)

> **blurp**

- Here's how you write **blurp.** Write **blurp** in the blank where Molly is talking. Raise your hand when you're finished. ✔
- Now you'll copy the names for the days of the week. You'll copy each name on the line right below it. But I'll have to warn you: One of those days is not right. When you find the day that is not right, bring your workbook up to me and show me the day. I'll show you how to write the correct day. **(Observe children and give feedback.)**
3. Later you can color the picture.

Scope
and
Sequence

Grade 1

	Phonics/ Vocabulary	Comprehension	Grammar/ Usage/ Mechanics	Writing/ Composition/ Speaking	Study Skills
Lesson 1	Opposites: 2	Classification: 1, 3, 4, 8 Listening Comprehension: 5 Recalling Details: 6 Following Directions: 7			
Lesson 2	Where: 2 Days Of Weeks: 3, 6 Opposites: 5	Classification: 1, 4, 10 Listening Comprehension: 7 Recalling Details: 8 Following Directions: 9			
Lesson 3	Where: 2 Days Of Week: 3, 6 Opposites: 5	Classification: 1, 4, 10 Listening Comprehension: 7 Recalling Details: 8 Following Directions: 9			
Lesson 4	Where: 2 Months Of Year: 3 Opposites: 5 Days Of Week: 6 Part/Whole: 9	Classification: 1, 4 Listening Comprehension: 7 Recalling Details: 8 Following Directions: 10			
Lesson 5	Actions: 1 Where/When: 3 Days Of The Week: 4 Months Of The Year: 4 Seasons: 4 Opposites: 5 Yesterday/Today: 6 Part/Whole: 9	Classification: 2, 10 Listening Comprehension: 7 Recalling Details: 8			
Lesson 6	Where: 2 Days Of The Week: 3 Seasons: 3 Months Of The Year: 3 Where/When: 4 Opposites: 6 Yesterday/Today: 7	Classification: 1, 5 Listening Comprehension: 8 Recalling Details: 9			
Lesson 7	Where: 1 Where/When: 2 Occupations: 3 Days Of The Week: 4 Seasons: 4 Months Of The Year: 4 Opposites: 5 Yesterday/Today: 6 Part/Whole: 8	Listening Comprehension: 7 Sequencing: 7 Classification: 9			
Lesson 8	Actions: 1 Where/When: 2 Days Of The Week: 3 Months Of The Year: 3 Seasons: 3 Same/Different: 4 Yesterday/Today: 6	Classification: 5, 9 Recalling Details: 7 Sequencing: 8 Following Directions: 10			
Lesson 9	Actions: 1 Where/When: 3 Opposites: 4 Days Of The Week: 5 Months Of The Year: 5 Seasons: 5 Same/Different: 6 Yesterday/Today: 8 Part/Whole: 11 Location: 12	Classification: 2 Reasoning: 7 Listening Comprehension: 9 Sequencing: 10			
Lesson 10	Actions: 1 Opposites: 3 Days Of The Week: 4 Months Of The Year: 4 Seasons: 4 Same/Different: 5 Yesterday/Today: 6 Location: 9	Classification: 2 Listening Comprehension: 7 Following Directions: 8			

	Phonics/ Vocabulary	Comprehension	Grammar/ Usage/ Mechanics	Writing/ Composition/ Speaking	Study Skills
Lesson 11	Actions: 1 Where: 3 Opposites: 4 Months Of The Year: 5 Days Of The Week: 5 Seasons: 6 Same/Different: 6 Yesterday/Today: 7 Location: 10	Classification: 2, 9 Sequencing: 8			
Lesson 12	All/Some/None: 1 Where: 3 Opposites: 4 Days Of The Week: 5 Months Of The Year: 5 Seasons: 5 Same/Different: 6 Yesterday/Today: 7 Part/Whole: 10 Location: 11	Classification: 2 Listening Comprehension: 8 Recalling Details: 9			
Lesson 13	All/Some/None: 1 Opposites: 3 Same/Different: 5 Months Of The Year: 6 Days Of The Week: 6 Seasons: 5 Today/Yesterday: 7 Part/Whole: 9	Classification: 2, 10 Reasoning: 4 Sequencing: 8			
Lesson 14	Actions: 1 Days Of The Week: 2 Months Of The Year: 2 Seasons: 2 Same/Different: 4 When/Where: 6 Location: 9	Sequencing: 3, 7 True/False: 5 Classification: 8			
Lesson 15	Actions: 1 Calendars: 3 Yesterday/Today: 4 Same/Different: 5	True/False: 2 Sequencing: 6 Listening Comprehension: 7 Recalling Details: 8			
Lesson 16	Actions: 1 Same/Different: 3 Materials: 4, 5 Calendars: 7 Yesterday/Today: 8 Part/Whole: 10 Location: 11	Sequencing: 2, 9 True/False: 6			
Lesson 17	Actions: 1 When: 2 Materials: 4, 5 Same/Different: 6 Opposites: 7 Calendars: 10 Part/Whole: 13	Reasoning: 3 Sequencing: 8, 11 True/False: 9 Character Extrapolation: 12 Following Directions: 14			
Lesson 18	Actions: 1 Materials: 2 Opposites: 3 When: 4 Calendars: 6 Location: 10	Only: 5 Sequencing: 7, 8 Listening Comprehension: 8 Asking Questions: 9			
Lesson 19	Actions: 1 Materials: 2 Opposites: 3 Yesterday/Today: 6 Calendars: 7	Only: 4 Sequencing: 5, 8 Listening Comprehension: 8			
Lesson 20	Actions: 1 Materials: 2 When: 3 Opposites: 4 Calendars: 5, 7 Who/Where/When: 6 Part/Whole: 10	Sequencing: 8 Asking Questions: 9			
Lesson 21	Actions: 1 Materials: 4 Opposites: 5 Who/Where/When: 7 Calendars: 8 Part/Whole: 12	Reasoning: 2 Only: 3 Classification: 6 Listening Comprehension: 9 Recalling Details: 10 Asking Questions: 11			

	Phonics/ Vocabulary	Comprehension	Grammar/ Usage/ Mechanics	Writing/ Composition/ Speaking	Study Skills
Lesson 22	All/Some/None: 1 When: 2 Calendars: 4 Materials: 6 Opposites: 7 Part/Whole: 11	Classification: 3 Only: 5 Listening Comprehension: 8 Sequencing: 9 Asking Questions: 10			
Lesson 23	Actions: 1 Opposites: 3 Calendars: 6 Yesterday/Today: 7 Location: 10	Only: 2 Reasoning: 4 Classification: 5 Sequencing: 8 Asking Questions: 9			
Lesson 24	Materials: 1, 6 Calendars: 2 Opposites: 4	Classification: 3 Who/Where/When: 5 Sequencing: 7			
Lesson 25	Opposites: 4 Calendars: 6 Location: 10	Asking Questions: 1 Only: 2 Who/Where/When: 3 Classification: 5 Listening Comprehension: 7 Recalling Details: 8 Asking Questions: 9			
Lesson 26	Calendars: 2 Yesterday/Today/ Tomorrow: 3 Opposites: 6 Part/Whole: 9	Only: 1 Asking Questions: 4, 8 Classification: 5 Sequencing: 7			
Lesson 27	Actions: 1 Calendars: 3 Opposites: 6 Yesterday/Today/ Tomorrow: 7 Location: 10	Only: 2 Who/Where/When/What: 4 Asking Questions: 5, 9 Sequencing: 8			
Lesson 28	Actions: 1 Calendars: 3 Opposites: 4 Yesterday/Today/ Tomorrow: 6 Asking Questions: 9 Classification: 10	Who/Where/When/What: 2 Classification: 5 Listening Comprehension: 7 Recalling Details: 8	Verb Tense: 1		
Lesson 29	Actions: 1 Calendars: 2 Opposites: 4 Yesterday/Today/ Tomorrow: 7	Classification: 3 Sequencing: 5, 8 Only: 6 Asking Questions: 9 Classification: 10	Verb Tense: 1		
Lesson 30	Actions: 1 Materials: 2 Opposites: 3 Today/Tomorrow/ Future: 4 Part/Whole: 9	Classification: 5 Asking Questions: 6, 8 Recalling Details: 7			
Lesson 31	Today/Tomorrow/ Future: 3 Part/Whole: 9	Classification: 1, 5 Opposites: 2 Who/When/What/Why: 4 Recalling Details: 6 Sequencing: 7 Asking Questions: 8			
Lesson 32	Today/Tomorrow/ Future: 3 From/To: 8 Location: 9	Classification: 1, 2, 5 Who/When/Why: 4 Asking Questions: 6 Sequencing: 7			
Lesson 33	Today/Tomorrow/ Future: 5	Classification: 1, 4 Who/What/Why: 2 Asking Questions: 3 Listening Comprehension: 6 Sequencing: 7			
Lesson 34	Today/Tomorrow/ Future: 3 Actions: 5 From/To: 7 Part/Whole: 8	Classification: 1, 2 What/Where/Why: 4 Sequencing: 5 Listening Comprehension: 6 Recalling Details: 6			
Lesson 35	Actions: 1 Today/Tomorrow/ Future: 2 Materials: 5 From/To: 7	Sequencing: 1, 6 Who/What/Why: 3 Classification: 4 Asking Questions: 8			

	Phonics/ Vocabulary	Comprehension	Grammar/ Usage/ Mechanics	Writing/ Composition/ Speaking	Study Skills
Lesson 36	Calendar: 3 Materials: 5 Today/Tomorrow/ Future: 7 From/To: 9	Classification: 1 Who/How/Why: 2 Classification: 4 Why/When/Where: 6 Sequencing: 8 Asking Questions: 10			
Lesson 37	Actions: 1 From/To: 2 Calendar: 4 Opposites: 5 Today/Tomorrow/ Future: 7	Why/When/Where: 3 Who/How/Why/Where: 6 Sequencing: 8			
Lesson 38	Calendars: 4 Today/Tomorrow/ Future: 7 Materials: 10	Classification: 1, 11 When/Where: 2 Deduction: 3, 5 Asking Questions: 6 Listening Comprehension: 8 Sequencing: 9 All/Some: 11			
Lesson 39	Opposites: 3 Today/Tomorrow/ Future: 4 From/To: 7 Materials: 8	Classification: 1 Deduction: 2 Sequencing: 5		Dramatic Activity: 6	
Lesson 40	Opposites: 4 Today/Tomorrow/ Future: 6 From/To: 8	Classification: 1, 7 Deduction: 2 Who/How/Why: 3 Why/Where: 5		Dramatic Activity: 9	
Lesson 41	Definitions: 1 From/To: 2 Things/Actions: 3 Today/ Tomorrow/ Future: 5 Part/Whole: 10	Classification: 1, 4, 9 True/False: 6 Recalling Details: 7 Sequencing: 8			
Lesson 42	Actions: 1 Definitions: 2 Today/Tomorrow/ Future: 4 From/To: 5 Things/Actions: 6, 7	Classification: 2, 3 True/False: 8			Data Collection: 9
Lesson 43	Actions: 1 Definitions: 2 Today/Tomorrow/ Future: 3 From/To: 10	Classification: 2, 6, 9 True/False: 4 Listening Comprehension: 7 Recalling Details: 8	Verb Tense: 5 Address: 8		
Lesson 44	Actions: 1 Today/Tomorrow/ Future: 3 From/To: 4, 9 Things/Actions: 5 Part/Whole: 10	Classification: 2 True/False: 6 Listening Comprehension: 7 Recalling Details: 8			
Lesson 45	Actions: 1 Things/Actions: 2, 6 Today/Tomorrow/ Future: 4	Who/What/When/Where/ Why: 3 Classification: 5, 10 True/False: 7 Listening Comprehension: 8 Recalling Details: 9 Following Directions: 11			
Lesson 46	Today/Tomorrow/ Future: 2 Things/Actions: 4 Opposites: 6	Classification: 3 Who/What/When/Where/ Why: 5 Sequencing: 8	Verb Tense: 1		Maps: 7 Cardinal Directions: 7
Lesson 47	Actions: 1 Today/Tomorrow/ Future: 2 Description: 4 Things/Actions: 7, 8 From/To: 12 Materials: 13	Classification: 3 Who/What/When/Where/ Why: 5 Reasoning: 6 Listening Comprehension: 10 Recalling Details: 10 Sequencing: 11			Maps: 9 Cardinal Directions: 9
Lesson 48	Actions: 1 From/To: 2 Today/Tomorrow/ Future: 4 Things/Actions: 5, 6 Description: 8 Materials: 13	Classification: 7, 12 Who/What/When/Where/ Why: 9 Sequencing: 11	Verb Tense: 3		Maps: 10 Cardinal Directions: 10

	Phonics/ Vocabulary	Comprehension	Grammar/ Usage/ Mechanics	Writing/ Composition/ Speaking	Study Skills
Lesson 49	Actions: 1 Today/Tomorrow/ Future: 3 Description: 4 Things/Actions: 5 Materials: 6 Analogies: 11 Locations: 12	Classification: 2 True/False: 7 Listening Comprehension: 9 Recalling Details: 10 Following Directions: 12			Maps: 8 Cardinal Directions: 8
Lesson 50	Actions: 1 Things/Actions: 3 Description: 4 Materials: 5, 11 Opposites: 6 Today/Tomorrow/ Future: 7 Analogies: 10	Classification: 2			Maps: 8 Cardinal Directions: 8 Data Collection: 9
Lesson 51	Actions: 1 Description: 2 Materials: 3, 4 Today/Tomorrow/ Future: 5		Verb Tense: 6	Sentences: 8	Maps: 7 Cardinal Directions: 7
Lesson 52	Actions: 1 Description: 3 Things/Actions: 4 Today/Tomorrow/ Future: 5 Analogies: 10	Classification: 2, 9 Listening Comprehension: 7 Recalling Details: 8			Maps: 6 Cardinal Directions: 6
Lesson 53	Actions: 1 Things/Actions: 2 Materials: 3 Today/Tomorrow/ Future: 6	True/False: 4 Classification: 5		Sentences: 8	Maps: 7 Cardinal Directions: 7
Lesson 54	Actions: 1 Materials: 2 Things/Actions: 3 Today/Tomorrow/ Future: 4 Materials: 8	Listening Comprehension: 5 Recalling Details: 6			Maps: 7 Cardinal Directions: 7
Lesson 55	Things/Actions: 1 Materials: 3 Opposites: 4 Today/Tomorrow/ Future: 5	Classification: 2		Sentences: 6	
Lesson 56	Things/Actions: 1 Opposites: 2 Calendars: 3 Materials: 5 Today/Tomorrow/ Future: 6 Locations: 9	True/False: 4 Listening Comprehension: 7			Maps: 8 Cardinal Directions: 8
Lesson 57	Description: 1 Opposites: 3 Calendars: 4 Things/Actions: 5 Materials: 6 Analogies: 9	True/False: 2 Character Extrapolation: 7 Classification: 8			
Lesson 58	Things/Actions: 1 Description: 2, 5 Opposites: 3 Calendars: 4 Locations: 9	Listening Comprehension: 6		Days Of The Week: 7	Maps: 8 Cardinal Direction: 8
Lesson 59	Things/Actions: 1 Actions: 3 Description: 5 Calendars: 6 Opposites: 7	Main Ideas: 4 Listening Comprehension: 8	Verb Tense: 2	Days Of The Week: 9	
Lesson 60	Description: 1, 3 Opposites: 4 Calendars: 5	Classification: 2 Listening Comprehension: 6		Dramatic Activity: 7 Days Of The Week: 8	
Lesson 61	Description: 1 Opposites: 4 Calendars: 5 Analogies: 8	True/False: 2 Who/What/Where/When/ Why: 3 Classification: 7		Sentences: 6	

	Phonics/ Vocabulary	Comprehension	Grammar/ Usage/ Mechanics	Writing/ Composition/ Speaking	Study Skills
Lesson 62	Things/Actions: 1 Description: 2 Opposites: 4 Calendars: 5 Analogies: 9	Who/What/Where/When/ Why: 3 Listening Comprehension: 6 Story Completion: 6 Recalling Details: 7			Maps: 8 Cardinal Directions: 8
Lesson 63	Actions: 1 Description: 3 Opposites: 4 Calendars: 5 Part/Whole: 8	Main Ideas: 2 Listening Comprehension: 6 Story Completion: 6 Classification: 7			
Lesson 64	Opposites: 2 Description: 3, 4 Calendars: 5	Classification: 1		Sentences: 6	
Lesson 65	Opposites: 1 Description: 3 Calendars: 5 Analogies: 6 Materials: 10	Main Ideas: 2 Classification: 4 Listening Comprehension: 7		Months Of The Year: 8	Maps: 9 Cardinal Directions: 9
Lesson 66	Description: 1 Analogies: 2 Opposites: 3 Calendars: 4	Listening Comprehension: 5 Recalling Details: 5		Months Of The Year: 6	
Lesson 67	Opposites: 1 Description: 2 Calendars: 3 Analogies: 5	Main Ideas: 4 Sequencing: 6		Dramatic Activity: 7	
Lesson 68	Opposites: 1, 3 Things/Actions: 2 Calendars: 4 Analogies: 5, 9	Listening Comprehension: 6 Classification: 8		Months Of The Year: 7	
Lesson 69	Actions: 1 Things/Actions: 2 Calendars: 3 Opposites: 4 Description: 5 Analogies: 6	Sequencing: 1 Recalling Details: 8		Dramatic Activity: 7	
Lesson 70	Analogies: 1, 8 Opposites: 3 Calendars: 4 Actions: 5	Main Ideas: 2 Character Extrapolation: 6 Classification: 7			
Lesson 71	Analogies: 1 Calendars: 2 Description: 3, 4 Materials: 8	Classification: 5 Sequencing: 6			Maps: 7 Cardinal Directions: 7
Lesson 72	Analogies: 1 Opposites: 2 Calendars: 3 Description: 4 Things/Actions: 6 Materials: 9	Why/When/Where: 5 Character Extrapolation: 7 Classification: 8			
Lesson 73	Description: 1 Analogies: 2 Calendars: 3 Things/Actions: 4	Classification: 5		Sentences: 6	
Lesson 74	Analogies: 1 Calendars: 3 Actions: 4 Things/Actions: 5 Materials: 9	True/False: 2 Who/What/When/Where/ Why: 6 Classification: 8		Sentences: 7	
Lesson 75	Analogies: 1 Calendars: 4, 6 Description: 5 Part/Whole: 9	Classification: 2, 8 True/False: 3		Sentences: 7	
Lesson 76	Calendars: 3 Description: 4 Analogies: 5, 10 Materials: 6	True/False: 1 Who/What/When/Where/ Why: 2 Reasoning: 7 Classification: 9		Sentences: 8	
Lesson 77	Materials: 1 Synonyms: 2, 6 Calendars: 3 Analogies: 4 Same/Different: 5 Description: 7	True/False: 8 Listening Comprehension: 9 Story Completion: 9 Recalling Details: 11		Dramatic Activity: 10	

	Phonics/ Vocabulary	Comprehension	Grammar/ Usage/ Mechanics	Writing/ Composition/ Speaking	Study Skills
Lesson 78	Things/Actions: 1 Calendars: 2 Analogies: 3 Synonyms: 4 Same/Different: 5 Description: 7	True/False: 6		Sentences: 8	
Lesson 79	Analogies: 1 Calendars: 2 Description: 3 Synonyms: 4 Materials: 5 Same/Different: 6	Classification: 7 Reasoning: 8 Listening Comprehension: 9 Sequencing: 11		Dramatic Activity: 10	
Lesson 80	Analogies: 1 Description: 2 Calendars: 3 Synonyms: 4 Materials: 5 Analogies: 9	Reasoning: 6 Classification: 8		Sentences: 7	
Lesson 81	Description: 1, 7 Analogies: 2, 10 Calendars: 4 Things/Actions: 5 Synonyms: 6	Reasoning: 3 Classification: 9		Sentences: 8	
Lesson 82	Analogies: 1, 5 Calendars: 2 Description: 4	Listening Comprehension: 6 Recalling Details: 6 Classification: 7			Maps: 3 Cardinal Directions: 3
Lesson 83	Analogies: 1, 10 Calendars: 3, 7 Synonyms: 5 Things/Actions: 6	Asking Questions: 2 Classification: 9		Sentences: 8	Maps: 4 Cardinal Directions: 4
Lesson 84	Calendars: 1, 2 Analogies: 3 Synonyms: 4	Classification: 7		Sentences: 5	Maps: 6 Cardinal Directions: 6
Lesson 85	Synonyms: 1 Description: 2 Calendars: 3	Who/What/When/Where/ Why: 5, 7 Asking Questions: 6 Reasoning: 8 Classification: 9 Listening Comprehension: 10 Sequencing: 10			Maps: 4 Cardinal Directions: 4
Lesson 86	Analogies: 1 Calendars: 2 Things/Actions: 3 Synonyms: 4 Synonyms/Opposites: 5 Description: 7 Materials: 11	Asking Questions: 5 Who/What/When/Where/ Why: 8 Classification: 10		Sentences: 9	
Lesson 87	Analogies: 1 Description: 2 Calendars: 3 Synonyms: 5	Asking Questions: 4		Sentences: 6	Data Collection: 7
Lesson 88	Analogies: 1 Calendars: 3 Description: 4 Synonyms: 5	Classification: 2, 7		Sentences: 6	
Lesson 89	Description: 2 Synonyms: 3 Calendars: 4 Materials: 6 Analogies: 9	Classification: 1, 10 Who/What/When/Where/ Why: 5 Reasoning: 7		Sentences: 8	
Lesson 90	Synonyms: 1 Description: 2 Analogies: 4 Calendars: 5	Asking Questions: 3 Classification: 8		Sentences: 6	Maps: 7 Cardinal Directions: 7
Lesson 91	Synonyms/Opposites: 1 Description: 2 Synonyms: 3 Analogies: 4 Calendars: 6	Who/What/When/Where/ Why: 5 Asking Questions: 8		Sentences: 7	
Lesson 92	Calendars: 3 Description: 4 Synonyms: 5	Who/What/When/Where/ Why: 1 Asking Questions: 2, 7		Sentences: 6	
Lesson 93	Analogies: 1, 4 Calendars: 2 Descriptions: 3, 5	Classification: 8		Sentences: 6	Maps: 7 Cardinal Directions: 7

	Phonics/ Vocabulary	Comprehension	Grammar/ Usage/ Mechanics	Writing/ Composition/ Speaking	Study Skills
Lesson 94	Description: 1 Synonyms: 2 Analogies: 4	Asking Questions: 3 Who/What/When/Where/ Why: 5 If-Then: 6		Sentences: 7	
Lesson 95	Analogies: 1 Description: 2 Synonyms/Opposites: 5 Materials: 8	Main Ideas: 3 Who/What/When/Where/ Why: 4 If-Then: 6 Classification: 7			
Lesson 96	Analogies: 1 Description: 2, 6 Synonyms/Opposites: 3	Main Ideas: 4 Asking Questions: 5 Character Extrapolation: 8		Sentences: 7	
Lesson 97	Synonyms: 1 Description: 3 Synonyms/Opposites: 4 Analogies: 5	Reasoning: 2 Asking Questions: 6 Classification: 7			
Lesson 98	Synonyms/Opposites: 1 Opposites: 3 Analogies: 4, 9 Description: 6	Main Ideas: 2	Verb Tense: 5	Sentences: 7	Maps: 8 Cardinal Directions: 8
Lesson 99	Description: 1 Synonyms: 2 Calendars: 3 Analogies: 4	Asking Questions: 5 Who/What/When/Where/ Why: 6 If-Then: 7		Sentences: 8	
Lesson 100	Opposites: 1 Analogies: 2 Description: 3 Synonyms: 4	Reasoning: 5 If-Then: 6		Sentences: 7	
Lesson 101	Analogies: 1 Opposites: 2 Description: 4 Synonyms: 5	Reasoning: 6 Classification: 9	Verb Tense: 3	Sentences: 7	Maps: 8 Cardinal Directions: 8
Lesson 102	Analogies: 1 Opposite: 2 Synonyms: 3 Materials: 4	Classification: 7	Verb Tense: 5	Sentences: 6	Maps: 8 Cardinal Directions: 8
Lesson 103	Analogies: 1, 7 Opposites: 2 Description: 4 Synonyms: 5	Classification: 3, 8		Sentences: 6	
Lesson 104	Analogies: 2 Opposites: 3	Who/What/When/Where/ Why: 4 Classification: 5, 8		Sentences: 6	Maps: 1, 7 Cardinal Directions: 1, 7
Lesson 105	Analogies: 1 Description: 4 Synonyms: 5	Main Ideas: 2 Classification: 3 Asking Questions: 7		Sentences: 6	
Lesson 106	Analogies: 1, 7 Opposites: 2 Description: 3 Synonyms/Opposites: 4 Calendars: 5 Materials: 8			Sentences: 6	
Lesson 107	Description: 2 Opposites: 3 Synonyms/Opposites: 5 Analogies: 7	Classification: 1, 8 Asking Questions: 4		Sentences: 6	
Lesson 108	Analogies: 1 Materials: 2 Description: 3 Opposites: 5	Reasoning: 4 Classification: 8		Sentences: 6	Maps: 7 Cardinal Directions: 7
Lesson 109	Analogies: 1 Opposites: 2 Description: 5	Asking Questions: 4 If-Then: 6	Verb Tenses: 3	Sentences: 7	
Lesson 110	Synonyms: 1 Description: 4 Analogies: 5	Reasoning: 2 Classification: 7	Verb Tenses: 3	Sentences: 6	Maps: 8 Cardinal Directions: 8
Lesson 111	Synonyms: 1, 2 Calendars: 3 Opposites: 4 Analogies: 8	Reasoning: 5 Classification: 7		Sentences: 6	

	Phonics/ Vocabulary	Comprehension	Grammar/ Usage/ Mechanics	Writing/ Composition/ Speaking	Study Skills
Lesson 112	Synonyms: 1 Description: 3, 5 Opposites: 7	Who/What/When/Where/ Why: 2 Classification: 8	Verb Tenses: 4	Sentences: 6	
Lesson 113	Opposites: 1, 3, 8 Actions: 2 Synonyms: 5 Analogies: 7	Asking Questions: 4		Sentences: 6	
Lesson 114	Synonyms: 1 Materials: 2 Description: 3 Calendars: 5	Main Ideas: 4 If-Then: 6		Sentences: 7	
Lesson 115	Opposites: 1 Synonyms: 3 Description: 4	Reasoning: 2 Listening Comprehension: 5 Recalling Details: 5			
Lesson 116	Opposites: 2, 8 Description: 3 Synonyms: 4, 5	If-Then: 1 Classification: 7		Sentences: 6	
Lesson 117	Synonyms: 2 Description: 3 Opposites: 4 Calendars: 5	If-Then: 1 Classification: 7		Sentences: 6	Maps: 8 Cardinal Directions: 8
Lesson 118	Synonyms: 3 Description: 4	Asking Questions: 1 Main Ideas: 2 If-Then: 5 Character Extrapolation: 6		Sentences: 7	
Lesson 119	Opposites: 1 Synonyms: 3 Description: 4, 5 Analogies: 9	If-Then: 6 Classification: 8	Verb Tenses: 2	Sentences: 7	
Lesson 120	Contractions: 3 Opposites: 4 Description: 5	Who/What/When/Where/ Why: 1 Reasoning: 2 Asking Questions: 7	Contractions: 3	Sentences: 6	
Lesson 121	Opposites: 3, 6 Contractions: 4 Analogies: 7	Asking Questions: 2	Verb Tenses: 1	Sentences: 5	
Lesson 122	Synonyms/Opposites: 1 Opposites: 4 Contractions: 5	Main Ideas: 3 Classification: 7	Verb Tenses: 2 Contractions: 5	Sentences: 6	Maps: 8 Cardinal Directions: 8
Lesson 123	Description: 2 Synonyms: 3 Contractions: 4 Opposites: 5	Character Extrapolation: 7	Verb Tenses: 1 Contractions: 4	Sentences: 6	
Lesson 124	Contractions: 1 Description: 3 Calendars: 4 Analogies: 7	Classification: 6	Contractions: 1 Verb Tenses: 2	Sentences: 5	
Lesson 125	Description: 2 Opposites: 3, 6	Main Ideas: 1 Reasoning: 4 Classification: 7		Sentences: 5	
Lesson 126	Contractions: 1 Actions: 2 Description: 3, 4 Opposites: 6		Contractions: 1	Sentences: 5	Maps: 7 Cardinal Directions: 7
Lesson 127	Contractions: 1 Description: 2	Asking Questions: 3 Who/What/When/Where/ Why: 4 Reasoning: 5 Listening Comprehension: 6 Story Completion: 6, 7 Recalling Details: 7	Contractions: 1		
Lesson 128	Description: 2 Contractions: 3 Opposites: 7	Reasoning: 4 Main Ideas: 5	Verb Tenses: 1 Contractions: 3	Sentences: 6	Maps: 8 Cardinal Directions: 8
Lesson 129	Synonyms/Opposites: 3 Description: 4 Contractions: 5 Analogies: 7	Main Ideas: 1 Reasoning: 2 Classification: 8	Contractions: 5	Sentences: 6	
Lesson 130	Contractions: 1 Actions: 2 Opposites: 4 Descriptions: 5		Contractions: 1 Verb Tenses: 3	Writing Stories About Characters: 6	